GLOBAL CORPORATE GOVERNANCE

GLOBAL CORPORATE GOVERNANCE

Edited by Donald H. Chew
and Stuart L. Gillan

Columbia University Press

NEW YORK

Columbia University Press
Publishers Since 1893
New York   Chichester, West Sussex
Copyright © 2009 Morgan Stanley Content Corporation
All rights reserved

Library of Congress Cataloging-in-Publication Data

Global corporate governance / edited by Donald H. Chew and Stuart L. Gillan.
    p.   cm.
    Includes bibliographical references and index.
    ISBN 978-0-231-14854-2 (cloth : alk. paper)—ISBN 978-0-231-14855-9
(pbk. : alk. paper)—ISBN 978-0-231-51997-7 (e-book)
    1. Corporate governance.   2. Corporate governance—International cooperation.
I. Chew, Donald H.   II. Gillan, Stuart L.   III. Title.
    HD2741.G56   2009
    338.6—dc22   2009016801

Columbia University Press books are printed on permanent and durable acid-free paper.

This book is printed on paper with recycled content.

Printed in the United States of America

c 10 9 8 7 6 5 4 3 2 1
p 10 9 8 7 6 5 4 3 2 1

References to Internet Web sites (URLs) were accurate at the time of writing. Neither the author nor Columbia University Press is responsible for URLs that may have expired or changed since the manuscript was prepared.

To our wives: Susan Emerson and Laura Gillan

Contents

Part III: Country-Specific Evidence on Ownership and Governance Structure

Part IV: The Role of Active Investors

Introduction

UNTIL FAIRLY RECENTLY, European companies were producing handsome stock returns, and companies in emerging markets were doing even better. Much of the explanation had to do with the economic cycle. After seeing their sales and profits fall during the worldwide recession at the start of this decade, European and Latin American and Asian companies all began to benefit from the general improvements in the global economy. But another, perhaps equally important, part of the story was the gradual strengthening of their corporate governance systems—a movement that, having been launched in the United States and the U.K. in the 1990s, has begun to go global.

Why should governance matter? The short answer is that effective governance—the set of controls on and incentives driving top management that come from *outside* as well as *inside* the firm—helps provide the assurance that investors need to commit their capital. And if this is true when buying stocks in one's own country, it is likely to be even more important when investing in companies in other countries, where information may be less reliable and investor influence (or protection) more limited.

Of course, such concerns about information and legal protection clearly have not prevented all investors from buying securities issued outside their homelands. In the last 30 years, the dollar amount of cross-border stock and bond transactions by U.S. investors has jumped from about 6% of U.S. GDP to more than 350%. And the massive cross-border capital flows, together with steady increases in global trade and production, have led some economists to make a number of bold predictions. Some capital markets theorists, for example, have suggested that investors everywhere will eventually end up holding the same "world market portfolio," with a proportional representation of all economies with traded assets. Macroeconomists have speculated that national investment and consumption levels will no longer be limited by national income and savings, since foreign capital should be readily available to make up any shortfalls. And corporate finance specialists have theorized that comparably profitable companies operating in the same industry but based in different countries will have similar capital and ownership structures, and roughly the same costs of capital and market values.

The reality, however, is that we continue to see significant cross-country differences in investment, financing, and internal governance structures. Much of this variation can be attributed to differences among countries in *external* corporate governance features—in the political, legal, and regulatory environments that help determine the vigor and effectiveness of the market for corporate control, and the degree of protection afforded outside (including foreign) providers of capital. But along with these country-level differences in external governance mechanisms, there is also considerable variation among companies in the design and effectiveness of *internal* governance systems—that is, in ownership and capital structures, payout policies, management incentives, and the degree of commitment to monitoring by boards of directors.

This book has two main messages. One is the fairly standard prescription that, in countries offering limited legal and regulatory protection for investors, policymakers can attract portfolio investors as well as direct foreign investment by strengthening the external features of their governance systems—their legal and regulatory frameworks, and the institutions that monitor corporate performance. And given the current conditions in today's global capital markets, this message has relevance for developed as well as emerging economies. The second message—perhaps more surprising—is that even in countries with limited external governance mechanisms, individual companies can take matters into their own hands in two ways: (1) by listing on overseas exchanges and thereby "borrowing"—at least to some degree—the strengths of a stronger governance regime; and (2) by buttressing their own internal governance systems with, for example, greater use of independent directors, a more effective dialogue with the investment community, and stronger management incentives.

This book consists of 15 chapters on aspects of international corporate governance that were previously published in the *Journal of Applied Corporate Finance*. The chapters are divided into four sections. Those that make up Part I, under the rubric "Governance, Markets, and Law," provide an overview of general corporate governance issues, along with a discussion of the relative importance of markets and laws in shaping how governance systems have evolved. The chapters in Part II provide insights into questions like the following: Can strong *internal* corporate governance systems counteract the negative effects on cost of capital and value in national regimes that offer limited protection for minority investors? And what kinds of companies seek to strengthen their internal governance systems? Part III consists of a series of chapters examining ownership and governance structures in specific countries, including Korea, France, Italy, and India. The fourth and final part contains three chapters that focus on the economic role of "active investors," significant owners such as LBO funds and some institutional investors that attempt to influence or participate directly in corporate strategic and financial decision-making.

We now provide a brief overview of the chapters in each of the four parts.

Part I: Governance, Markets, and Law

In January 2005, René Stulz, then President of the American Finance Association, devoted his presidential speech to the AFA to "The Limits of Financial Globalization." In the edited version of his talk that opens this book, Stulz begins by citing recent research suggesting that (1) investors continue to hold disproportionately large percentages of domestic securities in their portfolios (at the end of 2004, U.S. investors were holding only about a fourth of the "foreign" securities needed to form a global portfolio); (2) national investment and consumption continue to depend mainly on local savings and income; and (3) corporate ownership structures remain more concentrated, and capital structures more highly leveraged, in countries that offer less protection to outside investors.

In trying to explain the persistence of these cross-country differences in investment and financing, Stulz focuses on two kinds of governance problems, or what he refers to as the "twin agency problems." One is the tendency of controlling shareholders (said to be found in most listed companies outside the U.S. and the U.K.) to transfer value from the other ("minority") shareholders to themselves through self-dealing of various kinds. The other problem, which complicates and compounds the first, is the tendency of governments to expropriate wealth from *all* shareholders, controlling and minority.

To manage these problems, especially in countries with less investor-friendly legal and regulatory regimes, the controlling shareholders typically "co-invest" with outside minority investors by retaining large equity stakes. As Stulz argues, such co-investment is needed to reassure outsider investors that the interests of the controlling shareholders are largely consistent with their own, and that the insiders will attempt to shield outsiders from the depredations of the state. And when such companies need additional outside funding, instead of raising new equity, they show an unusually strong preference for debt—which preserves their concentration of ownership.

But if such co-investment improves the terms on which outsiders provide capital, it also has a big downside: The concentrated ownership and higher leverage mean that such companies are sacrificing the much larger risk-bearing capacity, and much lower cost of equity, that comes with having a large diversified shareholder base; and given the limits of their insiders' wealth, the companies are far more likely to pass up promising growth opportunities for lack of funding.

The twin problems can also have more subtle side effects. For example, a company operating under a confiscatory regime may find that, by increasing "transparency" for minority holders, it exposes the firm to further state expropriation and so reduces value. And in a similarly pessimistic note, Stulz mentions his own research that shows the difficulty for even well-governed companies to achieve high governance ratings from third-party agencies when the firms are based in countries with weak governance systems.

But for all his skepticism about the accomplishments of globalization, Stulz ends by repeating the predictions he and other economists made years ago. Both governments and the private enterprises within their jurisdictions have strong motives for finding more effective ways to manage the twin agency problems; and, "when they do," as Stulz says in closing, "the citizens of developing and developed nations alike will benefit from increasingly global financial markets."

In "The Political Roots of American Corporate Finance," Harvard law and economics scholar Mark Roe begins by observing that the ownership and governance structure of the large American corporation—with its dispersed shareholders, a board of directors that defers to the CEO, and a powerful, centralized management—is usually seen as a natural economic outcome of technological requirements for large-scale enterprises and substantial amounts of outside capital, most of which had to come from well-diversified shareholders. Roe, however, qualifies this story, arguing that U.S. corporate ownership structures are mainly the result of political forces that have restricted the size and activities of U.S. commercial banks and other financial intermediaries. Populist fears of concentrated economic power, interest-group maneuvering, and a federalist American political structure have all had a role in pressuring Congress to fragment U.S. financial institutions and limit their ability to own stock and participate in corporate governance.

In "International Corporate Differences: Markets or Law?" Frank Easterbrook responds to Roe's argument by attributing current differences in international corporate ownership and governance systems mainly to differences in the efficiency of capital markets, and not to differences in corporate law. Law, in Easterbrook's view, is largely a response to or an output of this process, not an input. In countries like the United States and the U.K. where financial markets are more efficient and there are few restrictions on cross-border cash flows, there is both less law and greater investor protection.

Moreover, Easterbrook argues that the effect of law on corporate governance and ownership is "far less pronounced" in America than in Europe and Japan. Restrictions on U.S. banks aside, corporate law in the United States is "enabling," allowing individuals considerable freedom in organizing, managing, and financing companies. By contrast, corporate law in Europe and Japan is described as "much more 'directory.'" And there is a straightforward explanation for this difference: When capital markets are efficient, the valuation process works better, which in turn provides investors with stronger assurances of fairness. When markets are less efficient, some substitute must be found—law, perhaps, or the valuation procedures of banks.

For this reason, then, banks play larger corporate governance roles in nations with less extensive capital markets—and corporate law is more restrictive. But with the current problems faced by banks and credit markets, as Easterbrook's thesis would also suggest, the United States and the U.K. are now clearly headed for more restrictive regulatory constraints, particularly on the risk-taking activity of financial institutions. As liquidity has dried up in many markets and prices appear to have become "disconnected" from fundamentals, U.S. and U.K. government officials have intervened heavily to correct what many (if not most) observers take to be a market failure. The extent, as well as the permanence, of such intervention, as Easterbrook's argument also suggests, is likely to depend on how quickly market confidence and liquidity are restored. The longer it takes for liquidity to return and markets to function normally, the more extensive and far-reaching the process of reregulation is likely to be—and with long-run effects that are not easy to predict.

In "Explaining Differences in the Quality of Governance among Companies: Evidence from Emerging Markets," Art Durnev and Han Kim provide a clear, and remarkably simple, answer to the question: What will cause governments and companies to upgrade their governance systems? In summarizing the findings of their study of nearly 900 companies in 27 emerging-market countries, Durnev and Kim report, first of all, a surprisingly large variation in the quality of corporate governance practices within the same country, with the greatest variation in countries that provide the least investor protection. They proceed to show that companies with the highest corporate governance and disclosure ratings appear to have the most investment opportunities and the greatest need for external financing—an association that is clearest in countries with the weakest safeguards for investors. Thus, the push for better governance appears strongest in companies with the greatest demand for outside capital—and the worse the country's reputation for protecting minority shareholders, the greater the demand by investors for effective internal governance.

Part II: Cross-Country Evidence on Governance Effectiveness and the Cost of Capital

In "Control Premiums and the Effectiveness of Corporate Governance Systems," Alexander Dyck and Luigi Zingales use the control premiums paid in large block sales to assess the quality of corporate governance systems (with large premiums interpreted as evidence of higher costs in removing inefficient management teams and hence less effective governance systems). The authors report significant variation in such premiums, with countries like the United

States and the U.K. showing premiums of less than 10% while premiums for countries like Brazil run in excess of 60%. The authors also use these measures to determine which institutions or mechanisms tend to be more effective in helping minority shareholders limit the expropriation of wealth by insider or controlling shareholders. Notable among such institutional variables are better accounting standards and effective legal protection of minority shareholders (both in terms of the laws on the books and their enforcement). At the same time, the authors also emphasize the importance of a number of extralegal factors, including more intense product market competition, diffusion of an independent press, and a high rate of tax compliance.

In "Globalization, Corporate Finance, and the Cost of Capital," René Stulz begins by noting that international financial markets have become progressively more integrated—a development that is contributing to higher stock prices in developed and developing economies. For companies that are large and visible enough to attract global investors, having a global shareholder base means having a lower cost of capital and hence a greater equity value for two main reasons. First, because the risks of equity are shared among more investors with different portfolio exposures and hence a different "appetite" for bearing certain risks, equity market risk premiums should fall for all companies in countries with access to global markets. Although the largest reductions in cost of capital resulting from globalization will be experienced by companies in liberalizing economies that are gaining access to the global markets for the first time, risk premiums can also be expected to fall for firms in long-integrated markets. Second, when firms in countries with less-developed capital markets raise capital in the public markets of countries (like the United States) with highly developed markets, they get more than lower-cost capital; they also import at least aspects of the corporate governance systems that prevail in those markets. For companies accustomed to less-developed markets, raising capital overseas is likely to mean that more sophisticated investors, armed with more advanced technologies, will participate in monitoring their performance and management. And in a virtuous cycle, more effective monitoring increases investor confidence in the future performance of those companies and so improves the terms on which they raise capital.

In addition to reducing market risk premiums and improving corporate governance, globalization also affects the systematic risk, or "beta," of individual companies. In global markets, the beta of a firm's equity depends on how the stock contributes to the volatility not of the home market portfolio but of the world market portfolio. For companies with access to global capital markets whose profitability is tied more closely to the local than to the global economy, use of the traditional Capital Asset Pricing Model (CAPM) will overstate the cost of capital because risks that are not diversifiable within a national economy can be diversified by holding a global portfolio.

In "Which Capitalism? Lessons from the East Asian Crisis," Raghuram Rajan and Luigi Zingales begin by noting that, during the 1980s and much of the 1990s, bank-centered, relationship-based economic systems were held up as an alternative (and in some respects superior) form of capitalism to the arm's-length, market-based, Anglo-Saxon systems of the United States and the U.K. But the weaknesses of such bank-reliant systems were clearly exposed by the Asian crisis of the late 1990s. This chapter attempts to explain both the heavy reliance of emerging economies on such relation-based systems and the vulnerability of such systems when attempting to manage large capital inflows.

According to Rajan and Zingales, relationship-based systems work well in environments where contracts are poorly enforced and reliable information and capital are scarce. In such a setting, relationships effectively substitute for contracts, and can achieve better outcomes than a primitive contractual system. But problems arise in such economies when capital becomes too plentiful, particularly when they open their markets to foreign inflows and effectively become "hybrid" economies (part relationship-based, part market-based).

The downside of relationship-based systems is their suppression of the price system and the signals it provides. Without the reliable price signals provided by market-based systems, relationship-based systems are more than usually prone to overinvestment when faced with large capital inflows, which in turn leads to capital flight (because investors have few contractual safeguards), plummeting currencies and asset prices, and recession. Thus, the contact between the two systems creates a fragile hybrid that, while mutually beneficial to relationship borrowers and arm's-length investors in normal times, is excessively vulnerable to shocks.

The authors suggest that while there may be some short-term benefits for emerging economies from reverting to pure relationship-based systems, in the long run such economies will be held back unless they develop the greater disclosure, contract enforcement, and competition of arm's-length systems. The current crisis may be an opportune moment for developing economies to begin to make the transition between systems and encourage the formation and growth of capital markets.

Part III: Country-Specific Evidence on Ownership and Governance Structure

Our next five chapters provide insights into five different national governance systems—those of India, Italy, Korea, the U.K., Germany, and France.

In "Corporate Governance in India," Rajesh Chakrabarti, William Megginson, and Pradeep Yadav note that the Indian corporate governance system has both supported and held back India's ascent to the top ranks of the world's economies. While on paper the country's legal system provides some of the best investor protection in the world, enforcement is a major problem, with overburdened courts and significant corruption. Ownership remains concentrated and family business groups continue to be the dominant business model, with significant pyramiding and evidence of tunneling activity that transfers cash flow and value from minority to controlling shareholders.

But for all its shortcomings, Indian corporate governance has taken major steps toward becoming a system capable of inspiring confidence among institutional and, increasingly, foreign investors. The Securities and Exchange Board of India, established as part of the comprehensive economic reforms launched in 1991, has made considerable progress in becoming a rigorous regulatory regime that helps ensure transparency and fair practice. And the National Stock Exchange of India, also established as part of the reforms, now functions with enough efficiency and transparency to be generating the third-largest number of trades in the world, just behind the NASDAQ and NYSE.

Among more recent changes, the enactment of Sarbanes-Oxley-type measures in 2004—which include protections for minority shareholders in family- or "promoter"-led businesses—has contributed to recent increases in institutional and foreign stock ownership. And while family- and government-controlled business groups continue to be the rule, India has also seen the rise of successful companies like Infosys that are free of the influence of a dominant family or group and have made the individual shareholder their central governance focus.

In "The Financial and Economic Lessons of Italy's Privatization Program," William Megginson and Dario Scannapieco summarize the accomplishments and disappointments of Italy's privatization program, assessing its impact on Italian capital markets, and offering lessons for other countries embarking on new privatization programs. Since 1994 the Italian government has sold equity stakes in some 75 large state enterprises, in the process raising over $125 billion—more than any other country during the same period. This chapter also describes the share issuance methods used by the government to execute several massive offerings, including the largest IPO in history.

The principal benefits of Italian privatization have been dramatic increases in the size and efficiency of Italy's stock markets and in the safety and stability of its banking system. Despite such improvements, privatization has failed to bring about the increased competition in key industries and lower prices for consumers that its planners originally envisioned. And based on this experience, the authors offer a number of lessons for government planners.

Perhaps most important, privatization is likely to yield decisive benefits only if the divestment program is properly designed and sequenced. Governments should begin by privatizing state-owned banks and other financial institutions, and as quickly as economically and politically feasible. Especially in less-developed economies, commercial banks are for many companies both the only suppliers of credit and the only effective source of market discipline—which helps explain why results have often been disastrous when governments have retained control of banks while privatizing other industries. Privatizing governments should also emphasize privatizations accomplished through share issuances rather than asset sales, with the aim of developing liquid and efficient stock markets and promoting effective corporate governance.

In "Changes in Korean Corporate Governance: A Response to Crisis," Han Kim and Woochan Kim start by noting that in the last months of 1997, the value of the Korean currency lost more than half its value against the dollar and the ruling party was swept from power in presidential elections. One of the fundamental causes of this national economic crisis was the widespread failure of Korean companies to earn their cost of capital, which contributed to massive shareholder losses and calls for corporate governance reform. Among the worst performers, and hence the main targets of governance reform, were family-controlled Korean business groups known as *chaebol*. Besides pursuing growth and size at the expense of value, such groups were notorious for expropriating minority shareholders through "tunneling" activities and other means.

The reform measures introduced by the new administration were a mix of market-based solutions and government intervention. The government-engineered, large-scale swaps of business units among the largest chaebol—the so-called big deals that were designed to force each of the groups to identify and specialize in a core business—turned out to be failures, with serious unwanted side effects. At the same time, however, new laws and regulations designed to increase corporate transparency, oversight, and accountability have had clearly positive effects on Korean governance. Thanks to reductions in barriers to foreign ownership of Korean companies, such ownership had risen to about 37% at the end of 2006, up from just 13% ten years earlier. And in addition to the growing pressure for better governance from foreign investors, several newly formed Korean NGOs have pushed for increased transparency and accountability, particularly among the largest chaebol.

The best governance practices in Korea today can be seen mainly in three kinds of corporations: (1) newly privatized companies, (2) large corporations run by professional management, and (3) banks with substantial equity ownership in the hands of foreign investors. The improvements in governance achieved by such companies—notably, fuller disclosure, better alignment of managerial incentives with shareholder value, and more effective oversight by boards—have enabled many of them to meet the global standard. And the governance policies and procedures of POSCO—the first Korean company to list on the New York Stock Exchange, as well as the recent recipient of a large equity investment by Warren Buffett—are held up as a model of best practice.

At the other end of the Korean governance spectrum, however, there remain many large chaebol-affiliated or family-run companies that resist such reforms.

Aided by the popular resistance to globalization, the lobbying efforts of such firms have succeeded not only in reducing the momentum of the Korean governance reform movement but also in reversing some of the previous gains. Most disturbing is the current push to allow American-style anti-takeover devices that, if successful, would weaken the disciplinary effect of the market for corporate control.

In "The Ownership Structure, Governance, and Performance of French Companies: Corporate Control and the Politics of Finance," Péter Harbula cites the important role of foreign institutional investors in spurring governance reform and performance improvements. While acknowledging the importance of such external market forces, Harbula's study also reinforces the critical importance of "co-investment" by insiders by showing that the performance of French companies improves as the percentage equity stakes of insiders increase. But this relationship holds only up to a point: Once the stakes rise above about 40%, performance begins to fall off, with the implication that insiders are entrenched and so in a position to take advantage of minority holders.

Harbula's results thus appear to suggest that, at least for companies without huge capital requirements, there may be an optimal level of insider ownership, in the range of 25–40%. What's more, and contrary to the conventional wisdom, there is now a growing body of evidence that insider ownership plays a similar role in many large U.S. public companies. Harbula's findings are remarkably similar to those of recent studies of U.S. family-owned companies, as well as to the findings of a series of studies of U.S. publicly traded companies by John McConnell and Henri Servaes. And in a study called "The Myth of Diffuse Ownership in the U.S.," Cliff Holderness reports that after "hand collecting" data on the insider ownership of a random sample of 375 U.S. public companies, he found that 96% of the companies had blockholders that in aggregate owned 39% of their total common stock. Thus, in the United States, as in France and elsewhere—and for all the specializing and delegating that goes on in modern economies—it may still pay to have large owners minding the shop.

In "Corporate Ownership and Control in the U.K., Germany, and France," Julian Franks and Colin Mayer note that the U.K. corporate ownership and governance system, like its U.S. counterpart, can be characterized as an outsider system with a large number of public corporations, widely dispersed ownership (though with growing concentrations of institutional shareholdings), and well-developed takeover markets. By contrast, the much smaller number and proportion of publicly traded German and French corporations are governed by insider systems—those in which the founding families, banks, or other companies have controlling interests and in which outside shareholders are not able to exert much control.

The different patterns of ownership in the U.K. and in France and Germany give rise to different incentives and corporate control mechanisms. Concentrated ownership would seem to encourage longer-term relationships between the company and its investors. But, while perhaps better suited to some corporate activities with longer-term payoffs, concentrated ownership could also lead to costly delays in undertaking necessary corrective action, particularly if the owners receive "private" benefits from owning and running a business. And, although widely dispersed ownership may increase the likelihood that corrective action will be sought prematurely (as outsiders rush to sell their shares in response to a temporary downturn), the presence of well-diversified public owners may also be more appropriate for riskier ventures requiring large amounts of new capital investment.

Thus, concentrated ownership, while having the potential to reduce information costs and to strengthen incentives to maximize value, can also impose costs in two ways: (1) by forcing managers and other insiders to bear excessive company-specific risks that could be transferred to well-diversified outsiders; and (2) by allowing insiders to capture private benefits at the expense of outsiders.

Part IV: The Role of Active Investors

Finance scholars have produced little evidence of the effectiveness of direct attempts by institutional shareholders to improve corporate performance. What studies we have—focused mainly on the activities of U.S. pension funds—show no clear effect on shareholder returns. But, as discussed by the panelists in the "London Business School Roundtable on Shareholder Activism in the U.K.," a recent study of shareholder activism in the U.K. looks promising.

The subject of the study is a "Focus Fund," launched in 1998 by the U.K. investment firm Hermes, whose aim is to identify underperforming companies, propose changes to their managements and boards, and—in contrast to the practices of the best-known U.S. shareholder activists—work mainly "behind the scenes" with the companies to bring about those changes. In keeping with the more private nature of U.K. activism, which reflects in part the fewer restrictions on communication between companies and their investors than in the United States, the study's method of investigation is also notably different from the methods used in studies of U.S. investors. Four academics were allowed to examine Hermes' records of its "engagements" with companies, including letters, recordings, and transcripts of telephone conversations, and the staff's personal notes and recollections.

Using this information, the researchers show that the Fund has been remarkably successful in bringing about three kinds of proposed changes: replacements of CEOs and Chairmen, changes in investment and financial policies (mainly increased payouts and more disciplined capital spending), and restructurings (typically leading to greater corporate focus). Of equal importance, the study also shows that the market reaction to the announcement of such changes has been significantly positive and that the cumulative effect of these positive reactions accounts for as much as 90% of the Fund's impressive "alpha" or market out-performance over its eight-year life.

As Michael Jensen has argued, the rise of leveraged buyouts (LBOs) in the United States during the 1980s can be viewed as the reemergence of "active investors" there—the modern-day counterparts of the J. P. Morgans of the turn of the twentieth century, who held positions and sat on the boards of U.S. companies. And particularly in the last decade, the U.S. LBO movement has spread to Europe—and, indeed, become a global movement.

In "Leveraged Buyouts in the U.K. and Continental Europe: Retrospect and Prospect," Mike Wright, Luc Renneboog, Tomas Simons, and Louise Scholes begin by pointing out that in 2005, buyouts accounted for half of all merger-and-acquisitions activity (as measured by value) in the U.K. And as in the U.S. during the 1980s, the greatest numbers of U.K. buyouts in recent years have been in management- and investor-led acquisitions of divisions of large corporations. In continental Europe, by contrast, the largest fraction of deals has involved the purchase of family-owned private businesses. But in recent years, increased pressure for shareholder value in countries like France, the Netherlands, and even Germany has led to a growing number of buyouts of divisions of listed companies. Like the U.K., continental Europe has also seen a small but growing number of purchases of entire public companies (known as private-to-public transactions, or PTPs), including the largest-ever buyout in Europe, the €13 billion purchase in 2008 of the Danish corporation TDC.

Finally, in "Sovereign Wealth Funds: A Growing Global Force in Corporate Finance," Shams Butt, Anil Shivdasani, Carsten Stendevad, and Ann Wyman note that sovereign wealth funds (SWFs) have emerged among the most important players in global financial markets. SWFs have shown a wide range of investment objectives, along with continually evolving time horizons and risk appetites. For example, some SWFs have become increasingly active in corporate acquisitions and other strategic transactions. Though many of these funds prefer to invest in debt or noncontrolling equity positions, a small but growing number are seeking substantial minority and controlling equity stakes.

SWFs have also recently become major participants in the financial institutions and alternative investment industries, with several high-profile investments in well-known private equity firms and financial services companies. In certain corporate transactions, their longer time horizons and willingness to employ larger percentages of equity have made them attractive alternatives to established private equity.

At the same time, however, the rising prominence and perceived lack of transparency of SWFs have raised concerns among governments and other market participants in countries where companies have been targeted for investment. For this reason, companies intent on obtaining funding from or investing with SWFs are advised to prepare for media and regulatory scrutiny, particularly if a transaction is perceived to involve a country's strategic or security interests. Government policymakers are urged to balance the perceived threats of SWFs against their potential benefits, particularly their ability to provide a stabilizing source of global liquidity in the current economic environment.

PART I

Governance, Markets, and Law

CHAPTER 1

The Limits of Financial Globalization

RENÉ M. STULZ

THE LAST 60 YEARS have seen a dramatic change in world financial markets. At the end of World War II, the capital markets of most countries were separated from one another by barriers of various kinds. For instance, many countries prohibited their investors from owning foreign securities or obtaining the foreign currency to purchase them. But since 1945, many countries have sharply reduced such barriers to cross-border trade in financial assets, giving rise to a development that is often called "financial globalization."

According to most economists, the globalization of financial markets is expected to have major economic benefits. In theory, it should lead to better sharing of risks among investors worldwide, allow capital to flow where its productivity is highest, and provide individual countries with greater opportunity to reap the benefits of their respective comparative advantages.[1]

In the process, moreover, significant cross-country differences in asset prices, investment portfolios, and corporate financial policies are eventually expected to disappear, resulting in a condition that economists refer to as "country irrelevance." According to this theoretical proposition, investors in all countries will end up holding essentially the same "world market portfolio," one that contains representative proportions of all global economies. And as a consequence, comparably profitable companies operating in the same industry but domiciled in different countries ought to have similar capital structures and roughly the same cost of capital and market valuations.

But the evidence in support of these predictions is at best mixed. While some studies have reported a positive effect of financial globalization on growth,[2] most of the evidence to date suggests limited benefits. Consider, for example, the following conclusion of a 2003 study of developing countries by the International Monetary Fund: "[W]hile there is no proof in the data that financial globalization has increased growth, there is evidence that some countries may have experienced greater consumption volatility as a result."[3] And contrary to the "country irrelevance" proposition espoused by economists, the bulk of the evidence also suggests that asset prices, investor portfolios, and corporate financial policies all continue to have significant "country-specific" components.

In this article, I argue that despite a dramatic increase in cross-border trade in financial assets, the positive impact of financial globalization has been surprisingly limited. My explanation for this puzzle is that the expected effects of increasingly global capital markets have been limited by what I call "the twin agency problems." These problems stem from the reality that, in pursuing their own interests, both the rulers of sovereign states and corporate insiders often take actions that reduce the value of companies to outside investors.

Why "twin problems" rather than two distinct problems? Because the problems tend to occur together and to feed on one another. When one agency problem is well managed, the other tends to be as well.

The severity of these problems varies across countries, depending on the soundness of a country's institutions. At one extreme are countries such as the U.K., Canada, and the U.S., where the twin problems are limited by well-established legal, regulatory, and market institutions. At the other extreme, countries like Russia provide minority shareholders with little protection against expropriation by either controlling shareholders or the state. In such countries, I show why corporations have a tough time attracting investment capital unless corporate insiders "co-invest" heavily with outside suppliers of equity.

One result of such co-investment is a highly concentrated ownership structure. While such ownership can certainly have benefits—for example, it has clearly played a critical role in the successes of LBOs, venture capital, and other forms of private equity—it also has two negative effects that can limit economic growth and the development of financial markets. First, it limits risk-sharing by forcing insiders to bear far more firm-specific risk than if they held diversified portfolios. Second, it means that a company's investment is limited by the wealth of its insiders, who can co-invest only to the extent they have the resources to do so.

As mentioned earlier, much of the expected benefit of financial globalization is assumed to come from the expanded risk-sharing that results from attracting investors from different countries with different risk exposures. The willingness of such investors to pay a "diversification premium" for a foreign company's shares is expected, all other things equal, to reduce the firm's cost of capital and thus stimulate investment. Unfortunately, however, in most international settings all other things are not equal. In countries that pose considerable risks for investors of expropriation by controlling investors and the state, the demand for co-investment effectively means that most of the risk of the firm must be borne by corporate insiders, not by well-diversified international investors. And this not only limits the gains from financial globalization for many nations, but creates the possibility that, in countries where such problems are particularly acute, the globalization of financial markets can at times end up *reducing* growth. The massive capital outflows experienced by a number of such countries during periods of crisis could not have happened had they not opened up their markets.

Some Evidence on Financial Globalization and Country Relevance

Since the end of World War II, there has been dramatic progress in reducing formal barriers to trading financial assets. In every year since 1950, the International Monetary Fund has published information on restrictions on international financial transactions. An index of "openness" compiled and updated by Dennis Quinn shows that such restrictions have almost completely disappeared in industrialized countries and have decreased considerably in developing countries.[4]

As can be seen in Figure 1.1, the volume of transactions in stocks and bonds between U.S. and foreign investors increased dramatically from 1977

FIGURE 1.1

Gross Cross-Border Securities Transactions for the U.S. (Sum of Purchases and Sales) to U.S. GDP (2006 Number Estimated from January–October Data)

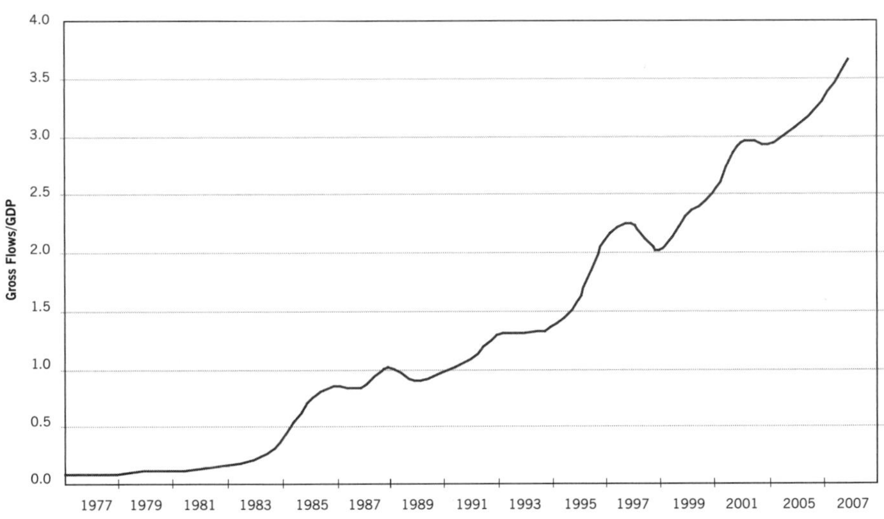

through 2006. During that period, the volume of such transactions as a percentage of GDP increased by a factor larger than 60, from just under 6% to over 365%. By comparison, the dollar volume of transactions on the NYSE grew from just over 7% of GDP to about 130% of GDP, or by a factor of 19.

With such a dramatic increase in cross-border trade in securities and the disappearance of many formal barriers to international investment, we would have expected institutional and other differences among countries to have steadily diminishing effects on both investors' and companies' investment and financing decisions. But it has not happened. According to a number of recent studies, "countries" continue to have a major influence on asset returns, investment portfolios, and corporate financial policies.

The evidence shows that countries continue to be important for portfolio choice. Investors continue to overweight domestic securities in their portfolios. Although such "home bias" has decreased over time, a study of global investor portfolios showed that, as of the end of 2004, the share of foreign equities in U.S. portfolios was roughly one-fourth of what it would have been had investors chosen to hold the "global market portfolio," with holdings in all the world's national economies in proportion to the size of their equity markets.[5]

Countries continue to be important for saving and investment. In a study produced more than 20 years ago, Martin Feldstein and Charles Horioka showed an extremely high correlation between domestic saving and investment.[6] This gave rise to what became known among economists as "the Feldstein-Horioka puzzle." The puzzle is this: As investors diversify internationally, saving (which depends on domestic income and wealth) and investment (which depends on local growth opportunities) should become less closely related to each other. Investment should be determined by the amount of promising growth opportunities within a country rather than the availability of funds. While there are signs of a decoupling of investment from saving in some countries, recent studies still find a surprisingly strong correlation. For instance, one study of emerging markets during the 1990s—the period when such markets began to take off—showed that the fraction of investment financed by foreign investors did not increase at all during that decade.[7]

Countries continue to be important for consumption. In a fully integrated world, consumption within a given country would not be tightly linked to, and would be more stable than, the country's income. To the extent they could, investors would effectively buy "insurance" against country-specific risks by holding internationally diversified portfolios and using hedging and risk-transfer mechanisms. Economists describe this phenomenon as "consumption risk-sharing." Recent studies, however, find at most a limited increase in consumption risk-sharing over time.

Countries continue to be important for corporate ownership. The composition of corporate ownership varies systematically across countries. In a widely cited 1999 study, Rafael La Porta, Florencio Lopez-de-Silanes, and Andrei Shleifer showed that, in most countries other than the U.S. and U.K., the representative company has a concentrated ownership structure.[8]

Figure 1.2 reports the median fraction of market capitalization held by blockholders in large companies representing 48 countries at the end of 2002.[9] The median ownership fraction for the 48 countries was just over 50%. The U.S. was at the "left tail" of the figure, with a median percentage of market capitalization held by blockholders of just over 15.5%. And the median percentage of blockholdings in U.K. companies, at 10.31%, shows a similarly dispersed ownership structure. By contrast, in a country like Italy, that fraction was over 40%.

Countries continue to be important for capital structure. Studies have found that corporate capital structures vary widely among countries. For instance, after studying the capital structures of public companies in 39 developed and developing countries, Joseph Fan, Sheridan Titman, and Gary Twite concluded that "a corporation's capital structure is determined more by the country in which it is located than by its industry affiliation."[10] More specifically, they found that companies in countries with weak governance institutions have significantly higher leverage than comparable firms in countries that provide greater protection for investors—a finding I will discuss later.

Countries continue to be important for governance. Countries explain a very large part of the variation in the quality of governance across companies. In a recent study, Craig Doidge, Andrew Karolyi, and I found that country characteristics explained more than 70% of the variation in companies' S&P corporate governance scores.[11] Thus, in countries with significant agency problems, even companies with highly effective governance systems are likely to find their capital choices limited by where they are domiciled (although, as I will argue later, volunteering to list on an overseas exchange can help address this problem).

Economists have worked hard to explain why countries matter as much as they do. There are more than 100 studies that attempt to explain the home bias of portfolios, with explanations centering on variables such as transportation costs, transaction costs, consumption preferences, and differences in information among investors. But this literature fails to be convincing. Much of it focuses, for example, on differences that are attributable to *distance*. As such reasoning goes, investors who are far away may be less well informed about securities than investors who are on the spot. But there is an obvious problem with this type of argument: According to the "distance" school of thought, portfolios of investors in San Diego should be more like the portfolios of investors in Tijuana than those held by investors in Philadelphia almost 3,000 miles away. But "distance" in this case is clearly at most a second-order effect. That San Diego and Tijuana are separated by a border is *much* more important than their proximity to one another. And if distance has limited explanatory power in accounting for differences in

Value-Weighted Average of the Percentage of Shares Held by Corporate Insiders for 48 Countries in 2002

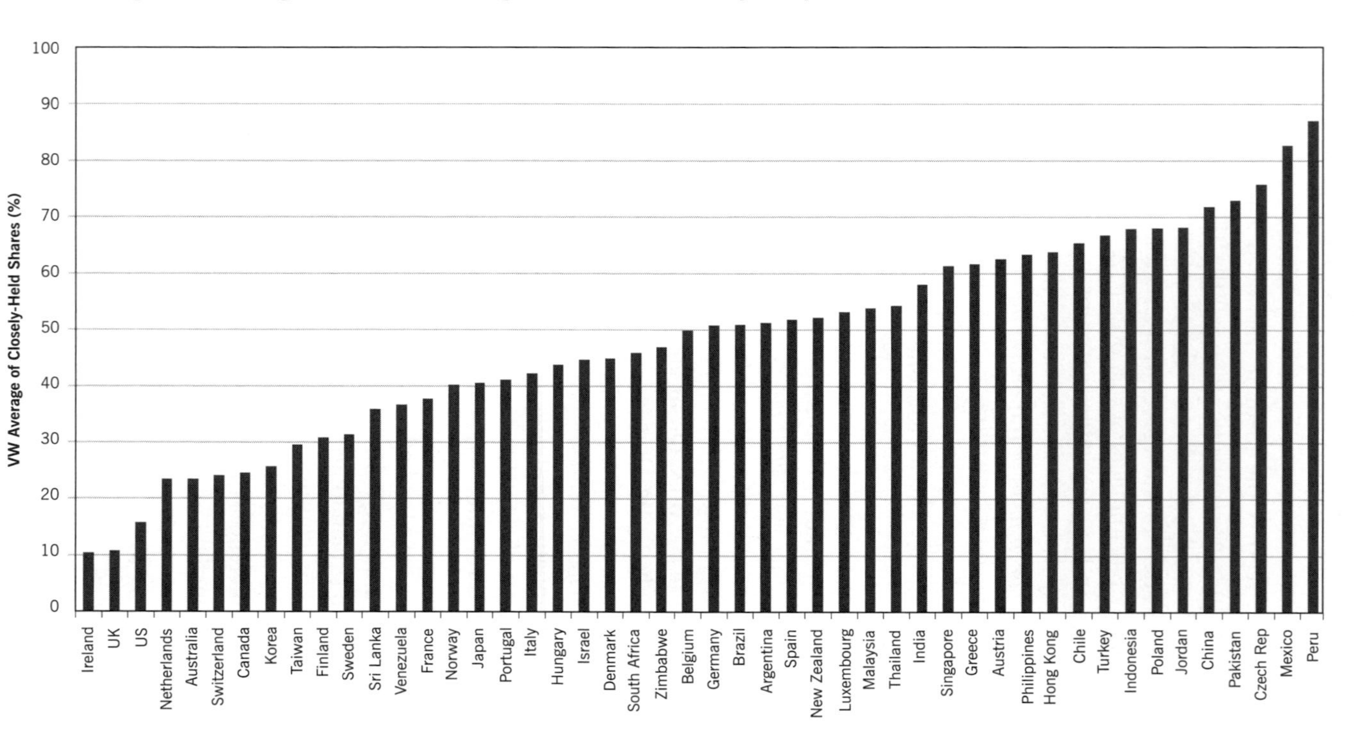

investor portfolios, it has even less to say about cross-country differences in, say, corporate capital structures. In this case, the differences have nothing to do with distance and everything to do with borders.

Why Countries Might Matter: The Twin Agency Problems

The key difference between explanations that rely on distance and those that rely on borders is the role of the sovereign state. There are two main reasons why the twin agency problems depend critically on the state: First, the sovereign state affects the extent of the agency problem between corporate insiders and other investors because it is a critical determinant of the extent of investor protection. Second, although the rulers of the sovereign state can expropriate investors, their powers to do so stop at the border.

To illustrate the implications of the twin agency problems for corporate ownership and risk-bearing, let's examine a simple example in which there are assumed to be two kinds of investors: entrepreneurs and portfolio investors. An entrepreneur has a unique investment opportunity. If she takes advantage of that opportunity, she starts a firm, sells equity to outside investors, and becomes a corporate insider. But if she decides to pass on the investment opportunity, she becomes a portfolio investor.

Let's consider now how the twin agency problems affect the entrepreneur and investors. Since the corporate insiders observe the cash flow produced by the company before anybody else, they have the ability to expropriate some of it before it comes to the attention of outsiders or representatives of the state. The rulers of the sovereign state are next in line; they can confiscate cash flows outright, tax them, redirect them to their favorite causes or allies, and so on. The cash flow left after expropriation by corporate insiders and the rulers of the sovereign state can then be (and let's assume for our example that it is) distributed to shareholders as a liquidating dividend.

Corporate insiders can transfer value from outside investors to themselves by consuming private benefits in relatively benign ways, such as buying fancy airplanes, or through more extreme ways, including outright theft. But it's important to keep in mind here that the corporate insiders, precisely *because of their ability to expropriate wealth from minority holders*, are limited in the amount of equity they can raise from outside investors. When pricing the equity offering, such investors assume that expropriation will take place. And given that the shares are priced to reflect such expected expropriation, insiders may have little choice but to expropriate; indeed, they can be viewed as having *already paid* for the "right" to expropriate in the discount at which the shares are sold.

The problem with such an "equilibrium," however, is that when they routinely expropriate minority shareholders, insiders also incur "deadweight costs" in the form of risk of embarrassment and possible exposure to legal sanctions. The size of such deadweight costs varies widely among countries. In countries such as the U.S. and U.K., expropriation is costly for insiders and so outside investors expect little of it to take place. But in countries where expropriation is expected, insiders can sell shares at a higher price (or, alternatively, reduce the deadweight costs associated with the possibility of expropriation) only by co-investing more with outside investors. As insiders increase their investment in a company, they have less to gain from expropriating minority shareholders.

To understand why, consider a simple example. Assume that the state expropriates 10% of a firm's cash flows after the controlling shareholders have already taken their cut in the form of private benefits. In that case, the outside shareholders receive dividends of 90 cents from each dollar of cash flow net of private benefits. And let's start by supposing that insiders own just 10% of the firm. In this case, by taking one dollar of private benefits, insiders would reduce the liquidating dividend by 90 cents, of which their share would be just 9 cents. As a consequence, the net gain to insiders of one dollar of private benefits before deadweight costs would be 91 cents in this case—and insiders would be expected to refrain from consuming this dollar of private benefits only if the associated deadweight costs exceeded 91 cents.

But now consider what happens when insiders own 50% of the company. In this case, each dollar of private benefits causes insiders to forgo 45 cents of dividends—and they accordingly stop consuming private benefits when the marginal deadweight cost reaches 55 cents. Thus, the net gain to insiders of a dollar of private benefits is reduced by increases in their ownership share. By co-investing more, insiders reduce their own incentives to extract private benefits. And the result of higher co-ownership is less expropriation of value by insiders, and thus higher values for all shareholders.

But, as already mentioned, there are two major costs associated with additional co-investment by insiders: the higher cost of capital that results from corporate insiders bearing risks they cannot diversify, and the constraint on the firm's investment and growth stemming from the limits of insiders' wealth and ability to co-invest.

What role does the state play in this corporate governance problem? A significant threat of expropriation by state rulers also encourages co-investment by corporate insiders. By "expropriation" I mean the (presumably self-interested) actions by state rulers that have the effect of reducing the returns of corporate investors. Although the case of Yukos comes to mind, the term "expropriation" covers a wide range of activities. Besides confiscating assets, state rulers can impose redistributive taxes, prohibit or limit value-adding activities (such as laying off redundant workers), favor friends and allies through permits and regulation, or demand bribes.

Such activities are, of course, by no means unknown in developed countries. In the U.S., we have evidence that the stock prices of S&P 500 companies with "Republican-connected" board members reacted positively to the Republican win in the election of 2000 and S&P 500 firms with Democratic board connections responded negatively.[12] And the widespread interference by the state and labor unions in most European countries has clear effects on how corporations are owned and organized.[13] But however common in developed nations, state intervention in business enterprise is likely to be even more pronounced, and destructive, in developing countries.

And such intervention has indirect as well as direct effects on corporate governance and behavior. One fairly direct effect is the heightened incentives of corporate insiders to reduce the state's proceeds from expropriation by increasing their own bargaining power with the state. The corporate insiders can accomplish this by building connections with the rulers and by making themselves more critical to the success of their companies through their choice of investment, contracting, and financing policies. But by making themselves more indispensable to a firm, insiders also become less subject to discipline by the market for corporate control and their outside shareholders—and so their incentive and ability to expropriate value increases, along with the associated deadweight costs. Thus the net result of such managerial entrenchment may be that the gains to minority shareholders from the reduced likelihood of expropriation by the state are completely offset by the losses from expropriation by insiders.

Furthermore, when management has a small ownership stake, it is more likely to use its entrenched position to extract the best deal from the state for itself instead of using its power to protect shareholders. This in turn means that when the expected costs of state expropriation are significant, the governance problems inherent in the separation of ownership and control are likely to become less manageable than when governments do not expropriate.

In sum, corporate insiders with large ownership stakes are more likely to make decisions that limit the potential for state expropriation. And their large ownership stakes can also work to assure outside investors that the insiders will make decisions that benefit *all* investors. Absent such a stake, they might be tempted to let the state expropriate minority shareholders at will in exchange for the right granted by the state to appropriate more private benefits.

How the Twin Agency Problems Blunt
the Effect of Financial Globalization

I've discussed each of the two agency problems separately, but now let's consider briefly how they feed on each other.

First, to the extent corporate insiders are connected with state rulers, they can use the state to transfer value from other investors. As Raghuram Rajan and Luigi Zingales show in their recent book *Saving Capitalism from the Capitalists*,[14] business incumbents routinely use laws and regulations to tilt the playing field in their favor, thus hindering the development of new competitors. Second, in countries with a significant threat of expropriation by the state, the consumption of private control benefits by insiders is actually encouraged by the fact that such consumption is easier to hide from the state than the corporate cash flows that remain after insiders have extracted their private benefits.

In a recent study investigating the relation between ownership concentration and the risk of state expropriation, I found that the fraction of companies that are widely held—defined as having no blockholder with a stake larger than 20%—was significantly higher in countries with less (below-median) state expropriation risk.[15] Furthermore, both the percentage of companies with family control and the percentage of insider owners (both in terms of numbers and value) were both significantly higher in countries deemed to have greater (above-median) risk of expropriation by the state.

Now, let's look more closely at how the twin agency problems work to limit the impact of financial globalization. As I mentioned at the beginning, theoretical models of financial globalization predict that lowering barriers to international investment will reduce the corporate cost of capital, thereby increasing both the present value of existing profit streams and the number of profitable investment opportunities. But although empirical studies provide some support for these predictions,[16] the changes in firm value detected by these studies seem disappointing.[17] The twin agency problems can help us understand why the impact of financial liberalization might fall short of expectations.

When cross-country barriers to financial trading are lowered, part of the anticipated increase in shareholder wealth is attributable to the expected profits from new investments that can be undertaken only if *more* capital is invested. But because of the twin agency problems, much of the increase in capital investment would have to come from insiders who may already be constrained by limits on their wealth and by their inability to diversify their holdings. In this fashion, the requirement for concentrated ownership could lead to far lower corporate investment than might be expected under a governance system that encouraged more dispersed ownership.

Even if foreign investors could be persuaded to take larger ownership stakes in overseas companies, the resulting decrease in ownership by corporate insiders could well lead, at least in the near term (and for reasons already discussed), to greater expropriation of outsiders by both state rulers and insiders. What's more, in countries where the risk of expropriation by the state is significant, there is also the real possibility that barriers to international investment could be reinstated. Witness the cases of Malaysia and Argentina.

Effect on New Business Formation. But all these considerations concern the effect of financial globalization on existing companies. Now let's look at this issue from the perspective of individual entrepreneurs contemplating the launch of new businesses. On the one hand, globalization reduces the cost of capital for the potential entrepreneur, making the expected earnings stream from the new business more valuable. At the same time, however, globalization could also provide alternative uses for the potential entrepreneur's capital that are more attractive than starting a company. Consider what might happen in a country where the state discourages entrepreneurs and offers few attractive investment choices, and then globalization suddenly provides more attractive investment opportunities outside the country. If the returns to being an entrepreneur were attractive before globalization, they may not be afterwards.

In sum, financial globalization can lead to fewer entrepreneurs and new companies when the twin agency problems are serious. Moreover, as portfolio investment becomes more attractive, insiders may also choose to reinvest less in their own firms, thereby reducing the amount of investment in existing companies as well.

Effect on Home Bias. When concentrated ownership is optimal because of limited investor protection, insiders cannot hold well-diversified portfolios. As a result, in countries with major twin agency problems, equity investment will continue to display a pronounced home bias—provided corporate insiders are local residents (which is almost invariably the case).

Saving and Investment Correlation. In countries where it is efficient for corporate insiders to have significant stakes in their companies, we would also expect saving and investment to be highly correlated. In such a country, if investment opportunities increase but income and wealth do not, companies will not be able to take advantage of the opportunities because insiders will not have enough wealth to co-invest with outsiders.

Effect on Consumption. Ownership concentration implies that a substantial fraction of equity is in the hands of investors whose wealth is not well diversified. This concentration of holdings resulting from the co-investment of insiders reduces the correlation of consumption across countries. So, for example, when a country with concentrated ownership experiences a disproportionately large drop in income and wealth, it is also likely to suffer a disproportionate (relative to other countries') drop in consumption.

Effect on Capital Structure. The twin agency problems also lead to higher leverage. Start by making the assumption that debt has to be repaid before consumption of private benefits by corporate insiders. In this case, financing with debt limits the amount that corporate insiders can use to consume private benefits. Because of this advantage of debt, we can expect that, all else equal, companies domiciled in countries where the agency problem of corporate insiders is important will have higher leverage. Higher leverage can also reduce the gains from expropriation by state rulers to the extent that equity claims are more easily expropriated than debt.

There is also one other "surprise" that can be explained by the twin agency explanation—namely, the possibility that what we can think of as effective corporate governance can actually prove counterproductive under states that expropriate. By investing in good governance, companies can commit to providing better protection for minority investors. However, the benefit from investments in good governance may turn out to be a cost because of the states' ability to expropriate such gains in efficiency and profits. As already mentioned, the possibility of managerial entrenchment, which worsens the agency problem associated with corporate insiders, can actually help preserve overall value by reducing the threat of state expropriation. Further, the threat of state expropriation limits the benefits from corporate transparency since it is harder for the state to expropriate a firm whose true situation is hard to evaluate. Finally, state intervention that prevents the enforcement of contracts or changes the interpretation of contracts reduces the ability of companies to use private contracting solutions to reduce the problem of expropriation by insiders.

The (Longer-Term) Promise of Financial Globalization

Up to this point, I have taken the twin agency problems as given. In so doing, I have ignored an important benefit of financial globalization: its potential to reduce the importance of these problems over time.

To begin with, financial globalization reduces the cost of external finance. As external finance becomes cheaper, companies have stronger incentives to be well governed, at least to the extent they have opportunities to make greater use of such capital.[18]

Financial globalization also provides tools for companies to reduce the agency problem associated with corporate insiders. In a world of segmented markets, companies are stuck with their country's institutions. If their country has weak financial markets or poor securities laws, firms have to live with them. But, as barriers to trade in financial assets fall, companies can "rent" the institutions of foreign countries. ADR programs, as I argued in a paper several years ago, effectively enable foreign companies to offer their investors some of the protection afforded by U.S. institutions.[19]

By giving resident investors what amounts to an exit option, financial globalization also reduces the state's ability to expropriate. Having reduced barriers to international investment, states are limited in their ability to expropriate unless they first restore barriers to international investment. If they attempt to do so, resident investors are likely to put their money elsewhere, foreign investors will go home, and local companies will become less competitive.

Since financial globalization gives investors an exit, it is not surprising that they use it when they feel threatened. This is what happens during times of financial crisis. But rather than viewing globalization and capital outflows as the fundamental *cause* of such instability, this view suggests that such capital flows and crises can be traced to governance. The real culprit in such cases is not the mobility of capital flows, but the source of the threat to investors: the twin agency problems.

Conclusion

Although barriers to international investment have fallen sharply over the last 60 years, the positive impact of financial globalization has been limited. Predictions by economists that cross-country differences in investment and financing would narrow or even disappear have largely failed to materialize, and thus countries still "matter" a great deal.

The main explanation for the surprising persistence of cross-country differences in investment, financing, and corporate governance centers on the importance of two agency problems: First, those who control a company can use their power to transfer value from minority shareholders to themselves. Second, those who control the state can use their powers to expropriate wealth from both controlling and minority shareholders.

In countries where these twin agency problems are significant, corporate insiders tend to co-invest more with outside investors, and ownership is thus more concentrated. Co-investment in turn limits the benefit of financial globalization, making it less likely that risks will be shared internationally and capital invested where it is most productive.

The twin agency problems also help explain a number of apparent paradoxes in international finance. Until such problems are addressed, they will limit the impact of financial globalization. But, as countries and companies continue to find ways to control these problems, the citizens of developed and developing countries alike will benefit from the progressive globalization of financial markets.

Notes

This chapter is an edited transcript of the author's presidential address to the American Finance Association in Philadelphia on January 6, 2005. It was previously published in *Journal of Applied Corporate Finance*, Vol. 19, No. 1 (Winter 2007): 8–15.

1. For a review of such advantages, see my article "Globalization, Corporate Finance, and the Cost of Capital," *Journal of Applied Corporate Finance*, Vol. 12, No. 3 (Fall 1999), 8–25.
2. For instance, Geert Bekaert, Campbell R. Harvey, and Christian Lundblad, "Does Financial Liberalization Spur Growth?," *Journal of Financial Economics,* Vol. 77, No. 1

(2005), conclude that a country's equity market liberalization leads to an increase in economic growth of 1%.

3. See Eswar Prasad, Kenneth Rogoff, Shang-Jin Wei, and M. Ayhan Kose, "Effects of Financial Globalization on Developing Countries: Some Empirical Evidence," International Monetary Fund (2003).

4. Dennis Quinn, "The Correlates of Change in International Financial Regulation," *American Political Science Review,* Vol. 91 (1997), 531–551.

5. Bong-Chan Kho, René M. Stulz, and Frank Warnock, "Financial Globalization, Governance, and the Home Bias," Unpublished working paper, The Ohio State University.

6. Martin Feldstein and Charles Horioka, "Domestic Saving and International Capital Flows," *Economic Journal,* Vol. 90 (1980), 314–329.

7. See Joshua Aizenman, Brian Pinto, and Artur Radziwill, (2004), "Sources for Financing Domestic Capital—is Foreign Saving a Viable Option for Developing Countries?," National Bureau of Economic Research, Working Paper 10624.

8. Rafael La Porta, Florencio Lopez-de-Silanes, and Andrei Shleifer, "Corporate Ownership Around the World," *Journal of Finance,* Vol. 54 (1999).

9. Using data reported in Worldscope.

10. Joseph P.H. Fan, Sheridan Titman, and Garry Twite, "An International Comparison of Capital Structure and Debt Maturity Choices," Unpublished working paper, University of Texas (2006).

11. Craig Doidge, G. Andrew Karolyi, and René M. Stulz, "Why Do Countries Matter So Much for Corporate Governance?" *Journal of Financial Economics,* Vol. 8, No. 1 (2007), 1–39.

12. Eitan Goldman, Jörg Rocholl, and Jongil So, "Does Political Connectedness Affect Firm Value?," Unpublished Working Paper, University of North Carolina (2006).

13. See Mark Roe, "Political Determinants of Corporate Governance," Oxford University Press (2003).

14. Raghuram G. Rajan and Luigi Zingales, *Saving Capitalism from the Capitalists* (New York: Random House, 2003).

15. These empirical results are contained in a more technical article which addresses the issues raised in my presidential address. See René M. Stulz, "The Limits of Financial Globalization," *Journal of Finance,* Vol. 60 (2005), 1595–1638.

16. See Geert Bekaert and Campbell R. Harvey, "Foreign Speculators and Emerging Equity Markets," *Journal of Finance* 55 (2000), 565–613; Peter Blair Henry, "Stock Market Liberalization, Economic Reform, and Emerging Market Equity Prices," *Journal of Finance,* Vol. 55 (2000), 529–564.

17. See my article "Globalization, Corporate Finance, and the Cost of Capital," *Journal of Applied Corporate Finance,* Vol. 12, No. 3 (Fall 1999).

18. See Art Durnev and E. Han Kim, "Explaining Differences in the Quality of Governance Among Companies: Evidence from Emerging Markets," *Journal of Applied Corporate Finance,* Vol. 19, No. 1 (2007), 16–24.

19. See note 1.

CHAPTER 2

The Political Roots of American Corporate Finance

MARK J. ROE

IN 1990, two of General Motors's largest institutional shareholders, unhappy with the company's declining market share and profits during the 1980s, sought to talk to GM's leaders about a successor to the retiring CEO. GM's senior managers rebuffed the shareholders. They could do that because the two large stockholders each owned less than 1% of the company's stock.

How such a corporate ownership structure—many shareholders with small percentage holdings and, until recently, little voice in governance—came to be the dominant form of large business enterprise in the U.S. is usually understood as a purely economic story, one of business adaptation to economies of scale and investor diversification. The reigning explanation of U.S. corporate ownership structure continues to be the one provided over 60 years ago by Adolf Berle and Gardiner Means in their classic, *The Modern Corporation and Private Property*. According to Berle and Means, economies of scale made possible by new technologies required U.S. companies at the turn of the century to become so large that their enormous capital needs could be satisfied only by selling stock to many outside investors—investors who, by and large, wanted diversified portfolios. Ownership was thus dispersed, and this dispersion shifted decision-making power over the firm from shareholders (or, more precisely, shareholder-managers) to professional managers. This had benefits: it facilitated the exit of company founders and their heirs, professionalized U.S. management, and set the stage for large mergers. But, as Berle and Means warned, the separation of ownership from control also had offsetting costs stemming from weakened managerial incentives and accountability.

What Berle and Means failed to foresee were the many corporate governance mechanisms that were devised by both corporate insiders and outside investors to reduce such "agency costs"—things like proxy fights, hostile takeovers, incentive compensation plans, and, more recently, active outside directors prodded by institutional investors. The continued domination of the large public corporation in the U.S. suggests that such governance mechanisms, coming on top of intense competition in American product markets, worked to minimize the problems from the separation of ownership from control. For if the U.S. system had failed to "adapt" in a way that solved this governance problem, the current U.S. ownership structure would have been supplanted by a more efficient alternative. Survival implies efficiency—or at least greater efficiency than available alternatives.

In 1994, I published *Strong Managers, Weak Owners: The Political Roots of American Corporate Finance,* in which I argued that this explanation, although correct as far as it goes, is incomplete. Economics alone cannot fully account for the evolution of the U.S. corporation into its present form. Politics, in the form of laws and regulations affecting commercial banks and other financial institutions, played a key role in fragmenting stock ownership beyond what was required to have big firms and well-diversified investors. From the middle of the 19th century onward, both state and federal laws restricted the growth and activities of the largest American financial institutions. U.S. commercial banks were prevented from branching nationally, and thus they lacked both the size and the information networks to fund big pieces of the capital required by the large American firms emerging at the end of the 19th century. Banks' products and portfolios were also restricted—most important, banks were barred from the securities business and from owning stock. U.S. insurance companies were barred from buying stock for most of this century. Mutual funds, thanks to rules established in the 1930s and 1940s, cannot easily devote their portfolios solely to big blocks; and they face legal problems if they go into the boardroom. And, finally, pension funds cannot take very big blocks without structural and legal problems; the big private pensions are under managerial control (not the other way around), and Employee Retirement Income Security Act (ERISA) rules make it more comfortable for pension managers to avoid big blocks than to take them.

The rules that restricted the size and scope of U.S. financial institutions were neither random nor economically inevitable. While the public interest goals of protecting financial institutions explain some rules, they do not explain all of them. Two major forces lay behind many of the restrictions: American populism, with its profound distrust of large private accumulations of power, and interest group politics. There were businesses and individuals—mostly local bankers—who gained from the early fragmentation of U.S. financial institutions. These winners in the political process had a large voice in Congress, in part because their private goals happened to line up well with popular sentiment.

The environment in which the large American firm evolved was conditioned by more than engineers' requirements for huge economies of scale and investors' demand for diversification. It was also a political environment that precluded very large-scale finance and raised the costs to financial institutions of participating in the governance of large firms. A richer story of evolution toward efficiency must account for political influences that shunted the large firm's evolution down some paths and not others.

The Limits of Economics in Explaining Corporate Ownership

Corporate finance and corporate governance are primarily economic matters. The financing goal is typically to secure funding for the corporation at the lowest possible cost; the governance goal is to maximize the value of the firm to its owners. Given these economic priorities, politics and law are rarely viewed as fundamental influences on the organization of finance and corporate governance. But the structure at the top of a nation's companies—the place where the board of directors, shareholders, and senior managers interact—is the outcome not just of economic evolution toward efficiency, but of political developments such as laws and regulations that limited the range of adaptive possibilities.

Of particular importance are historical events that influenced, and occasionally dictated, the ways in which financial intermediaries—particularly banks and insurance companies—channeled savings from households to firms. America's historical aversion to private concentrations of economic power sharply limited the size and activities of its financial institutions. Such restrictions in turn influenced how stock (and debt) has been owned in the U.S., in large part by making it costly—if not illegal—for such institutions to own large blocks of a single company's stock or play an active role in corporate governance.

To put the same thought a little differently, U.S. law and politics historically denied firms and investors the use of certain corporate governance tools, and so the American governance system evolved in ways that enabled them to make the best use possible of the other available tools. Corporate managers and investors used the tools at their disposal. Had more tools been available, some companies may well have chosen a different mix to make themselves as efficient as possible.

That politics affected the *forms* of corporate ownership seems likely. But did these political forces on U.S. corporate ownership structure also affect corporate *efficiency and security values?* Even if U.S. corporations and their investors successfully "adapted," it seems plausible that American laws reduced corporate efficiency and increased the cost of capital for some firms in some periods of U.S. history. Adaptation, after all, has costs. And, although the evidence is uncertain, it also seems plausible that denying use of a potentially effective governance tool could have continuing costs for some American firms.

In the next part of this chapter, I summarize the considerable evidence that U.S. politics, laws, and regulations influenced the forms of ownership and top-level governance of the American corporation. Evidence of large increases in costs of capital is harder to come by, and less persuasive. Nevertheless, in the second half of the chapter, I discuss three potential problems—(1) monitoring (or "agency") costs, (2) information costs, and (3) costs of coordinating long-term investments involving different parties—that could each raise the cost of capital for companies with fragmented ownership. By foreclosing the possibility of concentrated ownership, American politics denied U.S. companies one of the governance tools that could have helped to control these problems.

I close by offering some policy prescriptions. There is enough basis for arguing that concentrated ownership could at times be helpful that those restrictive rules lacking a policy justification ought to be pulled back. The reason to do so is not to favor one governance tool over another, but to encourage *both* ownership structures. Competition among alternative governance systems *within the U.S. economy* has the potential to increase the efficiency of American firms.

Political Roots

Political influences shaped American financial institutions and, in the process, American corporate finance and ownership patterns. Begin by looking at the large U.S. corporation as it emerged at the end of the 19th century. Coming near the close of the Second Industrial Revolution, this period saw remarkable advances in technology. One major consequence of the new technologies was enormous economies of scale, which meant that the cheapest production accrued to the firms with the largest operations. Among industrialized nations at the time, only America had a continent-wide economy with low internal trade barriers; and thus it alone provided a sufficiently large market for those enterprises that could achieve large-scale efficiencies.

But achieving the tremendous output necessary to realize the new scale economies required huge capital inputs to build the manufacturing facilities and the distribution system. Where could that capital come from? Much of it came from internal growth and retained earnings, some of it came from investors. Individuals, even when assembled into small groups, lacked sufficient capital to fund such undertakings. As Alfred Chandler described the railroads, the first of the modern business enterprises,

> Ownership and management soon separated. The capital required to build a railroad was far more than that required to purchase a plantation, a textile mill, or even a fleet of ships. Therefore, a single entrepreneur, family, or small group of associates was rarely able to own a

railroad. Nor could the many stockholders or their representatives manage it. The administrative tasks were too numerous, too varied, and too complex. They required special skills and training which could only be commanded by a full-time salaried manager. Only in the raising and allocating of capital, in the setting of financial policies, and in the selection of top managers did the owners or their representatives have a real say in railroad management.[1]

Even John Rockefeller, the richest man in America, ended up owning only a fraction of Standard Oil. New technologies allowed for vertical integration of several steps in production and distribution; transactions that once occurred across markets—making raw materials in one firm, manufacturing them into a final product in another, and distributing them in yet another—were brought inside a single firm, with managers visibly coordinating the steps of production. Managers had to avoid shortages at each stage of production and ensure a smooth flow from raw material to final sale. *Management* thus became an even more critical determinant of the success or failure of large enterprises.

Eventually these new large-scale enterprises had to draw capital from many different shareholders whose holdings tended to be small in relation to the size of the enterprise. Although the early growth was financed by the founders' own capital and by retained earnings, a growing firm's capital requirements tended to outstrip its ability to finance itself from its own earnings. Commercial banks would often lend capital to fund part of this growth, but banks could not play a full range of roles because of their size (national banks were limited to a single location) and limited powers (they could not own stock). In the U.S. at the turn of the century, there were no financial institutions of sufficient size and geographical diversity to provide the bulk of needed capital directly to America's new large enterprises.

For the large family-owned businesses that made up most of American industry at this time, founders (or their heirs) wanting to cash out thus had only two basic choices: (1) they could sell their stock into the securities market; or (2) they could merge with another firm, in which case the securities market would finance the merger. (Indeed, the primary role of the securities market at the turn of the century was not to raise new capital, but to finance the massive mergers at the end of the 19th century and to allow founders to cash out.)[2]

The dispersion of ownership that eventually resulted from such equity financing determined that professional, salaried managers (with perhaps modest stock holdings) would assume control of the day-to-day operations. Although descendants sometimes took over running the firm from the founders, that role tended to fall to hired managers. Then, over time, concentrated stock ownership dissipated into fragmented holdings as the heirs sold off the inheritance and the managers occasionally raised new capital in public markets.

The resulting combination of a large-scale enterprise, a professional (non-owner) management, and fragmented, diversified stockholders shifted control of public corporations from shareholders to managers. In contrast to business enterprises in Europe and elsewhere, dispersed shareholders and concentrated management became the distinguishing characteristics of the large American firm.

What Might Have Been? (Or the "Venture Capital" Model of Corporate Governance)

The separation of ownership and control proved functional and, in many cases, a major source of value in its own right.[3] Good managers replaced often less motivated or sometimes incompetent heirs. Specialization of risk-bearing and management meant that good managers didn't need to have their own source of capital to get to run large enterprises.

But separation via public stock markets was not the only plausible path. Some founders might have preferred that banks, insurers, or other financial institutions had instead become part owners of their businesses. Then the power of professional managers could have been balanced by financiers with large stakes and a continuing interest in the firm—much as happens in the small firms financed by U.S. venture capitalists.

Financiers like J.P. Morgan, it's true, were able to play a major role in corporate governance at the turn of the century even without holding big blocks of stock, particularly when the client firms needed outside capital. Like modern-day venture capital and merchant bankers, Morgan and other influential investment bankers sat on corporate boards and participated in strategic decision-making. But this role proved to be short-lived, at least partly because political reprisals against the "money-trusts" in the early 20th century induced Morgan and other bankers to keep a low corporate governance profile.[4]

Had national financing beyond the securities markets been available, a different pattern might have emerged. Larger financial institutions with nationwide scope may well have been able to finance more rapid expansion than that allowed by securities issuance or internally generated funds. Truly national financial institutions may also have been able to participate *as substantial owners* in the wave of end-of-the-century mergers and cash-outs. In that case, the institutions could have used their large blocks of stock to sit on the boards of the merged enterprises (much as venture capitalists and LBO firms like KKR do today) and so shared power with senior management. As I explain later, such a concentrated ownership and governance structure could have been one tool in the bundle to help control monitoring, information, and coordination problems that may well reduce the value of many U.S. companies today.

But, as things turned out, this "venture capital" model was not widely adopted for large firm governance in the United States. Shareholders, it's true, get to elect the board of directors, and the board appoints the CEO. But the actual flow of power, as everyone recognized, ran in reverse: the CEO recommended nominees to the board. Board members were typically either insider-employees or other CEOs with little reason to invest time and energy in second-guessing the incumbent CEO. The CEO's recommendation for the board went out to the shareholders, whose small shareholdings gave them little incentive—or means—to find alternatives; they checked off the proxy card and returned it to the incumbents. In this fashion, the CEO dominated the election and the firm. And, although the balance of power may have shifted with the increased shareholder and board-level activism, as recently as the 1980s many directors continued to "feel they are serving at the pleasure of the CEO-Chairman."[5]

Why U.S. Banks Were Not Ready for the Expansion

When the large American corporation was emerging around the turn of the century, the dominant financial institutions—commercial banks and insurance companies—were in no shape to hold large blocks of stock. Industrial companies had learned how to operate nationally, but banks and insurers operated locally and could not own stock. When industries needed capital for expansion or to fund consolidations during the end-of-the-century merger wave, they could not go directly to a handful of commercial banks, much less to a single bank, that could provide all of the needed equity and debt from their own sources. National banks were national in name only, able to operate only from a *single* physical location.

When attempting to identify the origins of such restrictions on banking, most people think of the New Deal legislation of the 1930s—particularly, the Glass-Steagall Act, which separated commercial banks from investment banks. But the most serious restrictions on both banks and insurers *came well before* the New Deal. For banks, they were in place at the end of the 19th century; for insurance companies, they came shortly after the turn of the century. The New Deal was important in confirming the financial and ownership structures that already prevailed—and in confirming them during a period of flux when those structures could have been changed, but were not.

Restrictions on Branching

As two Federal Reserve economists put it, "For much of its history, the United States has had a banking system like no other in the industrialized world. Since the early 1800s, the U.S. banking system has been highly fragmented, consisting of numerous small banks without extensive branch systems."[6] States chartered their own banks, and Congress, influenced by local interests, refused to charter national banks that could operate more extensively than the politically powerful local banks.

Every few decades, the lack of diversification resulting from such geographic restrictions either caused or aggravated a U.S. banking "crisis." This emboldened some political leaders to propose nationwide branching in order to strengthen the banking system. But, as happened when President Cleveland endorsed proposals to allow "national" banks to branch in 1895, the proposals were repeatedly blocked in Congress by well-organized unit bankers (bankers that operated from a single physical location). Indeed, the well-organized unit bankers not only stymied truly national branching for national banks, but induced Congress to reduce the capital requirement for rural national banks. The result was the establishment of many new banks, thus sowing the seeds for future bank crises and further strengthening the anti-branching banker constituency. Having more weak, local banks meant there were more players willing to invest in political action to block creation of national financial institutions.

Different political structures could have yielded different outcomes. Historically undemocratic Japan did not have the same open political structure that made American populism such a potent force. Japanese interest group configurations also differed from those in the U.S., and the national political structure was less responsive to local banking interests than the American structure. And, so, when the Japanese banking system faced a rash of failures in 1927, the Japanese authorities reacted by merging many banks into larger ones.

Such mergers were one of the major steps in the evolution of Japanese banks into the main banks that were at the center of the Japanese *keiretsu* after World War II. So, while American regulation was keeping banks small and local, Japanese regulation was making them much bigger. For better or worse, the Japanese banks had the financial strength to be able to take equity positions in most large firms after World War II. Large stock purchases of industrial firms by groups of four or five Japanese banks and insurers then produced the Japanese *keiretsu,* the networks of cross-ownership and influence among both industrial and financial firms that have dominated the Japanese economy since the 1950s.

Contrast Japanese policymakers' decision to concentrate finance during its 1927 banking crisis with the outcome of the American banking crisis that took place soon after. Instead of encouraging bank mergers and allowing nationwide branching, U.S. legislators responded to the Depression-era bank crisis by enacting deposit insurance (which was intended to *protect* small banks from larger competitors) and separating commercial from investment banking (to prevent concentration of power among the larger banking operations).

What explains the American result? The answer has much to do with differences in politics. Most members of the U.S. Congress, given the strength of their ties to their local districts, had an interest in keeping banks small and local.[7] Small-town American bankers were influential people; and, by exploiting the public sentiment against concentrated financial power, this interest group was consistently effective in Congress. And, so, Congress predictably chose to prop up the small banks with deposit insurance and other regulations designed to protect their ability to compete with larger banks at roughly the same time that an authoritarian Japan was concentrating its banking system.

Product Restrictions

Although geographic restrictions on U.S. banks were crucial, product restrictions also played an important role—and they too were in place well before the turn of the century. The National Bank Acts of 1863 and 1864 gave national banks only limited powers.[8] Control of an industrial company was not even contemplated and, hence, out of the question. And, in 1892, when the controversy over whether national banks could own stocks got the attention of the Supreme Court, the ruling came down that the power to own stock was not listed in the Act, and so it was not granted.[9]

Were Other Paths Possible?

We have already provided glimpses of alternative ownership structures in the form of the Japanese *keiretsu* and U.S. venture capital practices. But another way to see what might have been is to look at early American financial arrangements. Two of these are worth examining in some detail: (1) the close connections between banks and industry in New England in the early 19th century (before banking restrictions became as important); and (2) the structure and history of the Second Bank of the United States.

Economic historians have shown that, in the first part of the 19th century, New England entrepreneurs bound their operating firms to the local banks. Yet these banks did not grow into national financial institutions, and the ties between the entrepreneurs and their local banks eventually withered. The primary reason these relationships failed to grow appears to be that, as economic opportunities shifted from New England to the national economy, the New England banks could not get good information about distant firms, and the bankers were able to participate in the national economy only as passive buyers of short-term commercial paper. As economic historian Naomi Lamoreaux put it, "[F]irms could issue their IOUs through note brokers, who would market them to banks and financial intermediaries across the country . . . [and] banks lost their ability to assess a customer's total indebtedness."[10]

Since evaluating the creditworthiness of companies is usually a banker's strength, one wonders why the New England bankers ceded the profits to these note brokers. The most likely answer to this puzzle is that the bankers probably did not cede the profits voluntarily. Rather, because banks in regions with a capital surplus could not branch into capital-importing areas, the money could not move inside a single organization. But investment bankers could market notes and commercial paper throughout the country. Thus, entrepreneurs affiliated with banks could pursue economic opportunities to go national while their bankers, because of branching restrictions, could not. The commercial paper market—short-term IOUs from a debtor—was the way financiers and industrialists found to "contract around" the geographic restrictions on banks.

The Fate of America's First National Financial Institution

Ironically, one of the first American national business institutions was a bank, the Second Bank of the United States. Described by Alfred Chandler as the "first prototype of modern business enterprise in American commerce," its organizational structure allowed it to coordinate complex financial transactions through its many branches to enable capital to move across the nation to support the flow of trade.[11] But, as is well-known, Andrew Jackson killed this first national financial intermediary with his famous veto message refusing to recharter the Bank.

The Second Bank had a double importance for the history of U.S. banking. It was not only a precursor of the modern-day central bank necessary for a strong banking industry, it was also a semiprivate institution with an interstate branching network. Had it survived, its national branch network could have been a model for future private banking charters. The Second Bank, or more private but truly national banks, might have played a central financial role in the construction and merger of large national firms at the end of the 19th century.

Jackson's veto of the renewal of the Second Bank's charter can be attributed to both of the two key forces that would determine the future structure of U.S. financial institutions: interest group infighting and American populism. State banks felt threatened by the Second Bank, which competed with them and had some power to control them. This opposition was an early reflection of the local bank power that American federalism fostered and that tended to keep America's financial institutions small.[12]

Jackson's refusal to renew the Bank's charter also tapped the rich vein of populism in American politics. The veto message attacked the Bank as an elitist institution owned "by foreigners . . . and a few hundred of our own citizens, chiefly of the richest class." The Bank had the potential to be run by a small group of people. "It is easy to conceive that great evils to our country and its institutions might flow from such a concentration of power in the hands of a few men irresponsible to the people."[13] Jackson's forceful rhetoric helped imprint on the national psyche frightening images of an elitist concentration of private economic power. For decades following the veto, the message itself was assigned reading for schoolchildren.

Not until the 1990s were American laws changed to permit nationwide banks, at a time when banks were of diminishing importance in the economy.

How U.S. Insurers Lost Their Powers

Banks, though, were not the only powerful financial institution in the U.S at the turn of the century. In an era that preceded the rise of pension funds and mutual funds, life insurers were a central depositary for middle-class savings. Were they similarly affected by politics?

The early history of the life insurers suggests they were not. At the beginning of the 20th century, several of the largest American financial institutions were insurance companies, not banks. Although banks were confined to a single state, insurers were not. The largest New York insurers were twice as large as the largest banks and were moving into related financial activities. Some insurers were underwriting securities; some were buying bank stock and controlling large banks; and some were assembling securities portfolios with the potential for exercising control. Some insurance companies had already put as much as 12% of their assets into stock. Indeed, the three largest American insurers at the time—Equitable, Mutual, and New York Life—were growing so rapidly that they showed promise of developing into institutions that would rival the powerful German universal banks or the main banks in Japan. At the very least, they seemed ready to become much like the large modern British insurers, which hold considerable stock and play a more important governance role than their passive American counterparts.

But then politics intervened. In 1905, the insurance industry was rocked by scandal, revealing nepotism, insider financial chicanery, and bribery of legislatures. The New York legislature responded with a political inquiry, which came to be called the "Armstrong investigation" after the state legislator who chaired the committee. In 1906, new insurance laws barred insurers from owning stock, controlling banks, or underwriting securities. For the next 50 years, insurers were banned from owning any stock at all—and serious deregulation of this ban on stock ownership by insurance companies did not begin until the 1980s.

In short, American politics limited the insurance industry to its core business of writing insurance and investing in debt. Today, although insurance companies have stock holdings that amount to about 5% of the total market (which puts them a distant third behind mutual funds' share of about 10% and pension funds' 30%), they play a negligible role in corporate governance.[14]

Modern Times: Mutual Funds and Pension Funds

Mutual funds and pension funds, although long overshadowed by commercial banks and insurers, now account for the bulk of institutionally owned stock in the U.S., and their share of financial assets under management is expected to continue rising. Although the potential role of such funds in corporate governance has also been somewhat limited by legal and regulatory factors, political influences on laws and regulations that govern mutual funds and pension funds are less direct and clear-cut than those that constrained the historical structure of American banking and insurance. But such laws and regulations do raise the costs of such funds becoming involved in corporate governance—and it's too early to say whether the funds will come to play a bigger governance role.

For example, mutual funds face portfolio limits that stop them from deploying much of their assets in big block positions with boardroom influence.[15] And it is generally not worthwhile for funds with a small stake to attempt to play a big (which often means "expensive") public role in governance. The few public exceptions seem to arise when a mutual fund, or a complex of funds, finds itself with a sizeable block. For example, when Kodak was in crisis and Fidelity found that its group of funds owned about 7% of the company, Fidelity became involved.

As for pension funds, although the laws governing such funds do not explicitly bar big blocks and boardroom activity, such activities are deterred by the reality that funds that deviate from prevailing practice expose themselves to greater business risks and the threat of litigation.[16] Similarly, "little" mistakes with small ownership positions can be hidden and don't usually lead to a lawsuit against the pension funds' managers. But a misstep with a large block (even if embedded in a diversified portfolio) is more readily targeted for a lawsuit. Private pension funds are also typically under the control of the sponsor company's managements, and most senior managers have usually not supported strong corporate governance activity. The *public* pension funds, by contrast, have been more active. For example, CalPERS and others have prodded boards to set up governance and review procedures.

Although the new institutional activism is about a decade old, it is still too early to say where it will all end up. Current arrangements could be the long-term, continuing result—that is, occasional institutional activism, usually following bad firm performance, but with few big blocks of stock and little continuing inside-the-boardroom role. On the other hand, the current moderate levels of activism could be an evolutionary step *toward* new roles such as acquiring industry and governance expertise, and even putting institutional representatives in the boardroom (thus moving along a path once cut off).[17] But if this happens in a way that threatens corporate managers, one wonders whether the hostile takeover tensions of the 1980s will reemerge, and managers will once again call on state legislatures for protection.[18]

Modern Times: Securities Law Limits on Shareholders' Joint Action

With historical regulation of the banks and insurers barring big equity blocks, and with mutual funds and pension funds too new or too constrained for all but a few to be capable of taking big blocks in big industrial firms, *joint action* by a number of large shareholders may be today's most realistic corporate governance alternative to concentrated ownership for large U.S. firms. Given the institutionalization of stock ownership in the past couple of decades, ten or twenty owners of 1% of a firm could band together to involve themselves in corporate governance.

Obvious business reasons tend to frustrate this kind of coordination: some of the players don't want to work with a competitor (if you identify a problem, sell fast rather than alert competitors with whom you'd work to fix it), the institutions are only rarely going to be able to contribute functionally, and so on. But on top of this, securities rules discouraged joint shareholder action by, for example, classifying informal meetings (and even telephone calls) among a handful of investors as proxy solicitations requiring public filings with the SEC. Such laws saw to it that financial players who wanted to be active but keep a low profile could not do both; they instead needed their lawyers every step of the way and had to "go public" to be active. If the ownership stake was small, the profitable action was usually to do nothing.[19]

Then, in the early 1990s, the SEC relaxed its view that made many informal communications among investors come under rules requiring proxy filings. That change increased the activity of some investors with sizeable (though far from control) blocks in working with other investors to bring about change. As one example, Michael Price's actions in prodding Chase to merge with Chemical, taken largely through a mutual fund, were said to have been impossible before the SEC assured institutional investors that some forms of coordination would not be viewed as proxy solicitations.[20]

Potential Costs: Could Ownership Structure Affect Performance?

It is hard to deny that American politics contributed historically to smaller and weaker banks and insurers than would otherwise have developed. And it's quite possible that larger and stronger institutions would have taken bigger ownership stakes, such as those that are common in venture capital financing and in large firms in Japan and Germany. Big blockholding has costs in reducing diversification, and bigger institutions of course can hold bigger blocks at lower cost. But even if the form of corporate ownership was affected, long-term performance might not have been. Substitute tools accomplish at least part of what alternative ownership might do—and some of the substitute tools may well work better for some firms than ownership by a financial institution.

This brings us to the question posed at the beginning of this chapter: If the fragmented ownership of U.S. corporations was not economically inevitable, were the governance substitutes for concentrated ownership devised by U.S. firms and capital markets as efficient as the governance alternative that was foreclosed? To put the same another way, did the American adaptations demanded by U.S. law and politics end up imposing major costs on shareholders and the economy? Although such costs are difficult to quantify, they can be divided into two major categories: (1) the costs of the original adaptation; and (2) the continuing costs of a less than optimal governance system. First of all, even if the adaptations proved to be *perfect* substitutes, adaptation still cost something: new structures had to be built, experiments were tried and some failed, people who might have devoted themselves to another economic activity found themselves most profitably engaged in building these adaptive structures. As one example of such costs, some evidence indicates that at the time of one politically motivated restructuring—the Pujo investigation, which prompted Morgan and other investment bankers to leave the many boardrooms—the stock prices of Morgan's client firms declined.[21] While the reasons for the decline could have been several, one plausible interpretation is that the governance structure would be weakened, at least for a time. Adaptation, even if effective, usually isn't costless; the stockholders at the time adaptations take place pay a price.

The harder question is whether there are continuing costs from America's historical aversion to concentrated financial institutions with significant power in the boardroom. Given the many governance substitutes, it's hard to see how these costs can be very great—unless the main substitutes have problems or are themselves subject to political constraints. But if the substitute tools are less effective for some firms in some situations, then such companies may bear ongoing governance costs—say, reacting a little too slowly to a shift in demand in some cases, or failing to ramp up a new profitable project as fast as possible.

Three kinds of cost could affect companies even today: monitoring costs, information costs, and industrial organization costs. Each has the potential to raise a company's cost of capital and reduce its productivity.[22] The next three sections spell them out.

Monitoring Costs

Monitoring costs are well-known and hardly need explanation. As suggested earlier, the separation of ownership from control could weaken managerial incentives and accountability. Directors representing institutions with large blocks of stock would presumably have the means, and their institutions the incentive, for more effective monitoring of managers.

When Monitoring Is Likely to Be Important. Monitoring and corporate governance should matter least in highly competitive markets with little fixed, long-term capital and lots of growth opportunities. Managers who destroy value in such cases, or fail to increase it fast enough, will be unable to raise capital for growth and eventually be replaced. But when markets are concentrated, or the firms' fixed investments are large and its growth opportunities few, managers will be somewhat free from competitive and capital market pressures. In that setting, managers who fail to use their capital efficiently need not face the consequences of error immediately; whether because oligopoly provides "slack," or the firm has lots of long-lived capital in place, the firm can slowly waste away until one of the governance mechanisms kicks in to make managers do their job better (or replaces them).

Take the case of GM in the early 1990s. After almost a decade of shrinking market share and substandard stock-price performance, the company's competitive problems culminated in 1991 with a loss of $7 billion from North American operations. At this late stage, pressures from institutional shareholders finally combined with competitive failure to force GM's board to replace two senior management groups. If better internal governance mechanisms had been in place—ones that could have kicked in earlier—much of the loss in GM's competition position and shareholder value might have been avoided.

As this example is meant to suggest, pressures for better governance can be seen as reinforcing the effects of competition in product markets. Good governance encourages a quicker response to competitive forces, bad governance slows the response. Because many companies have long-term, fixed capital, and some U.S. and global markets are still oligopolistic, governance reform can play an important monitoring role.

A Qualification. One obvious qualification needs to be made at this point: because the institutional representatives would themselves be agents for others owning the stock, they would not be perfect monitors. Moreover, the blockholder itself, or the individuals managing the positions, could face conflicting incentives. For example, a commercial lender who is also a blockholder might overlook the poor shareholder returns of its borrowers while collecting fees and charging higher interest rates.

Thus, concentrated ownership by institutions is not a panacea, and some ownership forms could introduce their own monitoring costs.[23] But the question is not whether changes in ownership structure would be costless (although public policy concerns must of course be considered when deciding to allow such changes). The question is whether block ownership and boardroom representation would reduce the overall agency costs faced by the corporation and its investors.

Information Costs

When information about a company's strategy or prospects is complex or "soft" (i.e., difficult to quantify), management often finds it hard to communicate it to outsiders. Stockholders with small holdings—and the equity analysts who write research reports for them—may not have the incentives to spend much time trying to understand complex, technological information; so they might choose to ignore it and just look at the bottom line. And managers with good, but *proprietary* information would not want to reveal such information to the stock market because it could benefit their competitors. In either event, the stock market never gets the information; and, to the extent the market discounts share values for greater uncertainty (i.e., assumes the worst), information costs end up raising the firm's cost of capital.

But such soft, complex, or proprietary information may be more readily conveyed to those who sit regularly in the boardroom. The ability to communicate the prospective value of a high-quality and cohesive middle management team, or the import of technical data generated inside the firm, may well be greatly improved by regular, private interaction between large stable stockholders and managers. In this sense, concentrated ownership may be able to lower the cost of capital by reducing information costs.

Another potentially important source of information costs are distortions of management's incentives that could occur when managers are unable to communicate effectively with the market. If managers increase the long-run value of the firm in ways that investors cannot see right away, the managers may not get the "credit" right away (say, in the form of bonuses or payoffs from short-term stock options) their performance merits. Managers may then pass up profitable investments with long-term payoffs while blaming the "short termism" of the stock market. And both managers and markets will be behaving "rationally"—managers because they believe their superior performance will not be rewarded during their tenure, and investors because they lack both the information necessary to evaluate the profitability of such investments and the influence to bring about necessary changes if managers are wrong. Managers may even try to insulate themselves from the stock market (as many did during the hostile takeovers of the 1980s) by erecting anti-takeover defenses.

In theory, then, concentrated ownership structures can improve the flow of information from inside the firm to large shareholders, thus helping to deter the short-term propensities often seen in managerial behavior and sometimes in the stock market. Large holdings give the owner the scale economies needed to justify investing in the capability to acquire and process complex information. Big blockholders can afford to hire an engineering or marketing consultant that a small stockholder wouldn't think of hiring. Finally, size and board-room presence give large stockholders a strong incentive to protect proprietary information (because to behave otherwise would reduce the value of their own large stock positions).

Coordination Costs in Joint Long-Term Investments

Multiple complex investments need coordination: An auto company builds an assembly line and needs a supplier to build a big facility to make the chassis or the transmissions or the engines. What stops one of them from extorting the other later on, after the other has built specific machinery that can't be used for anything else? What stops the one who is stuck from finding their supply prices driven down to their variable costs, so that it can't recover its original investment in the factory and machines?

This problem of coordinating joint long-term investments recurs in organizing industry, and *can be especially costly* when highly specific contracts cannot be written to govern the investments. The specific contracts can't be written many times because business will change in ways the two parties can't anticipate or because pricing formulas can't be made before the business gets going.

One solution to this "contracting and coordination" problem is, of course, complete vertical integration: the customer—the assembly-line firm—buys up the supplier firms, or builds itself all of the necessary machinery, parts, and distribution systems. Although this "solves" the coordination and hold-up problems, it creates other problems, which can be more costly. Combining customers and their suppliers within a single firm tends to reduce managerial accountability for each and blunts incentives for efficiency.

A promising alternative lies in the multiple cross-holdings of stock by customers and suppliers, especially when a half-dozen suppliers and customers must simultaneously make such commitments. A customer that partly owns, say, 5% of the stock of a supplier has less incentive to exploit the supplier than one who doesn't. A customer that is a 5% stockholder and sits on a supplier's board gets information with which to monitor management not just as a buyer of the supplier's products, but also as a board member and stockholder. If the customer tried to take advantage of the supplier after the supplier has committed itself, a "*keiretsu*-like" coalition of shareholders could intervene to stop the opportunism.[24]

A third-party financier could cement these partial relationships, acting as an "escrow" agent that owns some of the equity of both the suppliers and the customers. Financial institutions big enough to hold, say, 5–10% of the stock of each of the suppliers and customers in a network could play this role. Although there's evidence of this in Japan,[25] one could also imagine a role for such arrangements in the U.S. Using such financing, for example, the bust-ups of the 1980s could have taken a somewhat different course. In the U.S. the choice has tended to be an "either/or" one, with possibilities lying only at the ends of the spectrum of independence versus integration. But, with third-party financing, some related companies might have been broken off from large vertical organizations, but networks of coordination could have been retained when it was important to do so. Under such arrangements, the financing institutions would broker deals when disputes between customers and suppliers came up, and smooth relationships during normal times.[26]

The Case for Competing Governance Systems

Today, each nation tends to have its own semi-proprietary governance system, in which the largest public companies have relatively homogeneous ownership structures. In Japan, main banks both lend to and own 5% of the stock of large firms, with other banks taking 5% blocks as well. In Germany, a handful of banks and insurers have many large blocks of stock, some owned directly, some built from custodial holdings for individual investors. Thus, whereas most large U.S. companies have fragmented ownership structures, most large Japanese firms and many European firms have large-block shareholders. There is little diversity within national economies.

One major advantage of the U.S. financial system is its flexibility. When large organizational structures become inefficient in the U.S., entrepreneurs set up new firms that compete with old firms—and, through the securities markets, small competitors can often quickly raise the financing they need to be viable. And, by competing with the large organizations, small firms either end up improving the large firms, or replacing them. American-style hostile takeovers, though much reduced since the 1980s, also help bring about such changes. The U.S. system also seems to excel at big-leap improvements, because whole new structures (MCI is a good example) can be quickly built by American entrepreneurs using venture capital financing and a vibrant securities market.

By contrast, in centralized financial systems like those of Japan and Germany, the central players seem less willing to finance new ventures, either because they fail to see the advantages of the innovation or because the new ventures would compete with their own large corporate clients. On the other hand, foreign bank–centered systems may be able to make stronger commitments to established firms that help enable those companies to make steady improvements in known technologies. To the extent they are successful in reducing the information and monitoring costs faced by outside investors, bank-dominated systems may enable such companies to carry out their investment plans during difficult periods.

But, for purposes of public policy, where does this comparison leave us? The recognition that the U.S. securities markets have greater flexibility, but less ability to make long-term commitments, than bank-centered economies like Japan and Germany, might seem to fail to yield any clear policy recommendations. It would be a mistake to list the advantages and disadvantages of all the different systems, weigh them, and then pronounce one the winner. It would also be a mistake to decide that if there is no clear winner—or even if the securities markets were the winner—we ought then to preserve *all* aspects of the current American system.[27]

Such arguments are flawed because they exclude an important middle ground: the possibility of encouraging *competition* among organizational forms in the same national economy. Competition between the two forms should bring out the best of both. Indeed, a national economy with competing forms of governance should, all else equal, eventually outperform an economy dominated by a single form. A mixed system could enable its firms to make more rapid and productive responses to changes in their markets and technologies.

Here's the basic idea: Begin by imagining that the ownership structure of the firms in two industries, A and B, are evenly divided between American-style fragmented ownership and Japanese-German concentrated ownership. Industry A is a high-tech, high-growth industry with lots of investment opportunities and large requirements for new capital. By contrast, Industry B is a low-tech, slow-growth industry with few investment requirements and excess capital.

High Growth, Shortage of Capital. Assume that in Industry A the value of a certain technology becomes apparent to inside managers, but the payoff from such investment is not the kind that can be communicated effectively to scattered outside stockholders. In that case, the managers of the 50% of the firms in that industry with fragmented ownership choose not to invest because they expect to be penalized in the short run (with smaller salary increases or reductions in the value of their stock options). At the same time, the managers of the other half of Industry A's firms can talk privately to their large-block stockholders, who are able to understand the needed change. In these circumstances, the firms with concentrated ownership get a competitive advantage by reacting faster. Eventually, however, product market competition brings even the slower-moving, diffusely owned firms into line, as they react with a lag.

And here's the benefit of competing governance systems: if none of the firms in the industry had large blockholders, managers of all companies might be more reluctant to make the investment because of their fear that the stock market would punish them until the supporting information was diffused throughout the economy.

Low Growth, Excess Capital. Now let's turn to Industry B, with limited growth opportunities and heavy fixed capital. In this case, it is likely to be those companies with concentrated ownership that respond most slowly. The insiders—a group that includes the managers and the big blockholders—may be reluctant to acknowledge that downsizing outmoded facilities is necessary because demand isn't going to come back to the industry. In this scenario, companies with dispersed ownership sometimes may act first. After the stock price is driven down, either insiders are forced to reform from within, or outsiders launch a hostile takeover and oust the incumbents. And then, once this information gets pounded into the industry in the form of higher stock prices for the downsized firms, then the big blockholders might help to speed change in their own firms.

As these two examples are intended to suggest, competition among different governance forms can speed change and adaptation. Product market competition, to be sure, will eventually bring about necessary change if all else fails. But even the increasingly global character of product market competition is no guarantor that the needed changes will be the quickest and most productive possible. Better governance can speed along needed change.

One might mistakenly imagine that global competition is enough to bring about change and that governance is therefore irrelevant. But this isn't true; a nation can insulate its firms from competitive forces. It must pay a price in lower living standards, but that doesn't mean that insulation can't be bought.

Imagine a nation that resists building a modern governance system and perpetuates some state ownership of enterprises, entrenches old managerial elites in the private businesses, or keeps outmoded labor arrangements. Let's assume further that such entrenchment leads to substandard management in the majority of that nation's firms. Must this governance system collapse under the threat of heightened international competition? Is it unstable?

The answer is "no" to both; it need not collapse and it could be stable. While global competition pressures that country's firms to improve, it doesn't *require* that they change. What counts is whether the firms produce competitive products that can be sold. The firm can continue to compete with an outmoded governance structure if it "saves" somewhere else with an offsetting advantage. It can save somewhere else by paying its employees (or some other immobile input) less. This result, while reducing that nation's standard of living relative to others', does not necessarily lead to economic instability. Stability depends as much on a nation's politics as it does on global competition.

Conclusion

America's fragmented ownership, a shift in power to professional managers, and the suppression of large owners did not threaten the widely held American corporation as an organizational form because the U.S. firm and its investors adapted. Even if the structure had some weaknesses, its weaknesses were outweighed by its strengths. While the separation of ownership from control reduced managerial accountability and incentives, and made the communication of strategic information more difficult, dispersed ownership facilitated economies of scale and the substitution of professionalized management for the often less capable heirs of the founders.

Competition often makes companies efficient regardless of their governance structure. Competition in product markets—and in managerial labor and capital markets as well—helped to align the interests of shareholders and managers, because the firm must get out a competitive product to survive in the long run. In the 1930s, 1940s, and 1950s, America was the world's only continent-wide open market, which meant that nowhere else in the world could several firms in an industry reach economies of scale *and* have workable competition *and* political stability. Markets abroad were closed, other nations were too small, transportation and communication costs were too high, and political upheaval was common.

But, besides the stimulus provided by competition, the large U.S. public firm also prevailed primarily because of its (and its investors') ability to strengthen managerial accountability and incentives. Through both internal and external adaptations, the public corporation succeeded in balancing the problems of managerial control with the demand for outside capital and diffusion of risk. Internally, the firm controlled managerial agency problems with outside directors, with a managerial headquarters staff responsible for overseeing the operating divisions, and with the use of managerial incentive compensation. Externally, hostile takeovers, proxy contests, and the threat of both further disciplined managers. A remaining question, however, is whether another tool in the governance toolbox—more concentrated ownership—would have helped some firms to adapt more quickly or with fewer costs.

Today, stock is moving from individuals to institutions. This trend toward greater institutional ownership and voice is critically important, and we can interpret it in two ways. Seen through the sweep of 100 years of American financial history, it can be viewed as yet one more adaptation to political constraints on U.S. financial institutions. But it can also be understood as the long-delayed breakout of more concentrated ownership and shareholder voice after previous institutional alternatives—concentrated ownership by banks and insurers—were suppressed.

That a dispersed ownership system may have costs does not, of course, mean that we should force firms to have more concentrated ownership structures—or that we should "subsidize" big blocks, or "tax" fragmented holders who trade vigorously. But we should also resist the temptation to add up the costs and benefits of each national governance system, pronounce one the winner, and then use law to move a system to the preferred governance model. Even if securities markets are better overall than concentrated ownership, concentrated ownership might be better for enough firms now and then that allowing such ownership structures could encourage better overall corporate performance in the future. There are enough tantalizing possibilities that we should permit outcomes that have been discouraged by laws and regulation. In America, that would mean loosening restrictions such as some of the current residual portfolio rules and securities law hindrances.

No corporate governance silver bullet will cure whatever governance ills occasionally afflict some American firms. Since a casual look at the concentrated governance systems in Germany and Japan shows lots of governance failures, one should be skeptical of any claim that concentrated ownership is superior and thus should be adopted by most companies. Institutional strength has obvious defects. It creates severe conflicts of interest, particularly if the institution sells something—a product, debt, or financial services—to the firm in which it owns stock. Such relationships could deteriorate into mutual managerial self-protection and, in so doing, discourage entrepreneurial initiative and leadership. And increased institutional power could lead to political pressure for more government intervention, which has tended not to work well in the U.S., and may yet prove to work poorly abroad. These imponderables are so large that any policy conclusion must be tentative, keeping in mind that where there are expected benefits there are likely to be some costs, too.

At the same time, one should not collect the stories of foreign failures at Metallgesellschaft, Daimler-Benz, and others, and then unequivocally endorse American-style corporate governance (with its own failures, such as ADM and the decade-long delay before GM seriously addressed its problems). Rather one should recognize that each system has strengths and weaknesses. Because America is big and capable of absorbing multiple governance systems, the U.S. has a greater potential than other nations of facilitating both organizational forms (and their hybrids), and allowing them both to compete.

So, my policy prescription is simple: since no governance form seems obviously superior for all firms at all times, we ought to allow competition among governance systems. Vestigial rules that serve little public purpose but hinder the emergence of competing governance structures should be revised. In most nations where the evidence is available, politics has favored some forms of organization and ownership over others. In Germany, bank influence has been favored, stock markets suppressed. In Japan, regulation blocked the growth of public capital markets and channeled postwar financing through banks. America, as we have seen, has not been immune to these political influences, which have favored liquid public markets and small-town bankers at the expense of concentrated finance. In suppressing alternatives to the diffusely held public corporation, American law and political history have suppressed competition among ownership forms.

Notes

1. Alfred Chandler, *The Visible Hand: The Managerial Revolution in American Business*, 87 (1977).
2. Ibid., 373.
3. William Lazonick, "Controlling the Market for Corporate Control: The Historical Significance of Managerial Capitalism," in *Industrial and Corporate Change*, 445, 447, 462–63 (1992).
4. A notable focus for such political reprisals was the Pujo investigation early in the 20th century. Chandler, cited in note 1, pp. 491–92.
5. Jay Lorsch and Elizabeth MacIver, *Pawns or Potentates: The Reality of America's Corporate Boards* (1989).
6. Robert T. Clair and Paula K. Tucker, "Interstate Banking and the Federal Reserve: A Historical Perspective," *Federal Reserve Bank of Dallas, Economic Review*, Nov. 1989, at 1.
7. Federal Reserve Committee on Branch, Group, and Chain Banking, Branch Banking in the United States 174 (1937); Eugene N. White, "The Political Economy of Banking Regulation, 1864–1933," 42 *Journal of Economic History* 33, 35 (1982); Eugene N. White, "The Regulation and Reform of the American Banking System, 1900–1929," *Journal of Economic History*, at 65, 161 (1983).
8. National Bank Act of 1864, ch. 106, 13 Stat. 99 (1864) (codified as amended at 12 U.S.C. § 38 (1988)).
9. California Bank v. Kennedy, 167 U.S. 362 (1892); National Bank Act of Feb. 25, 1863, ch. 58, §11, 12 Stat. 665; 12 U.S.C. §24 (Seventh) (1988). State member banks of the Federal Reserve System were later similarly restricted. 12 U.S.C. § 335 (1988).
10. Naomi R. Lamoreaux, "Information Problems and Banks' Specialization in Short-Term Commercial Lending: New England in the Nineteenth Century," in *Inside the Business Enterprise: Historical Perspectives on the Use of Information*, 161, 180 (Peter Temin, ed., 1991).
11. Chandler, cited in note 1, pp. 30–31, 42–43. Temin evaluates it as an inter-regional financier and a crypto-central bank. Peter Temin, *The Jacksonian Economy*, 28–58 (1969).
12. Bray Hammond, "Jackson, Biddle, and the Bank of the United States," *Journal of Economic History* 7, 1 (1947).
13. Edward L. Symons, Jr., and James J. White, *Banking Law: Teaching Materials*, 13–16 (3d ed., 1991).
14. Warren Buffett's insurers are property and casualty companies, not life insurers; property and casualty insurers overall have a much smaller asset base than the life insurers have. Buffett's authority to use even the property and casualty insurers for big blocks of stock required changes in the governing law, changes made in the 1980s.

15. To be sure, mutual funds' positions rarely even come near these limits, but this could be the result of such limits in combination with other constraints that have prevented mutual funds from taking large blocks in the past.

16. And, because the historical structures and rules for banks and insurers have not looked kindly on governance activity, the pension law's imitation rules favor the diversified, fragmented structures. See Mark Roe, "Mutual Funds in the Boardroom," *Journal of Applied Corporate Finance* 5, no. 4 (Winter 1993); Roe, *Strong Managers, Weak Owners* (1994), ch. 8 (mutual funds), ch. 9 (pension funds).

17. See Ronald Gilson and Reinier Kraakman, "Reinventing the Outside Director: An Agenda for Institutional Investors," *Stanford Law Review* 43, 863 (1991). The in-the-boardroom models haven't been adopted, and the first data results don't suggest that the from-the-distance governance role has yet become profitable. John Wagster and Andrew K. Prevost, "Wealth Effects of the CalPERS' 'Hit List' to SEC Changes in the Proxy Rules."

18. Roe, *Strong Managers,* ch. 10 (takeover politics), and chs. 16 and 21 (speculating on possible political influences today and in the future).

19. Roe, "Political Roots"; Bernard S. Black, "Next Steps in Proxy Reform," *Journal of Corporation Law* 18 (1992).

20. Andrew E. Serwer, "Mr. Price Is on the Line," *Fortune,* Dec. 9, 1996, 70 (Price takes bigger blocks through mutual funds when he can use proxy law rollback to coordinate with other owners to engineer changes at Chase.)

21. Miguel Cantillo, "The Rise and Fall of Bank Control in the United States: 1890–1920" (University of California at Berkeley, Working Paper No. 254, Oct. 1995).

22. See Roe, *Strong Managers,* chs. 17, 18, and 19.

23. See Roe, *Strong Managers,* pp. 260–62 ; Jonathan Macey and Geoffrey Miller, "Corporate Governance and Commercial Banking: A Comparative Examination of Germany, Japan, and the United States, *Stanford Law Review* 48, no. 1 (Nov. 1995): 73–112.

24. Ronald J. Gilson and Mark J. Roe, "Understanding the Japanese Keiretsu: Overlaps Between Corporate Governance and Industrial Organization," *Yale Law Journal* 102, 871 (1993).

25. David Flath, "The Keiretsu Puzzle," 10 *Journal of the Japanese and International Economies* 101–102 (1996).

26. To be sure here, cross-ownership is not without its own costs in creating conflicts of interest—a supplier may ignore bad management if it gets a better price. Industrial companies are not set up for stock ownership and are taxed unfavorably on their stock returns.

27. Nor is it correct to "measure" how much politics shaped the institutions of governance and pronounce as the winner the nation that had the "least" political influence. That is, in France, Germany, and Japan, politics probably had more impact on the structure of the corporation and the institutions that own them than it had in the U.S. In Germany, securities markets were stifled, mandatory codetermination was added, and a rigid corporate law was kept in place. Therefore, one might (mistakenly) reject the idea that politics influenced the form and possibly the costs of organizing the large American firm.

CHAPTER 3

International Corporate Differences

Markets or Law?

FRANK H. EASTERBROOK

STRONG MANAGERS, WEAK OWNERS: The Political Roots of American Corporate Finance is a constructive response to the fallacy that whatever is, is best. Many of us whose scholarly interests center around corporate law and finance have verged on, if not committed, this fallacy, though usually unintentionally. Many economic studies show that what is, is *not* best. Statutes are among the worst offenders; many are designed to transfer wealth, and they reduce it in the process. Institutions of corporate law and governance can be flawed for the same reason. Still, we must understand that American corporate structure has evolved through long competitive pressure to maximize welfare, *given the constraints*. This caveat avoids the fallacy Roe's book identifies.[1]

The constraints include politics. If some external force really means that American mutual funds can't own more than a few percent of the shares of any large corporation, that handicap may lead to a reduction in efficiency; but such a reduction does not imply that investors, managers, and corporations have fallen short of optimality. Organizations, like species, adapt to their surroundings.

One wonders only briefly whether businesses can't control their surroundings, instead of the other way round. More than one thoughtful person has believed that business leaders could have defeated efficiency-reducing bills by applying the tools of political suasion, but that they were content instead to negotiate the terms of surrender. Yet this occurs because, as Michael Jensen has pointed out more than once, the "corporation" is as diffuse and disorganized as voters at large. Corporations are numerous, have different agendas, are at each others' throats in product and financial markets alike, and can't organize well because they can't overcome their free riding problem—a very serious one, given the liquidity of capital markets.[2] Laws imposing handicaps on some businesses create market opportunities for others, who support them even as consumers and investors lose ground. So it may be inevitable that well-organized segments of the financial-services industry will combine with ill-informed public sentiment to secure and defend laws such as the National Bank Act and the Glass-Steagall Act—laws that increase their own profits while injuring the investors in the short run, and depressing the rate of growth (by reducing return on investment) and hence injuring society as a whole in the long run.

Corporations usually must take law as given and adapt. It doesn't take chaos theory to show that the evolutionary path will diverge in different nations,[3] as it has in nature (a trip to Australia will make that point). Nor does it take great wisdom to see that increasing connections among finance systems worldwide will create pressure to extirpate these differences. Paring the maladapted laws from the statute books is a slow process, but it is inevitable. Nations that do not adapt will lag behind in competition. Change is going on now, but the need to assemble political coalitions makes for halting, two-steps-forward-and-one-step-back movement.

Politics versus Economics

The most interesting question is whether the existing (or historical) legal differences among economic systems matter very much. Roe believes that they do, but this is unproven. American politics may be uniquely populist, as Roe contends—though one wonders why it should be—but there are lots of ways for small firms to play with the big boys. The Second Bank of Burlap can raise money locally and participate in a syndicated loan to IBM. Huge ownership blocks can then coexist with low levels of concentration in the banking business.[4] J.P. Morgan didn't own the House of Morgan; other people's money predominated. And I have a lot of difficulty with the idea that modern money managers tremble in fear of Ferdinand Pecora, whose hearings recessed 62 years ago, or that insurance companies disdain the corporate control market because, as a result of repealed legislation, they lack the expertise to play. Expertise can be hired.

Consider how little the legal system matters to what seem to be important aspects of corporate organization and control. When U.S. law is changed to allow mutual funds and insurance companies to hold larger positions, they don't take advantage of that opportunity (Roe develops the details of this non-event nicely). Warren Buffett of Berkshire Hathaway is an outlier. (Other insurers and mutual funds, such as Oppenheimer, that have elected to use the options recently allowed in the United States have declined to take seats on their portfolio firms' boards.) In the United Kingdom, the law has long allowed banks to hold large blocks of shares, but English firms *do not* do this—although their counterparts on the other side of the Channel (and the Pacific) do.

These differences require an explanation more powerful than reluctance or political fear or missing expertise. Political reactions *never* stop competition, unless the market is so concentrated as to be monopolized—which finance is not. It is less concentrated in the United States than elsewhere, and we should therefore expect more risk-taking, and more novel forms of organization, rather than fewer (as Roe believes). If Firm A's financing innovations bring the glare of klieg lights and hearings down on the industry's head, what of it? In the interim, Firm A makes a lot of money; afterward it makes the normal rate of return. One paper after another by students of industrial organization shows how firms innovate and boost their output even though they know that in the long run prices will fall, and profits vanish. The industry would be better off if each firm refused to build that new plant, but each reasons that if it does not build, someone else will, and take the profits.

Just so in financial markets. If Insurer X or Investment Bank Y refuses to acquire blocks of stock, and if that step is profitable, someone else will do so. Tender offers make this point nicely. Until the mid-1960s, one could have said of the market for corporate control what Roe says about mutual funds and banks and insurers: managers just don't muscle in on friendly firms, and "reputable" investment banks didn't like the hostile tender offer. But firms at the fringes of respectability began to assemble financing, and before long all the white-shoe firms had to follow suit. Throughout the 1970s and 1980s there was an explosion of tender offers, leveraged buyouts, spinoffs, split-ups, and related restructuring devices. As many predicted, this brought retaliation in the legislature. Did that risk cause anyone to back off? Not at all; someone else (Michael Milken, in particular) would have taken even more of the business. So legislation happened, and clever people have found ways around *that*—with the result that corporate control transactions are on an upswing, and in 1996 set a record despite the tighter laws and antitrust scrutiny.[5]

These developments readily could have been replicated in miniature, by taking 10% blocks rather than by taking 51% or 80% or 100% blocks. But they were not. We need an economic rather than a political or sociological explanation for why this is so rare. Financial intermediaries and investors cannot be at once dynamic and risk-taking (as the takeover wars show) yet passive and risk-averse (as Roe tells us American financial intermediaries are). Unfortunately, Roberta Romano and Mark Ramseyer, who have had a lot to say about this question,[6] are not with us today. So I offer an explanation of my own—not quite the same as theirs, but with some elements in common.

Not Populism, but the Politics of Self-Interest

Let us put populism aside as an explanatory variable. Populist talk is cheap, but the wishes of the unwashed rarely explain laws or economic institutions even for a few years; for popular sentiment to dominate an entire century is out of the question. Milk producers win higher prices in the political arena even though they are few in number and opposed to the most popular cause of all—good nutrition for children. Why should things be different in financial markets? More to the point, why is there so little resistance to the laws and rules that fracture holdings in the United States? And why is England's structure of holdings so similar to that of the United States, even though its laws are like those of Japan and Germany?

If not populism, then what? There are real interest groups, with money at stake. Securities dealers want to keep other financial intermediaries from poaching; local banks want to restrict competition from securities dealers; and so on. This has the makings of a good coalition to suppress money-center banks and other financial institutions.

None of this is inconsistent with anything in Professor Roe's book. The big question is why there is so little fighting back. Roe attributes this to the ghost of Ferdinand Pecora, but I would rather attribute it to the nature of the stakes. Money-center institutions don't fight back for two reasons: first, they are not an effective interest group for the same reason corporations as a whole are not an effective group—they can't solve their free riding problem given the ease of exit in financial markets; second, it is the existence of these very markets that make fighting back not worthwhile. Securities markets in the United States are as close as one gets to Adam Smith's atomistic competition. Information is plentiful, transaction costs low.

With efficient markets, there is no money to be made by holding undiversified blocks in public corporations.[7] Competition bids down the price of securities so that the excess risk created by the lack of diversification is not compensated. Even when the holder has inside information, the likelihood that the information will come out before the investor can capitalize by selling is high. Concentrated earnings therefore create uncompensated risk. Why should the money-center financial intermediaries expend political capital to win the right to reduce their earnings?

Public markets meanwhile put managers under the same kind of pressure that concentrated holdings would do. And because entrepreneurs can't raise as much capital with inefficient governance devices as with good ones—for the entrepreneurs themselves bear the cost of inefficiency in a lower price realized for stock—they choose whichever device has the lowest total costs. If public markets were inefficient, entrepreneurs would arrange for large blocks of stock, just as they grant powers of control to venture capitalists. Managers' incentives are in the long run aligned with investors' incentives.

No surprise, therefore, that even when banks, mutual funds, and insurers are allowed by law to increase the concentration of their holdings, they don't do so—not in the United States, and not in the United Kingdom, whose financial markets also are quite large and efficient. Capital is freely imported and exported, so financial markets in both countries are *world* markets. The United

States and the United Kingdom have this in common even when the United Kingdom is experiencing one of its occasional bouts of socialism; and I think the two nations' similar financial structure is explained by this commonality in the markets rather than by legal differences. Put otherwise, the law of corporate finance is endogenous rather than exogenous; that is to say, current corporate law should be viewed more as the consequence of other forces than as the primary cause of corporate structure.

Developments Abroad

While efficient markets in the United States and the United Kingdom allowed these developments, much of Europe and Asia was under corporative, fascist, or even feudal organization. Public markets were rare and inefficient. After World War II, revitalization took time, and many of the investments had to be large, producing concentrated holdings (much like the United States at the end of the 19th century) that take time to dissipate. Often markets were confined by law to a single country; and the market in Illinois (or France) is much less liquid than the market in the United States (or the European Union). The United States and England have large, efficient, internal markets and welcome capital from outside. This is not universally true; often politics works the other way (in Japan, banks got the upper hand and squelched trading markets); and as the size of the public market decreases, or outside capital is disfavored by the government, the debt-equity ratio and concentration of ownership must be higher to compensate. To be fair, I must acknowledge that Roe discusses this possibility at page 185, for a single paragraph. But I think he dismisses it too quickly, without subjecting it to analysis or an empirical test (on which more below).

Let me put this in a different way. There are many substitute means of controlling the agency costs that arise from professional management and the separation of ownership from control. Concentrated holdings are one; forcing managers to return often to capital markets is another. Greater concentration of ownership means that the firm has curtailed or foregone the ability to raise money in capital markets from diversified investors, a major loss. The large blockholder is taking undiversified risk, which requires compensation; and to deal with the risk the blockholder will monitor more closely, which also must be paid for. Other investors have to pay for these risk-bearing and monitoring services. Less concentration means that risk can be diversified away, liquidity increased, and the cost of capital lowered. As long as the agency costs of management do not rise by more than the savings from diversification, there is a social gain. There is on average less concentration in the United States than in the European Union, and costs of capital in the United States are lower, which implies that there is a net gain. And there is a related point: a *really* large firm can't have concentrated total investment because no one has enough wealth, even if one person is willing to bear the risk. Concentration comes through financial intermediation, and the intermediary has the same problems the firm itself did. Greater concentration *among equity investors* is not necessarily the same as greater concentration among all investors. One way to have votes concentrated, while reducing the total stake of the largest investor (and thus the undiversified risk-bearing that needs to be compensated), is to increase the debt-equity ratio. Take an extreme case: a firm with 99% debt and 1% equity can be controlled by a person holding 51% of the equity, or only 1/2% of the firm's capital. Some holding companies with pyramidal structures achieved such ratios but such companies generally have not survived in competition. Why? The "concentrated" equity owner can control management, but it is in his own interest to exploit debt investors *ex post* by increasing volatility. Debt investors know this and charge more for capital. Debt-heavy holding company structures lose out in competition with rivals that hire capital more cheaply. So too with nonvoting shares, which are functionally equivalent to debt (or preferred stock) with respect to their effect on control (that is, they leave control to someone else) but without the mandatory payout that for debt offsets the separation of control from the residual claim.

I suggested a decade ago[8] that the principal role of dividends is to force firms into capital markets. If companies pay money out, they have to raise it too. The need to raise money, rather than any formal "governance" device, is the principal constraint on managers—since they must pay the current price for money, reflecting the market's evaluation of their willingness and ability to pay investors. If the cost of money rises, the firm fails in its product markets; to avert this, managers repay investors and make credible promises of future controls.

Michael Jensen has made the same point about public debt[9]—and of course debt ordinarily entails a mandatory distribution, while dividends are optional (though there is a price to be paid for reducing or omitting them). One should say the same thing about bank debt. I suspect that, in the long run, most "governance" devices are insignificant compared to the discipline of capital markets. Unless they are planning to liquidate, firms need to raise money—if only from trade creditors, whose financing is often vital. To raise new money they must repay old money; otherwise promises are not believed. And *if* they can raise money at competitive prices in public markets, they don't need concentrated holdings, which create uncompensated risk.

One occasional response to an argument of this kind is that mature firms do not return to capital markets. This is not so. It confuses equity markets with capital markets. Mature firms raise capital all the time—from banks, from bondholders (debt is issued in series to require periodic payments and therefore periodic rollovers of debt), and in commercial paper markets. The institution of "commercial paper," essentially confined to mature firms, shows how managers find it in their interest to be in capital markets continually. Raising new money and repaying existing investors *at the same time* is puzzling until you see this function. Commercial paper has a short maturity (nine months or less), so firms that issue it are always under the scrutiny of capital markets, and small changes in risk bring perceptible changes in interest rates. Even a few basis points are costly, and they catch other investors' eyes.

When managers raise new money, firms must pay the rate of return appropriate to their *current* strategies and risk. In a nation with large and efficient capital markets, this valuation is done on the fly, for new securities and existing ones. Efficiency means accurate valuation on average—and "accurate" compared not with an ideal but with alternatives such as discounted cash flow analysis, done by large blockholders who can't rely on trading markets. Cash flow analysis has high error rates indeed. Because assembling capital in large markets cuts down risk through diversification, the cost is lower. We should therefore expect nations with more efficient capital markets to have less concentration of ownership, and this is exactly what occurs. Law appears to have little independent force. The less efficient is the valuation process in charging managers with the true, current cost of capital, the more substitution toward banks or other block holdings. As the European Union becomes increasingly integrated, concentration among investors will fall.

This leads to a suggestion for an empirical test: examine the relation between ownership concentration and cost of capital. Average return on public investment (which is to say, the cost of capital) should fall as concentration of holdings falls. But I think that Mark Roe would predict the opposite: that when concentration is low, agency costs of management rise, and capital can be attracted only by higher returns to public investors.

Enabling versus Real Rules of Law

So like Roe I think that history and culture matter; but I do think that these are aligned with, rather than opposed to, the economics of agency cost control. Indeed, I think that the influence of law on corporate governance and structure is far less in the United States than in Europe and Japan. Perhaps the courts play a larger role in the United States, in the course of enforcing contracts and fiduciary duties, but law plays less.

Corporate law in the United States is "enabling"—which is to say that it lets people do largely what they want in organizing, managing, and financing the firm. Europe and Japan are much more directory. There are rules, which people must follow even if everyone would prefer to do things differently. Even the features of U.S. law that look prescriptive—for example, the regulation of securities—have little to do with corporate governance. Firms must make disclosures when issuing stock, but the shares can carry most any *substantive* rights people can dream up, and they sell for whatever price investors are willing to pay. Even the vaunted "fiduciary duty" of managers is just a matter of enforcing agreements. If the manager writes himself a bonus check, that's fine; if he takes the same amount without authorization, that's theft; the difference is approval by authorized corporate actors, not any decision of the state. Fiduciary duty means keeping one's promises. Courts in the United States sometimes try to interpolate terms into incomplete contracts, but they do this to achieve what parties would have bargained for had they thought about the question.[10] Courts almost never fail to enforce terms actually bargained for. When they try to do more, they generally fail.[11]

By contrast to the enabling structure of U.S. corporate governance, the European Union and its constituent member states use real rules of law. If in the United States you want to create a firm in which one person contributes capital and the other labor, and they get equal amounts of stock, that's fine. If in the European Union you want to do this, you can't; the Second Directive forbids the issuance of stock in exchange for a promise to perform services. If investors in the United States want to authorize their firm to sell new stock to outsiders without first offering it to insiders, that's fine. In the European Union, they can't do so; preemptive rights are mandatory.[12] Now preemptive rights help guard against dilution, so investors could benefit from them—though, given the differences among firms, *universal* preemptive rights are surely a bad idea. My point here, though, is not to debate the wisdom of preemptive rights, but rather to note that in Europe they are achieved by law, and in the United States they are achieved, if at all, by contract. In the United States equity investors have no right to dividends; a firm can go from cradle to grave without issuing them, and investors cannot force dissolution to get at undistributed profits. In the European Union, according to the Fourth Directive, firms must announce anticipated dividends and adhere to these schedules, and compulsory dissolution is available.

Devices such as these in the European Union affect markets, too. Because firms cannot create and offer the full menu of devices, some risk-return combinations will be missing from the trading markets. As a consequence, the markets will be less efficient—and the lack of efficiency makes them less liquid (and still less efficient) by inducing substitution toward large blocks.

Firms make many promises in the United States, and courts enforce them, while law in the European Union is more bureaucratic. This explains my paradoxical statement that the United States relies more on courts but less on law. Good thing, too! For judges are just bureaucrats with general portfolios. Bureaucrats have poor information and worse incentives—they have their own agendas and do not share in the firm's profits and losses. Just so with judges. Even the Chancery Court of Delaware, our greatest corporate tribunal, mixes corporate mergers with divorces and child-custody cases. Few judges are chosen for business expertise, and none are fired for poor decisions. Professor Jensen thinks that managers' profit share of 0.3% in the United States is too low to align incentives properly;[13] judges' share is 0.0%. Interest-alignment devices thought essential to make corporations work, when applied to judges, are called bribes.

On the other hand, judges can enforce contracts. For then the investors and managers themselves lay down the rules. Judges serve as neutral umpires, enforcing the contracts without regard to who gains and who loses in a particular case. The contents of the contracts, however, come from competition in financial markets, rather than from law.

Markets are costly and imperfect, but they beat the political process every time. And the more efficient financial markets are, the better competition among entrepreneurs works. This is a point Jensen and Meckling made a generation ago.[14] Entrepreneurs make promises to investors. If these promises are not optimal from investors' perspective, then investors pay less and the entrepreneurs themselves bear the costs of suboptimality. Of course, this mechanism depends on investors being able to evaluate the promises made to them. When capital markets are efficient, the valuation process works better; when markets are less efficient, some substitute must be found—law, perhaps, or the valuation procedures of banks. Thus we have greater bank roles in nations with less extensive capital markets—and, as the European Union's company directives show, we have more law, too. European corporate law is today about as meddlesome and directory as U.S. law was in the late 19th century, before U.S. capital markets became efficient.

What would *really* be nice is for Europe and Japan to abolish their meddlesome restrictions on corporations and financial markets, while the United States abolishes its meddlesome restrictions on banks and other financial intermediaries, and everyone abolishes meddlesome restrictions on trans-border investments. Then we might see where competition takes us. On this subject, Mark Roe and I agree wholeheartedly, but we both know it won't happen—too many interest groups.

One may ask how corporate law came to be enabling rather than directory in the United States. The answer lies in competition among jurisdictions—still another form of investor protection. States that tried inefficient regulation would drive capital and corporate structures out of their jurisdictions. Ease of movement within the large U.S. market made this possible. So states lost the ability to do substantial injury. Could they do good? Well, they could be more hospitable to competition, and the structure of federalism in the United States made this possible. Courts restricted states' ability to discriminate against corporations that had their headquarters in other states. Firms could move their charters without moving their operations—quite unlike the "real seat" doctrine in Europe, which was created by France in the 19th century to block competition from England! And it happened that Delaware was small enough to make a binding *commitment* to have an efficient law. It gathers about 20% of the state budget from corporate charter fees, a bond of good faith toward corporations that lack votes in the legislature. No surprise when the head of the committee that drafted the most recent version of the Delaware Code became Chief Justice of Delaware.

To sum up: international differences in corporate governance are attributable more to differences in markets than to differences in law. Law is an output of this process, not an input. When financial markets are more efficient and interjurisdictional competition blooms, there will be less law and more investor protection at the same time.

Notes

1. See generally Frank H. Easterbrook & Daniel R. Fischel, *The Economic Structure of Corporate Law* 22–39 (Cambridge: Harvard University Press, 1991).
2. See Frank H. Easterbrook, "The Demand for Judicial Review," 88 *Northwestern L. Rev.* 372 (1993), which addresses the question why corporations file suits (and pay taxes) that in the aggregate make them worse off. The answer is the same as the reason why corporations increase output and reduce prices, even though that prevents them from making monopoly profits: competition.
3. Roe extends on this point nicely in "Chaos and Evolution in Law and Economics," 109 *Harv. L. Rev.* 641 (1996). See also Theodor Baums, Richard M. Buxbaum, & Klaus J. Hopt, eds., *Institutional Investors and Corporate Governance* (Berlin: de Gruyter, 1994) (chapters discuss the law and economics of arrangements in many nations); Mats Isaksson & Rolf Skog, *Aspects of Corporate Governance* (Stockholm: Juristffir-laget, 1993) (similar project); Gary Gorton & Frank A. Schmid, "Universal Banking and the Performance of German Firms," 58 *J. Fin. Econ.* 29 (2000); Andre Shleifer & Robert W. Vishny, "A Survey of Corporate Governance," 52 *Journal of Finance* 37 (1997); Andre Shleifer & Robert W. Vishny, "A Survey of Corporate Governance" (paper presented at the Nobel Symposium on Law and Finance, Stockholm, August 1995); William J. Carney, "The Political Economy of Competition for Corporate Charters," 26 *J. Legal Stud.* 303 (1997); Takeo Hoshi, Anil Kashyap, & David Sharfstein, "The Role of Banks in Reducing the Costs of Financial Distress in Japan," 27 *J. Fin. Econ.* 67 (1990); David G. Litt, Jonathan R. Macey, Geoffrey P. Miller, & Edward L. Rubin, "Politics, Bureaucracies, and Financial Markets: Bank Entry into Commercial Paper Underwriting in the United States and Japan," 139 *U. Pa. L. Rev.* 369 (1990); Stephen D. Prowse, "Institutional Investment Patterns and Corporate Financial Behavior in the United States and Japan," 27 *J. Fin. Econ.* 43 (1990); J. Mark Ramseyer, "Legal Rules in Repeated Deals: Banking in the Shadow of Defection in Japan," 20 *J. Leg. Stud.* 91 (1991).
4. If it even makes sense to compute concentration among banks by country—as if the levels of concentration among Pennsylvania banks mattered! Concentration of ownership from the firms' side is more important, and ownership of the American corporation is considerably more concentrated than most people suppose. See, for example, Harold Demsetz & Kenneth Lehn, "The Structure of Corporate Ownership: Causes and Consequences," 93 *J. Pol. Econ.* 1155 (1985).

5. According to the *Wall Street Journal,* the U.S. merger and acquisition business in 1996 was $659 billion, an all-time top (Section 3, page R8 (Jan. 2, 1997)).

6. See Roberta Romano, *The Genius of American Corporate Law* 118–47 (Washington, D.C.: American Enterprise Institute, 1993); Romano, "A Cautionary Note on Drawing Lessons from Comparative Corporate Law," 102 *Yale L .J.* 2021 (1993); J. Mark Ramseyer, "Columbian Cartel Launches Bid for Japanese Firms," 102 *Yale L. J.* 2005 (1993).

7. The qualifier "in public corporations" is important. There may be substantial gains from taking a corporation private by a leveraged buyout or similar transaction. Many of these gains come not from the greater concentration of holdings *per se,* but from the radical alteration in the incentives (including compensation) that managers face. Once the firm is closely held, however, large blocks are essential to facilitate monitoring, for the market institutions serving this function are gone. For discussions of the sources of gain in going-private transactions, see Michael C. Jensen, "Active Investors, LBOs, and the Privatization of Bankruptcy," 2 *J. Applied Corp. Fin.* 35 (1989); Frank H. Easterbrook, "High-Yield Debt as an Incentive Device," 11 *Int'l Rev. L. & Econ.* 183 (1991). Once these changes have accomplished their goal of reforming corporate operations, many of these firms return to public ownership so that investors may avoid the risk of holding these undiversified blocks.

8. Frank H. Easterbrook, "Two Agency-Cost Explanations of Dividends," *Am. Econ. Rev.* 74, 650–59 (1984).

9. Michael Jensen, "Agency Costs of Free Cash Flow, Corporate Finance, and Takeovers," 76 *Am. Econ. Rev.* 323–29 (1986).

10. See Frank H. Easterbrook & Daniel R. Fischel, "Contract and Fiduciary Duty," 36 *J. L. & Econ.* 425–46 (1993); see also John H. Langbein, "The Contractarian Basis of the Law of Trusts," 105 *Yale L. J.* 625, 657–69 (1995).

11. Litigation designed to improve the managers' fidelity often depresses stock prices; courts' inability to separate good from bad management, coupled with the risk aversion of managers, leads to settlements that do not respect the probable merit of the claim. See Janet Cooper Alexander, "Do the Merits Matter? A Study of Settlements in Securities Class Actions," 43 *Stan. L. Rev.* 497 (1991). See also Reinier Kraakman, Hyun Park, & Steven Shavell, "When Are Shareholder Suits in Shareholder Interests?," 82 *Geo. L. J.* 1733 (1994); Janet Cooper Alexander, "The Value of Bad News in Securities Class Actions," 41 *UCLA L. Rev.* 1421 (1994); Roberta Romano, "The Shareholder Suit: Litigation Without Foundation?," 7 *J. L. Econ. & Org.* 55 (1991); Mark L. Cross, Wallace N. Davidson, & John H. Thornton, "The Impact of Directors' and Officers' Liability Suits on Firm Value," 56 *J. Risk & Insurance* 128 (1989); Daniel R. Fischel & Michael Bradley, "The Role of Liability Rules and the Derivative Suit in Corporate Law: A Theoretical and Empirical Analysis," 71 *Cornell L. Rev.* 261 (1986). But see Joel Seligman, "The Merits Do Matter," 108 *Harv. L. Rev.* 438 (1994).

12. William J. Carney, "The Political Economy of Competition for Corporate Charters," supra note 3, canvasses many of these details.

13. Michael Jensen, "Performance Pay and Top Management Incentives," 98 *J. Pol. Econ.* 225 (1990).

14. Michael Jensen & William Meckling, "Theory of the Firm: Managerial Behavior, Agency Costs, and Ownership Structure," 3 *J. Fin. Econ.* 305–60 (1976).

CHAPTER 4

Explaining Differences in the Quality of Governance among Companies

Evidence from Emerging Markets

ART DURNEV AND E. HAN KIM

THE DOT-COM MELTDOWNS, along with the recent wave of governance scandals and large corporate bankruptcies around the world, have moved corporate governance to the center of investors' and policymakers' radar screens. The progressive globalization of capital and product markets has put increased pressure on companies to practice better governance, regardless of their location on the world map.

Recent studies show that good governance yields higher returns for shareholders, suggesting that efforts to improve governance can be worth the cost.[1] But, along with mounting evidence of the value-increasing effects of better governance, the research also shows that companies around the globe continue to have strikingly different governance structures. A number of studies have attempted to explain such variation by focusing on country-wide differences in corporate governance systems (that is, how does the governance system of a representative U.K. company differ from that of a representative firm in Italy?); and in so doing, they have provided valuable insights into the effects of different regulatory and legal environments.[2] But several important questions remain unanswered, especially at the level of individual companies.

In a recently published study entitled, "To Steal or Not to Steal,"[3] we attempted to answer the following questions: Do all companies in countries with weak legal protection for investors suffer from poor corporate governance? And do the vast majority of companies in strong legal regimes practice high-quality governance? Using data on 859 companies in 27 countries, our study revealed considerable variation in governance and disclosure practices within the same country, with the variation increasing as the legal environment becomes less investor-friendly.

This finding in turn raised a number of other questions: Is the wider variation in governance in countries with weaker investor protection simply a reflection of the greater latitude permitted by lower minimal standards?

Or does it also reflect differences in how companies adapt to a permissive legal environment, with some firms choosing to adhere to governance practices far stricter, than those that are required by law? And to the extent companies are making such choices, is there a systematic pattern in which certain kinds of companies choose higher-quality governance? If so, what corporate attributes tend to be associated with stronger governance practices? And, finally, are differences in the quality of governance priced by the stock markets and, if so, are the effects large enough for corporate decision-makers to take notice?

The findings of our study serve, first of all, to dispel the popular misconception that all companies in countries with weak investor protection have weak corporate governance systems. Indeed, we were surprised both by the number of high-quality governance firms in such countries, and by the variation in governance scores within the same country.

Our study also identified three key attributes that, in countries with strong and weak investor protection alike, tend to distinguish companies with better corporate governance and disclosure practices: (1) abundant investment opportunities, (2) greater need for external financing, and (3) higher concentration of cash flow (as opposed to just voting) ownership rights. Finally, and perhaps most important, we find that the positive impact of good governance on firm value is more significant—and the relation between the above corporate attributes and governance practices is stronger—in countries with less investor-friendly regulatory oversight.

Why Do Companies Provide Better Governance Than the Law Requires?

The "intuition" behind the three key corporate attributes—investment opportunities, need for external financing, and cash flow ownership concentration—that appear to drive a company's governance choice is fairly straightforward. First, profitable investment opportunities provide the controlling shareholder with incentives to make value-maximizing uses of investor capital rather than divert corporate resources for personal gain. When investment opportunities are more profitable, the controlling shareholders' share of the return from such investments is larger relative to the benefits of diverting resources (a useful analogy here is that people are less likely to resort to crime when they have a stake in the status quo, something valuable to lose). In the absence of valuable investment opportunities, controlling shareholders are likely to be tempted to appropriate resources for private use rather than following the value-maximizing course of returning excess capital to other investors.

Second, companies that rely more heavily on external financing can use a reputation for effective governance to raise global equity and debt at lower costs. In other words, a good governance system effectively increases a company's value by reducing its cost of capital.

Third, concentrated ownership makes it less likely that the controlling shareholder will divert corporate resources for private benefits. As an owner's share of cash flow rights increases, the owner bears a higher percentage of the costs associated with diverting resources and otherwise failing to maximize value.

What's more, these three corporate characteristics should have greater influence on a company's choice of governance in weak legal environments since investors' demand for reassurance is greater. In other words, companies in weak legal regimes have stronger incentives to structure their own governance so as to take fuller advantage of profitable investment opportunities, to overcome the negative effects of poor investor protection on their ability to raise external capital, and to resolve conflicts between controlling and outside shareholders.

Finally, companies with better governance and more transparency should be valued more highly in the stock market because of investors' greater confidence that they will end up with their fair share of firm profits. And, as stated, this positive effect of good governance on firm value is likely to be stronger in countries with weak legal systems. To put it another way, good corporate governance should be valued more highly in countries where it is scarce—namely, in weaker legal regimes.

International Governance and Disclosure Rankings

In our study, we tested these hypotheses with governance rankings provided by Credit Lyonnais Securities Asia (CLSA) and disclosure rankings by Standard & Poor's (S&P). In 2001, CLSA issued reports on the governance practices of 494 companies in 24 countries, providing scores on the quality of governance during 2000. The companies were based in East and South Asia, Latin America, and Eastern Europe. The governance scores assigned to each firm by CLSA were based on responses by financial analysts to 57 questions, which were then used to construct scores on a 1–100 scale, where a higher number indicates better corporate governance. All questions have binary answers (yes/no) with the aim of limiting analysts' subjectivity.

The 57 questions were grouped into one of the following seven categories, each designed to measure a different aspect of a company's governance system: discipline (managerial incentives and behavior in terms of value-maximizing actions); transparency (timely and accurate disclosure); board independence; board accountability; responsibility (enforcement and management accountability); protection of minority shareholders; and reputation for social responsibility and ethical practices. For each of the 494 companies, we computed a composite governance index, *COMP*, by taking a simple average of the first six categories (while, as discussed later, designing a separate test for the issue of social responsibility).

CLSA claims that its rankings are objective, showing no favoritism to their clients.[4] But, to test the reliability of CLSA composite scores as a measure of the quality of governance, we examined the relation between the CLSA scores and corporate misdeeds. Specifically, we looked for evidence of scandals involving 84 companies in the 14 countries that had CLSA scores for at least 12 companies. For each country, we selected the top three and bottom three firms in CLSA composite scores and did a manual scan of the Lexis-Nexis database for reports of misdeeds by these companies during the three-year period 1999 through the end of 2001. The following were considered misdeeds: asset expropriation, accounting misreporting, earnings manipulation, stock price manipulation, insider trading, share dilution, and illegal projects. After we identified 49 such events, we found the number of scandals reported for each firm to be negatively and significantly correlated with the CLSA composite score (correlation coefficient=−0.36, p-value=0.0), indicating that firms with low CLSA scores are more likely to have governance scandals.

As a robustness check for the results based on CLSA rankings, we also used Standard & Poor's disclosure scores for 573 companies in 16 emerging markets and three developed countries in 2000. S&P identified the 91 most common disclosure items after examining the annual reports and accounts of leading companies around the world. The S&P disclosure scores are simply the number of items disclosed. The inclusion of each item is scored on a binary basis representing 'yes' (included) or 'no' (not included) answers to ensure objectivity. Each 'yes' answer is equal to one point. These items are then grouped into three sub-categories: *ownership* (ownership structure and investor relations, 22 items), *disclosure* (financial transparency and information disclosure, 34 items), and *board* (board and management structure and process, 35 items). For each company, we then summed the scores for each of the three categories to come up with an aggregate transparency index that we called *TRAN*.

The advantage of S&P scores, as suggested, lies in their objectivity, whereas CLSA scores are more comprehensive but susceptible to subjectivity. S&P scores, however, depend only on the number of disclosures, and do not reflect the content. They are best viewed as a measure of transparency and not a comprehensive measure of corporate governance. But despite such differences, the two sets of rankings turned out to be fairly consistent, with companies that score high on CLSA's corporate governance typically scoring high on S&P's disclosure as well.[5]

Our measure of the strength of the legal environment for a given country was based on both *de jure* and *de facto* aspects of regulation. For our *de jure* measure of investor protection, which we called *INVESTOR,* we used the "anti-director rights" (shareholder rights) index from a widely cited study of the shareholder friendliness of different international legal systems.[6] To measure the strength of *de facto* regulation, called *ENFORCE,* we used the International Country Risk Guide's rule-of-law index, which is a numerical assessment of the strength of a country's tradition of law and order. To construct a measure that reflects both aspects of regulation, we multiplied *INVESTOR* by *ENFORCE* and called it *LEGAL.*

As shown in table 4.1, our sample of 27 countries covers a broad range of legal regimes, with *LEGAL* scores ranging from 3.33 (Mexico) to 41.65 (Hong Kong and Chile). As can also be seen in the table, both the CLSA and S&P scores for individual companies reveal significant variation in corporate governance and disclosure within a single country. For CLSA, the average spread between maximums and minimums for countries with more than two companies was 38.46, as compared to the mean score of 47.03 (out of 100). For the S&P disclosure measure, the average spread was 29.56, as compared to the mean of 34.37 (out of 91).

To examine whether and the extent to which the within-country variation in governance is related to the strength of legal protection for investors, we followed a two-step procedure. First, we regressed each company's CLSA composite score on the three determinants of governance: investment opportunities, need for external financing, and control variables. Then we regressed the absolute values of the fitted residuals—the unexplained part of governance, if you will—of the first-stage regression on the country variable *LEGAL.* The coefficient on *LEGAL* turned out to be negative (and significant at the 1% level of statistical significance), indicating that within-country variation in governance is larger when the legal environment is less investor-friendly.[7]

What Explains the Variation in Governance and Transparency among Companies?

In testing our hypotheses about governance and corporate attributes, we regressed individual companies' governance scores on measures of investment opportunities, external financing needs, ownership concentration, and legal environment (while controlling for country-random effects, industry, and other firm characteristics). Investment opportunities were measured as lagged growth in sales. External financing requirement was defined as the difference between the firm's actual growth rate and the growth rate that could be sustained with retained earnings, while maintaining a constant debt-to-assets ratio. In the case of our third corporate attribute, we measured the concentration of cash flow ownership rights, *OWN_CASH,* as the share of cash flow rights held by the largest shareholder. The regressions also included a variable called

TABLE 4.1

Summary Statistics of Legal Regime Variables, CLSA Composite Governance Score, and S&P Transparency Ranking by Country

This table reports the legal regime variables, the mean, standard deviation, minimum, and maximum of CLSA composite corporate governance scores, COMP, and S&P transparency rankings, TRAN, by country. The variable INVESTOR is the antidirector index; ENFORCE is rule of law; and LEGAL is INVESTOR×ENFORCE. N is the number of firms in the country.

| Country | Legal Regime Variables | | | CLSA Composite Governance Score, COMP | | | | | S&P Transparency Ranking, TRAN | | | | |
	INVESTOR	ENFORCE	LEGAL	Mean	St. Dev.	Min	Max	N	Mean	St. Dev.	Min	Max	N
Argentina	4	8.33	33.32	60	–	60	60	1	23.44	8.37	12	35	9
Australia	4	10	40	–	–	–	–	–	56.69	7.19	37	66	26
Brazil	3	3.33	9.99	53.76	7.97	38.78	68.22	30	27.3	10.46	16	51	30
Chile	5	8.33	41.65	57.02	5.38	43.4	65.04	16	29.44	10.48	13	50	18
China	1	8.13	8.13	43.56	11.24	21.62	64.5	25	41.88	10.14	24	56	16
Colombia	3	2.64	7.92	47.87	–	47.87	47.87	1	–	–	–	–	–
Czech Rep.	2	8.33	16.66	51.42	–	51.42	51.42	1	–	–	–	–	–
Greece	2	5.07	10.14	52.11	5.15	48.47	55.76	2	–	–	–	–	–
Hong Kong	5	8.33	41.65	56.28	11.37	35.04	83.49	38	41.76	4.02	33	54	42
Hungary	3	8.61	25.83	49.49	8.33	43.61	55.38	2	–	–	–	–	–
India	5	6.67	33.35	47.58	10.03	29.1	83.27	79	33.66	9.58	15	55	41
Indonesia	2	3.33	6.66	33.56	11	10.59	56.57	18	32.73	6.36	22	43	11
Japan	4	9.24	36.96	–	–	–	–	–	44.3	7.87	19	59	150
Korea	2	6.67	13.34	38.57	6.35	29.7	52.86	24	39.49	10.25	12	54	47

(continued)

TABLE 4.1 (*continued*)

Country	Legal Regime Variables			CLSA Composite Governance Score, COMP					S&P Transparency Ranking, TRAN				
	INVESTOR	ENFORCE	LEGAL	Mean	St. Dev.	Min	Max	N	Mean	St. Dev.	Min	Max	N
Malaysia	4	5.28	21.12	50.65	13.65	19.47	72.83	47	39.54	6.73	30	56	50
Mexico	1	3.33	3.33	55.68	7.3	43.55	63.96	8	22.81	8.37	13	47	16
N. Zealand	4	10	40	–	–	–	–	–	51	–	51	51	1
Pakistan	5	5	25	27.83	12.71	15.53	60.02	11	31.56	6.71	20	43	9
Peru	3	5	15	68.84	–	68.84	68.84	1	19	3.56	16	26	7
Philippines	3	5.9	17.7	36.03	12.16	17.46	57.92	20	23.44	5.73	11	30	9
Poland	3	7.15	21.45	34.53	0.81	33.96	35.1	2	–	–	–	–	–
Russia	5	5	25	13.77	–	13.77	13.77	1	–	–	–	–	–
Singapore	4	10	40	59.05	8.45	40.83	77.37	43	51.27	8.33	28	68	26
South Africa	5	3.54	17.7	61.01	7.96	38.36	75.9	40	–	–	–	–	–
Taiwan	3	6.67	20.01	47.16	8.85	25.8	67.07	47	18.33	6.23	13	31	39
Thailand	2	8.33	16.66	48.58	12.31	25.5	71.12	20	42.08	11.54	15	57	26
Turkey	2	6.04	12.08	36.23	9.87	21.09	51.09	17	–	–	–	–	–
Average	3.3	6.6	22.25	47.11		34.32	60.81		35.25		21.05	49.05	
Total								**494**					**573**

TABLE 4.2

Country Random-Effects Regressions of CLSA Governance and S&P Transparency Scores on Investment Opportunities, External Financing Needs, and Legal Environments

This table reports the results of regressions of CLSA composite corporate governance score, *COMP*; investor protection, *PROTECT*; social awareness, *SOCIAL*; or S&P transparency ranking *TRAN* on *INV_OPP* (investment opportunities), *EXT_FIN* (external financing needs), *LEGAL* (quality of legal environment), *INV_OPP * LEGAL, EXT_FIN * LEGAL* (interaction terms for investment opportunities and external financing needs with the quality of legal environment). All regressions control for industry fixed effects, firm size, research and development expenditures, export intensity, cross-listing dummy, and financial statements consolidation dummy (coefficients are not reported). ***, **, * indicate significance at 1%, 5%, and 10% levels.

	CLSA COMP	CLSA PROTECT	CLSA SOCIAL	S&P TRAN
INV_OPP	14.089***	21.270**	6.421	35.737***
EXT_FIN	4.363*	16.223***	−9.900*	9.154
LEGAL	0.490***	1.013***	−0.091	0.352***
*INV_OPP * LEGAL*	−0.525***	−0.579*	−0.466	−1.125***
*EXT_FIN * LEGAL*	−0.083	−0.443**	0.258	−0.302
R2	0.240	0.224	0.137	0.231
Companies	344	334	334	439

WEDGE to take account of possible differences between cash flow and control or voting rights.[8] A greater gap between cash flow rights and control rights makes it easier for the controlling shareholders to divert corporate resources for private benefits that are not shared by minority shareholders, while making the private cost of diversion less costly for the controlling shareholder.

As reported in table 4.2, the results of our regressions provided strong support for our hypotheses. In particular, the CLSA composite scores (*COMP*), the CLSA minority shareholder protection scores (*PROTECT*), and S&P's transparency rankings (*TRAN*) all had significant positive relations with variables representing companies' investment opportunities and external financing requirements.[9]

Moreover, the governance and transparency scores were also positively correlated with the strength of the local country legal regimes (*LEGAL*), which confirms the results of earlier country-level studies that stronger legal institutions improve the quality of governance.

Also worth noting, the regression terms intended to capture the interaction of the legal regime with the effects of investment opportunities and external financing on the company-specific governance measures (*COMP, PROTECT,* and *TRAN*) had negative coefficients. This result suggests that the positive effects of investment opportunities and external financing on governance are larger in weaker legal environments.

As reported in table 4.3, the regression results with ownership concentration also show a significant positive coefficient on cash flow rights, *OWN_CASH*.[10] And as also expected, the coefficient for *WEDGE* is negative and significant for *PROTECT,* CLSA's measure of minority investor protection. For ownership concentration, *PROTECT* is more relevant than *COMP,* because *COMP* includes measures of transparency and other governance criteria that are unlikely to be influenced by ownership concentration. Controlling share-

TABLE 4.3

Country Random-Effects Regressions of CLSA Governance and S&P Transparency Scores on Ownership Concentration and Legal Environments

This table reports the results of regressions of CLSA composite corporate governance score, *COMP*; investor protection, *PROTECT*; social awareness, *SOCIAL*; or S&P transparency ranking *TRAN* on *OWN_CASH* (the share of cash flow rights held by the largest shareholder), $(OWNER\_CASH)^2$ (squared term for cash flow ownership), *WEDGE* (dummy variable, equal to one if *CONTROL - OWN_CASH* $\geq$ 10% and zero, otherwise, where *CONTROL* is the share of voting rights held by the largest shareholder), *LEGAL* (quality of legal environment), *OWN_CASH*LEGAL* (interaction term for the share of cash flow rights held by the largest shareholder with the quality of legal environment). All regressions control for industry fixed effects, firm size, research and development expenditures, export intensity, cross-listing dummy, and financial statements consolidation dummy (coefficients are not reported). ***, **, * indicate significance at 1%, 5%, and 10% levels.

	CLSA COMP	CLSA PROTECT	CLSA SOCIAL	S&P TRAN
OWN_CASH	0.575**	1.691***	−0.595	0.192
$(OWN\_CASH)^2$	−0.005**	−0.015***	0.005	−0.001
WEDGE	−0.829	−8.640*	1.371	−0.803
LEGAL	0.864***	1.447***	−0.220	0.599***
OWN_CASH LEGAL*	−0.010	−0.030*	0.017	−0.005
R2	0.442	0.326	0.118	0.344
Companies	173	173	173	240

A Case of Good and Improving Governance in Korea

Developments at Hana Bank in Korea can be used to illustrate some of the key points of this article, as well as other important aspects of corporate governance. Hana received the top ranking by CLSA among the 28 Korean companies it covered in 2001, the last year CLSA allowed public access to its individual company ranking.*

Hana is one of the two major private Korean banks that came through the Korean financial crisis and its aftershock in relatively good financial standing; the other was Shinhan Bank. Unlike most other local banks, Hana and Shinhan were purely private and had direct foreign investor involvement from their inception. Hana was established as an investment finance company in 1971 with 40% foreign ownership: the International Financial Corporation with a 20% stake, and 5% each from Goldman Sachs, Bankers Trust, Nomura, and PICA. In 1991 Hana was converted into a bank. Shinhan was established mostly with investments from a group of Japanese investors. In both cases, foreign investments had the partly unforeseen benefit of shielding the two banks from government interference in lending practices. Most local banks were subject to frequent government intervention until the Korean financial crisis, which prompted serious attempts at financial sector reforms. Although not completely immune to government interference, the foreign block-holder participation in Hana enabled the bank to develop and maintain more objective lending policies based on sound credit assessment, which in turn allowed the bank to escape the devastation resulting from the collapse of the Daewoo Group in 1999.

By the time the Asian financial crisis hit Korea in 1997, most of the original foreign block holders had sold their shares. The same year, Seung Yu Kim, who had been with Hana since its start as a finance company, became the president and CEO. Kim immediately started an aggressive campaign to attract large foreign investors, successfully bringing back the IFC as a 7% block holder. By early 2001, when Kim became the chairman as well, the bank had representatives of several large block holders sitting on its board of directors, a practice extremely rare among Korean firms. Its board had representatives from Allianz (11.82% ownership), the IFC (6.64% ownership), and five local companies, each with 3% or more ownership. (The rest of the board consisted of three independent directors, including a U.S. finance professor, five executives, and an auditor.) At the end of 2005, Hana had four large foreign block holders: Goldman Sachs (9.34%), TEMASEK (9.06%), Templeton (8.13%), and Allianz (4.84%). It also added another foreign representative, from Goldman Sachs, to the board in addition to those from Allianz and IFC.

continued

The unique composition of the board has had a strong influence on Hana's shareholder value focus. For example, during several preliminary merger and acquisition talks with potential targets, the top management and the board did not hesitate to back away from potential bidding wars when prices escalated beyond economically sensible levels. Shareholder value has long been the board's primary criterion for decision-making. Although many companies pay lip service to this ideal, the reality is that once merger talks get started, the heat of negotiation often pushes the bidding firm to overpay, leading to destruction of shareholder value.** It is also well known that during takeover contests, a bidding company's top executives often let hubris overcome rationality and that resisting such temptation requires undivided attention to shareholder value creation.

How did Hana become a data point in our study? In 2000 its CLSA overall governance was ranked fourth among 24 Korean firms, and 281st among 494 companies worldwide. Its investment opportunity set was assigned a score of 0.55, three times the average of 0.18 for Korean firms. The numerical values assigned for external financing needs and ownership concentration were 0.16 and 16.1, respectively, lower than the 0.31 and 27 averages of other Korean companies. And its Q ratio was 1.01, also lower than Korea's average Q of 1.19. Nevertheless, between 2000 and 2001, CLSA increased Hana's overall governance score from 47.2 to 71.6, making it first among 28 Korean firms and 18th among 500 firms worldwide.

The largest improvement in Hana's 2001 governance score was in the category called "discipline," which measures managerial incentives and behavior in terms of value-maximizing actions. With newly consolidated power in 2001, Kim led Hana's renewed focus on shareholder value. It introduced stock option plans and jumpstarted an active investor relations campaign, dedicating a full page to corporate governance in its 2001 annual report—another rarity among Korean firms at that time. And such governance improvements have produced results for shareholders. Over the four-year span from the end of 2001 to the end of 2005, Hana's stock price rose by 173%, comparing quite favorably to the 99% increase in KOSPI (Korea Stock Price Index) and an average 99% increase in Korean bank stocks.

*See note 4 for why it blocked public access starting 2002.
**See M. Bradley, A. Desai, and E. H. Kim, "The Rationale behind Inter-Firm Tender Offers: Information or Synergy?" Journal of Financial Economics (1983), pp. 183–206, and see M. Bradley, A. Desai, and E. H. Kim, "Synergistic Gains from Corporate Acquisitions and Their Division Between the Stockholders of Target and Acquiring Firms," Journal of Financial Economics (1988), pp. 3–40.

holders with greater cash flow rights have their self-interest better aligned with those of minority shareholders, resulting in better protection of minority shareholder interests; however, there is no obvious reason why they will advocate greater transparency. And since there is no reason to expect firms with concentrated ownership to disclose more, it's not surprising that when we used S&P transparency scores as the dependent variable, all the coefficients had the right signs, but most lost significance.

In sum, we concluded that investor protection improves with the concentration of cash flow rights, but decreases as the controlling shareholder acquires control rights in excess of cash flow rights. Furthermore, the positive effect of ownership concentration on investor protection is stronger in weaker legal regimes. This makes sense because, for companies operating in countries with weak legal investor protection, concentrated ownership of cash flow rights should serve as a more important tool to resolve agency conflicts between controlling and minority shareholders.[11]

Good Governance Is Valued More Highly Where It Is Scarce

Better governance and disclosure practices should increase investor confidence, which in turn should have a positive effect on firm valuation. Since high-quality governance is relatively scarce in weak legal regimes, the comparatively few companies with good governance are likely to be valued more highly in a poor legal environment. Thus, we expect the impact of the quality of governance on firm valuation to be larger in weaker legal regimes.

To test these arguments about valuation and governance, we used Tobin's Q (the sum of total assets plus the market value of equity less book value of equity, all divided by total assets) as a proxy for firm valuation. The most important independent variables in the regression were the CLSA or S&P scores, a variable for the legal regime, and another reflecting the interaction of the legal regime with corporate governance or disclosure scores. And, in order to control for other possible influences on value, we also included variables representing industry effects, past sales growth, firm size, R&D expenditures, export intensity, and cross-listing and financial statements consolidation dummies.[12]

As reported in table 4.4, the results of these regressions suggest that companies with better governance command higher values. Both the CLSA composite score and the S&P measure of transparency are positively related to firm valuation (Tobin's Q). Moreover, the results are not only statistically, but also economically significant in the following sense: The coefficient on *COMP* indicates that a one standard deviation increase in a company's overall governance score is associated with an 0.17 increase in its Q ratio (which amounts to about 9% of the sample average Q ratio of 1.89).

TABLE 4.4

Country Random-Effects Regressions of Firm Valuation on CLSA Governance or S&P Transparency Scores and Legal Environments

This table reports the results of regressions of firm valuation on *CORP_GOV (CLSA's COMP* or *SOCIAL*, or S&P transparency ranking, *TRAN*), *LEGAL* (quality of legal environment), and *CORP_GOV * LEGAL* (interaction term for *CORP_GOV* with the quality of legal environment). All regressions control for industry fixed effects, firm past investment opportunities, size, research and development expenditures, export intensity, cross-listing dummy, and financial statements consolidation dummy (coefficients are not reported). ***, **, * indicate significance at 1%, 5%, and 10% levels.

Dependent Variable	Valuation			
CLSA COMP	1.950*			
CLSA SOCIAL	0.436			
S&P TRAN			0.905**	
LEGAL	0.010	0.001	0.016	0.017***
*CORP_GOV * LEGAL*	−0.026*	0.030	−0.006***	
R2	0.344	0.361	0.282	0.321
Companies	344	334	438	344

The quality of the legal environment, *LEGAL,* also has the expected positive sign, which is consistent with the findings of earlier studies.[13] But, perhaps more interesting, when *LEGAL* enters the regression with either CLSA or S&P scores, it loses statistical significance. Only when the same regression is estimated without governance or transparency scores does the *LEGAL* coefficient become significant (the last column in the table). The message of this finding is that an individual company's reputation for effective governance and transparency scores is more important than the surrounding legal environment in determining its value; or to put it another way, companies can rise above their legal settings.

Reinforcing this argument, the interaction term with *LEGAL* has the expected negative sign for both *COMP* and *TRAN* and is significant, implying that the positive relation between governance and valuation is stronger in weaker legal regimes. The coefficient on the interaction term for *COMP* can be interpreted as saying that in a weak legal regime, such as that of Mexico (*LEGAL*=3.33), a one standard deviation increase in the governance score is associated with an increase in the Q ratio of 0.24, a 13% increase relative to the average Q of 1.80 for Mexican firms. By contrast, in a strong legal regime like that of Hong Kong (*LEGAL*=41.65), the same increase in the governance score is

A Russian Case

Wimm-Bill-Dann Foods Company (WBD), a Russian producer of dairy products, juices, baby foods, and mineral water, is a good example of a transparent company operating in a country plagued by problems of weak institutions and corruption. WBD was founded in 1992 by five entrepreneurs, who still control the company. Having experienced rapid growth both through expansion of existing assets and acquisition of food companies in different regions of Russia, WBD now owns over 30 plants, operates distribution centers in more than 45 Russian cities, controls over 40% of the market, and employs more than 17,000 people. WBD has traded as a Level 3 ADR on the NYSE since 2002.

According to a report by CLSA, Russia experienced substantial improvements in governance legislation in the first years of this decade.* For example, in November of 2001, the Russian government implemented a "corporate governance code" urging all publicly listed corporations to follow better governance. The key provisions of the code give more power to shareholders to dismiss top managers, prohibit insider trading, and define in general how a company should deal with interested parties and conflicts of interests between board members and the company. To improve enforceability of the code, the Russian government started awarding contracts only to companies that adopted the code. Despite these efforts, some Russian companies with large state ownership have been accused of corporate governance abuses.

WBD has been continuously praised by many rating agencies, including Standard & Poor's, for its sound governance and disclosure practices. In S&P's 2001 transparency and disclosure survey, WBD scored a respectable 71 (out of 91), which made it second among 42 rated Russian companies (and 266th among all 1,026 international firms). During this period, WBD also had relatively high levels of investment opportunity (measured as 0.2, as compared to an average 0.18 for all Russian firms) and reliance on external financing (0.3 in relation to a Russian average of 0.18). Moreover, WBD was rewarded for its sound governance practices and high disclosure levels with a market-to-book value of 1.54 in 2002. (For comparison, the average values for all Russian and world companies were 0.83 and 1.53, respectively.)

As a Level III ADR company, WBD adheres to strict disclosure requirements prescribed by the Securities and Exchange Commission and the Sarbanes-Oxley Act. Press accounts have noted that the information packages prepared for shareholders before general meetings are comprehensive and include financial statements prepared according to U.S. GAAP along

continued

with a 20-F annual report. Moreover, S&P's governance report in 2003 points to a number of specific governance strengths of WBD:

- Unlike many other Russian companies, WBD fully discloses its ownership structure providing the names of major owners. WBD employs an established, international auditor, Ernst & Young, for both its U.S. GAAP and Russian Accounting Standards financial statements.

- The controlling group is committed to following strong governance practice, which is formalized in the Shareholders' Agreement and the company's Corporate Governance Code. (This commitment was demonstrated by the openness of the board's decision making when appointing a new CEO in 2002.)

- The board has an independent majority and wide range of skills. The effectiveness of the board is supported by three committees and is involved in a wide range of issues, including risk management, internal controls, acquisitions, executive succession, and remuneration.

- There is a dedicated disclosure committee composed of senior management and chaired by the CEO. WBD discloses individual board member compensation.

* CLSA Emerging Markets, "Saints and Sinners: Who's Got Religion?" (Hong Kong: CLSA, 2001).

associated with an increase in Q of only 0.11, which represents less than 5% of the average Q of 2.41 for firms in Hong Kong.

These findings are also consistent with the findings of McKinsey & Co.'s 2000 survey of governance premiums around the world.[14] According to that survey, institutional investors were then paying premiums for good governance ranging from 12–14% in North America and Western Europe, 20–25% in Asia and Latin America, to more than 30% in Eastern Europe and Africa.

One last point: The results reported in table 4.4 also provided no evidence that investors assign a higher value to corporate policies and behaviors that are defined as "socially responsible" by CLSA. As financial economists like Michael Jensen have long argued, it pays for companies to invest in social causes as long as there is a payoff to such investment, whether in terms of public goodwill (translating into a stronger "brand") or relief from possible political and regulatory interference. The apparent absence of any link between social investment and value can be traced either to the fact that social investment tends to be at best a zero NPV project, or to disagreement about the worth of some of the causes supported. CLSA's social index includes child labor practices, political legitimacy, environmental responsibility, equal employment policy, and ethical behavior. Several of these criteria are contentious. As one example, economists question whether blanket prohibitions of child labor in low-income economies are truly helpful in societies where the next-best alternatives could be starvation, prostitution, or drug peddling.

In Closing: Hope for Companies in Emerging Markets

Our study of 859 companies in 27 countries in Asia, Latin America, and Eastern Europe identified three corporate attributes—profitable investment opportunities, significant capital requirements, and concentrated ownership—that appear to lead companies to adopt governance and disclosure practices that go beyond those stipulated by local law and regulation. What's more, these associations with effective governance are stronger in countries with weaker investor protection. And perhaps most important, our study provides evidence that companies with higher governance and transparency scores command higher values—and that this governance valuation effect is more pronounced in countries with weaker legal systems.

These results send a powerful message of hope to companies, investors, and policymakers in emerging economies with limited institutional protection of minority shareholders. Companies that establish and maintain reputations for good governance and transparency are likely to be rewarded by investors with higher valuations. Policymakers should trust the market at least to the extent of allowing companies with significant funding requirements to improve their governance in ways that meet the demands of potential (in some cases international) investors. On the other hand, the companies that require policymakers' attention are those with limited investment opportunities, little need for external financing, and controlling shareholders with voting control disproportionate to their claims on cash flow. These firms have little private incentive to improve governance.

Our results also have implications for the perennial debate over "pro-growth" versus "redistributionist" national economic and fiscal policies. To the extent pro-growth policies succeed in generating more profitable investment opportunities, companies in need of funds will have stronger private incentives to improve governance practices on their own, without prodding from regulators. Moreover, allowing companies to experiment with their own forms of governance and disclosure is likely to be more productive than imposing a "one-size-fits-all" set of requirements. By contrast, redistributionist-oriented policies that tend to weaken property rights, and dampen incentives to make investments and raise external capital, will make the policymakers' job much more demanding.

Notes

We are grateful to Don Chew for his very helpful suggestions and comments. This research was funded by Mitsui Life Financial Research Center at the University of Michigan. Art Durnev thanks the Institut de Finance Mathématique de Montréal (IFM2) for providing research funding.

1. These studies include R. La Porta, F. Lopez-de-Silanes, A. Shleifer, and R. W. Vishny, "Investor Protection and Corporate Valuation," *Journal of Finance* (2002), pp. 1147–1170; C. Doidge, G. A. Karolyi, and R. M. Stulz, "Why Are Foreign Firms Listed in the U.S. Worth More?" *Journal of Financial Economics* (2003), pp. 205–238; P. Gompers, J. Ishi, and A. Metrick, "Corporate Governance and Equity Prices," *Quarterly Journal of Economics* (2003), pp. 107–155; A. Durnev and E. H. Kim, "To Steal or Not to Steal: Firm Attributes, Legal Environment, and Valuation," *Journal of Finance* (2005), pp. 1461–1493; and B. Black, H. Jang, and W. Kim, "Predicting Firms' Governance Choices: Evidence from Korea," *Journal of Corporate Finance* (2006), pp. 660–691.

2. See R. La Porta, F. Lopez-de-Silanes, A. Shleifer, and R. W. Vishny, "Legal Determinants of External Finance," *Journal of Finance* (1997), pp. 1131–1149; A. Demirguc-Kunt and V. Maksimovic, "Law, Finance, and Firm Growth," *Journal of Finance* (1998), pp. 2107–2137; R. Rajan and L. Zingales, "Financial Development and Growth," *American Economic Review* (1998), pp. 559–586; K. Kumar, R. Rajan, and L. Zingales, "What Determines Firm Size?" NBER Working paper no. 7208; J. Wurgler, "Financial Markets and the Allocation of Capital, *Journal of Financial Economics* (2000), pp. 187–214.

3. A. Durnev and E. H. Kim, "To Steal or Not to Steal: Firm Attributes, Legal Environment, and Valuation," *Journal of Finance* (2005), pp. 1461–1493.

4. In support of this claim, the *South China Morning Post* reported in 2001 that CLSA lost much of its corporate finance business with companies given low corporate governance scores and that, because of the lost business, CLSA was considering stopping compiling the scores (S. Seawright, "Rankings a Dangerous Exercise," *South China Morning Post* (2001), A2). CLSA has continued publishing general, aggregate governance reports; however, it has blocked public access to firm-specific governance scores starting 2002.

5. The correlation coefficient between CLSA's *COMP* and S&P's *TRAN* is 0.20 (p-value=0.0).

6. R. La Porta, F. Lopez-de-Silanes, A. Shleifer, and R. W. Vishny, "Law and Finance," *Journal of Political Economy* (1998), pp. 1113–1155.

7. Many previous studies have failed to detect a statistically significant relation between governance and firm performance in the U.S., due partly to small variations in the observed variables for the quality of governance. Because of the relatively strict U.S. regulations concerning governance and transparency, the variation in the observable measures of governance among U.S. firms (prior to bankruptcies and reports of scandals in media) is small relative to that in other countries. We avoid this problem by constructing a sample of international firms that allows for greater variation in the observed quality of governance and transparency.

8. Control rights exceed cash flow rights in companies with pyramidal structures, cross-holdings, and dual-class shares. For example, if the controlling shareholder owns 10% of company A's outstanding stock, which in turn owns 30% of firm B's stock, then she is considered to control 10% of firm B, the weakest link in the chain of control rights. However, the cash flow rights of firm B owned by the controlling shareholder is only 3% (10%*30%).

9. The regression coefficients for *COMP* in particular can be interpreted as saying that a one standard deviation increase in growth rates *(INV_OPP)* increases the governance score by 4.86, an increase of 9.97% over the sample mean of 48.74, while the same increase in external financing needs raises *COMP* by 2.13, an increase of 4.37%.

10. At the same time, the results show a significant negative coefficient on a variable called *(OWN_CASH)*2 for *COMP*. Apparently corporate governance improves with the concentration of cash flow rights, but at a decreasing rate, consistent with earlier findings of R. Morck, A. Shleifer, and R. W. Vishny, "Management Ownership and Corporate Performance: An Empirical Analysis," *Journal of Financial Economics* (1988), pp. 293–315; and J. McConnell and H. Servaes, "Additional Evidence on Equity Ownership and Corporate Value," *Journal of Financial Economics* (1990), pp. 595–612. They argue that greater ownership concentration by insiders may align their interests with those of minority shareholders, but at some point it may also result in a greater degree of managerial entrenchment.

11. The sizes of the coefficients also indicate that the effects are economically significant. For *PROTECT,* one standard deviation increase in cash flow rights increases the score by 12.67, a 21.02% increase relative to the 60.27 sample mean, while increasing control rights by 10% above cash flow rights decreases the score by 8.64.

12. Past sales growth is added to control for a possible spurious relation between governance and valuation because growth opportunities, proxied by sales growth, are related to both valuation and corporate governance.

13. This is consistent with the findings of R. La Porta, F. Lopez-de-Silanes, A. Shleifer, and R. W. Vishny, "Investor Protection and Corporate Valuation," *Journal of Finance* (2002), pp. 1147–1170, that firms located in better legal environments enjoy higher valuation.

14. See *McKinsey Quarterly,* "Putting a Value on Corporate Governance" (1999).

PART II

Cross-Country Evidence on Governance Effectiveness and the Cost of Capital

CHAPTER 5

Control Premiums and the Effectiveness of Corporate Governance Systems

ALEXANDER DYCK AND LUIGI ZINGALES

THE LAST DECADE has witnessed a tremendous increase of interest in corporate governance, which in turn has triggered a search for the key elements of an effective governance system. To evaluate the effectiveness of different corporate governance systems, it is necessary to develop an objective measure of effective corporate governance. The main gauge used by most economists and policy makers—the size of a nation's equity market—is generally considered too indirect to provide a useful guide for analysis or reform. In this chapter, we begin by summarizing the findings of our published research that presents a more direct measure of the success of corporate governance systems. Then we use this newly constructed measure as a basis for identifying the most important elements of a well-functioning national governance system.

One useful definition of corporate governance is "the ways in which suppliers of finance to corporations assure themselves of getting a return on their investment."[1] If we adopt this definition, then one measure of the *shortcomings* of a corporate governance system is the proportion of a company's value that does not accrue to all shareholders on a per share basis, but is instead captured by inside shareholders who control and sometimes manage the firm. Economists refer to this extra value captured by insiders as the *"private* benefits of control."* This name reflects the reality that effective control of a corporation confers the opportunity not only to improve performance and increase value, but also to divert wealth away from shareholders and other groups in favor of the controlling coalition.

To illustrate the concept of private control benefits, take the case of company (or individual) A that buys a controlling interest in company B. One way for A to realize private benefits is simply to *transfer* value—say, by getting B to sell its product to A at below-market prices or getting B to buy inputs from A at above-market prices (whether or not such behavior is legal and the likelihood that if illegal it will be sanctioned depends on the domicile of both companies

A and B). Another possibility, which does not involve an actual *transfer* of wealth, is for company A to profit from an investment opportunity that it learns about as a direct consequence of its involvement with B (and that might have instead been undertaken by B).

This kind of wealth diversion reduces what minority shareholders are willing to pay for shares, lowering the value of all companies where such behavior represents a real possibility. And by raising the cost of finance, it limits the ability of such firms to fund attractive investment projects. But how can we tell how much of this activity goes on within a national economy? By their nature, such private control benefits are difficult to observe and even more difficult to quantify in a reliable way. (After all, if such value transfers could be observed and quantified, it would be relatively easy, at least where such transfers are illegal, for non-controlling shareholders to stop them.)

Financial economists have come up with two methods of estimating the size of private benefits. One is to look at differences across firms and among nations in the size of premiums paid for voting stock relative to non-voting stock.[2] If superior voting stock trades at a premium while having equal or inferior dividend rights, this means that control is valuable. But such control should command additional value only if controlling shareholders expect to receive some benefits not available to minority shareholders. And thus large premiums can be viewed as an indication of inadequate protections for minority shareholders and a weak corporate governance system.

Cross-country studies of voting premiums suggest widespread weakness in corporate governance as well as significant variation among countries. The earliest, single-country studies concluded that voting rights tend to be worth 10% to 20%, on average, of the value of common stock, with countries such as the United States (5.4%), Sweden (6.5%), and the United Kingdom (13.3%) reporting relatively low premiums, moderate premiums in Switzerland (20.0%) and Canada (23.3%), and much higher premiums in countries like Israel (45.5%) and Italy (82.0%).[3] A study of 18 countries by Nenova (2001a), using a common methodology and for a common year, reported an average premium across all countries of 13%, with low levels in countries like the United States (2%) and Sweden (1%) and much higher premiums in countries like Italy (29.4%) and Mexico (36.4%). (These high average premiums, as well as the variation among countries, were evident even when the studies controlled for possible inter-country differences in economic rights and liquidity across voting and non-voting shares.)

But this method of evaluating corporate governance systems clearly has limitations. One concern is the possibility that companies that choose to have multiple classes of stock are fundamentally different from other publicly traded companies in those countries. But perhaps even more limiting is the fact that the method cannot be applied to the governance systems of the many nations that prohibit multiple classes of stock.

The second method of estimating private control benefits, which was pioneered in a 1989 study by Michael Barclay and Cliff Holderness, focuses on differences in the price per share paid in a privately negotiated transfer of a controlling block and the price that can be observed in the market once investors have absorbed the fact that there will be a new controlling shareholder. The rationale for this method is that the price per share an acquirer pays for the controlling block reflects *both* the cash flow benefits it expects to receive as a shareholder (which include the value of any improvements it expects to make in the firm's performance) and any private benefits stemming from its controlling position. By contrast, the market price of a share just after the change in control is announced should reflect only the cash flow benefits that *all* shareholders expect to receive under the new management.

Hence, as Barclay and Holderness have argued, the difference between the price per share paid by the acquiring party and the price per share prevailing on the market should reflect the differential payoff accruing to the controlling shareholder. And after some adjustments (discussed below), this difference can be used as a measure of the private benefits for the controlling shareholder.

In a study that was published this year in the *Journal of Finance,* we used the Barclay and Holderness method to infer the value of private benefits of control in companies representing 39 different countries. Based on 393 control transactions that took place between 1990 and 2000, we found that control premiums averaged 14% of the equity value of a firm. As in other studies, we found considerable cross-country variation in the premiums, with 14 countries having average premiums of less than 3% and 10 countries with premiums of 25% or more (including Brazil, with an average premium of 65%).

After performing a series of tests to convince ourselves that these estimates were in fact likely to be measures of private benefits, we then used this measure to explore the following question: What factors within a national economy work to limit such wealth transfers and thereby strengthen its corporate governance system? Perhaps the most common factor associated with lower private benefits is the presence of laws that protect minority shareholders from abuses by insiders. In fact, the extent of such legal protections is often taken to be the measure of the strength of a governance system. But although our study investigated the explanatory power of corporate law, our investigation was not limited to legal factors. Given significant gaps between the laws on a country's books and what takes place in practice, most systems develop less formal, non-contractual ways of limiting self-dealing by insiders. In exploring this possibility, our study considered a number of extralegal mechanisms and institutions that have been proposed by scholars as controlling private benefits—notably product market competition, labor pressures, and moral norms. To these well-known mechanisms, we added two of our own: public opinion and corporate tax enforcement. We hypothesized that in countries with many independent communications media, particularly a thriving business press, the desire of insiders to maintain their public reputation and of organizations to maintain a reputation for fair treatment of minority stockholders should act to limit abuses by controlling shareholders.[4]

We also reasoned that, for most companies, governments represent in effect the largest minority shareholder as a result of their corporate income tax claim; and that the government and minority shareholders have a common interest in preventing insiders from "tunneling" income out of the firm. In this sense, the ability of a government to ensure compliance with tax claims can be viewed as a measure of the effectiveness of this additional monitor of corporate affairs. And, as we discuss below, our study showed that an independent and widely circulating press, high rates of tax compliance, and a high degree of product market competition are all associated with lower private benefits of control.

How to Measure Private Benefits

Consider a company whose stock trades at $8 per share. One day a large block—say, 40%—changes hands (outside of the stock market) at a price of $14 per share. The difference between $8 and $14 can be broken down into two components: (1) the increase in the value of the company expected under the new management team and (2) the private benefits the new shareholder expects from its control of the company. By observing a market price the day *after* the transfer of control has taken place—which gives the market the opportunity to assess the strength of the new management team—we can separate the expected increase in company value from the expected private benefit of control.

To illustrate, let's say that after the transfer has been announced, the stock jumps from $8 to $10. The $2 increase reflects outsiders' expectation of improved corporate performance, presumably resulting from more effective oversight or better management by the buying firm (or individual). But what accounts for the difference between $14 and $10? In some cases, the $4 difference will reflect buyers' greater confidence in, or better information about, their own ability to improve the firm's performance. But on average—and provided the market does a good job of capturing expected gains in its near-term price reactions—the new controlling shareholders must expect to receive the additional $4 in *private* benefits—that is, benefits that do not accrue to outside minority shareholders (and may in fact come at their expense).

Since this premium has been paid only on 40% of the stock, we normalize it by the total value of the company [0.4*((14−10)+10)=0.161]. Hence, in this case we estimate the value of control to be 16% of the value of the company. (Note that the control premium can also be negative even if the new buyer pays a premium over the existing stock price; this would happen if the price on the exchange rises above the negotiated price of the block sale.)

Data and Descriptive Statistics

One limitation of this method is that it can be applied only to publicly traded companies that experience a transfer of a controlling block. In performing our study of such transactions, we started by compiling a list of all control block transactions reported by Securities Data Corporation for the period 1990–2000. After imposing a set of criteria to ensure homogeneity, we were left with a sample of 393 observations from 39 countries.[5]

Table 5.1 presents the characteristics of the deals in our sample, while table 5.2 reports descriptive statistics of the block premiums from our sample according to the country in which the acquired firm is located. The sample includes more than 40 observations each from active equity markets such as the United Kingdom and the United States. For some countries, we have relatively few observations as a result of the combination of weak coverage by Datastream, few reported prices for control sales, and limited observability of control premiums as a result of laws regulating tender offers in the case of control sales. The rank ordering of countries by control premium is very similar using mean and median values, suggesting that our results are not driven by a few outliers.

The first column of table 5.2 presents the average control premium by country, computed as the coefficient of fixed country effects in a regression where the dependent variable is the control premium as defined at the beginning of this chapter. Overall, the average control premium was 14% when each country was given an equal weighting, but only 10% when each transaction received equal weight (which means that countries with smaller control premiums tend to have more transactions). In 10 of our 39 sample countries, the average control premium exceeded 25% of equity value. The countries in our sample with the highest private benefits (bad governance) were Argentina, Austria, Colombia, the Czech Republic, Israel, Italy, Mexico, Turkey, Venezuela, and Brazil, which had the highest estimated value of 65%. At the other extreme were 14 countries for which private benefits were estimated at 3% or less. These countries were Australia, Canada, Finland, France, Hong Kong, Japan, Netherlands, New Zealand, Norway, Singapore, South Africa, Taiwan, the United Kingdom, and the United States.

Of course, control premiums differ across firms for a variety of reasons related to specifics of the deal and characteristics of the firm. If such variation were more pronounced in some countries than others, this would make country averages misleading indicators of the underlying strength or weakness of

Transaction Characteristics

This table presents the summary statistics of the specific characteristics of all the 412 transactions analyzed in this chapter.

Variable	Number of Observations	Mean	Std. Dev.	MM	Max
The difference between the security value of the buyer (market price at t+2) and of the seller (market price at t-30) normalized by the market price at t+2	412	0.06	0.24	−1.84	0.90
Buyers proportion of change in security value	412	0.02	0.09	−0.43	0.40
Initial shareholding as a percent of total shares	412	1.31	3.72	0.00	20.00
Size of control block as a percent of total shares	412	37.71	17.51	6.00	90.00
Fixed assets as a percentage of total assets (U.S. 3-digit SIC)	412	0.29	0.23	0.00	0.77
INDICATOR VARIABLES					
Transactions with blocks greater than 20%	412	0.27			
Transactions with another large shareholder	412	0.16			
Financial distress in target in year of transaction (EPS<=0)	412	0.26			
Financial distress in target in year before transaction (EPS<=0)	412	0.22			
Domestic acquirer	412	0.62			
Control block created by issuing new shares	412	0.16			
Agriculture, forestry, & fishing (SIC 01-09)	412	0.05			
Mining (SIC 10-14)	412	0.04			
Construction (SIC 15-17)	412	0.01			
Manufacturing (SIC 20-39)	412	0.39			
Transportation & pub. utilities (SIC 40-49)	412	0.09			
Wholesale trade (SIC 50-51)	412	0.03			
Retail trade (SIC 52-59)	412	0.06			
Finance, insurance, & real estate (SIC 60-67)	412	0.23			
Services (SIC 70-89)	412	0.10			
Seller an individual (news stories)	412	0.18			
Seller government (news stories)	412	0.03			
Seller unidentified (news stories)	412	0.08			
Seller public company (news stories)	412	0.54			
Acquirer public company (SDC)	412	0.42			
Acquirer subsidiary (SDC)	412	0.13			
Acquirer private (SDC)	412	0.40			
Acquirer government (SDC)	412	0.01			
Acquirer unknown (SDC)	412	0.03			

Block Premium as Percent of Firm Equity

Country	Mean	Median	Standard Deviation	Minimum	Maximum	Number of Observations	Number of Positive Observations
Argentina	0.27	0.12	0.26	0.05	0.66	5	5
Australia	0.02	0.01	0.04	−0.03	0.11	13	9
Austria	0.38	0.38	0.19	0.25	0.52	2	2
Brazil	0.65	0.49	0.83	0.06	2.99	11	11
Canada	0.01	0.01	0.04	−0.02	0.06	4	2
Chile	0.15	0.12	0.18	−0.08	0.51	9	8
Colombia	0.27	0.15	0.34	0.06	0.87	5	5
Czech Republic	0.58	0.35	0.80	0.01	2.17	6	6
Denmark	0.08	0.04	0.11	−0.01	0.26	5	3
Egypt	0.04	0.04	0.05	0.01	0.07	2	2
Finland	0.02	0.01	0.06	−0.07	0.13	14	9
France	0.02	0.01	0.10	−0.10	0.17	5	3
Germany	0.10	0.10	0.13	−0.24	0.32	18	15
Hong Kong	0.01	0.03	0.05	−0.12	0.05	9	7
Indonesia	0.07	0.07	0.03	0.05	0.09	2	2
Israel	0.27	0.21	0.32	−0.01	0.89	9	8
Italy	0.37	0.16	0.57	−0.09	1.64	8	7
Japan	−0.04	−0.01	0.09	−0.34	0.09	21	5
Malaysia	0.07	0.05	0.10	−0.08	0.39	41	31
Mexico	0.34	0.47	0.35	−0.04	0.77	5	4
Netherlands	0.02	0.03	0.05	−0.07	0.06	5	4
New Zealand	0.03	0.03	0.09	−0.17	0.18	19	14
Norway	0.01	0.01	0.05	−0.05	0.13	14	9
Peru	0.14	0.17	0.11	0.03	0.23	3	3
Philippines	0.13	0.08	0.32	−0.40	0.82	15	11
Poland	0.11	0.08	0.11	0.02	0.28	5	5
Portugal	0.20	0.20	0.14	0.11	0.30	2	2
Singapore	0.03	0.03	0.03	−0.01	0.06	4	3
South Africa	0.02	0.00	0.03	0.00	0.07	4	2
South Korea	0.16	0.17	0.07	0.04	0.22	6	6
Spain	0.04	0.02	0.06	−0.03	0.13	5	4
Sweden	0.06	0.02	0.08	−0.01	0.22	13	12
Switzerland	0.06	0.07	0.04	0.01	0.15	8	8
Taiwan	0.00	0.00	0.01	−0.01	0.00	3	2
Thailand	0.12	0.07	0.19	−0.08	0.64	12	11
Turkey	0.30	0.09	0.55	−0.03	1.41	6	5
United Kingdom	0.02	0.01	0.05	−0.06	0.17	43	23
United States	0.02	0.02	0.10	−0.20	0.40	47	28
Venezuela	0.27	0.28	0.21	0.04	0.47	4	4
Average/ Number	**0.14**	**0.11**	**0.18**	**−0.04**	**0.48**	**412**	**300**

national governance systems. To address this concern we next produced revised estimates of how control premiums differ across countries that were based on a regression that controlled for company and transaction characteristics.

1. Differences in the Extent to Which the Block Conveys Control

First of all, in calculating our initial control premiums, we assumed that all transactions in our sample transfer absolute control. But this is probably incorrect because the transfer of, say, a 20% block does not carry the same amount of control as the transfer of a 51% block. Similarly, the transfer of a 30% block when there is another shareholder controlling 20% likely carries less control than the transfer of the same block when the rest of the shares are dispersed. Thus, control blocks above 50% are likely to fetch a higher price. Similarly, the presence of another large shareholder (a stake in excess of 20%) should reduce the premium.[6]

As shown in table 5.3 (column 2), for our sample of 393 transactions, an absolute majority of votes, all other things equal, had the effect of increasing the value of a controlling block by 9.5% of the total value of equity (with statistical significance at the 5% level). But contrary to our prediction, the presence of another large shareholder also had a small positive (though not statistically significant) effect on the control premium.

2. Differences in the Extent of the Seller's Bargaining Power

In estimating the private benefits of control, we assumed that the seller's bargaining power is constant across all deals. But in cases where sellers have greater-than-average bargaining power, control premiums should be higher. And the converse is also true—namely, that for a given amount of private benefits of control, the lower the seller's bargaining power, the lower our estimates of control premiums.

We tried to control for these differences in bargaining power with three proxies:

First, if the selling company is in financial distress, it is more likely to be forced to sell and hence to have less bargaining power. As a proxy for financial distress, our study created a dummy variable that takes the value 1 when earnings per share are 0 or negative in the year of the block trade or the year preceding the block trade.[7] As expected, companies in financial distress exhibited a control premium that is 5.4 percentage points lower than otherwise identical companies that are not.

Similarly, when the acquisition of a controlling block takes the form of an equity infusion, this probably indicates that a company needs to raise equity, a sign of a weak bargaining position. We inserted a dummy if the block was formed by newly issued equity. Contrary to expectations, the creation of a

TABLE 5.3

Estimated Block Premia by Country

The dependent variable is the block premium as a percent of firm equity. Each regression includes country fixed effects. In addition, in column (2) we introduce several deal characteristics: whether it is a majority block, whether there is another large shareholder, whether the firm is in financial distress, whether the block was created by issuing new shares, whether the buyer is a foreigner, and if the firms' shares are cross-listed in the United States. In column (3) we introduce several industry and seller/buyer characteristics: identity of the buyer (individual, government, subsidiary, dispersed), identity of the seller (individual, government, unknown), 2-digit SIC code industry dummies, and the proportion of fixed to total assets. In column (4) we introduce in addition interactions between foreign acquirer and cross-listing dummy and the difference in governance rules between acquiring country (or U.S. for cross-listed firms) and target country. All regressions are estimated by OLS. Robust standard errors are in parentheses.

		Dependent Variable: Block Premium				
INDEPENDENT VARIABLES	(1)	(2)		(3)		(4)
Buyer's proportion of change in security value		−0.323	(0.211)	−0.319	(0.209)	−0.336 [0.211]
Stake greater than 50%		0.095**	(0.039)	0.095**	(0.039)	0.087** [0.0391
Another large shareholder		0.041	(0.043)	0.018	(0.040)	0.02 [0.039]
Financial distress in selling firm		−0.054*	(0.028)	−0.043	(0.028)	−0.044 [0.028]
Sold through new share issue		0.041	(0.057)	0.034	(0.059)	0.026 [0.058]
Buyer is foreign		0.069**	(0.034)	0.065*	(0.036)	0.06* [0.036]
Cross-listed in the U.S.		−0.062	(0.040)	−0.067*	(0.039)	0.113 [0.083]
Interaction of relative strength of antidirector rights (home-target nation) and foreign acquirer						−0.029*** [0.011]
Interaction of relative strength of antidirector rights (U.S.–target nation) and cross-listed in the U.S.						−0.07** [10.034]
Buyer individual or private				−0.042	(0.026)	−0.045* [0.026]
Buyer government				0.008	(0.046)	0.011 [0.049]
Buyer subsidiary				−0.001	(0.049)	0.013 [0.049]
Buyer dispersed or unknown				−0.039	(0.044)	−0.031 [0.043]

(continued)

TABLE 5.3 (*continued*)

		Dependent Variable: Block Premium						
INDEPENDENT VARIABLES	(1)		(2)		(3)		(4)	
Seller individual					0.021	(0.029)	0.024	[0.029]
Seller government					0.008	(0.100)	−0.008	[0.0971
Seller unknown					0.028	(0.031)	0.026	[0.031]
Fixed assets as percent of total					−0.097	(0.062)	−0.09	[0.062]
Industry-Agriculture, forestry, fishing					−0.03	(0.050)	−0.027	[0.0501
Industry-Mining					−0.071	(0.071)	−0.068	[0.072]
Industry-Construction					−0.027	(0.042)	−0.058	[0.071]
Industry-Transportation & utilities					0.066*	(0.031)	0.064**	[0.032]
Industry-Wholesale trade					0.046	(0.047)	0.037	[0.046]
Industry-Retail trade					−0.057	(0.055)	−0.046	[0.055]
Industry-Finance, insurance, real estate					0.055	(0.045)	0.054	[0.044]
Industry-Services					−0.024	(0.038)	−0.012	[0.0381

Country Fixed Effects

	(1)		(2)		(3)		(4)	
Argentina	0.268**	(0.111)	0.158	(0.131)	0.197	(0.123)	0.183	(0.113)
Australia	0.020	(0.013)	−0.001	(0.034)	0.051	(0.052)	0.052	(0.051)
Austria	0.383***	(0.099)	0.318	(0.054)	0.309***	(0.050)	0.319***	(0.051)
Brazil	0.650***	(0.252)	0.606***	(0.229)	0.652***	(0.245)	0.653***	(0.245)
Canada	0.013	(0.017)	−0.06	(0.056)	−0.055	(0.075)	−0.052	(0.083)
Chile	0.183***	(0.069)	0.149**	(0.065)	0.165**	(0.067)	0.16**	(0.065)
Colombia	0.273*	(0.142)	0.197	(0.137)	0.242*	(0.132)	0.325**	(0.128)
Czech Republic	0.578*	(0.312)	0.462	(0.297)	0.555*	(0.325)	0.563*	(0.330)
Denmark	0.077	(0.048)	0.039	(0.050)	0.036	(0.070)	0.027	(0.065)
Egypt	0.038	(0.024)	−0.050	(0.061)	0.025	(0.082)	0.112	(0.093)
Finland	0.025	(0.016)	−0.016	(0.027)	−0.010	(0.036)	0.002	(0.037)
France	0.019	(0.052)	0.040	(0.059)	0.080	(0.077)	0.084	(0.078)
Germany	0.095***	(0.034)	−0.020	(0.052)	0.016	(0.059)	0.041	(0.058)

	Model 1		Model 2		Model 3		Model 4	
Hong Kong	0.003	(0.019)	0.045	(0.033)	0.040	(0.044)	0.008	(0.048)
Indonesia	0.072***	(0.017)	−0.034	(0.040)	0.043	(0.047)	0.043	(0.045)
Israel	0.270**	(0.107)	0.238**	(0.108)	0.259**	(0.114)	0.252**	(0.116)
Italy	0.369*	(0.199)	0.323*	(0.191)	0.311	(0.192)	0.349*	(0.199)
Japan	−0.043**	(0.021)	−0.070	(0.044)	−0.038	(0.054)	−0.039	(0.051)
Malaysia	0.072***	(0.017)	0.063***	(0.018)	0.093***	(0.032)	0.089***	(0.033)
Mexico	0.345**	(0.146)	0.296**	(0.143)	0.322**	(0.144)	0.396***	(0.133)
Netherlands	0.016	(0.020)	−0.054	(0.068)	−0.015	(0.060)	−0.015	(0.062)
New Zealand	0.027	(0.024)	−0.028	(0.042)	0.026	(0.046)	0.028	(0.045)
Norway	0.015	(0.014)	0.007	(0.026)	0.052	(0.041)	0.061	(0.043).
Peru	0.142***	(0.053)	0.067	(0.080)	0.060	(0.082)	0.08	(0.075)
Philippines	0.129	(0.083)	0.115	(0.081)	0.142*	(0.079)	0.148*	(0.080)
Poland	0.133***	(0.052)	0.003	(0.081)	0.041	(0.092)	0.039	(0.092)
Portugal	0.203***	(0.073)	0.159***	(0.052)	0.197***	(0.059)	0.207**	(0.059)
Singapore	0.030*	(0.016)	0.024	(0.035)	0.042	(0.069)	0.038	(0.062)
South Africa	0.017	(0.015)	−0.045	(0.061)	0.005	(0.072)	−0.014	(0.074)
South Korea	0.157***	(0.027)	0.086	(0.066)	0.088	(0.086)	0.137*	(0.081)
Spain	0.041	(0.027)	0.021	(0.042)	0.047	(0.058)	0.058	(0.052)
Sweden	0.074***	(0.027)	0.033	(0.047)	0.041	(0.057)	0.047	(0.056)
Switzerland	0.063***	(0.015)	−0.073	(0.056)	−0.067	(0.074)	−0.051	(0.073)
Taiwan	−0.004	(0.004)	−0.047	(0.039)	−0.040	(0.074)	−0.038	(0.073)
Thailand	0.125**	(0.054)	0.073	(0.080)	0.121	(0.084)	0.107	(0.080)
Turkey	0.371	(0.246)	0.276	(0.232)	0.346	(0.249)	0.363	(0.246)
United Kingdom	0.014*	(0.007)	0.000	(0.019)	0.040	(0.033)	0.02	(0.033)
United States	0.01	(0.013)	0.002	(0.031)	0.044	(0.038)	0.035	(0.038)
Venezuela	0.270***	(0.094)	0.256**	(0.105)	0.221**	(0.112)	0.268**	(0.119)
Number of Observations	393		393		393		393	
R-Squared	0.389		0.431		0.459		0.470	

*significant at 10% level; **significant at 5% level; ***significant at 1% level

block through a new equity offering had a positive (though not statistically significant) effect on the premium.

This method was particularly common in Japan, where in a majority of cases control was transferred by financially distressed companies through private placements of new equity. The concentration of such transactions in Japan underscores the importance of controlling for company and deal characteristics rather than focusing on the raw averages across countries.

Finally, foreign acquirers generally face more competition, at the very least because their involvement implies that the transactions are open to foreign buyers and thus there is a larger pool of potential acquirers. Thus, the bargaining power of the seller in these transactions is likely to be bigger. We find that foreign buyers pay a premium of 6.9% (statistically significant at the 5% level).

3. Cross-Listing in the United States

Finance and legal scholars have argued that foreign companies that list in the U.S. exchanges thereby submit themselves to tougher governance rules and limit their own ability to extract private benefits.[8] Since we wanted to capture how "typical" firms across different countries compare in their governance outcomes, and firms that cross-list are unlikely to be "typical," we controlled for the presence of cross-listing. For this purpose we inserted a dummy variable equal to 1 for any selling company that is cross-listed in the United States as well as in its home market.[9] As expected, cross-listed companies had lower private benefits (although given the dearth of dually listed companies in our sample [23], the statistical significance of this effect is below conventional levels).

4. Adjusted Estimates of Private Benefits Controlling for Differences in Deal and Firm Characteristics

After inserting all these deal and company characteristics in our basic regression, we re-estimated the country fixed effects. The results are reported at the bottom of column 2 in table 5.3. Since many of the control variables included capture part of the value of control, the country fixed effects can no longer be interpreted as the estimates of the average value of private benefits in that country, but only as relative rankings. Including these controls dramatically lowers the ranking for countries characterized by the higher-than-average presence of foreign acquirers and sales of majority stakes like Germany, Switzerland, Egypt, and Poland.

On the one hand, these estimates represent an improvement over our raw data because they adjust for deal characteristics. But they suffer from an econometric problem. To estimate the impact of these deal and firm characteristics, we had to assume that this impact is constant across countries. In some cases this assumption might be untenable. For example, the difference between acquiring a 51% stake rather than a 30% one might be huge in a country where private benefits of control are large, but it might be small or even irrelevant in a country where the private benefits of control are very tiny.[10] The regression, however, attributes the same effect to all the countries, underestimating differences across countries.

In the remainder of our study, where we explored the effects and causes of these cross-country differences, we used a refined measure that incorporates controls to keep constant deal (and other) characteristics. But recognizing that these deal characteristics may not be constant across countries, we also tested and reported results without controls.

5. Differences in Industry and Buyer/Seller Characteristics

Cross-country differences could also arise because of other differences in industry and deal characteristics. Private benefits might differ across industry. The media industry, for instance, is often mentioned as an industry where private benefits are larger.[11] Similarly, individuals might value opportunities for private benefits more highly than corporate blockholders).[12] We wanted to ensure that our cross-country comparison was not affected by any systematic difference in the industry characteristics of the deals or the nature of the seller and the buyer. For this reason we re-estimated the country averages, controlling for differences in industry characteristics and identity of the controlling party.

To capture industry differences, we introduced an industry dummy based on the two-digit SIC code of the acquired firm. About three-quarters of our transactions were accounted for by manufacturing (39%), finance insurance and real estate (24%), and services (10%). In a crude way, these controls capture differences in private benefits linked to product market competition. Second, we constructed a measure of tangibility of assets (percentage of total assets that are fixed) based on the three-digit SIC code of the acquired firm. The rationale for this control was that insiders will have more difficulty diverting resources if assets are tied down and easily observable, as is the case with tangible assets.[13]

As shown in column 3 of table 5.3, companies with more tangible assets were found to have lower private benefits. Firms in wholesale trade, finance (financial, insurance, and real estate sector), and transportation and utilities had a higher level of private benefits than manufacturing firms (although these results are not significant).[14]

We also collected information on the identity of the acquirers and the sellers, attempting to determine whether the seller was an individual, the company itself (through new share issues), or a corporate entity. We found the most common seller is a corporation, followed next by individuals (18%), new share issues (16%), and governments (3%). We used SDC data to identify whether the acquirer was a public company, subsidiary, the government, or a private company. The transactions in our sample were almost equally divided between public acquirers (41%) and private acquirers (also 41%). We provided a further classification using news stories and the SDC synopsis field. We identified 13% of our transactions as involving individual acquirers, and 4% as involving a financial intermediary that purchases the shares and then resells them to institutional investors. We interpreted these latter acquisitions as the dispersal of the controlling stake. None of these buyer or seller characteristics turned out to be significant.

At the bottom of column 3 of table 5.3, we report the estimates of the country average level of private benefits after we control for the above differences in level of private benefits across industries. The relative ranking, however, does not seem to be affected very much by these industry controls.

Alternative Interpretation of Control Premiums

While conducting our study, we also considered the possibility that the block premiums were not really measuring private benefits, but something else. The most plausible alternative interpretation is that such control premiums reflect a tendency of buyers to overpay. We tested for this possibility by looking at the announcement effect on the stock price of the acquiring company. If these premiums reflect overpayments, acquiring firms should experience negative returns at the announcement of the transaction.

Of the 393 transactions in our sample, there were 115 in which the acquirer was a publicly traded company and the stock price reaction was reported in Datastream. But inconsistent with the overpayment hypothesis, the mean value of the announcement effect (not reported) was in fact slightly positive (0.5%) and not statistically different from zero. Another implication of the overpayment hypothesis is that the buyer's announcement return should be negatively related to the size of the control premium. But our study found that although the coefficient was negative, it was neither economically nor statistically significant (coefficient of -0.018, p-value of 0.64).

A second possible alternative interpretation—particularly for larger premiums in underdeveloped and therefore less efficient markets—is that buyers have better information (than the market) about the expected payoff from a transaction and there is therefore a delay in incorporating new information. On average, such delays will inflate our estimates of private benefits.

To test for this possibility, we re-estimated the private benefits using the market price 30 days after the announcement instead of just two days after. But our results were virtually identical. If anything, the average premium in developing countries like Brazil was higher rather than lower. We also examined the cumulative abnormal returns to shareholders in target firms from two days to

30 days after the announcement and tested whether the initial level of private benefits was related to the subsequent cumulative abnormal returns. But we found no such effect (with an insignificant relationship between control premiums and post-announcement returns (coefficient of 0.009, p-value of 0.80).

Finally, we were concerned about a possible distortion stemming from selective nondisclosure of the terms of a transaction. In fact, one of the criteria we had to impose to obtain our estimates was the observability of the price paid for the controlling block. A major concern was the possibility that, in countries with better protection of investors, controlling parties were more reluctant to disclose large premiums. If that were the case, then our study would report lower private benefits in the United States not because they are indeed lower, but because large premiums are less likely to be disclosed.

To check for this possibility, we computed the percentage of deals we had to drop from our sample because the terms were not disclosed. On average, 33% of the deals did not disclose the terms, ranging from 0% in Taiwan to 70% in Austria and 82% in the Czech Republic. Contrary to the selective nondisclosure argument, we found that countries with higher premiums tend to have a higher percentage of deals whose terms are not disclosed. Similarly, when we used as a proxy for protection of minority shareholders the "antidirector rights" index constructed by La Porta et al. (1997), we found (not surprisingly) that in countries with greater shareholder protection a larger percentage of deals are disclosed. In sum, if selective nondisclosure biased our results, it did so in a way that understated rather than exaggerated cross-country differences.

Are We Really Estimating Private Benefits?

While we were able to reject these alternative interpretations, what evidence did we have that our estimates were really reflecting private benefits of control?

At the anecdotal level, there are several studies documenting the pervasiveness of self- dealing transactions in countries like Italy (such as Zingales, 1994) and the Czech Republic (Glaeser et al., 2001). It is thus reassuring that our estimates of private benefits for these two countries are both very high (37% and 58%, respectively). It is particularly interesting to stress the differences between our estimates for Poland and the Czech Republic. Both of them are former socialist countries, with a similar level of GDP per capita. Nevertheless, consistent with the analysis of Glaeser et al. (2000), who document differences in the protections for minority shareholders, our estimates are very different (11% for Poland, 58% for the Czech Republic).

A more subtle test of whether these estimates really reflect the ability to extract private benefits is whether our estimated private benefits depend not only on the institutional variables of the country of the company whose control has been acquired, but also on those of the country of the acquiring company (when the two are different).[15] In other terms, an acquirer from a country with less investor protection is likely to be better able to siphon out corporate resources from a subsidiary than a company coming from a country with very rigid rules. This should be reflected in a higher willingness to pay higher control premiums. Thus, we should observe higher estimated private benefits in cases where a foreign acquirer comes from a country with poor protection of investors.

To test this possibility, we re-estimated our basic specification inserting as additional explanatory variables two interaction terms: between the difference in governance rules and the foreign acquirer's dummy (equal to 1 if the acquirer comes from a country different from the target), and between the difference in governance rules and the cross-listing dummy. Our proxy for the difference in governance rules was the difference between countries of the antidirector rights index mentioned earlier. As shown in column 4 of table 5.3, companies coming from more investor-friendly countries paid control premiums that were 2.8% less, on average (and this effect was statistically significant). We also found a statistically significant negative effect of the superiority of governance rules on the control premiums for cross-listed firms. This result implies that the reduction in private benefits resulting from cross-listing is greater for firms from countries with weaker investor protections. (At the foot of table 5.3 we present country fixed effects with these controls—and such controls were applied in all the tests reported in the remainder of this chapter.)

Besides providing some comfort that our estimates were indeed capturing private benefits of control for company insiders, these findings also provided some new evidence that bears on the ongoing debates about governance. On one hand, the results suggest the possibility for firms in countries with weak investor protection to raise their value by "borrowing" another country's institutions—either by selling a block to a firm in that country or, say, by cross-listing in the United States. These results provide direct support for the contention of studies (such as Coffee, 1999; Reese and Weisbach, 2001; and Doidge et al., 2001) of a link between cross-listing and private benefits. But perhaps more important, the results cast some doubt on the prospects for the convergence of different corporate governance systems. For example, Coffee (1999) predicts that companies from countries with better protection of investors will end up buying companies from countries with weaker protection. Our result suggests that, in the context of controlling blocks, companies from countries with better investor protection may be more limited in their ability to extract private benefits and so less willing to bid high premiums for controlling blocks. This raises the possibility that controlling blocks may end up in the hands of companies from the countries with the worst rules, not the best.

An Analysis of Outliers

In Brazil we estimated private benefits to be 65% of the value of equity. Could private benefits really be this large, or was this finding the result of some problem with the way we measured them? We did some further analysis of this extreme outlier to help ascertain the reliability of our method.

As part of a study of the impact of legal reform on private benefits in Brazil, Nenova (2001b) independently collected information on control sales in Brazil between 1995 and 2000. In so doing, she identified 8 transactions that met our initial sample selection criteria.[16] For those transactions, she reported an average value of private benefits of 42%, reasonably close to our estimate. In addition, we asked a Brazilian investment bank to give us all the privatization data for transactions in which the government sold a controlling block of an already listed firm.[17] Their search produced 23 privatization transactions with the requisite data, including 21 transactions that were not included in our original data set.[18] The average control premium in this sample was 129%.

In sum, independent estimates lead to a very similar conclusion: Private benefits of control in Brazil are extremely high.

Within-Country Variation in Private Benefits

Another check to verify whether our method captures private benefits was to see whether our estimates changed when there are changes in external conditions that affect the ability to extract private benefits. While the fact that we had relatively few transactions from many countries limited our ability to systematically explore time series variation, for three events we had this possibility.

The first event we explored was the passage in Italy of a corporate governance reform in 1998 known as the Draghi reform. Among other things, this reform made it easier for minority shareholders to sue management appointed by the controlling shareholder. Such a reform should limit the ability to extract private benefits. When we segmented our data into observations before and after July 1998, we found that before the reform the average value of private benefits was 47%, while after the reform the average value was only 6%.[19]

The second event we explored focuses on Brazil in the 1990s where, as Nenova (2001b) reported, there were two important changes in corporate law. The first change occurred on May 5, 1997, when Law 9457 was adopted. This law, designed in part to enhance government revenues when they sold controlling stakes in privatization transactions, eliminated mandatory disclosure of the price of sales of blocks, eliminated minority shareholders' right to withdraw from the firm in the case of significant transactions such as mergers and spin-offs and to receive a price per share based on the book value of the firm, and eliminated a requirement for acquirers to make a mandatory offer to other holders of voting shares at the same price and terms as that for the controlling block. The elimination of withdrawal rights gives controlling shareholders another avenue to extract private benefits, while the equal opportunity provision theoretically has more mixed effects on the ability to extract private benefits (see Bebchuk, 1999). The second change, passage of Instruction 299 by the Brazilian securities and exchange commission (CVM), reinstated these disclosure, withdrawal, and equal opportunity provisions, and added even more disclosure requirements.

These legal changes suggest that private benefits will differ depending on which legal regime is in effect, with private benefits expected to be greatest in the period when Law 9457 was in effect, and lower both before and after. This is in fact what we found in our sample of transactions; the average premium was highest in the 9457 period, at 119%, with lower levels in the pre-9457 period at 53% and 37% in the post-instruction 299 period. A similar trend was revealed in our privatization sample where we had data only for the first two periods (with values of 109% in the pre-9457 period increasing to 131% in the 9457 period).

The third event we explored focuses on changes in the economic environment rather than changes in the legal regime to protect investors. It has been suggested that stealing will increase when the expected return on investment declines and that the Asian crisis presents such an event. We tested for this possibility, examining whether the levels of private benefits were different for emerging markets in Asia during the Asian crisis (of 1997 and 1998).[20] Based on a regression of private benefits with country fixed effects, we found that the Asian crisis period was indeed associated with higher private benefits (coefficient of 0.068), although this is not significant at conventional significance levels (p-value=0.162).

In sum, in all the three instances our estimates of private benefits were consistent with our theory. Having established some degree of confidence in our estimates, our study next turned to an exploration of the key factors that lead to better performance.

What Works to Limit Private Benefits?

What sorts of institutions help to constrain abuses? And what types of corporate governance reforms—both by firms and governments—will ultimately deliver the greatest returns?

The prevailing view is that the law and a country's legal origin are the primary institutional factors that work to limit corporate abuses. This view focuses clearly on the interests of financial investors and the specific contractual and legal mechanisms that are designed to constrain managerial misconduct. Accordingly, we examined the importance of legal institutions for governance outcomes. But we did not limit our empirical investigation to just these institutions. There are other stakeholders in firms that take an interest in governance and have the potential to influence the extent of abuses. As a result, we also explored whether explicit contracts with other stakeholders (for example, the government through its tax claim) and non-legal constraints on management behavior (such as concerns about reputation and avoiding criticism by the press) help limit the consumption of private benefits.

The Role of Legal Institutions

The Legal Environment. The ability of a controlling shareholder to appropriate some of the value generated is limited by the possibility of being sued. Thus, a greater ability to sue should translate into smaller private benefits of control (see Zingales, 1995a). The same reasoning applies to any legal right attributed to non-controlling shareholders (La Porta et al., 1997). Accordingly, our study attempted to examine the explanatory power of legal rights that give minority investors leverage over insiders. More specifically, we focused our attention on the level of shareholder rights in the country of the target firm (as proxied for by the La Porta "antidirector rights" index for the transition countries in our sample).

Disclosure Standards. Disclosure standards regulate the information available to non-controlling shareholders. The more accurate is this information, the more difficult it is for a controlling shareholder to appropriate value without incurring legal penalties or at least reputational costs. Thus, we expected our measures of the quality of disclosure to be negatively correlated with the size of private benefits of control.

Enforcement. The strength of legal protections depends on the expectation of speedy and predictable enforcement. Thus, we included as one of our contractual variables a measure of the strength of a country's law and order tradition as measured by the country risk rating agency International Country Risk. This rule of law index is scaled from 0 to 10.

Extralegal Institutions

The potential constraints imposed by extralegal institutions have not been prominent in current debates, at least in part because of a lack of empirical examination. We focused our attention on five institutional factors that, at least in theory, have the potential to raise expectations of penalties for activities that produce private benefits for controlling shareholders. Some of these factors that can raise the costs to the controlling shareholder for wealth-diverting activities (such as the penalties produced by product market competition and by public opinion pressure) are constraints that are *external* to the firm. Other factors (such as the sanctions that can be introduced by moral norms, labor, and the government as tax collector) are more "internal" to the firm.

Product Market Competition. The degree of product market competition affects the opportunity to appropriate private benefits in two main ways. First, the more competitive markets are, the more verifiable prices become. When prices are more "objective," it is more difficult for a controlling shareholder to tunnel out resources using manipulated transfer prices without incurring legal or reputational costs. Second, in a competitive market, the distortions produced by the extraction of private benefits are more likely to jeopardize the survival of the firm. Hence, competition represents a natural constraint on the extraction of private benefits. In regressions in our study, we included controls for industry characteristics and used as our cross-country proxy for the extent of product market competition the general response to the survey question, "Do competition laws prevent unfair competition in your country?," as reported by the World Competitiveness Yearbook for 1996.

Public Opinion Pressure. Controlling shareholders might limit their efforts to divert firm resources not out of fear of legal sanction by financial investors but rather out of concern for their reputation. But for concern about reputation to act as a deterrent, it is necessary to have a "public opinion"—that is, an independent press that publicizes the facts and a large set of educated investors who read newspapers and have some (collective) power to punish improper behavior (Zingales, 2000). As one example, shareholder activist Robert Monks succeeded in initiating some major changes at Sears not by means of the norms of the corporate code (his proxy fight failed miserably), but through the pressure of public opinion. He paid for a full-page announcement in the *Wall Street Journal* where he exposed the identities of Sears' directors and called them "non-performing assets" (Monks and Minnow, 1995). The embarrassment for the directors was so great that they implemented all the changes proposed by Monks. Likewise in Russia, one of the top-performing investment funds has achieved its returns in part by publicizing abuses and so embarrassing insiders and regulators to take corrective action (Dyck, 2002). In a study we published two years ago (Dyck and Zingales, 2002), we attempted a systematic examination of this potential corporate governance role of the media. Specifically, we tested whether indicators of the presence of the press are correlated with lower levels of abuse. As our measure of press presence, we used an indicator of newspapers' "diffusion," measured as the circulation of daily newspapers normalized by population.

Internal Policing through Moral Norms. Regardless of the reputational cost or the legal punishment associated with private benefits, a controlling shareholder might choose not to appropriate value as a result of moral considerations. Coffee (2001) proposed the violent crime rate as a proxy for these moral norms, while Stulz and Williamson (2001) focused on culture as an indicator of norms. To test for an impact of moral norms, we used both proposed measures: the number of violent crimes (as reported by the World Competitiveness Yearbook based on Interpol data for 1993) and Stulz and Williamson's classification of countries by their primary religious orientation.

Labor as Monitor. Additional constraints on controlling shareholders might come from the presence of economic entities with a direct interest in firm decisions that could penalize efforts to extract private benefits directly without having to turn to the courts. Labor is privy to inside information on customers and suppliers and can hold up the controlling shareholder by threatening to withhold services and, in some cases, through its position on the board of directors. On the other hand, because labor's interests are not the same as minority shareholders', it is not clear that labor can be counted on to constrain private benefits; in many cases, it may choose to align itself with the controlling shareholder against outside investors. We tested for the effect of labor on private benefits using as a cross-country measure of the extent of potential labor power the degree of employee protection. This measure is available for all OECD countries.

Government as Monitor through Tax Enforcement. Like labor, government has an economic interest in corporate profitability and decision making, and it can take actions to reduce private benefits without having to turn to the courts. What has received little recognition, though, is how the presence of the state's claim (e.g., corporate income tax) and how the state enforces that claim can influence governance and have spillover effects on minority shareholders. We make a distinction between the effect of tax rates and tax enforcement. While the presence of taxes can make governance problems worse, by providing an additional incentive to steal from minority shareholders (see Desai, Dyck, and Zingales, 2003), tax enforcement can improve the situation for shareholders. This is because tax authorities and non-controlling shareholders have a common objective: to ascertain the value produced by a company and get a share of it. For example, a principle of corporate taxation for transfer pricing is the use of an arm's-length price based on what independent parties in a competitive market would charge. How tax authorities enforce their rules on transfer pricing affects the incentives to reallocate returns through transfer pricing, with strict enforcement reducing the likelihood that a controlling shareholder will use transfer prices to siphon out value at the expense of minority shareholders. Therefore, better tax enforcement should lead to smaller private benefits of control. Hence, to test for the effect of taxes on governance in our study, we used as a measure of the effectiveness of a taxation system an index developed by the World Competitiveness Report that assesses the level of tax compliance.

The Tests

In our study, we then ran a series of tests examining, first, the impact of each institution in isolation on private benefits (the results of which are reported in table 5.4) and, second, their effects in combination with each other (see table 5.5). (For both of these regressions, we included all of the control variables used in the test reported in table 5.3 as well as an indicator variable that identifies countries that have any form of tender offer requirement.) In the "univariate" tests whose findings are reported in table 5.4, we included log GNP per capita and rule of law variables to capture important sources of additional variation across countries. In multivariate tests reported in table 5.5, we did not include these control variables.

We started by estimating the impact of "legal" factors—those factors that directly or indirectly rely on the court enforcement of certain rights. Because information disclosure is a prerequisite for any legal action, we started with the quality of the accounting standards, as measured by the CIFAR index. As reported in column 1 of table 5.5, companies in countries with better accounting standards have lower private benefits of control. This effect is both statistically and economically significant. A one standard deviation increase in our measure of accounting standards reduced the value of control by 9.0 percentage points. Viewed together with the other control variables, accounting standards explained 25% of the variation in private benefits of control (the firm-specific control variables alone explained just 15%).

The second variable we examined was the extent of legal protections for minority investors, measured, again, using the La Porta et al. index of antidirector rights. As reported in column 2, countries with greater antidirector rights have lower private benefits of control. A one standard deviation increase in the La Porta index reduced the value of control by 4.4 percentage points. Together with the firm-specific variables, antidirector rights explained 22% of the variation in private benefits of control. In sum, we found that legal institutions are strongly associated with lower levels of private benefits.

We also tested the explanatory power provided by extralegal institutions, which are suggested by a functional rather than an institutional perspective. Here we focused on crude country-wide measures of product market competition, size and extent of reputational penalties, moral norms, employee protections, and diligence of tax authorities.

As reported in column 3 of table 5.4, we found that, after controlling for industry type, countries with more competitive product markets—at least as measured by this survey of the World Competitiveness Report—have lower

TABLE 5.4

Institutional Determinants of Private Benefits of Control-Univariate Analysis

The dependent variable is the block premia as a percent of firm equity. The explanatory variables include all of the variables introduced in Table 5.3 except the country fixed effects, but including a dummy to indicate the presence of a mandatory tender offer law. In place of the country fixed effects, we include as controls log gnp per capita and rule-of-law index, then introduce one at a time several institutional variables: (1) accounting standards index; (2) antidirector rights index; (3) an index of the extent of competition laws; (4) diffusion of the press as measured by the newspaper circulation/population; (5) incidence of violent crimes; (6) extent of legal protections for labor; (7) a dummy variable if primary religion is Catholicism; and (8) tax compliance index. Standard errors, which are reported in parentheses, are robust and clustered by country.

	Legal Institutions		Extralegal Institution					
Independent Variables	1	2	3	4	5	6	7	8
Accounting standards	−0.004 [0.002]*							
Antidirector rights		−0.026 [0.011]*						
Competition laws			−0.066 [0.034]*					
Newspaper circulation/population				−0.021 [0.012]*				
Violent crime incidence					0.000 (0.000)			
Labor protection						0.027 [0.020]		
Catholicism is primary religion							0.064 [0.058]	
Tax compliance								−0.069 [0.025]**

(continued)

TABLE 5.4 (*continued*)

Independent Variables	Legal Institutions		Extralegal Institution					
	1	2	3	4	5	6	7	8
Variables Controlled for:								
Buyer bargaining power	y	y	y	y	y	y	y	y
Ownership variables	y	y	y	y	y	y	y	y
Financial distress	y	y	y	y	y	y	y	y
Foreign acquirer	y	y	y	y	y	y	y	y
Cross-listed in the U.S.	y	y	y	y	y	y	y	y
Buyer identity	y	y	y	y	y	y	y	y
Seller identity	y	y	y	y	y	y	y	y
Industry group	y	y	y	y	y	y	y	y
Tangibility of assets	y	y	y	y	y	y	y	y
Interaction of relative strength of antidirector rights (home–target nation) and foreign acquirer dummy	y	y	y	y	y	y	y	y
Interaction of relative strength of antidirector rights (U.S.–target nation) and cross-listed in the U.S. dummy	y	y	y	y	y	y	y	y
Presence of takeover law	y	y	y	y	y	y	y	y
Log gnp per capita	y	y	y	y	y	y	y	y
Rule of law	y	y	y	y	y	y	y	y
Constant	y	y	y	y	y	y	y	y
Number of observations	381	393	393	393	377	233	393	393
Countries included	36	39	39	39	36	18	39	39
R-squared	0.250	0.220	0.210	0.220	0.230	0.200	0.220	0.240

TABLE 5.5

Institutional Determinants of Private Benefits of Control-Multivariate Analysis

The dependent variable is the block premia as a percent of firm equity. The explanatory variables include all of the variables introduced in table 5.3 except the country fixed effects, but including a dummy to indicate the presence of a mandatory tender offer law. As institutional variables in specification (1) we use the antidirector rights index and the rule-of-law index. In specification (2) we use a dummy variable if the primary religion is Catholicism, a tax compliance index, the diffusion of the press as measured by the newspaper circulation/population, and the index of the extent of competition laws. The independent variables in specification (3) are the antidirector rights index, rule-of-law index, tax compliance index, and diffusion of the press as measured by the newspaper circulation/population. Standard errors, which are reported in parentheses, are robust and clustered by country.

Independent Variables	Dependent Variable: Block Premium		
	(1)	(2)	(3)
Antidirector rights rule of law	−0.026**		−0.003
	(0.012)		(0.019)
	−0.026***		−0.006
	(0.010)		(0.011)
Catholicism		0.019	
		(0.056)	
Tax compliance		−0.064***	−0.061*
		(0.021)	(0.033)
Newspaper circulation/population		−0.020**	−0.018*
		(0.009)	(0.010)
Competition laws		−0.042	
		(0.036)	
Variables controlled for:			
Buyer bargaining power	y	y	y
Ownership variables	y	y	y
Financial distress	y	y	y
Buyer characteristics	y	y	y
Seller characteristics	y	y	y
Foreign acquirer	y	y	y
Cross-listed in the U.S.	y	Y	y
Industry type	y	y	y
Tangibility of assets	y	y	y
Interaction of relative strength of antidirector rights (home–target nation) and foreign acquirer dummy	y	y	y
Interaction of relative strength of antidirector rights (U.S.–target nation) and cross-listed in the U.S. dummy	y	y	y
Presence of takeover law	y	y	y
Constant	y	y	y
Number of observations	393	393	393
Countries included	39	39	39
R-squared	0.213	0.245	0.243

*significant at 10% level; **significant at 5%; * * *significant at 1% level

private benefits of control. A one standard deviation increase in our measure of competition reduced the value of control by 6.0 percentage points. Together with the firm-specific variables, competition explained 21% of the variation in private benefits of control.

As reported in column 4 of table 5.4, consistent with the idea that public opinion pressure might curb insider abuse, countries where newspapers are more diffused (as measured by the number of copies sold per 100,000 inhabitants) have lower private benefits of control. Diffusion captures both the importance of public opinion and the credibility of newspapers (assuming that less credible newspapers sell fewer copies).[21] A one standard deviation increase in newspapers' diffusion reduced the value of control by 6.4 percentage points. Together with the firm-specific variables, newspapers' diffusion explained 22% of the variation in private benefits of control. The findings reported in columns 3 and 4 suggest that institutions external to the firm help to limit private benefits.

Columns 5 and 7 report the findings of our tests of the idea that countries with higher moral norms might have lower private benefits. Consistent with Coffee's prediction, countries with worse norms as proxied by higher violent crime rates have higher private benefits of control, but the effect is economically and statistically insignificant. To investigate moral norms as proxied by primary religion, we introduced indicator variables for the four main religions (Buddhist, Catholic, Muslim, and Protestant). As a country religion, we used the dominant one (see Stulz and Williamson, 2001). We found that Catholic countries have higher private benefits (although the result is not significant) while those in Protestant countries were significantly lower. The effects of the Muslim and Buddhist religions were not significant.

Reported in columns 6 and 8 are our tests of the extent to which the strength of other corporate stakeholders are associated with lower levels of private benefits. In column 6, we report the estimated effect of labor as a monitor of private benefits. As an index of potential labor strength, we used both an unweighted and a weighted (not reported) index of employee protections based on average indicators on regular contracts and short-term contracts from OECD data compiled in Pagano and Volpin (2000).

The restriction to OECD countries admittedly limits our number of countries and observations, but gives perhaps a purer test of the contention that labor can work as monitors since this literature has focused on organized labor in developed economies. Inconsistent with the hypothesis that labor is an effective monitor (but consistent with Pagano and Volpin's counter-contention that entrepreneurs and workers will align themselves against the interests of minority investors), we found that increased labor power is associated with higher private benefits, although this result is not statistically significant (p-value of 0.204 for employee protections, 0.13 for weighted employee protections).

Finally, we investigated the possibility that a government interested in enforcing tax rules can reduce private benefits. As reported in column 8, countries with a higher degree of tax compliance, as measured by the World Competitiveness Report, have lower private benefits of control. A one standard deviation increase in our measure of tax compliance reduced the value of control by 8.6 percentage points, a significant amount. Together with the firm-specific variables, tax compliance explained 24% of the variation in private benefits of control.

In interpreting these results, one should keep in mind that tax compliance is an "equilibrium outcome," one that is affected both by tax enforcement and by the attitude of citizens toward cheating on their taxes. To try to identify the impact of tax enforcement, we included (in an unreported regression) a measure of willingness to cheat on taxes as measured in the World Value Survey. In this survey people are asked to rate from 1 to 10 the statement "cheating on taxes if you have a chance is . . . ," where 1 is never justifiable and 10 is always justifiable. We found this variable to be insignificant, while the coefficient on tax compliance remained significant, suggesting that the effect of tax compliance comes from tax enforcement and not from differences in moral values across countries. We also examined the robustness of this result to the inclusion of the marginal tax rate and our results were unchanged.

Table 5.5 (column 2) reports the combined effect of the four extralegal institutions that individually had a statistically significant effect. All four variables retained the predicted sign, but the magnitudes of their coefficients fell and only tax compliance and newspaper diffusion remained statistically significant at the 5% level. Together these four variables were able to explain 24% of the variation in private benefits.

Thus, all the evidence reported thus far is consistent with both the legal and the extralegal institutions playing a role in constraining private benefits. In fact, a crude R-squared test suggests that *both* sets of institutions have roughly the same explanatory power. Next we asked ourselves, can we design a test that would enable us to distinguish which is more important?

There are two obstacles to doing so. First, many of these institutional variables are highly correlated. Shareholder's protection, however, showed no correlation with newspaper circulation and had a correlation of only 0.4 with tax compliance. Second, and most important, all these proxies are measured with error. Hence, their statistical significance in a multivariate analysis may well be more related to the level of noise in these measures than to their actual importance.

Nevertheless, we thought it would be interesting to try and put all these variables in one regression. When we did so, as reported in column 3 of table 5.5, of all the institutional variables we found to be significant in the previous regressions, only newspapers' diffusion and tax compliance remained significant. The paucity of observations and the high degree of multi-colinearity caution us against drawing any strong conclusion from this comparison. What we can say, however, is that the results are inconsistent with an exclusive focus on legal factors as institutional curbs to private benefits.

Conclusions

In a study published in the *Journal of Finance,* we attempted to measure the quality of a corporate governance system by computing the level of private benefits enjoyed by insiders. We then used these estimates to determine which institutions help shareholders limit the diversion of wealth by insider or controlling shareholders.

We found that many institutional variables, taken in isolation, seem to be associated with a lower level of private benefits of control: better accounting standards, better legal protection of minority shareholders, better law enforcement, more intense product market competition, diffusion of an independent press, and a high rate of tax compliance.

The possible role of tax enforcement in reducing private benefits, and thus indirectly enhancing financial development, is probably the most important new insight that emerges from our analysis. Improving the corporate taxation system is well within the range of feasible reforms. If this is indeed a primary mechanism by which private benefits of control can be curbed and financial markets fostered, the benefits of financial development might be within reach for many more countries.

Notes

This chapter draws on and summarizes the findings of I.J. Alexander Dyck and L. Zingales, "Private Benefits of Control: An International Comparison," *Journal of Finance,* Vol. 59, No. 2 (2004), pp. 537–600.

1. For a broader definition, see Zingales (1998). Full citations for all studies mentioned in the text are supplied in the references at the end of the article.
2. See, generally, L. Zingales, "The Value of the Voting Right: A Study of the Milan Stock Exchange Experience," *Rev. Fin. Stud.,* Vol. 7 (Spring 1994).
3. See R. Lease, J. McConnell, and W. Mikkelson, "The Market Value of Control in Publicly Traded Corporations," *Journal of Financial Economics,* Vol. 7 (1983); K. Rydqvist, "Takeover Bids and the Relative Prices of Shares That Differ in Their Voting Rights," Stockholm School of Economics Working Paper (1992); W. Megginson, "Restricted Voting Stock, Acquisition Premiums, and the Market Value of Corporate Control, "*The Fin. Rev.,* Vol. 25 (1990); Homer, "The Value of the Corporate Voting Right," *J. Banking & Fin.,* Vol. 12 (1988); Robinson and White, "The Value of a Vote in the Market for Corporate Control," York University Working Paper (1990); Levy, "Economic

Evaluation of Voting Power in Common Stock," *Journal of Finance,* Vol. 38 (1982); and Zingales (1995b).

4. Zingales (2000); Dyck and Zingales (2002).

5. For a complete description of the criteria imposed and their justification, see Dyck and Zingales (2004).

6. In Canada and Australia, we used 15% since exceeding 20% would trigger a mandatory offer for remaining shares.

7. While other measures of cash flow are preferable, earnings per share is one of the few data items consistently repotted in Datastream for the companies in our database.

8. Coffee (1999), Reese and Weisbach (2001), and Doidge et al. (2001).

9. We obtained the list of cross-listing from Doidge et al. (2001). We thank Andrew Karolyi for kindly providing us with the data.

10. Since we have enough observations for the United States (46), we can assess the realism of our assumption by estimating the same specification restricted to U.S. data. While the other coefficients are very similar to the ones reported in table IV, the coefficient of the majority block dummy is small and insignificant. "Imposing" to the United States the same majority dummy effect as other countries, thus, will distort its average level of private benefits upward.

11. See, for example, Demsetz and Lehn (1985).

12. See, for example, Barclay and Holderness (1989).

13. To avoid potential endogeneity problems, we used U.S. averages (see Rajan and Zingales (1998)). We derived U.S. measures in a two-step procedure. First, we computed the average ratio of fixed assets (property plant and equipment) to total assets for all companies in each three-digit SIC code for the period 1990–1999. Then we took the median value across all companies. We then impute this value for all of the companies in our sample.

14. Including both types of industry controls in a sense "over-controls" for industry effects, with tangibility (coefficient of -0.11, p-value of 0.033) and financial industry (coefficient of 0.076, p-value of 0.019) being significant in regressions that include these industry variables separately (not reported).

15. For example, Coffee (1999), Reese and Weisbach (2001), and Doidge et al. (2001) argue that foreign companies list in the United States to pre-commit themselves to extract fewer private benefits of control.

16. Her approach, albeit very similar, is not strictly comparable with our own, as she uses the price on the date of sale and compares the sale price with the price of voting shares on the exchange.

17. This sample only includes transactions where the sale price is cash. That is, we excluded privatizations where sale price could include so-called privatization currencies that include government debt that was trading at a discount.

18. They identified 12 transactions where the stake sold was 19.26% which we excluded because this level was below our selection criteria, but in Brazil accounted for 50.1% of the voting shares in the company. In addition, they were able to identify stock market prices for a number of firms that we were not able to collect using Datastream or were not identified by SDC.

19. The p-value for the equality of the two means is only 21%, but this is not surprising given that we have only six observations before and two afterward.

20. Specifically, this test includes Hong Kong, Indonesia, Korea, Malaysia, Philippines, Singapore, Taiwan, and Thailand.

21. In Dyck and Zingales (2002b) we study the determinants of newspapers' diffusion. We find that the type of dominant religion and the degree of ethnolinguistic fractionalization

explain 41% of the variation in press diffusion. When we use these as instruments for press diffusion, the results are unchanged.

References

Aghion, Philippe and Patrick Bolton, 1992, "An Incomplete Contract Approach to Financial Contracting," *Review of Economic Studies*, Vol. 59, pp. 473–494.

Barclay, Michael and Clifford Holderness, 1989, "Private Benefits of Control of Public Corporations," *Journal of Financial Economics*, Vol. 25, pp. 371–395.

Bebchuk, Lucian, 1999, "A Rent-Protection Theory of Corporate Ownership and Control," NBER Working Paper No. 7203.

Bebchuk, Lucian and Christine Jolls, 1999,"Managerial Value Diversion and Shareholder Wealth," *Journal of Law, Economics, and Organization*, Vol. 15, No. 2, pp. 487–502.

Black, Bernard, Reinier Kraakman, and Anna Tassarova, 2000, "Russian Privatization and Corporate Governance: What Went Wrong?," *Stanford Law Review*, Vol. 52, pp. 1731–1808.

Burkart, M., D. Gromb, and F. Panunzi, 1998, "Why Higher Takeover Premia Protect Minority Shareholders," *Journal of Political Economy*, Vol. 106, pp. 172–204.

Coffee, John, 1999, "The Future as History: The Prospects for Global Convergence in Corporate Governance and Its Implications," *Northwestern University Law Review*, Vol. 93, No. 3, pp. 641–708.

Coffee, John, 2001, "Do Norms Matter? A Cross-Country Examination of Private Benefits of Control," Mimeograph, Columbia University Law School.

DeAngelo, H. and L. DeAngelo, 1985, "Managerial Ownership of Voting Rights," *Journal of Financial Economics*, Vol. 14, pp. 36–39.

Demsetz, H. and K. Lehn, 1985, "The Structure of Corporate Ownership: Causes and Consequences," *Journal of Political Economy*, Vol. 93, pp. 1155–1175.

Desai, Mihir, Alexander Dyck, and Luigi Zingales, 2003, "Corporate Governance and Taxation," Harvard Business School Working Paper Series, No. 04–001.

Djankov, Simeon, Clara McLeish, Tatiana Nenova, and Andrei Shleifer, 2001, "Who Owns the Media?" NBER Working Paper No. 8288.

Djankov, Simeon and Peter Murrell, 2000, "The Determinants of Enterprise Restructuring in Transition: An Assessment of the Evidence," Working Paper, University of Maryland.

Doidge, C., G. Andrew Karolyi, and R. Stulz, 2001, "Why Are Foreign Firms Listed in the U.S. Worth More?" Ohio State University Working Paper.

Dyck, I.J. Alexander, 2000, "Ownership Structure, Legal Protections, and Corporate Governance," in Boris Pleskovic and Nicholas Stern, eds., *2000 Annual World Bank Conference on Development Economics*, pp. 291–330. World Bank, Washington, D.C.

Dyck, I.J. Alexander, 2001, "Privatization and Corporate Governance: Principles, Evidence, and Future Challenges," *World Bank, Research Observer,* Vol. 16, No. 1, pp. 59–84.

Dyck, I.J. Alexander, 2002, "The Hermitage Fund: Media and Corporate Governance in Russia," Harvard Business School Case 703–010.

Dyck, I.J. Alexander and Luigi Zingales, 2002, "The Corporate Governance Role of the Media," in *The Right to Tell: The Role of Mass Media in Development* (Washington, D.C.: The World Bank).

Dyck, I.J. Alexander and Luigi Zingales, 2004, "Private Benefits of Control: An International Comparison," *Journal of Finance,* Vol. 59, No. 2, pp. 537–600.

Federov, Oleg, 2000, "Case Studies on Abusive Self-Dealing," OECD/World Bank Corporate Governance Roundtable for Russia, February 24–25.

Glaeser, Edward, Simon Johnson, and Andrei Shleifer, 2001, "Coase vs. the Coasians," *Quarterly Journal of Economics,* Vol. 116, pp. 853–900.

Grossman, Sanford and Oliver Hart, 1980, "Takeover Bids, the Free Rider Problem, and the Theory of the Corporation," *Bell Journal of Economics,* Vol. 11, pp. 42–69.

Grossman, Sanford and Oliver Hart, 1988, "One Share One Vote and the Market for Corporate Control," *Journal of Financial Economics,* Vol. 20, pp. 175–202.

Harris, Milton and Artur Raviv, 1988, "Corporate Governance: Voting Rights and Majority Rules," *Journal of Financial Economics,* Vol. 20, pp. 203–235.

Holderness, Clifford and Dennis Sheehan, 1988, "The Role of Majority Shareholders in Publicly Held Corporations: An Exploratory Analysis," *Journal of Financial Economics,* Vol. 20, pp. 317–346.

Holthausen, R.W., R.W. Leftwich, and D. Myers, 1990, "Large Block Transactions, the Speed of Response, and Temporary and Permanent Stock Price Effects," *Journal of Financial Economics,* Vol. 26, pp. 71–95.

Johnson, Simon, Rafael La Porta, Florencio Lopez-deSalines, and Andrei Shleifer, 2000, "Tunneling," *American Economic Review,* Vol. 90, pp. 22–27.

La Porta, Rafael, Florencio Lopez-de-Salines, and Andrei Shleifer, 1999, "Corporate Ownership around the World," *Journal of Finance,* Vol. 54, pp. 471–517.

La Porta, Rafael, Florencio Lopez-de-Salines, and Andrei Shleifer, 2000, "Investor Protection and Corporate Governance," *Journal of Financial Economics,* Vol. 59, pp. 3–27.

La Porta, Rafael, Florencio Lopez-de-Salines, Andrei Shleifer, and Robert W. Vishny, 1997, "Legal Determinants of External Finance," *Journal of Finance,* Vol. 53, pp. 1131–1150.

La Porta, Rafael, Florencio Lopez-de-Salines, Andrei Shleifer, and Robert W. Vishny, 1998, "Law and Finance," *Journal of Political Economy,* Vol. 106, pp. 1113–1155.

Lease, Ronald C., John J. McConnell, and Wayne H. Mikkelson, 1983, "The Market Value of Control in Publicly-Traded Corporations," *Journal of Financial Economics,* Vol. 11, pp. 439–471.

Lease, Ronald C., John J. McConnell, and Wayne H. Mikkelson, 1984, "The Market Value of Differential Voting Rights in Closely Held Corporations," *Journal of Business*, Vol. 57, pp. 443–467.

Lopez-de-Silanes, Florencio, 1997, "Determinants of Privatization Prices," *Quarterly Journal of Economics*, Vol. 4, pp. 965–1025.

Megginson, William L., Robert C. Nash, Jeffrey M. Netter, and Annette B. Poulsen, 2000, "The Choice Between Private and Public Markets: Evidence from Privatizations," Working Paper, University of Georgia.

Milgrom, P. and R. Weber, 1982, "A Theory of Auctions and Competitive Bidding," *Econometrica*, Vol. 50, pp. 1089–1122.

Monks, Robert and Nell Minow, 1995, *Watching the Watchers: Corporate Governance for the 21st Century* (Malden, MA: Blackwell Publishing).

Morck, Randall, Bernard Yeung, and Wayne Yu, 2000, "The Information Content of Stock Markets: Why Do Emerging Markets Have Synchronous Stock Price Movements?" *Journal of Financial Economics*, Vol. 58, pp. 215–260.

Nenova, Tatiana, 2001a, "The Value of Corporate Votes and Control Benefits: A Cross-Country Analysis," Mimeograph, Harvard University.

Nenova, Tatiana, 2001b, "Control Values and Changes in Corporate Law in Brazil," Working Paper, World Bank.

Nicodano, G. and A. Sembenelli, 2001, "Private Benefits, Block Transaction Premiums, and Ownership Structure," Università di Torino Working Paper.

Pagano, Marco and Paolo Volpin, 2000, "The Political Economy of Corporate Governance," Working Paper, London Business School.

Pistor, Katherina, Martin Raiser, and Stanislaw Gelfer, 2000, "Law and Finance in Transition Economies," *Economics of Transition*, Vol. 8, pp. 325–368.

Rajan, Raghuram and Luigi Zingales, 1998, "Financial Dependence and Growth," *American Economic Review*.

Reese, W. and M. Weisbach, 2001, "Protection of Minority Shareholder Interests, Cross-Listings in the United States, and Subsequent Equity Offerings," NBER Working Paper.

Roe, Mark, 2001, "Rents and Their Corporate Law Consequences," Discussion Paper, Columbia Law School.

Rydqvist, K., 1987, "Empirical Investigation of the Voting Premium," Northwestern University Working Paper No. 35.

Shleifer, Andrei and Robert Vishny, 1997, "A Survey of Corporate Governance," *Journal of Finance*, Vol. 52, pp. 737–783.

Stiglitz, Joseph, 1985, "Credit Markets and the Control of Capital," *Journal of Money, Credit and Banking*, Vol. 17, No. 2, pp. 133–152.

Stulz, René and Rohan Williamson, 2001, "Culture, Openness, and Finance," NBER Working Paper No. 8222.

Zingales, Luigi, 1994, "The Value of the Voting Right: A Study of the Milan Stock Exchange Experience," *Review of Financial Studies*, Vol. 7, pp. 125–148.

Zingales, Luigi, 1995a, "What Determines the Value of Corporate Votes?" *Quarterly Journal of Economics,* Vol. 110, pp. 1047–1073.

Zingales, Luigi, 1995b, "Insider Ownership and the Decision to Go Public," *Review of Economic Studies,* Vol. 62, pp. 425–448.

Zingales, Luigi, 1998, "Why It's Worth Being in Control," in George Bickerstaffe, ed., *The Complete Finance Companion* (London: FT Pitman Publishing).

Zingales, Luigi, 2000, "In Search of New Foundations," *Journal of Finance,* Vol. 55, pp. 1623–1653.

CHAPTER 6

Globalization, Corporate Finance, and the Cost of Capital

RENÉ M. STULZ

WHEN MALAYSIA IMPOSED ITS RESTRICTIONS on capital flows last year, the world financial community was stunned. Yet, for many years after World War II, such capital controls would have seemed quite normal. After the war, almost all countries had tight controls on currency conversion, which meant that outside investors could invest in foreign markets only if they could get access to often-scarce foreign currencies. In addition, most countries also had explicit restrictions on foreign investment. Some countries prohibited their own citizens from buying foreign shares. In many cases, foreign investors were forbidden to buy local shares. And in countries where foreign investors were allowed to buy local shares, the shares often carried lower (or no) voting rights—and there were typically limits to the percentage of a firm's shares that could be owned by foreigners. In addition to these legal and regulatory constraints, there were also less formal deterrents to international investment. Besides political risks such as the possibility of expropriation, there were major obstacles to hedging foreign exchange rate risk as well as a near-total lack of coordination of accounting standards among countries.

Over the last 50 years, the legal and regulatory barriers to international investment have largely disappeared among developed economies. And, in the past decade, such barriers have fallen dramatically in many emerging markets. As a result of these changes, U.S. investors can now buy securities of companies in many foreign countries with almost no restrictions. Large U.S. corporations today raise funds in different financial markets throughout the world—sometimes in simultaneous offerings in onshore and offshore markets. Asian investors now worry about how the U.S. markets performed while they were asleep because they believe that the fate of their markets during the day depends on what happened in New York in the past twelve hours. And morning news shows in the U.S. routinely discuss the overnight returns of the Nikkei and Hang Seng indices in an effort to forecast the performance of U.S. markets.

Though economists and financial academics have generally welcomed this process of globalization and emphasized its benefits to investors and corporations, many policy makers have questioned whether the process has gone too far and whether controls on capital flows should be reinstated. In this chapter, I attempt to evaluate how the globalization of capital markets is affecting the corporate cost of capital and equity values.

The remainder of the chapter falls into four main sections. In the first I investigate how globalization affects the discount rate that investors use in valuing a given stream of equity cash flows. In so doing, I present a number of arguments for why globalization is reducing investors' required rate of return on stocks of companies in developed as well as developing economies.

In the second section, the focus shifts to a different, generally neglected perspective on the cost of capital. John D. Rockefeller said that the greatest challenge in his career was "to obtain enough capital to do all the business I wanted to and could do" (Chernow, *Titan* (Random House, 1998)). To understand this problem of raising capital, consider a firm with a large project that management must finance. Based on the cash flows that *management* expects the project to generate, the rate of return on the project exceeds the cost of equity capital dictated by the capital markets. However, the cash flows that matter when raising equity from outside investors are the cash flows that *investors* believe they will eventually receive from the firm in the form of dividends or capital gains. If capital markets expect the project to contribute less to the value of the firm than management does, the company will be forced to sell equity at a price below what management thinks it is worth. In management's view, being forced to sell equity at a "discount" increases the effective cost of capital; and if the additional cost is large enough, management may forgo the project.

The difference between management's and investors' assessments of the project's value could exist for at least two reasons. First, management typically has more information about the profitability of a project than do investors, and it is often hard for management to communicate that information credibly. This problem is referred to by academics as the "information asymmetry" problem. Second, investors might be concerned that management will make poor use of the capital because its own objectives differ from those of investors. This shareholder-manager conflict is often called the "agency cost" problem.[1] As a result of these two problems, management might not be able to raise enough funds to launch the project. And even if the firm is able to raise the necessary funds, these two problems could make equity capital prohibitively expensive.

Because of these information and agency cost problems, a firm's cost of capital will depend critically on its corporate governance system. By "corporate governance system," I mean not only the internal controls such as independent boards and effective incentive compensation plans, but also external elements such as legal protection for minority shareholders, sophisticated and activist institutional investors, and well-functioning takeover markets. My argument here, in brief, is that companies in national economies with more effective corporate governance are likely to raise capital on better terms because such firms are more likely to invest the capital wisely and to reinvest the firm's cash flows in ways that do not destroy shareholder wealth. Thus, in the second part of the chapter, I maintain that globalization improves corporate governance and thereby lowers the cost of external financing by reducing information and agency costs.

The third section of the chapter offers a brief review of the growing body of empirical evidence on the impact of globalization on the cost of capital. What evidence we have provides some, though by no means overwhelming, support for the above arguments—and I attempt to explain why the evidence is not more conclusive. The fourth and final section discusses the implications of the theory and evidence for corporate strategy and practice.

Why Globalization Is Reducing the Cost of Capital: The Portfolio Perspective

Consider a market that, for whatever reason, is isolated from the rest of the world. In this market, shares issued locally must be held by local investors, and local investors cannot diversify internationally. In such circumstances, because local investors have to bear more risk than if they were free to diversify their holdings across international markets, they will have required rates of return for holding local stocks that are higher than the rates required by well-diversified, global investors for holding the same stocks. As a consequence, the prices of local shares will be lower than if the local market were integrated with global markets.

A striking confirmation of this argument was provided by the Swiss firm Nestlé's decision, in November of 1988, to eliminate restrictions on foreign ownership on both classes of its shares. Until that time, Nestlé had two types of shares that differed only in ownership restrictions.[2] One type of shares, called *bearer shares,* was available to all investors, foreign as well as Swiss. A second type, *registered shares,* was available only to Swiss investors. Both registered and bearer shares had the same voting rights and the same dividends.

If restrictions on foreign ownership do not affect share values, one would expect the registered shares to sell for about the same amount as the unrestricted bearer shares. But the registered shares sold at a consistently large discount to the bearer shares. Indeed, the shares available only to Swiss investors were typically *only about half as valuable* as the shares available to foreign investors.

Then, on November 17, 1988, Nestlé announced that it was removing the restrictions on foreign ownership of its registered shares. During the week of the announcement, the price of the registered shares rose from SFr. 4,245 to 5,782, an increase of over 36%. And although the value of the bearer shares fell by about 25% (presumably because arbitrageurs were selling them while buying the registered shares), Nestlé's total market capitalization—the sum of the values of both classes of shares—increased by 10%.

The lesson from this example is that, where barriers to international investment segment a national capital market from global markets, the local investors bear all the risk of the economic activities in their economy. And, for bearing this risk, such investors require a higher risk *premium* that effectively reduces the value that local investors are willing to place on the stock relative to what a globally diversified investor would pay if given the chance.

The Local CAPM

To understand why investors in segmented markets are likely to require higher rates of return, consider the simple "mean-variance" model of investor behavior for which Harry Markowitz was awarded the Nobel Prize in 1990. Suppose that investors can invest only in their own countries and that, as the Markowitz model suggests, they care about only the expected return of their portfolio of assets and the variance of that return. Such investors will measure risk by the volatility of the return of their portfolio; and, as the volatility of their country's market portfolio increases, the risk premium required by investors for holding the market portfolio will increase along with it. For instance, assuming investors across countries have similar attitudes toward risk, a country where the variance of the market portfolio is twice what it is in another country will have twice the risk premium of the other country.

To estimate the cost of equity capital for a particular company operating in a segmented financial market, one could use the following "local" version of the capital asset pricing model (CAPM):

$$E(R_C) = R_f + \beta_H \times [E(R_H) - R_f],$$

where $E(R_C)$ is the required rate of return on the company's stock by local investors; R_f is the risk-free rate; β_H is the beta of the company's stock price in relation to the local or home-country market; and $E(R_H)$ is the expected return of the home country market portfolio.

The cost of equity so calculated serves both as a discount rate for valuing the company's equity cash flows and, when adjusted for debt financing, as the "hurdle rate" for corporate investments. So, for example, when a firm considers whether to take on a project, the present value of the project for its shareholders is estimated by discounting the expected cash flows from the project at the CAPM-determined required rate of return.

Now consider what happens to the cost of capital when this country decides to open up its markets to foreign investors. To do that, let's take the real economic activities of the country as given; in other words, if a country has invested in the production of widgets, we assume that the expected value and the variance of the profits from producing widgets are not affected by globalization.[3] By keeping the degree of globalization in markets for goods and services unchanged, we can focus just on the impact of *financial* globalization.

When a country opens up its capital market to foreign investors and lets its own residents invest abroad, the residents of the country no longer have to bear all the risks associated with the economic activities of the country. They can be shared with foreign investors who, by investing in the country, bear some of these risks. In exchange, domestic investors bear foreign risks by buying foreign securities. For both groups of investors, the benefit from bearing foreign as well as domestic risks is that some of these risks offset each other through the process of diversification. By investing in many countries with economic cycles or events that are partly offsetting, investors can reduce the risk of their portfolios substantially without reducing their expected return. For example, although studies of international diversification differ as to the extent of these benefits, most conclude that exchanging a portfolio of U.S. stocks for an internationally diversified portfolio will reduce the standard deviation of the returns by at least 20%.[4]

To see the effect of diversification on investors when countries liberalize their capital markets, it is useful to consider an example. Assume there are a large number of countries integrated into world markets, that each country represents a very small fraction of the total global market, that the return on each national market portfolio has the same expected value and variance of return, and that the return on the market portfolio in each country is completely uncorrelated with the return of the market portfolio in every other country. Once the markets in all countries become open to each other, all investors (who, again, care only about the expected return and variance of their portfolios) are assumed to hold the world market portfolio to take full advantage of the benefits from diversification.

With this set of assumptions, the expected return on an investor's portfolio remains the same regardless of how his wealth is invested across countries. At the same time, the variance of the return falls with each additional country added to the portfolio. In the extreme case where the number of countries is very large, the variance of the return approaches zero, and the world market portfolio has no risk and hence no risk premium. In such a case, all stocks in all countries would be priced as if investors required only the risk-free rate of return.

Of course, it is unrealistic to think that all risks could be completely diversifiable internationally. In particular, business cycles, as we saw once again during the Asian crisis,[5] have a tendency to cross country boundaries. It is also obviously a gross exaggeration to think that *all* publicly traded companies would have access to global capital markets. This would likely be true only for the largest and most visible firms—or at most those included in a major national index of stocks.

But if the above example is clearly unrealistic, it nevertheless serves to illustrate an important point: if investors truly care only about the expected return and the variance of their portfolios, they will respond to new opportunities for global diversification by creating portfolios that promise either a lower volatility for the same expected return or a higher expected return for the same volatility. And this means that risk premiums and the cost of capital can be expected to fall not only in previously segmented markets, but in long-integrated markets as well. As one would expect, the largest reductions in cost of capital resulting from globalization will be experienced by companies in liberalizing economies that are gaining access to the global markets for the first time. (Recall, again, the dramatic effect of Nestlé's decision to open its registered shares to foreign investors.) But companies in integrated economies like the U.S. are also benefiting from increasing capital flows from investors in once isolated markets because this allows the firms' risks to be shared by a much larger pool of investors with different risk exposures and hence different appetites for bearing the risks of these companies. Indeed, I would argue that globalization's effect on the cost of capital over the past decade or so is a significant contributor to the current level of U.S. stock prices.

The Global CAPM

Besides falling risk premiums in all integrated (or integrating) capital markets, the above example has a second major implication for the corporate cost of capital. As already noted, if global diversification of equity portfolios minimizes volatility and risk premiums, then investors in all countries have incentives to hold the same global portfolio that includes the equities of companies all over the world. For this reason, it is useful to think of the equity markets that are integrated with each other as forming essentially one worldwide market portfolio. And for all companies that are large or visible enough to be traded in such a global equity market, the proper risk measure, or beta, would be computed in relation not to the home-country portfolio, but to the world market portfolio. That is, in integrated markets, investors with globally diversified portfolios will measure the risk of individual stocks by how they contribute to the volatility *not* of their home-country portfolios, but to the volatility of the global portfolio. For example, a U.S. investor—and, for that matter, a Japanese or a Swiss investor—considering the purchase of IBM shares will evaluate the beta of IBM not in relation to the S&P 500, but rather in relation to a global index like the Morgan-Stanley Capital International (MSCI) World Index.

In sum, the CAPM holds for all integrated markets together rather than on a country-by-country basis. Therefore, in calculating the cost of capital for a given firm, we should use a global CAPM like the following:

$$E(R_G) = R_f + \beta_G \times [E(R_G) - R_f],$$

where R_G denotes the required expected return on a stock when markets are global; R_f is still the local country risk-free rate; β_G is the global beta of the company in question; and R_G denotes the return of the global market portfolio (again, like the MSCI World Index).

Presented in this context, the global CAPM is especially useful in showing the two distinct effects of global diversification on the cost of capital. Besides reducing market risk premiums for both home countries and for the world equity market as a whole, gaining access to global markets also effectively reduces the betas of most companies. More precisely, globalization reduces the beta of all companies whose profits and values are more strongly correlated with their local economies than with the global economy. For example, returning to the case of Nestlé, when the company eliminated the Swiss ownership requirements on its registered shares in 1988, the company had a Swiss beta of 0.9, but a global beta of only 0.6. And even if we assume the global market risk premium was equal to (instead of lower than) the Swiss market premium, that reduction in beta alone translated into a 150 basis-point reduction of Nestlé's cost of equity capital.[6]

But, as suggested earlier, it is not only companies from once-segmented markets like Nestlé that are benefiting from globalization. Although the reduction in cost of capital is likely to be greatest for large companies based in small countries with limited capital markets, the fall in the global risk premium means that even firms in well-established financial markets like the U.S. and U.K. are benefiting from the global diversification of investors' portfolios. This is a benefit that increases the value of all firms whose cost of capital is determined in global markets.

Globalization Reduces Capital Costs by Improving Corporate Governance

The above arguments for why globalization reduces the discount rate of investors are compelling, but they do not capture the whole impact of globalization on the cost of capital. To understand why, let's focus on a company that has to raise equity to finance a new investment. In many ways, the ability of firms to raise equity from the public is a paradox. In an equity issue, the firm receives cash from outside investors without a contractual agreement to give anything back. For equity financing to be possible, shareholders must expect to receive sufficient cash flows to provide them with an expected return comparable to what they would expect to earn on other investments of the same risk. But, as discussed in the introduction, managers face difficulties in convincing shareholders that they will receive such cash flows. This is because managers (1) have information that shareholders do not have about the firm's investments, and (2) have incentives both to issue equity when they feel their stock is overvalued and to take projects that do not necessarily increase shareholder value.

Because of these information and incentive problems, a firm may have good projects but be unable to finance them because its managers cannot convince shareholders that the projects are value-adding. Though we focus first on companies where shareholders are widely dispersed and managers are "in power," many of the issues that we discuss are the same if there is a large, controlling shareholder instead. We address the latter case toward the end of this section.

Consider a firm whose management believes it has valuable projects. In other words, if management could convince investors that the projected cash flows will materialize—and eventually accrue to them in the form of higher dividends or capital gains—the shareholders would benefit from the firm's investment in these projects. Managers will often have difficulty convincing investors that such projects have value because managers can benefit from corporate investments even if they fail to earn the cost of capital. Managers tend to benefit—in the form of higher salaries, increased social standing, and so forth—when the firm simply gets bigger, which often leads them to invest even in unprofitable projects rather than pay out larger dividends or buy back stock.

Management will be less able to pursue its own goals at the expense of shareholders when there is effective monitoring. By "monitoring" I mean all the processes whereby boards of directors and other interested parties examine the actions and policies of management and use the outcome of their examination to influence management's actions and policies. When necessary, boards of directors, active shareholders, and potential bidders can all take actions to reverse managerial decisions or even replace management. And, as managers increasingly come to understand that decisions that hurt shareholders affect their own tenure and compensation, managerial decisions are more likely to be value-increasing.

But monitoring, of course, is itself a costly activity and does not provide a complete solution for corporate governance. For one thing, because monitoring is costly, it is much more likely to take place after poor performance. If the firm loses money, for example, investors will often devote significant resources to figure out what is happening. But it is much harder for outsiders to figure out that managers did not take actions that would have made a successful firm even more successful. It is especially in these situations that incentives are likely to play a key role: they can lead managers to maximize shareholder wealth even when no monitoring takes place.

In sum, the extent to which management finds it in its own interest to maximize shareholder wealth depends critically on the firm's corporate governance system. If the firm's corporate governance system makes it possible for management to be monitored efficiently—particularly when it also has strong incentives to increase value—the firm's stock price will be higher and management will find it easier to raise funds.

Let's now consider in more detail how investor monitoring of management takes place and how it is likely to be affected by globalization.[7] We consider in turn each of six important mechanisms used to monitor management:

1. **The Board of Directors.** In principle, a firm's board of directors is the most direct mechanism for monitoring management. Managers report to the board and the board can fire management. Board members have a duty to be informed about what management is doing. One problem with this arrangement, however, is that when the firm has diffuse shareholders, managers generally determine the composition of the board. This clearly limits the board's ability to discipline management if it becomes necessary.

Having a board that lacks credibility may not be a problem for a company that does not need outside capital. But if the firm wants to raise funds in the capital markets, it becomes an important issue because a weak board is less likely to discipline managers—or replace them if necessary—when performance proves inadequate. For this reason, unless management has a strong track record and clear incentives to increase value, investors are likely to expect lower cash flows from companies with weak boards.

This has important implications for firms from segmented economies attempting to raise capital in *global* markets. For such firms to succeed, investors in these markets must have confidence that the use of the funds they provide will be monitored. As we are now seeing in countries like Japan and Korea—and as we saw in the early 1990s in the United States—this demand for monitoring is leading to more active boards that are increasingly independent of management.

2. **The Capital Markets.** To sell securities, managers hire investment bankers who play a key *certification* role by risking their reputations in marketing the securities to their investor clients. When raising capital

in global markets, companies from less developed markets gain access to a broader range of investment banks. And provided such companies have the right qualifications and good prospects, they can choose to issue securities with banks that have stronger reputations or more specialized knowledge about the firms' industries than their local bankers. Because such investment banks are in a better position to evaluate the firms' prospects, while also having more reputational capital at risk, securing the help of such banks conveys positive information to the markets about the companies themselves.

3. **The Legal System.** The legal system plays two roles.[8] First, it limits the ability of management to expropriate resources from investors. In legal systems with few protections for (minority) shareholders, managers can almost literally steal corporate assets with something close to impunity. But, as the legal system improves, shareholders have greater recourse and the deterrents to managerial self-dealing and fraud become more effective. Second, the legal system provides a mechanism for investors to monitor management and exercise their rights. When shareholders discover management policies or actions that hurt them, they can use the legal system to force management to change those policies and, in some cases, receive compensation for lost value.

With globalization of financial markets, companies based in countries with little protection of minority shareholders that raise funds and list in countries with stronger protection expose themselves to legal actions from investors in these countries. As a result, minority shareholders in such firms end up with better legal protection than they had before.

4. **Active Shareholders.** Small shareholders have little incentive to monitor management. Monitoring, as we have seen, is expensive. And since these shareholders have a small stake, even if their monitoring efforts would lead to a value-increasing improvement in management's policies, the benefits to these investors would likely be small relative to the costs incurred. Large shareholders benefit much more from their own monitoring efforts. As a result, companies with large shareholders, all else equal, are likely to be monitored more closely than firms with only small shareholders.

Globalization makes it possible for investors from other countries to take large stakes in a firm and monitor management. As suggested earlier, there is a potential problem with large shareholders: namely, their tendency to use their influence to obtain benefits from management that do not accrue to the other shareholders. But since the large shareholders produced by globalization are foreigners and thus presumably "outsiders," they are much more likely to perform the arm's-length monitoring that ends up increasing firm value and benefiting minority stockholders.

5. **The Market for Corporate Control.** When internal governance systems fail, the market for corporate control—that is, takeovers, LBOs, and the like—makes it possible to remove management if it does not maximize shareholder wealth. Moreover, even in the absence of a takeover bid, the mere possibility of takeover has a disciplinary effect on management since it knows that if the firm performs poorly, it could become a takeover target.

Of course, takeovers are effectively, if not legally, prohibited in many national economies. But provided there is some possibility for investors to remove underperforming managers, opening up a capital market to foreign investors immediately creates a much larger pool of investors that can compete for control of firms within that market. This leads to greater competition for control among investors, which benefits existing shareholders directly. Moreover, even if takeovers are currently prohibited, the opening of capital markets to foreign investors tends to create a set of economic forces that exert pressure for opening up the market for corporate control.

6. **Disclosure.** Public disclosure of information by firms is required by laws and regulations. But most larger companies would disclose information even if they were not required to do so. Failure to provide adequate information would make it very expensive, if not impossible, to raise funds from the public capital markets. In that case, the firm would have to resort to banks and other financial intermediaries—a capital-raising process in which private disclosure takes the place of public disclosure.

When a firm raises funds from public markets, it must not only provide extensive disclosure at the time of issuance but also commit to furnish information on an ongoing basis (at least through the term of the financing). The more information a company provides initially—and the stronger its commitment to provide continuing disclosure—the less costly it is for investors to monitor management and, hence, the more favorable the other terms and conditions of the financing.

One problem here, however, is that it is difficult for firms in countries with minimal disclosure requirements to commit themselves to ongoing disclosure. The choice of a stricter regulatory environment (say, the U.S., which means oversight by the SEC) is one way for companies to commit to continuous disclosure. Another is listing on an exchange (like the NYSE or Nasdaq) with extensive disclosure requirements. Thanks to globalization, companies can commit to higher disclosure standards simply by seeking additional listings on exchanges that have higher standards than their local market.

Of course, those firms that feel they are getting a higher stock price by maintaining their ability to conceal poor performance (say, by means of the "smoothing" allowed by the "reserve accounting" popular outside the U.S. and U.K.) are unlikely to volunteer to meet SEC requirements. But since this logic implies that firms with the best prospects are the ones most likely to choose to list on stricter exchanges, the mere announcement that a company intends to list on such an exchange tends to be interpreted by the market as good news.[9]

Why Globalization Increases Monitoring for All Companies

In this analysis, then, globalization increases the monitoring of management and thereby reduces information and agency costs. As a result, globalization reduces the costs of external finance for companies *in addition to* reducing the expected rate of return required by investors. This reduction in the costs of external finance resulting from improved corporate governance can be viewed as a decrease in the cost of capital in the following sense: it can turn value-reducing projects—projects that might otherwise have been abandoned because of the high cost of funding them—into value-adding projects. It does so by increasing investors' estimates of the cash flows they will receive from the companies they invest in. The strengthening of corporate governance systems associated with globalization raises the probability that management will work harder and make more value-increasing decisions for its investors while having fewer opportunities to pursue goals that are not in investors' interests.

Yet, based on our analysis, one might conclude that globalization increases the monitoring of management only for those firms that decide to participate in the global capital markets. But this is not the case: once a company has a choice between participating and not participating in global capital markets, the choice not to participate may reveal important information about the value of that firm.

To see this, let's go back to the issue of disclosure. Firms that want to participate in global markets must meet disclosure standards that allow them to compete for funds in these markets. But if a firm is large enough to access global markets and chooses not to do so mainly to avoid complying with stricter disclosure requirements, investors are likely to conclude that management prefers less disclosure because it allows them to conceal poor performance—or at least a failure to maximize value. Thus, companies that stay local and continue to meet only local disclosure requirements may be "signaling" their investors that they are worth less than previously thought. And, in this fashion, globalization can be seen as exerting pressure for better performance and greater transparency on all firms large enough to raise capital in global markets.

The Special Case of Large Shareholder-Controlled Firms

Our discussion has focused thus far on the case of publicly traded companies with highly fragmented ownership where management is in control. This is an apt characterization of most large, public firms in the U.S. and the U.K. But, in the case of even the largest "quoted" companies in most other countries, there tend to be large shareholders—such as banks, other corporations, and founding families—with controlling interests.[10] As noted earlier, although such shareholders presumably have strong incentives to monitor management, they also have incentives, along with the power, to force management to take actions that benefit themselves at the expense of other shareholders and other investors. The working of such incentives can be seen clearly in accounts of South Korean chaebols (and also in the case study of Union Bank of Switzerland by Claudio Loderer).

This ability of controlling shareholders to expropriate value from other investors creates a problem for firms in raising capital. For instance, outside investors who buy equity in a firm controlled by a large shareholder will discount the price they are willing to pay to reflect the fact that the firm's profits might be siphoned off to companies controlled by the large shareholder. This discount might be large enough that the firm cannot "afford" to raise new funds.

To avoid this problem, minority shareholders have to be protected. In addition to monitoring management, minority shareholders need a way to monitor the large shareholder. They can do so using all of the mechanisms discussed above except the board of directors—since the large shareholder will effectively control the board. By listing on exchanges with high standards for protecting minority shareholders, a firm expresses its commitment to respect the rights of these shareholders. In cases where the local exchange does not offer much protection for minority shareholders, globalization enables companies to seek listings on foreign exchanges that provide such protection. Such listings increase firm value both by ensuring that the firm's policies are more likely to increase shareholder wealth and by allowing the firm to raise funds on more favorable terms.

Globalization and Transactions Costs

Thus far, we have ignored the costs of buying and selling securities. Globalization is reducing these costs for many firms, and such cost reductions increase firm value both directly and indirectly. In 1986, Yakov Amihud and Haim Mendelson published the first of several academic studies to show that the size

When Globalization Undermines Governance: The Case of Japan

Globalization does not necessarily increase the monitoring of management, at least in the short run. The reason for this is that the opening of capital markets can disrupt existing relationships within a country that once contributed to the monitoring of management or large shareholders. Take the case of Japan. In the Japanese economy, monitoring until recently took place primarily through banks, and through the networks of firms called *keiretsu* that are often organized around a bank. Japanese banks held equity stakes in their customers and played a much larger role than U.S. banks both in the financing and governance of corporate borrowers. As a result, Japan was said to have a bank-centered, "relationship-based" governance system, as contrasted with the "market-based" systems of the U.S. and the U.K., with hostile takeovers as one of their central features.

Before 1980, Japanese firms were prevented by both formal and informal restrictions from raising debt in public markets—a policy that benefited Japanese banks. And, as virtually a monopoly supplier of (debt) funds to Japanese firms, the banks' ability to monitor management came in large part from their ability to threaten to withhold funds. But globalization, by enabling Japanese firms to raise funds outside of Japan (which in turn caused restrictions on Japanese public debt markets to be eased), had a dramatic impact on Japanese corporate governance by loosening the corporate ties to banks.[*]

To the extent our theory is correct, foreign investors should begin to exert a monitoring effect on Japanese firms. In particular, a growing pool of active institutional shareholders and potential bidders should begin to emerge. But such effects, as the Japanese experience of the 1990s suggests, do not happen overnight. And the continuing presence of large corporate shareholders (as distinguished from the banks) in Japanese firms, and other impediments to a well-functioning corporate control market, have made the expected monitoring benefits of globalization slow in coming.

In sum, globalization appears to have created a corporate governance vacuum in Japan—at least in the short run—by failing to substitute the monitoring power of the market for the monitoring power of banks. Nevertheless, recent developments suggest that capital markets are beginning to assume a monitoring role,[**] and that many Japanese companies are adopting important elements of Western-style corporate governance with greater attention to management incentives and stock prices.

continued

* See Jun-Koo Kang, Yong-Cheol Kim, K. Park, and René M. Stulz, "An Analysis of the Wealth Effects of Japanese Offshore Dollar-Denominated Convertible and Warrant Bond Issues," *Journal of Financial and Quantitative Analysis* 30 (1995), 257–270.
** Consider, for example, the recent dramatic restructuring of Nissan, brought about by pressure from its largest foreign shareholder, Renault. For an account, see Tim Burt, "Nissan Jobs to Go in $9 bn Restructuring," *Financial Times*, October 19, 1999, p. 1.

of the bid-ask spread affects the market's required rate of return on securities.[11] The reasoning is that if investors have to pay more to transact a security, they have to be compensated with a greater expected return *before* transaction costs to offset these costs.

With globalization, one expects the bid-ask spread on securities to decrease for several reasons. For one thing, the pool of potential investors increases significantly. Second, directly related to our analysis of governance, the greater disclosure by firms associated with globalization reduces opportunities for insider trading. This means that market makers and investors without access to inside information worry less about being taken advantage of by insiders when they trade. And to the extent such assurances increase the number of investors and market makers willing to transact in a firm's securities, this leads to greater liquidity and a lower bid-ask spread.[12] In support of this proposition, a 1997 study by Katherine Smith and George Sofianos shows that firms that list abroad experience an increase in volume even in their home market, which is consistent with the argument that globalization leads to greater liquidity and hence a lower cost of capital.[13]

Third, globalization means greater competition in market-making and investment banking services. Companies that enter the global capital markets have access to investment banks that can compete for their business and hence lower prices. These firms can also choose to list on exchanges that are more efficient, thereby reducing the cost of transacting their securities.[14]

Besides reducing transactions costs, the greater liquidity resulting from globalization has an indirect impact on the monitoring of management. First, with greater liquidity, the market for a firm's equity becomes more efficient in the sense that it more quickly and accurately reflects information about the firm. This makes the firm's stock price more informative and hence more useful in monitoring management. Second, greater liquidity makes it easier for active investors to accumulate positions in a stock and to sell these positions as well.

Empirical Evidence on the Impact of Globalization on the Cost of Capital

Having discussed the theory of how globalization should affect the cost of capital, let's now examine the empirical evidence. We will do this in four steps: First, I review studies of the explanatory power of the global CAPM. Second, I discuss the problems with using traditional methods of estimating the risk premium with time-series data in order to evaluate the impact of globalization on the cost of capital. Third, I discuss indirect approaches to assessing the effect of capital market liberalization on the cost of capital. Fourth and last, I offer a number of suggestions why the measured impact of globalization—though typically statistically significant—is not greater than the studies report.

Globalization and the Capital Asset Pricing Model

Tests of the CAPM in an international setting have been conducted in two ways. First, there have been tests of the global CAPM using country portfolios, and these tests have been remarkably supportive of the model. For example, a classic study by Campbell Harvey published in 1991 uses almost 20 years of historical returns of 17 different countries to assess the explanatory power of the global CAPM.[15] As noted earlier, the global CAPM predicts that the risk premium in each country should be roughly equivalent to the risk premium on the world market portfolio multiplied by the beta of the country portfolio relative to the world market portfolio.

Harvey's study reports that, from February 1970 to May 1989, the average monthly return of the Morgan-Stanley Capital International World Index in excess of the 30-day bill was 0.553%, or 6.6% on an annualized basis. This number provides an estimate of the risk premium on the world market portfolio over that period.

Harvey's study provides support for the global CAPM in the following sense: Of the 17 countries in his sample, 14 had average excess returns that were statistically indistinguishable from the average returns predicted by the global CAPM. For example, he obtains an estimate of the global beta for Germany of 0.70. And, according to the global CAPM, the risk premium for Germany is its global beta (0.70) multiplied by the risk premium on the world market portfolio of 0.55% per month, or 0.39% per month. The average monthly excess return of the market portfolio of Germany over the sample period was 0.5%, which is not statistically different from the predicted return of 0.39%.

Nevertheless, there were three countries for which the model provided a poor "fit": Japan, Norway, and Austria. For example, the global beta of Japan over the sample period was 1.42, implying a risk premium of 0.78% (1.42×0.55) per month. But the average excess return in Japan was a much higher 1.34% per month (clearly a statistically significant difference). The reason for the failure of the model in this case was the very large positive returns of Japanese stocks in the 1980s, which had the effect of overstating the Japanese risk premium (a problem that we take up in the next section).[16]

In a study published in 1992, K.C. Chan, Andrew Karolyi, and I tested a different prediction of the global CAPM: namely, to the extent that national capital markets are integrated, significant changes in the volatility of major components of the global portfolio should affect the risk premiums of other markets in the portfolio. In support of this proposition, we found that changes in the variance of both the Japanese stock market and the Morgan-Stanley Europe, Asia, and Far East Index were directly correlated with changes in the risk premium of U.S. stocks. Our findings suggest, for example, that a sharp drop in the volatility of the Japanese market can be expected to reduce the risk premium in the U.S. and, indeed, in all integrated economies.[17]

The studies on the world CAPM discussed so far focus on equity markets that are reasonably well-integrated with the global equity market. But what about countries whose markets are not part of the global markets? As suggested earlier, for securities priced in a closed market, the local CAPM should hold. But once that security begins to trade in a relatively open market, the global CAPM becomes the relevant pricing model.

One important study focuses directly on this transition. In an article published in 1995, Geert Bekaert and Campbell Harvey examine the pricing of equity in emerging markets.[18] They begin by noting that, for such markets, globalization is not a linear development. Most countries do not steadily become more integrated with world markets, but instead proceed in fits and starts—and in some cases, as the imposition of Malaysian capital controls suggests, they take major steps backward. As Bekaert and Harvey hypothesize in their study, when a country becomes more integrated with the world market, its cost of capital should depend more on its beta in relation to world markets; but when, like Malaysia, it takes steps that make its markets less integrated, its cost of capital should depend more on local market volatility. And their study provides considerable statistical support for this argument.

To see the implications of Bekaert and Harvey's study, let's look at the case of Chile. From 1976 to 1992, the annual average return in dollars on Chilean stocks was a very high 37%, but the standard deviation, at 40%, was also very large. In the conventional method of applying the (local) CAPM, this historical data would be used to predict future expected returns, and so a number like 37% would end up serving as an estimate of Chile's current cost of capital. Now, if Chile was still a completely closed market, one might have been justified in estimating its risk premium in this fashion. But, given the present extent of Chile's integration with world markets, 37% is clearly a gross overstatement of the country's *current* expected return. The global beta of Chile, reflecting its relatively low correlation with world markets, is generally no higher than 0.50. And, using a global CAPM, the excess expected return (in dollars) for Chile, assuming a risk-free dollar rate of 6% and a world market risk premium of 6.6%, would be less than 10% (6% + (0.5 × 6.6%)) instead of its historical average of 37%. The key insight here is that, if Chile's cost of capital was once anywhere close to 37%, then the integration of world markets must be bringing about a dramatic reduction in the cost of capital. And these results for Chile are representative of emerging markets in general, since these countries also tend to have high standard deviations and low betas.[19]

But what evidence do we have that annual expected returns in Chile, and in other emerging markets, are now in fact closer to 10% than to 30%? Perhaps the most suggestive piece of evidence are the higher stock returns achieved by most of these nations in the 1980s and 1990s, at least prior to the Asian crisis. Such large positive returns, as I will argue in the next section, are consistent with falling risk premiums. Also furnishing evidence of smaller risk premiums is another study by Bekaert and Harvey that shows that the dividend yields of emerging market equities fall as their markets become more integrated with world markets.[20]

In sum, there is a dramatic difference in estimates of the risk premium that use historical estimates versus those that assume the global CAPM. And the results of Bekaert and Harvey's study, as well as the other evidence just cited, suggest that the global CAPM now provides a more reliable guide to pricing emerging-market stocks than the local CAPM. But if the global CAPM does a good job of explaining the risk premiums of *country* portfolios, it fares less well when applied to specific portfolios of stocks within countries. However, this should not be taken as a criticism of the global CAPM *per se;* the problems that arise when applying the global CAPM to individual companies outside the U.S. are fundamentally the same as those that researchers have found when testing the local U.S. CAPM on U.S. companies. That is, the pronounced tendency of both smaller U.S. firms and those with high book-to-market ratios to produce higher-than-expected returns also shows up clearly in studies of companies outside the U.S.[21]

And just as these shortcomings do not rule out use of the CAPM for U.S. stocks, they should not deter us from applying the global CAPM. The fact that countries that are integrated with world markets have risk premiums that depend on their covariances with the world market portfolio suggests that the global CAPM offers the most promising approach to estimating cost of capital—at least as a first approximation. Adjustments can then be made in cases where there are likely to be problems—say, in the case of small firms and those with market-to-book ratios well below 1.0.

Time-Series Evidence

The traditional approach to evaluating a market's risk premium is to compute its average excess return over a long period of time. For instance, it is common in the U.S. to use past excess returns on the U.S. stock market since the 1920s. The argument for proceeding this way is the presumption that the future is likely to be similar to the past. One has to use long periods of time because the stock market is volatile. Over shorter periods of time, one might conclude that the risk premium is either negative (if the market fell during the period), or extremely high (if the market increased dramatically). For instance, if you were using rolling 20-year periods to estimate the risk premium, you would conclude that the risk premium increased. From 1976 to 1995, the estimate of the risk premium for the U.S. using the Ibbotson data is 7.31%; but from 1978 to 1997 it is 9.36%!

A market's capitalization is the present value of the cash flow shareholders expect to receive from the securities traded in that market, where the discount rate is computed using the risk premium of the market. This implies that even if the cash flows expected by shareholders remain unchanged, when the risk premium falls, stock prices and market capitalizations will increase to reflect the reduction in investors' discount rates. And this means that there will be a negative relation between changes in the risk premium and changes in equity values.

Because of this negative relation between the risk premium and stock prices, the use of past returns to estimate the risk premium is a reliable approach only if one believes that the risk premium is relatively stable over time. In this case, the longer the period over which one estimates the risk premium, the better the estimate one obtains. Unfortunately, the variance of stock returns is high enough that, *even* when one uses fairly long periods of time, one reaches very different conclusions about the size of the risk premium depending on the estimation period chosen. For instance, the U.S. risk premium estimated over the last 70 years—about 8% (when using arithmetic averaging)—is substantially higher than the U.S. risk premium estimated over the last 200 years—about 4%.

There is little reason to believe that the risk premium is stable over long periods of time. From our discussion in the previous section, we know that there are good reasons for the risk premium to be related to the variance of returns—and this variance clearly changes over time. And, as we have seen, the market portfolio also changes over time. As markets become more integrated when barriers to international investment fall, more countries become part of the world market portfolio. And, as the world market portfolio includes more countries, its variance will continue to fall because of the benefits of international diversification.

In sum, the lack of stability in the risk premium means that the time-series averaging method for estimating cost of capital will not capture the effect of globalization on the cost of capital. Globalization has been taking place over the last 40 years; and if our theory about the impact of globalization on the cost of capital is right, the cost of capital should have been falling over that period. But, to those who ignore the impact of globalization on the cost of capital, the higher stock prices and returns associated with the past 40 years will mistakenly suggest that risk premiums have increased.

Event-Study Approaches

Rather than assessing the impact of globalization on the cost of capital by estimating the mean excess return on the market, one could take a more direct approach: namely, investigate the effect of particular globalization "events" on the equity capitalization of firms and countries. By "events" I mean announcements of market openings or other forms of liberalization. If equity markets incorporate information efficiently, one would expect events that lead investors to believe that an equity market will be more open to foreign investors—and that investors in a country will be better able to invest abroad—to have an immediate impact on equity values in that country.

In another study, Peter Henry ran a series of statistical tests designed to measure the stock market impact of capital market liberalizations in 12 countries.[22] In his first test, he considers the impact of liberalization during a period that starts four months before the announcement and ends three months after the announcement. Over that period, stock returns are higher by 4.6% per month on average, for a total cumulative abnormal return of 36.8%. He then proceeds to investigate whether this impact of globalization still holds when he controls for several variables that influence stock returns, in particular macroeconomic variables. When he does so, the impact of liberalization falls somewhat, to about 30%, but the impact is still statistically as well as economically significant. His evidence therefore suggests that liberalization increases shareholder wealth substantially.

What does an increase in stock prices of 30% imply for the cost of capital? Because the value of equity is the present value of cash flows expected to accrue to the shareholders, we can use the following experiment to produce an estimate of the impact of globalization on the cost of capital for the countries in Henry's sample. Let's begin with a simple valuation model known as the Gordon dividend growth model. This model assumes that cash flows to shareholders consist solely of expected future dividends and that dividends are expected to grow at a constant growth rate. The model then uses the following perpetuity formula to value the future dividends as follows:

$$V = d/(r-g),$$

where V is the value of equity, d is the dividend payment at the end of the period, r is the cost of capital, and g is the growth rate of dividends.

If we assume that d and g are given (and let's set d equal to \$1 and g to 5%), we can "back out" the impact of liberalization on the cost of capital from the price change by using the following formula:

$$\text{Price after} - \text{Price before} = [d/r_{\text{After}} - g] - [d/r_{\text{Before}} - g] \tag{1}$$

From Henry's study, we have the price change in percentage terms (again, 30%), which we define as Δ. We can then use Δ to solve the above equation to obtain:

$$r_{\text{After}} = (1/1 + \Delta) \times r_{\text{Before}} + (\Delta/1 + \Delta) \times g \tag{2}$$

Using this equation to estimate the impact on the cost of capital, we find that if the cost of capital before liberalization was, say, 20%, the 30% increase in equity capitalization reported by Henry would be consistent with a new cost of capital of 16.5%.

But this estimate of the reduction in cost of capital obtained from Henry's study should be used with some caution. First, although we keep the growth rate of dividends constant as liberalization takes place, one would expect liberalization to lead to faster growth in corporate profits, a higher growth rate of dividends, and hence a lower estimate of the change in the cost of capital. Second, to the extent that countries liberalize after (and in part because) their stock market has done well, Henry's estimate could overstate the gains from liberalization. Third, Henry does not include all liberalization events, which might understate the total impact of liberalization. But if each of these effects is potentially important, it is not clear that they together produce any obvious bias in the estimated effect on the cost of capital.[23]

The Case of ADRs. If none of the firms in a country has access to international capital markets, the initiation of an ADR program by a single company in that country can be construed as evidence of liberalization of the capital market of that country. Nevertheless, one would expect the primary effect of initiating an ADR program to be on the cost of capital of the company that undertakes such a program. As a result, there has been a large number of studies that investigate the stock-price impact on individual firms of ADR introductions.[24]

Based on our earlier analysis, we would expect that a firm that succeeds in having its equity valued at the global market cost of capital rather than the cost of capital of a segmented market would typically experience a substantial increase in value. As an example, suppose that the risk premium of the country is 10%, the company has a beta with respect to the country market portfolio of 1.0, the dividend growth rate is 4%, and the risk-free rate is 5%. Suppose further that the firm has a world beta of 0.5 and that the risk premium on the world market portfolio is only 6%. In this case, if the firm suddenly (and unexpectedly) gained access to the world markets, the global CAPM predicts that its value will increase by 57%.

Contrary to this example, empirical studies have not found evidence of large increases in firm value by focusing on a narrow window around the announcement of the ADR program or the listing of the ADRs. Two studies—one by Stephen Foerster and Andrew Karolyi published in 1999, and another by Darius Miller in 1998[25]—investigate both the return around the announcement of an ADR program and the return around the day when the actual listing takes place. Both studies find positive returns around the announcement date *and* around the listing date. However, the returns are small. For example, in examining 153 ADR listings on the Nasdaq, AMEX, and NYSE from 1976 to 1992, Foerster and Karolyi (1999) find an abnormal return of 1.2% during the week of listing. And, for the 45 listings for which they also have an announcement date, they find an insignificant positive abnormal return of 0.2% on the day of announcement. In Miller's study, the average announcement abnormal return for 53 ADRs listed on NYSE or Nasdaq from 1985 to 1995 is 2.63%.

Miller's study also distinguishes between firms from emerging markets and firms from developed markets. To the extent that emerging markets have more barriers to international investment than developed markets, one would expect a greater abnormal return for firms from emerging markets. Confirming this expectation, Miller finds that the abnormal return of firms from emerging markets is almost twice the abnormal return of firms from developed markets.

Both Foerster and Karolyi (1999) and a study by Vihang Errunza and Darius Miller (1998) estimate returns before the initiation of an ADR program and afterwards.[26] Strikingly, Foerster and Karolyi find that firms that list experience an unexpected increase in their stock price of 19% for the year before the listing; but this increase is followed by a decrease of 14% in the year after listing. Before rushing to interpret such results, however, it is useful to keep in mind that the significantly negative returns after listings have also been documented for U.S. firms going public on U.S. exchanges or listing on the NYSE after having traded on the Nasdaq. This suggests that the negative returns after ADR listings reported by Foerster and Karolyi may have little to do with the fact that the listing is an ADR listing but much to do with the fact that firms tend to list (or go public) following exceptional performance.[27]

At the level of individual companies, it is also possible to conduct an analysis that directly compares the valuation of firms in a given country that have ADR programs with the values of those that do not. For example, a 1996 study by Denis Logue and Anat Sundaram examines changes in price-to-book, price-to-cash earnings, and price-to-earnings ratios around the month in which the firms list. The study finds that each of these three ratios increases for firms that list ADRs relative to a control group of comparable firms. Such increases in valuation ratios are all consistent with a decrease in the cost of capital.

The evidence discussed so far in this section focuses on non-U.S. firms gaining access to the global markets. But this is not the whole story. There is also evidence that U.S. companies benefit from using the global markets. Offshore markets—notably the Euro-dollar market—are playing a large and growing role in the financing of many large U.S. firms. My own study (with Yong-Cheol Kim) of the stock market reaction to offshore debt financings by U.S. companies reports significant positive returns, in contrast to the small negative reaction to announcements of U.S. domestic debt offerings.[28] And studies of U.S. firms that issue equity in global markets also report evidence of a more favorable stock market reaction—one that is consistent with a lower cost of capital.[29]

Why Is the Decrease in the Cost of Capital Not Larger?

Although we now have considerable evidence that globalization reduces the cost of capital, the decrease in the cost of capital observed when a country liberalizes its markets or when a firm enters the global capital markets is less than one would expect. I offer a few reasons why the existing studies may not be capturing the full effect of globalization.

Because the studies just cited all investigate how stock prices react to globalization, this immediately suggests a reason why they might find smaller effects than expected. If financial markets are efficient, we expect them to incorporate information in prices very quickly, if not "instantaneously." Thus, when a country liberalizes or a firm accesses global capital markets, it is possible that the market has already anticipated this event to some degree. In the extreme case where the market knows that a firm will undertake an ADR program, the impact of that program on shareholder wealth on the date of listing will be negligible. The same holds for the liberalization of a country. For this reason, event studies of globalization have a fundamental problem. If globalization is so advantageous that it becomes largely predictable, event studies will never be able to detect its impact. To be sure, the country studies do report finding some effect. But to be able to gauge the full impact of globalization on the cost of capital from an event study, one has to have some idea of the extent to which the liberalization is anticipated—and this, of course, is very difficult to determine.

Market anticipation is not the only reason why the existing studies are likely to underestimate the benefits of globalization. The studies effectively make the assumption that a country liberalizes or a firm accesses global capital markets in such a way that they are immediately and completely integrated in world markets. But this, of course, is rarely the case. It is a well-established finding that investors are not as well-diversified internationally as the theory suggests they should be.[30] For example in 1996, U.S. investors held 90% of the value of their stock portfolio in U.S. stocks, even though U.S. stocks represented less than half of the world market capitalization of stocks. And such a home bias exists in all foreign countries for which statistics on ownership are available.

There are several explanations that have been offered for the existence of the home bias. One focuses on the fact that, although many laws and regulations limiting foreign portfolio investment have disappeared, there are still many restrictions and additional costs faced by investors investing abroad. Information asymmetries between domestic and foreign investors, the existence of different consumption baskets, political risk, and behavioral biases can all lead to a preference for domestic assets. Political risk, for example, can make information asymmetry a major deterrent to foreign investors. The informational advantage of home country investors will depend on the disclosure and regulatory environment of a country, with weaker regimes providing a greater advantage for local investors.

As a consequence, when some countries liberalize, few foreign investors may choose to invest because the institutional "infrastructure" in such countries may be inadequate. If a country liberalizes, but markets do not expect investors to take advantage of the liberalization, then liberalization will not affect the cost of capital. If a firm starts an ADR program but foreign investors do not buy the ADRs, most of the benefits of the program will fail to materialize. In support of this view, Foerster and Karolyi (1999) show that while many ADR programs significantly expand the shareholder base, many others do not—and the extent to which an ADR program broadens the shareholder base is a crucial determinant of whether the ADR program is associated with an increase in stock price.

Globalization, Corporate Practice, and Corporate Strategy

What are the lessons from the globalization of securities markets for corporations? This chapter makes three important points for international financial managers:

1. *International financial markets are progressively becoming one huge, integrated, global capital market, which in turn is contributing to higher stock prices in developed as well as developing economies.* As a consequence of the globalization of equity markets, large companies everywhere can raise capital from foreign as well as local investors. Having a global shareholder base means having a lower cost of capital and hence a greater equity value.

Shareholders benefit from globalization for two main reasons:
First, the risks of equity are shared among more investors with different portfolio exposures and hence a different "appetite" for bearing certain risks.

With the resulting global diversification of investor portfolios, companies with access to global markets experience a reduction in market risk premiums and hence a lower cost of capital. And a lower cost of capital means a higher stock price for a given level of cash flows or earnings.

Second, when firms in countries with less-developed capital markets raise capital in the public markets of countries (like the U.S.) with highly developed markets, they get more than lower-cost capital; they also import at least aspects of the corporate governance systems that prevail in those markets. For companies accustomed to less-developed markets, raising capital overseas means that more sophisticated investors, institutions, and technologies will participate in monitoring their performance and management. And, in a virtuous cycle, more effective monitoring will increase investor confidence in companies' future profitability and so improve the terms on which such firms raise capital.

This process of globalization of equity markets continues to proceed vigorously, both at the level of national governments and capital markets and within individual companies. With the growth of the Internet, moreover, the limits to further globalization of equity markets are primarily political rather than economic or technological. Shareholders can now trade a firm's shares wherever they are, provided country governments do not prevent them from so doing.

2. *Market risk premiums are not stable, and long-run past returns do not provide a reliable guide when estimating current premiums.* The reduction in the cost of equity capital brought about by globalization is hard to detect when one focuses on historical data. The reason for this is that the global diversification of investor portfolios and the resulting expansion in the shareholder base (of all companies with access to global markets) has the effect of increasing equity values as it decreases the global risk premium and cost of capital. For this reason, one who uses historical returns on equity as a basis for estimating future required returns could easily conclude that the cost of equity capital has increased when in fact it has fallen. For example, using U.S. stock returns over just the last 20 years would yield estimates for the U.S. market risk premium as high as 10%—estimates that make it very hard indeed to explain the current level of U.S. stock prices. A better approach is likely to be one that computes a risk premium that is consistent with current equity valuations and reasonable growth estimates for earnings.[31]

3. *In measuring the risk of individual firms and projects, use the global (not the local) CAPM.* In global markets, the risk of a firm's equity depends on how the stock contributes to the volatility not of the home market portfolio, but of the world market portfolio. For companies with access to global capital markets whose profitability is tied more

closely to the local than to the global economy, use of the local CAPM will overstate the cost of capital because risks that are not diversifiable within a national economy can be diversified by holding a global portfolio. Thus, to reflect the new reality of a globally determined cost of capital, all companies with access to global markets (even those in the U.S.) should consider using a global CAPM that views a company as part of the global portfolio of stocks.

Another common problem in calculating cost of capital is the tendency of managers evaluating overseas investments to add an extra risk premium—over and above the premium in the CAPM—to account for the special risks associated with foreign projects. Such an approach is hard to justify. If the extra risk premium is used to compensate for country risks, then it must be demonstrated that those risks are not diversifiable and that shareholders charge a risk premium to bear those risks. In a world where the firm has a global shareholder base, it makes little sense to think that shareholders will require a higher risk premium simply because the firm invests abroad. There are, to be sure, large country-specific risks in world markets; and management may well want to hedge such risks to avoid default or reduce costs associated with financial distress. But such risks should not be viewed as increasing the cost of capital for a project. Country-specific risks may reduce the expected cash flows of a project; but as globalization progresses, a firm's shareholders care less about where the expected cash flows come from, and focus simply on how big they are—and how they affect a global portfolio.

Notes

This chapter presents the implications for corporate finance of my working paper entitled "Globalization of Equity Markets and the Cost of Capital," which is available at http://www.cob.ohio-state.edu/fin/faculty/stulz under the heading "working papers." I am grateful for research assistance from Ed Gladewell, Jan Jindra, and Dong Lee; and for comments from Yakov Amihud, Bernard Dumas, Peter Henry, Andrew Karolyi, John McConnell, Nils Tuchschmid, Ingrid Werner, and participants at the NYSE–Bourse de Paris Conference on Global Equity Markets in Paris and the BSI Conference in Lugano. I also thank the New York Stock Exchange and the Bourse de Paris for financial support.

1. More precisely, it is called the "agency cost of managerial discretion" problem. For a detailed analysis of this problem, see my paper "Managerial Discretion and Optimal Financing Policies," *Journal of Financial Economics* 26, no. 1 (1990), 3–26.
2. There were also differences in anonymity. Investors could buy bearer shares anonymously, whereas purchasers of registered shares had to register their shares with the company to obtain full ownership rights.
3. In fact, globalization is likely to change real economic activities—and improve efficiency—by encouraging economies that have been previously segmented from global markets to focus increasingly on their areas of comparative advantage. For an article that shows how globalization allows countries to specialize more and undertake

riskier projects because individuals in a country can diversify risks by investing abroad, see Maurice Obstfeld, "Risk-Taking, Global Diversification, and Growth, *American Economic Review* 84 (1994), 1310–1329.

4. For a recent estimate of the benefits from diversification, see Giorgio DeSantis and Bruno Gerard, "International Asset Pricing and Portfolio Diversification with Time-Varying Risk," *Journal of Finance* 52 (1997), 1881–1913.

5. Some observers have expressed concern that correlations increase during crises. For example, correlations seemed to increase during the recent Asian crisis, and then to fall afterward. More generally, there is a concern that the progressive integration of global economic activity is leading to greater synchronization of global economic cycles and rising correlations during bear markets. Geert Bekaert and Campbell Harvey find that when countries open their capital markets, they experience a small increase in their home market's correlation with global markets, but not sufficiently large to change our general argument about the impact of globalization on the cost of capital. (See Bekaert and Harvey, "Foreign Speculators and Emerging Markets," *Journal of Finance* 55, no. 2 (2000), 565–613.)

6. For the details of this calculation, see my 1995 article, "Globalization and the Cost of Capital: The Case of Nestlé," *Journal of Applied Corporate Finance* 8, no. 3 (Fall 1995).

7. For a recent review of the literature on corporate governance, see Andrei Shleifer and Robert Vishny, "A Survey of Corporate Governance," *Journal of Finance* 52 (1997), 737–784.

8. See Shleifer and Vishny (1997).

9. For two articles that develop theoretical models where firms reveal their good prospects by listing abroad, see Salvatore Cantale, "The Choice of a Foreign Market as a Signal," working paper, Tulane University, 1998; and O. Fuerst, "A Theoretical Analysis of the Investor Protection Regulations: Argument for Global Listing of Stocks," working paper, Yale School of Management, 1998.

10. See Rafael LaPorta, Florencio Lopez-de-Silanes, Andrei Shleifer, and Robert W. Vishny, "Corporate Ownership Around the World," *Journal of Finance* 54 (April 1999), 471–517.

11. Yakov Amihud and Haim Mendelson, "Asset Pricing and the Bid-Ask Spread," *Journal of Financial Economics* 17 (1986), 223–249.

12. For evidence of the link between disclosure and the cost of capital—more specifically, that U.S. firms with a limited analyst following that disclose more have a lower cost of capital—see Christine Botosan, "Disclosure Level and the Cost of Equity Capital, *The Accounting Review* 72 (1997), 323–349.

13. See Katherine Smith and George Sofianos, "The Impact of a NYSE Listing on the Global Trading of Non-US Stocks," working paper 97–02, New York Stock Exchange, 1997.

14. Although one might think that the U.S. has not benefited from global competition in financial services, this has not been the case. Over the last 30 years or so, the largely unregulated offshore markets have put pressure on U.S. financial service companies and played a key role in limiting their regulatory burden. To understand the importance of the offshore markets, think of the omnipresence of LIBOR in the financial industry. No U.S. institution that is active in financial markets can ignore this interest rate. While it is a dollar rate, it is not determined in the U.S. but rather in London (since it stands for the London Interbank Offer Rate). Another telling example of this offshore pressure occurred just after the LTCM crisis. The popular clamor for greater regulation of domestic hedge funds led to great concern that more regulation would drive these funds offshore.

15. Campbell R. Harvey, "The World Price of Covariance Risk," *Journal of Finance* 46 (1991), 111–158.
16. Our discussion focuses on table VI of Harvey (1991). He also implements his model allowing betas to change over time, and this leads to a smaller but still statistically significant mistake for Japan. More recent support for the global CAPM was provided by DeSantis and Gerard (1997), cited earlier. Using different methods from Harvey, this study calculated monthly returns from January 1970 to December 1994 for eight large countries, and also reached conclusions that were supportive of the world CAPM.
17. K.C. Chan, G. Andrew Karolyi, and René M. Stulz, "Global Financial Markets and the Risk Premium on U.S. Equity," *Journal of Financial Economics* 32 (1992), 137–167.
18. Geert Bekaert and Campbell Harvey, "Time-Varying Market Risk Premiums," *Journal of Finance* 50 (1995), 403–444.
19. In my working paper referenced in the unnumbered note above, I derive a condition that must be met for a country to experience a reduction in investors' required rate of return as a result of becoming integrated with world markets. The condition can be stated fairly simply: the variance of the small country market portfolio must exceed its covariance with the world market portfolio. This condition will always be met when the small country market portfolio is much more volatile than the world market portfolio. When I tested this condition on 37 different using weekly returns countries over a 10-year period from 1988 to 1998, all 37 countries—even the U.S. and the U.K.—satisfied this condition. But, not surprisingly, some countries appear to gain much more from risk-sharing than others. Argentina is the country that over that sample period seems to gain the most from risk-sharing because of its combination of high volatility and low correlation with the world market portfolio. Interestingly, in our list of countries, the country that benefits the most from risk-sharing after Argentina is China, where the stock index is composed of the Chinese shares available to foreign investors.
20. However, Bekaert and Harvey interpret their results as consistent with a fairly modest reduction in costs of capital, less than 200 basis points. See Geert Bekaert and Campbell Harvey, "Foreign Speculators and Emerging Markets," *Journal of Finance* 55, no. 2 (2000), 565–613.
21. For a study that shows that a world CAPM understates the expected returns of small firms across countries, see Robert Korajczyk and Claude Viallet, "An Empirical Investigation of International Asset Pricing," *Review of Financial Studies* 2 (1989), 553–585. For a study that shows that value stocks earn a premium across countries and makes the case for a world value factor, see Eugene Fama and Kenneth French, *Journal of Finance* (1998).
22. Peter B. Henry, "Stock Market Liberalization, Economic Reform, and Emerging Market Prices, *Journal of Finance* 55, no. 2 (2000), 529–564.
23. The study by Bekaert and Harvey, cited in note 20, also shows that liberalization leads to a significant decrease in the cost of capital—but one that is considerably smaller than that found by Henry.
24. For a review of these studies, see G. Andrew Karolyi, "Why Do Companies List Shares Abroad? A Survey of the Evidence and Its Managerial Implications," *Journal of Applied Corporate Finance* 11, no. 3 (Fall 1998).
25. Stephen R. Foerster and G. Andrew Karolyi, "The Effects of Market Segmentation and Investor Recognition on Asset Prices: Evidence from Foreign Stocks Listing in the U.S.," *Journal of Finance* 54 (June 1999); and Darius Miller, "The Market Reaction to International Cross-Listings: Evidence from Depositary Receipts," *Journal of Financial Economics* 51 (1999).

26. Vihang R. Errunza and Darius P. Miller, "Market Segmentation and the Cost of Capital in International Equity Markets," unpublished working paper, Texas A&M University, College Station, TX, 1998.
27. See Bala G. Dharan and David Ikenberry, "The Long-Run Negative Drift of Post-Listing Stock Returns," *Journal of Finance* 50 (1995), 1547–1574.
28. Yong-Cheol Kim and René Stulz, "The Eurobond Market and Corporate Financial Policy: A Test of the Clientele Hypothesis," *Journal of Financial Economics* 22, no. 2 (1988).
29. See Susan Chaplinsky and Latha Ramchand, "The Impact of Global Equity Offerings," *Journal of Finance,* 55, no. 6 (2000), which shows that the average negative market reaction (of slightly more than 2%) to the announcement of equity offerings is reduced by about one-third in global offerings.
30. For these numbers, see Linda Tesar and Ingrid Werner, "The Internationalization of Securities Markets Since the 1987 Crash," Brookings-Wharton Papers on Financial Services, 1998, 281–372.
31. See Aswath Damodoran, "Estimating Equity Risk Premiums," Stern School of Business working paper.

CHAPTER 7

Which Capitalism?

Lessons from the East Asian Crisis

RAGHURAM G. RAJAN AND LUIGI ZINGALES

JUST A FEW YEARS AGO, it was fashionable to decry the shortsightedness of the American financial system, the widely alleged tendency of U.S. financial markets to ignore longer-term corporate prospects while focusing on quarterly earnings reports. There were repeated calls for the U.S. to adopt new laws that would permit financiers to take a longer view of their investments, and to move toward the more relationship-based investing model that prevails in Japan.[1]

It is amazing what a banking crisis or two will do to popular fashion. Now the talk is all about the virtues of "the market," the importance of competition and disclosure, and the horrors of crony capitalism. Why did these relationship-based financial systems, which have been credited with fueling the miraculous growth of East Asia, suddenly implode? Is the current crisis a temporary setback to an otherwise successful system or does it herald its demise? Does the slow but steady ascendance of the public markets, even in Germany, suggest the eventual supremacy of the arm's-length, market-based Anglo-Saxon system?

Relationship versus Arm's-Length Systems

To answer these questions, let's begin with a sketch of the salient features of these two kinds of systems. Like all sketches, this one has elements of caricature, but this is the price we have to pay to avoid being distracted by the details.

A financial system has two primary goals: to channel resources to their most productive uses and to ensure that an adequate portion of the return flows to the financier. The latter is, of course, crucial to the former. Without a guarantee of an adequate return, funds will not be made available for investment.

Relationship-based systems ensure a return to the financier by granting her some form of power over the firm being financed. The simplest form of power is when the financier has (implicit or explicit) ownership of the firm. The financier can also serve as the sole or main lender, supplier, or customer. In all of these forms, the financier attempts to secure her return on investment by retaining some kind of monopoly power over the firm she finances. As with every monopoly, this requires some barriers to entry. These barriers may come from regulation, or lack of transparency—or "opacity"—of the system, which substantially raises the costs of entry to potential competitors.

Contrast this with the arm's-length, Anglo-Saxon system, where the financier is protected by explicit contracts. In such systems, contracts and associated prices determine the transactions that are undertaken. As a result, institutional relationships matter less and the market becomes a more important medium in determining the terms of transactions.

An important distinction between these two systems is their different degree of reliance on legal enforcement. Relationship-based systems can survive in environments where laws are poorly drafted or contracts not enforced. The relationship is largely self-governing; parties intent on maintaining their "reputations" honor the spirit of agreements (often in the absence of any written contract) in order to ensure a steady flow of future business within the same network of firms. By contrast, the prompt and unbiased enforcement of contracts by courts is a precondition for the viability of a market-based system. Moreover, since contracts are typically hard to write with the wealth of detail necessary to fully govern transactions, it is important that the law offer a helping hand. Under common law, the court tries to follow the spirit rather than the letter of a contract, thus enabling contracts to offer greater protection. For this reason, it is perhaps no surprise that market-based systems are found largely in countries with a common-law tradition (hence the "Anglo-Saxon" model).[2]

Another distinction between the two systems is the relative importance of transparency. Market-based systems require transparency as a guarantee of protection. In the words of Franklin Roosevelt, "Sunlight is said to be the best of disinfectants; electric light the most efficient policemen."[3] By contrast, relationship-based systems are designed to preserve opacity, which has the effect of protecting relationships from the threat of competition.

An Example: Credit

Before going further, let us consider the example of a transaction—the extension of credit—in each of the two systems. In a relationship-based system, a bank will have close ties with a potential borrowing firm, perhaps because of frequent past contacts or because of ownership links. In assessing the borrowing needs of the firm and its ability to pay interest and principal, the bank will consider not only the firm's current debt-servicing capability, but also its long-term ability to repay and the various non-contractual levers the bank can push to extract repayment.[4] The interest rate charged will be repeatedly negotiated over time, and may not have a direct relationship to the intrinsic risk of the project.

In an arm's-length system, by contrast, the firm will be able to tap a wider circle of potential lenders because there will be more financial information about it. The loan will be contracted for a specific period, and the interest rate will be a competitive one that compensates the lender for time and the risk of the particular loan.

Limitations on competition in a relationship system do not just give the financier power, but also strengthen his incentive to cooperate with the borrower. Studies show that the main banks of Japanese keiretsus went out of their way to help financially distressed borrowers within their keiretsus. For example, Sumitomo Bank not only effectively guaranteed Mazda's debts when it got into trouble after the first oil shock, but also orchestrated a rescue, in part by exhorting employees within its keiretsu to buy Mazda cars.[5] Sumitomo's incentive to help would have been considerably weaker if Mazda had had the option of giving the lion's share of its business, once it emerged from distress, to some other bank. As this example suggests, the effective limitations on outside competition imposed by the keiretsu system enable lenders to "internalize" a greater share of the benefits accruing to borrowers than is possible in an arm's-length, competitive banking environment.

The absence of competition and disclosure in a relationship-based system imply that there are really no price signals to guide decisions. Unlike an arm's-length system, where a number of competitive lenders can give a borrowing firm independent assessments of the costs of undertaking a project, the cost a borrower faces in the relationship-based system is simply what the relationship lender and the borrower negotiate. Since there can be substantial value created in the relationship, and the negotiation and allocation of this "surplus" is a function of each party's power, the effective cost can deviate substantially from the true risk-adjusted cost over a long period.

Do Relationship-Based Systems Always Lead to Worse Investment Decisions?

But is this necessarily a bad thing? Are lending and investment decisions always inefficient if the cost of funds differs from their true cost? Are there no redeeming features of a relationship-based system? The answer to all these questions is no. In the real world with all its "imperfections," an imperfect cost of funds can sometimes produce the right investment decisions.

For instance, consider our previous example of a firm in distress. Taking into consideration all the value that the firm adds to society—to workers, customers, and local governments as well as shareholders—the company may be worth saving. But, *in the short run,* the true cost of funding may far exceed what the firm can pay without creating further investment distortions.[6] And in the competitive arm's-length system, a lender may not be able to recoup or "internalize" enough of the firm's value in the long run to be able to offer it subsidized financing in the short run. So the firm is much less likely to be bailed out in the competitive, arm's-length system. By contrast, a lender in a relationship-based system, confident in the strength of the relationship (and the protection it affords from competition), can offer a below-market rate in the short run and then recoup its losses with an above-market rate over the long run when the firm is healthy and can afford high payouts. In sum, relationship banks can be viewed as using their monopoly power to charge above-market rates in normal circumstances in return for an implicit agreement to provide below-market financing when their borrowers get into trouble.

A recent study (involving one of the present writers) provides evidence of such relationship lending practices even in the U.S.[7] In examining bank loans to small businesses in different banking "markets" throughout the U.S.,[8] the study finds that in "concentrated" markets (those where most of the lending is done by a handful of banks) more credit is available to young firms than in more competitive banking markets. To the extent that young firms are subject to more credit "rationing," as many observers have suggested, the evidence suggests that the relationship-based system does a better job of ensuring that value-adding projects get funded.

The study also finds that the interest rates charged younger firms are lower, on average, in concentrated markets than in competitive markets, with the effect reversing for older firms. This suggests that banks in concentrated markets can offer more credit on economic terms because their relationships allow "intertemporal cross-subsidies"—that is, below-market rates for younger firms that are compensated for by above-market rates for more mature firms with greater ability to pay. Such subsidies, as suggested earlier, would not be possible in more competitive markets.

Clearly, it is this kind of ability to "internalize joint surplus"—that is, to trade off short-run losses for longer-run gains—that led so many observers, including many economists, to defend the efficiency of relationship-based systems. But it is easy to see the problems that can arise in such systems. Perhaps most important, the relationship-based system does not pay much attention to market or price signals. And this indifference to price signals becomes self-fulfilling: If investment decisions are not driven by prices, then prices become less effective in providing economic direction because they reflect less information.

This is not to say that the arm's-length system is a perfect allocator of re-sources. Because outsiders have little power under normal circumstances, management can indulge in considerable "empire-building" without triggering an intervention by outsiders (a problem that has been called "the agency costs of free cash flow" by Michael Jensen). Nevertheless, the arm's-length system can use hostile takeovers and LBOs to correct this problem when it gets out of hand.[9] In relationship-based systems, by contrast, the problem of misallocation of resources due to the lack of price signals is more troublesome, because such systems lack a self-activating corrective mechanism. In fact, even if the price signals were accurate, the power structures in relationship-based systems may not allow movement in the direction indicated by the prices.

Evidence of this unwillingness to respond to market signals was provided by a 1991 study by Hoshi, Kashyap, and Scharfstein.[10] The study looked at a sample of Japanese firms in the late 1970s and early 1980s that had close ties to banks and compared their investment behavior with a sample that had no such ties. The investments of firms that had no bank ties were very sensitive to the cash flow the firms generated from operations; when operating cash flows de-creased sharply, so did investment spending—and vice versa. By contrast, the investments of firms with strong ties to the banks were significantly less sensi-tive to the firms' operating cash flow.

As suggested earlier, one possible interpretation of these findings is that bank-ing relationships make it easier for firms to obtain external funding for value-adding investments, thus making them less dependent on their own cash flows. But recent events in Japan suggest a different explanation. More often than not, the companies' continuous access to bank funding on favorable terms allowed them to ignore the signal sent by their poor cash flows and to continue investing. By continuing to invest in these circumstances, such firms may well have been destroying long-term value rather than increasing or preserving it. And, even if the banks were failing to provide the managers of these firms with the right sig-nals, it appears that the stock market was attempting to do so. For, as the study also reported, the firms with strong bank ties in their sample had lower "Tobin's q" (or market-to-replacement cost) ratios than firms without bank ties. To the ex-tent Tobin's q is a reliable proxy for a firm's investment opportunities, the stock market was expressing skepticism about the likely payoff from such investments.

Moreover, another study of Japanese firms published in 1998 suggests that such market skepticism was warranted. For although Japanese firms with close bank ties had greater access to funds when their operating cash flows declined, such access did not enable them to achieve higher profits or growth rates than their peers.[11]

Yet another recent study provides additional evidence that relationships can distort the allocation of funds.[12] In the early 1990s, Japanese banks in-creased their lending to the U.S. commercial real estate market. At their peak in 1992, the U.S. subsidiaries of Japanese banks accounted for one fifth of all commercial real estate loans held in the U.S. banking sector. Then, in response to a severe decline in real estate prices in Japan, the Japanese banks cut back their lending in the U.S. even as U.S. prices were rising (and lending by non-Japanese banks increasing); at the same time they expanded their lending in the domestic Japanese market, where prices were plummeting. Thus, rather than cutting their losses in Japan—or at least not abandoning their profitable opportunities in the U.S.—Japanese banks poured more money into their unprofitable Japanese relationships.

In sum, the message from the existing research is that although relationships may increase or preserve value in some cases—particularly when contracts are hard to write or enforce—they also have the downside that they do not rely on price signals. The consequence has been a widespread and costly misallocation of resources.

By contrast, market-based economies like the U.S. and the U.K. sustained high levels of corporate investment throughout most of the 1990s while still producing enough profit to reward shareholders. The relative prosperity of these economies can be attributed in no small part to their reliance on market prices to allocate resources. And indeed there appears to be a virtuous cycle at work here: in the process of relying on prices for guidance, the arm's-length transactions that predominate in these economies also have the beneficial effect of making prices more informative. Thus, the more transactions that come into the market, the more likely decisions made on the basis of price are likely to be the right ones. As we will argue below, in economies with a sufficient degree of contractual "infrastructure" to support them, arm's-length transactions are likely to lead to better decisions.

The Costs and Benefits of Conglomerates: Some Evidence of When Relationships Add Value

But, if relationship-based systems generally allocate resources less efficiently than market-based economies, how do we account for their popularity? After all, almost all economies, including the U.S., have at some point in their history relied heavily on relationships, particularly in earlier stages of development.[13] Thus, one promising hypothesis for the durability of the relationship-based system is that it works better than an arm's-length system in relatively less developed economies—those where contracts are ineffective and price signals from the market relatively uninformative.

Some support for this argument comes from recent research on the performance of conglomerate organizations. Conglomerates can be thought of as the ultimate relationship-based financial system in the sense that the different business units that make up the organization receive financing from an internal capital market.

Several studies of conglomerates in the U.S. have shown that they trade at substantial discounts relative to stand-alone firms.[14] Moreover, these studies—including one that we recently completed (with Henri Servaes)—show that the size of the discount is related to the extent of the conglomerate's investments in relatively unprofitable segments. In particular, our study shows that both the discount and the degree of overinvestment in unprofitable businesses increase as the diversity of businesses within a conglomerate increases.[15]

Taken together, then, the evidence on U.S. conglomerates suggests that they trade at a significant discount relative to stand-alone firms, and that such discounts appear to be a direct function of the extent of resource misallocation. But do conglomerates perform better in less-developed economies?

There is some evidence for this, most of it fairly recent. In 1995, this journal published a study showing that the South African "groups" (collections of publicly traded companies with a pyramid ownership structure) have traded at consistent premiums to their net asset values (NAVs).[16] A more recent study finds that large diversified groups in India outperformed smaller unaffiliated firms between 1989 and 1995.[17] And a 1998 study of conglomerates in 35 countries reports that the relative value of diversification in a country is related to the country's income level.[18] Specifically, in low-income countries they find either a diversification *premium* or no discount, while in high-income countries they find a significant diversification discount.[19]

Perhaps the most telling evidence for conglomerates, however, is the continuing dominance of this organizational form in Asia, Latin America, and much of Western Europe—indeed, almost everywhere outside the Anglo-Saxon world.[20] Of course, such dominance does not necessarily imply that they will continue to prevail, only that they have proved efficient in certain (possibly now past) circumstances.

A Framework for Thinking about the Value of Relationships

From our discussion above, two factors seem important in determining whether relationships work well in an environment relative to arm's-length transactions. The first is the adequacy of the contractual "infrastructure" ("contractibility" for short) in that environment. If much of the surplus value in a transaction can be contractually allocated, there is little role for a controlling financier to add value by reallocating the surplus to facilitate transactions. For this reason, the development of property rights, laws, and institutions (such as auditors and regulators) that facilitate transactions will reduce the relative value of relationships.

The second factor is the importance of price signals. In a situation of extreme capital scarcity, when it is relatively easy to determine that certain investments have positive net present values, decisions based on relationships are not likely to go very wrong. But in situations where the clearly profitable investments have been made and there is abundant capital chasing relatively few opportunities, price signals are very useful in helping to guide investment and relationships. In such cases, obscuring price signals can lead to investment that ends up destroying substantial value.

Figure 7.1 may be a useful way to summarize our framework. On the x-axis is the ratio of available capital to investment opportunities, on the y-axis is the degree to which institutional development facilitates contracting. As shown in the lower left corner of the figure, a relationship-based system is clearly better than an arm's-length system when there is little available capital relative to opportunities *and* when contractibility is low. As shown in the upper right, an arm's-length system dominates when both are high. When the ratio of capital to opportunities is low but contractibility is high, both systems work reasonably well—though, in most developed economies, the arm's-length system tends to supplant the relationship system over time.[21] This is because a well-functioning contractual system creates very good opportunities outside the relationship, and narrows the amount of give and take that is possible inside it. Finally, neither system works well when capital is relatively abundant and contractibility is low. The relationship system cannot allocate the capital effectively (it can easily lead to overinvestment) while the arm's-length system has limited ability to recover funds once they are invested.

Figure 7.1 begs the question: What brings about a change in the environment? The main force for such change appears to be major changes in invest-

FIGURE 7.1

Systems Most Consistent with Different Environments

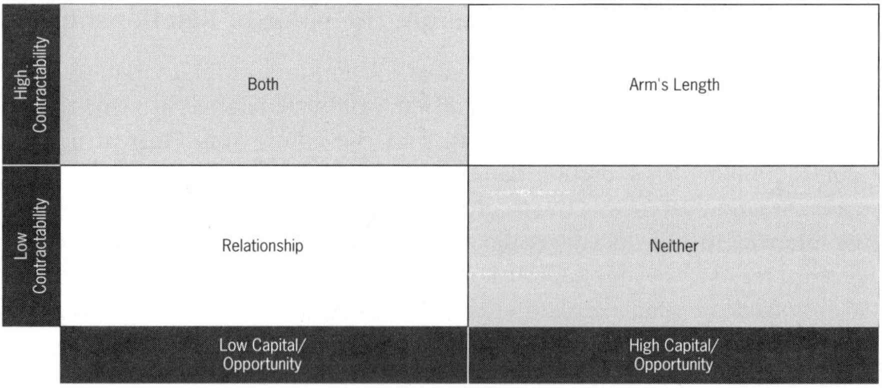

	Low Capital/ Opportunity	High Capital/ Opportunity
High Contractability	Both	Arm's Length
Low Contractability	Relationship	Neither

ment opportunities or capital flows; institutional infrastructure changes tend to follow them, though often with a considerable lag. Moreover, there is no guarantee that institutional changes will keep pace with the changes in capital flows, or that the system itself will change to be consistent with the environment.

For example, consider a relationship system in a situation with low contractibility and high capital availability relative to opportunities (in short, the condition of East Asia and most emerging economies a few years ago). An improvement in institutional infrastructure and the move toward an arm's-length system has the potential to improve matters. But there is no reason to believe that institutional change will be rapid or that the vested interests in the relationship system will permit such a move. The resulting inconsistency of the system with the environment can lead to distortions.

Let us now try to make some sense of the recent events in East Asia in the light of this framework.

Making Sense of the Asian Crisis

Until the end of the 1980s, the East Asian economies were overwhelmingly relationship-based systems.[22] At the outset of liberalization, the volume of profitable investment opportunities greatly exceeded the available capital. This capital shortage in turn prompted a momentous change in the environment: namely, the opening up of these economies to capital flows—a development that coincided with the increased desire of Western banks and fund managers for international diversification.

But, as figure 7.1 would suggest, there was a potential problem. A flood of foreign capital poured into these countries at a time when the institutional infrastructure was not adequately developed to permit direct contracting between these sources of capital and borrowers. Essentially, the arm's-length capital was lent to a relationship-based system that did not have adequate price signals to deploy the massive inflow of capital properly.[23] The economies moved from the lower left-hand box in figure 7.1 to the lower right-hand box, an environment where neither system can be expected to work very well.

Not only did foreign lenders not always know whether their funds were being deployed appropriately, they also did not have the institutional safeguards to protect their investment.[24] Therefore they took the next best route— they kept their loans and investments short term so that they could pull out at any indication of trouble.[25] So long as the countries could not offer adequate institutional safeguards, short-term financing was the cheapest way for the countries to obtain the large amounts of capital that were on offer. Both sides were happy provided the economies continued to hum along.

But then prospects changed. It is hard to say whether the trigger was the depreciating yen (driven down because of loose Japanese monetary policy), poor macroeconomic policies, or the realization that capital was being poorly invested by the relationship system. At any rate, once some foreign arm's-length capital started to pull out, it did not make sense for any to stay in. Since the relationship system would ensure that the pain would be spread through invisible cross-subsidies and the like, and not contained within a few specific "bad" institutions, it made sense for every outsider who could to pull out. This was not necessarily a panic, but a "rational" move to the exits by arm's-length capital providers who knew they had inadequate protection for the long run, and were not sufficiently part of the relationship system to get any of the benefits of staying. Of course, it is easy to see how the subsequent development of the crisis took place.

We do not rule out the possibility that moral hazard may have been behind some of the investment that flowed in, or that there was some panic in the search for exits. Yet it seems to us that much of what happened can be explained as the consequence of two financial systems that are essentially incompatible coming into contact with each other. Not having either the power that is the currency in relationship systems or contractual safeguards that are essential to an arm's-length system, foreign investors protected themselves by keeping the exits clear. An unexpected bad shock led them to head for the exits. The mistake, if any, may have been on the part of the East Asian countries in underestimating the risk involved in accepting such flows, without a clear plan to reform their institutions once the flows had been accepted.

One clear policy implication of this analysis is that a country faced with the prospect of substantial financial inflows has to either accept the risk of financial fragility or improve its financial infrastructure before it accepts the flows. Institutions such as exchanges and custodial services have to be set up, monitors such as rating agencies, auditors, and supervisory authorities have to be established or strengthened, accounting standards and disclosure laws improved, and bankruptcy and contract law made more effective. Not only does such institutional development improve the way foreign inflows are invested, it also makes the system more resilient to adverse shocks by "localizing" them within a few institutions.

In short, unfettered flows should be allowed only after the financial infrastructure is in place. The notion that investors will create their own institutions after they come in is a version of Say's Law that should be laid to rest.

Where Do We Go from Here?

Given the flight of foreign capital and the ensuing capital shortage now confronting them, East Asian economies might appear to be justified in returning to their traditional relationship-based systems. But is a return to the old system likely to restore these economies to their former strength? And is a relationship-based system really a viable, long-run solution for these economies?

Our analysis thus far would suggest that a return to relationships is the best way to go in the short run. That is, until foreign capital shows signs of renewed interest in these economies, staying in the lower left-hand corner of figure 7.1 would appear to be the best course of action. Yet there is a fundamental problem with relationship systems, one that we have largely glossed over until now: namely, their resistance to change. The opacity and collusive practices that sustain a relationship-based system entrench incumbents at the expense of potential new entrants. Moreover, the very lack of transparency also makes it hard for democratic forces to detect all of the abuses in the system. This strengthens the hand of incumbents in resisting reform.

One of the effects of a crisis is to create such immense problems that even the relationship system cannot hide them. The evidence of gross abuse can be a powerful weapon for democratic and liberal forces in pressing for reform. An example is the financial legislation that was rushed through Congress soon after the onset of the Great Depression, in 1933 and 1934. Of course, much of that legislation—including the Glass-Steagall Act and the Securities Act of 1934—has been attacked by economists as politically motivated[26] and a source of inefficiency in the U.S. economy.[27] What is rarely pointed out, however, is that such legislation laid the framework for the modern U.S. financial sector. The crisis of the Great Depression provided an opportunity for democratic forces to combat the concentration of power on Wall Street; and the legislation that resulted from the crisis essentially ended relationship-based finance in the United States. In so doing, Glass-Steagall and the Securities Acts can be seen as providing the initial impetus for the present variety and competitiveness of U.S. financial institutions.

In the near term, then, East Asia's crisis and capital shortage provides a rare opportunity for institutional reform. Over the longer run, however, such economies can be expected to move from their current condition of capital shortage to situations that once again test the systems' ability to allocate capital. When that day comes, the arm's-length system is likely to be more efficient. If the current crisis can be weathered, the long run need not be that long for the East Asian economies. Rather than reconstituting the old monopolies and inside deals, these economies would be well advised to follow the U.S. example in the 1930s and take advantage of the financial crisis to improve transparency and accountability in their financial system.

But how do these economies weather the short-run crisis? The problem is that while a large portion of foreign capital has fled, some is still in the system, along with domestically supplied capital. As the financial mess is untangled and the underlying problems revealed, more capital will disappear, either outside the country or under the mattress. Furthermore, there is likely to be a ratchet effect in the disclosure process. Because the markets suspect insiders of dissembling as in the past, any disclosures will be discounted as understating the true extent of the problems. But this makes it hard for reforming insiders to confess everything since the market continues to discount their disclosures.[28] For example, if the market's past experience with the system causes it to multiply the size of disclosed loan losses by two, an admission of the true size of loan losses may cause tremendous capital flight since, at least in the short run, the market might believe the true losses are twice the actual ones. Since confidence is so critical to markets, it may paradoxically be impossible to clean up the system and restore long-run credibility without risking further short-run flight.

This would suggest that if there is a serious intention to clean up the system, a temporary government guarantee—with clearly defined time limits—of the financial institutions, together with a temporary restriction on capital flows, may be necessary to give the system the latitude to purge itself.[29] The danger in this course, however, is that such restrictions would make it easier to continue with the status quo because the market would no longer reflect the state of the system. Therefore, it is crucial that there be genuine political will to reform the system before such drastic measures are contemplated. Other institutional reforms should follow in the longer run, and these reforms will provide Asian economies not only with the capacity to absorb arm's-length foreign capital when fashion and sentiment turn, as surely they must, but also with the much-needed information to allocate this capital to the highest-value use. Therein lies the best hope for restoring long-term growth.

Notes

1. See, for example, Michael Porter, "Capital Choices: Changing the Way America Invests in Industry," *Journal of Applied Corporate Finance* 5, no. 2 (Summer 1992), 4–16.
2. See Rafael la Porta, Florencio Lopez de Silanes, Andrei Shleifer, and Robert Vishny, "The Legal Determinants of External Finance," *Journal of Finance* 52 (1997).
3. In Joel Seligman, *The Transformation of Wall Street* (Boston: Northeastern University Press, 1995), 42.
4. For example, the bank may refuse to extend a blanket guarantee to the firm's other creditors, or refuse to provide new financing or even take a piece of it, if the firm is not cooperative.
5. See Takeo Hoshi, Anil Kashyap, and David Scharfstein, "The Role of Banks in Reducing the Costs of Financial Distress in Japan," *Journal of Financial Economics* 27 (1990), 67–88.
6. For example, too high an interest rate could lead the firm to take riskier, negative NPV projects. See Michael Jensen and William Meckling, "Theory of the Firm, Managerial Behavior, Agency Costs, and Capital Structure," *Journal of Financial Economics* 3 (1976).
7. See Mitchell Petersen and Raghuram Rajan, "The Effect of Credit Market Competition on Lending Relationships," *Quarterly Journal of Economics* 110 (1995), 407–443.
8. The idea of distinct banking markets makes sense in this case because small firms rarely do business with a bank outside their local banking market; the median borrower in the above-cited study is only two miles from its bank.

9. If anything, managerial empire-building may be less of a problem in relationship-based systems precisely because financiers have the power to intervene extensively and absorb free cash flows from successful firms.

10. Takeo Hoshi, Anil Kashyap, and David Scharfstein, "Corporate Structure, Liquidity, and Investment: Evidence from Japanese Bank Data," *Quarterly Journal of Economics* 27 (1991), 33–60.

11. See David Weinstein and Yishay Yafeh, "On the Costs of a Bank-Centered Financial System: Evidence from the Changing Main-Bank Relations in Japan," *Journal of Finance* 53 (1998), 635–672.

12. See Joe Peek and Eric Rosengren, "The International Transmission of Financial Shocks: The Case of Japan," *American Economic Review* 87 (1998), 495–505.

13. See Charles Calomiris and Carlos Ramirez, "The Role of Financial Relationships in the History of American Corporate Finance," *Journal of Applied Corporate Finance* 9, no. 2 (Summer 1996), 52–74.

14. See, for example, Larry Lang and René Stulz, "Tobin's Q, Corporate Diversification, and Firm Performance," *Journal of Political Economy* 102 (1994), 1248–1291; and Philip Berger and Eli Ofek, "Diversification's Effect on Firm Value," *Journal of Financial Economics* 37 (1995), 39–65.

15. See Raghuram Rajan, Henri Servaes, and Luigi Zingales, "The Costs of Diversity: The Diversification Discount and Inefficient Investment," mimeo, University of Chicago, http://gsblgz.uchicago.edu.

16. Graham Barr, Jos Gerson, and Brian Kantor, "Shareholders as Agents and Principals: The Case for South Africa's Corporate Ownership Structure," *Journal of Applied Corporate Finance* 8, no. 1 (Spring 1995). Part of the groups' superior performance is attributed to the opportunities for diversification they provide large South African investors—opportunities that are likely to be valuable in regimes, like South Africa's, with relatively binding capital controls.

17. See Arun Khanna and Krishna Palepu, "Corporate Scope and Institutional Context: An Empirical Analysis of Diversified Indian Groups," Harvard Business School Working Paper (1997).

18. See Larry Fauver, Joel Houston, and Andy Naranjo, "Capital Market Development, Legal Systems, and the Value of Corporate Diversification: A Cross-Country Analysis," University of Florida Working Paper (1998).

19. This evidence should be viewed as preliminary, because Lins and Servaes find a conglomerate discount in six of the seven emerging markets they examine (see Karl Lins and Henri Servaes, "Is Corporate Diversification Beneficial in Emerging Markets?," London Business School Working Paper (1998).

20. See Khanna and Palepu, cited earlier.

21. For example, even Germany is moving toward U.S. accounting standards and has recently developed a vibrant market for high-tech initial public offerings.

22. For an excellent overview of the East Asian Crisis, see the articles on Nouriel Roubini's web page at http://www.stern.nyu.edu/~nroubini/asia/AsiaHomepage.html. In particular, see Nouriel Roubini, Giancarlo Corsetti and Paolo Pesenti, "What Caused the Asian Currency and Financial Crisis?," New York University Working Paper (1998); and Steve Radelet and Jeffrey Sachs, "The Onset of the East Asian Financial Crisis," Harvard University Working Paper (1998).

23. These countries had stock markets, which could have been a source of price signals. But disclosure rules were often inadequate and the monitoring institutions that exist in more developed economies—such as auditors, analysts, and rating agencies—are still relatively undeveloped.

24. For example, even if creditors could learn enough to know the firm was defunct, bankruptcy laws existed largely on the books.
25. This is very similar to the way depositors keep bank management in check by threatening to run in case of trouble (see Charles Calomiris and Charles Kahn, "The Role of Demandable Debt in Structuring Optimal Banking Arrangements," *American Economic Review* 81 (1991), 497–513; and Douglas Diamond and Raghuram Rajan, "Liquidity Risk, Liquidity Creation and Financial Fragility: A Theory of Banking," Working Paper, University of Chicago).
26. See George Benston, *The Separation of Commercial and Investment Banking* (Oxford: Oxford University Press, 1990), and Randall Kroszner and Raghuram G. Rajan, "Is the Glass Steagall Act Justified? Evidence from the U.S. Experience with Universal Banking, 1921–1933," *American Economic Review* 84 (1994), 810–832.
27. See Raghuram Rajan, "Why Bank Credit Policies Fluctuate: A Theory and Some Evidence," *Quarterly Journal of Economics* 109 (1994), 399–442.
28. See Raghuram Rajan, "Why Bank Credit Policies Fluctuate: A Theory and Some Evidence," *Quarterly Journal of Economics* 109 (1994), 399–442.
29. For another view on the necessity of capital controls, see Paul Krugman, "Saving Asia: It's Time to Get Radical," *Fortune* (September 7, 1998).

Country-Specific Evidence on Ownership and Governance Structure

Corporate Governance in India

RAJESH CHAKRABARTI, WILLIAM L. MEGGINSON,
AND PRADEEP K. YADAV

ONE OF THE MAJOR ECONOMIC DEVELOPMENTS of this decade has been the recent take-off of India, with growth rates averaging in excess of 8% for the past four years, a stock market that has more than tripled in as many years, and a steady inflow of foreign investment. In 2006, total equity issuance reached $19.2 billion in India, up 22% from the year before. Indian companies were also among the world's most active issuers of depositary receipts in the first half of 2006, accounting for one in three new issues globally. Debt issuance reached an all-time high of $13.7 billion, up 28% from a year earlier. And merger and acquisition volume was a record $27.8 billion, up 38%. Much of that increase in M&A was driven by a 371% increase in "outbound" acquisitions—purchases by Indian companies of non-Indian firms—which exceeded inbound deal volumes for the first time.

The equity shares of about 5,000 companies are now listed and traded on India's two major stock exchanges, the Bombay Stock Exchange (BSE) and the National Stock Exchange of India (NSE). As can be seen in figure 8.1A, this is comparable to the number of companies traded on the NASDAQ and the New York Stock Exchange *combined,* and well above the number traded on the London Stock Exchange or Euronext. What's more, in both 2005 and 2006, the number of trades on the NSE was the third highest in the world, just behind NASDAQ and the NYSE, and several times the number of trades on the LSE or Euronext (see figure 8.1B). And the number of derivatives trades on the NSE is also several times that of Euronext or London, and is catching up with U.S. derivatives exchanges (see figure 8.1C). But, unlike anywhere else in the world, most (78%) of the trading interest in derivatives is in *individual* company stock futures and options rather than index derivatives. And more than half (though only 36% by value) of the trades in individual equities are by individual traders rather than institutions or corporate entities.[1] All this suggests increased corporate ownership by individual investors, which in turn

Panel A: Number of Companies Traded in India and on Other Major Stock Exchanges

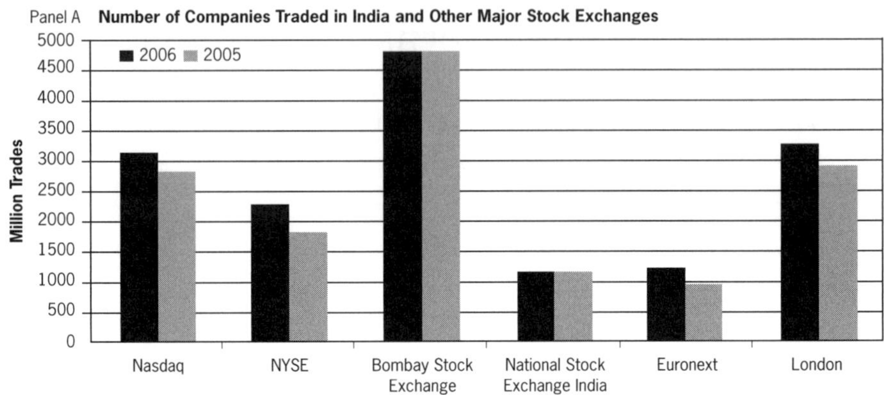

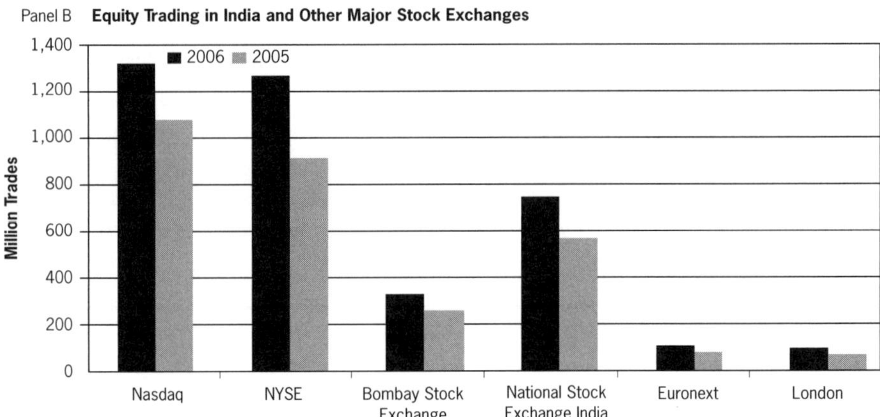

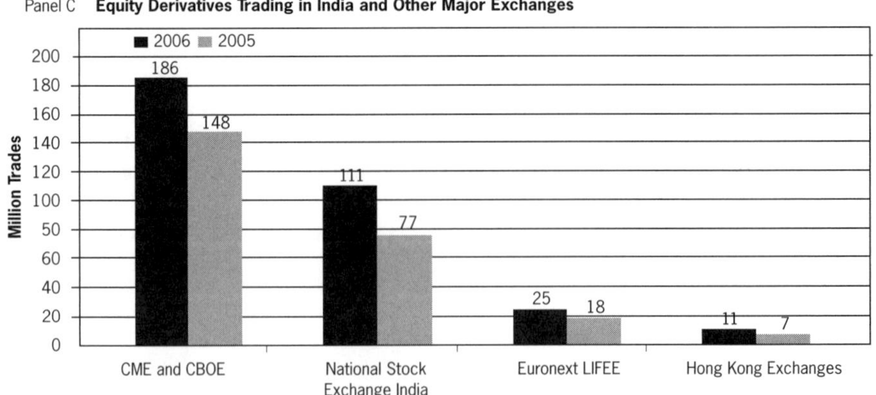

Source: World Federation of Exchanges 2006 Annual Report.

could provide significant incentives for the growth of effective corporate governance practices in India.

But widely dispersed stock ownership by individuals, as commonly exists in the U.S. and the U.K., is by no means the norm in Indian companies. And one of the biggest challenges facing Indian corporate governance is reflected by—and to a certain extent stems from—the ownership structure of its companies. Even among India's largest publicly traded companies, shareholdings remain relatively concentrated, and *de facto* control even more so, with family business groups and, to a lesser extent, state-owned (or public sector) enterprises continuing to dominate the corporate sector. As recently as 2006 (see figure 8.2), some 60% of India's 500 largest companies (comprising about 65% of the total market capitalization of the Bombay Stock Exchange) were affiliated with these business groups.[2] And another 11% of these companies (accounting for another 22% of the market capitalization) are companies wholly or significantly owned by the central (federal) government or state governments.

Such concentration of ownership is not surprising. In fact it tends to be the norm in developing economies (and in many developed economies as well), providing all but the largest business enterprises with an effective means of dealing with information and contract enforcement problems that arise from relatively weak legal protection of minority stockholders (and property rights generally).[3] In this sense, India's current ownership structure can be viewed in large part as a legacy from its weak governance system of the past. But if such concentrated ownership has contributed to India's past growth, it also provides the controlling shareholders with both the temptation and the means to exploit the minority or non-family holders. Studies of Indian business groups have produced evidence of significant "tunneling" activity—that is, related company transactions that have the effect of transferring assets and cash flows from minority to controlling shareholders.[4] Facilitating this activity, and compounding the problem of "outside" investors, the actual ownership within these companies is far from transparent, with widespread pyramiding, cross-holding, and the use of non-public trusts and private companies for owning shares in group companies.

Even in companies that are not controlled by families, the widespread presence and influence in Indian corporate governance of what are called "promoters" are, at least potentially, cause for concern. A "promoter" is generally understood to mean the "entrepreneur"—whether an individual, a corporate entity, or a government institution[5]—that establishes and continues to have effective control of the business. And since the status of "promoter" gets effectively transferred through sale of the business to a new owner, perhaps a better definition is an individual or entity with a "controlling interest" in the business (with 20% or more equity holding, according to the definition of the *Securities and Exchange Board of India* [SEBI]).

Distribution of 500 Largest Indian Companies among Different Ownership and Control Categories

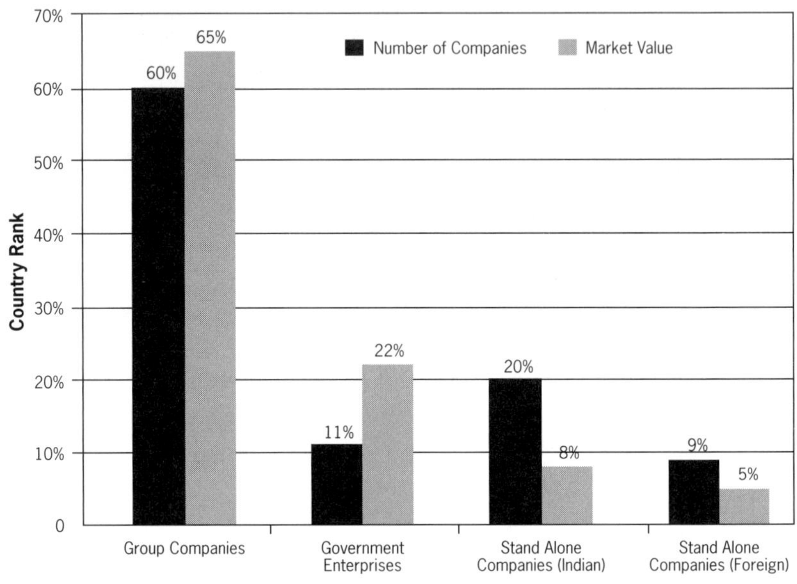

Source: Prowess.

As one indication of the pervasiveness of promoters, a 2005 study of the shareholdings of some 2,500 Indian listed manufacturing companies at the end of 2002 reported that promoters held roughly 48% of the shares, accounting for about 51% of the shares of the family group companies and 46% of the shares of the other, so-called stand-alone firms.[6] By comparison, the Indian public's share amounted to just 35% of the total sample, including 28% of the group companies and 38.5% of the stand-alone firms. Moreover, as reported in a follow-up study by the same authors, there were very few Indian companies with widely held ownership and no significant "single-promoter control." In 2003, as the study reported, less than 2% of the 500 largest Indian companies had no single shareholder with at least 5% ownership—and less than 6% of the companies lacked a single blockholder with at least 15%. At the same time, 88% of the companies had promoters with at least 25% positions, and 46% had single shareholders with 50% ownership or more.[7]

To provide the reader with a better sense of the identity and influence of such promoters, figure 8.3 shows the percentage shareholdings of different kinds of shareholders for the same 500 largest Indian companies described in figure 8.2. On average, as already suggested, promoters own just over 50% of

FIGURE 8.3

Types of Promoters in the 500 Largest Companies in India

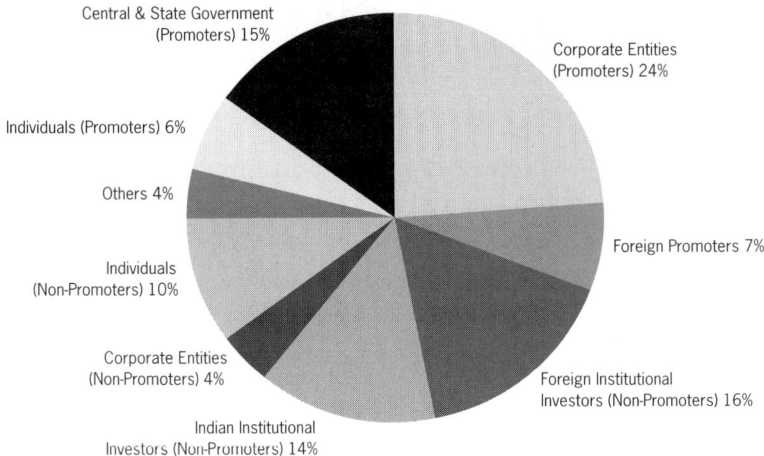

Source: Prowess.

the shareholding of these companies. Of this total, Indian corporate promoters account for the largest share (24%), while governments account for about 15%, Indian individuals for 6%, and foreigners (mostly companies) for 7%.

But it's important to remember that this picture of Indian corporate ownership is a snapshot of the past. And while the present probably doesn't look much different, the future, thanks to some fairly recent changes in Indian corporate governance, could look quite different. As one suggestive indicator of future developments, figure 8.3 shows significant (non-promoter) holdings (14%) in India's largest companies by Indian institutional investors, mainly banks, financial institutions, mutual funds, and insurance companies. And even more telling, at least in terms of the future of Indian corporate governance, foreign institutional investors accounted for 16% of the shares.

In the next section of this chapter, we describe the historical evolution of corporate governance in India, while focusing on reforms that have been initiated since the start of the major economic liberalization in the early 1990s. Then we offer a current assessment of the legal and institutional aspects of investor protection and corporate governance in India, both the letter of the law and the reality of its implementation. Finally, we review the recent academic literature on corporate governance in India. As described in the pages that follow, the recent history of Indian corporate governance, while clearly not without problems and challenges, is rich in accomplishments and perhaps richer in promise.

Historical Background

The historical development of Indian corporate law and regulation has been marked by many contrasts. At independence in 1947, India inherited one of the world's poorest economies, but one with a manufacturing sector that accounted for a tenth of the national product. The country also inherited four functioning stock markets with the Bombay Stock Exchange predating the Tokyo Stock Exchange, with clearly defined rules governing listing, trading, settlements, a well-developed equity culture (if only among the urban rich), and a banking system with well-developed lending norms and recovery procedures.[8] Thus, in terms of its corporate laws and financial system, India emerged far better endowed than most other former colonies, British or otherwise. The 1956 Companies Act built on this foundation, as did other laws governing the functioning of joint-stock companies and protection of investors' rights.

Early corporate developments in India were dominated by the rise and spread of what is known as the "managing agency system." This set of ownership structures and financing arrangements contributed to the birth of a limited kind of dispersed equity ownership—one that enabled management to achieve "control rights" that were disproportionate to their stock ownership. Moreover, the turn toward socialism in the decades after independence, marked by passage of the 1951 Industries (Development and Regulation) Act and the 1956 Industrial Policy Resolution, put in place a regime and a culture of licensing, protection, and red tape that bred corruption and stifled the growth of the corporate sector. The situation worsened in subsequent decades, and corruption, nepotism, and inefficiency became the hallmarks of the Indian corporate sector. Exorbitant tax rates encouraged creative accounting practices and gave companies incentives to develop complicated emolument structures with large "under-the-table" compensation at senior levels.

Under these circumstances, India predictably failed to develop deep and liquid equity markets. And in the absence of a stock market capable of raising equity capital efficiently, three central (federal) government development finance institutions (the Industrial Finance Corporation of India, the Industrial Development Bank of India, and the Industrial Credit and Investment Corporation of India), together with about 30 other state government-owned development finance institutions, became the main providers of long-term credit to companies. Along with the central government-owned and managed mutual fund, the Unit Trust of India, these institutions also held (and continue to hold) large blocks of shares in the companies to which they lent, and had board representation in the form of nominee directors who typically played very passive roles in the boardroom.

The corporate bankruptcy and reorganization system also had serious problems. Until recently India's system has been driven primarily by the 1985

Sick Industrial Companies Act (SICA), which considers a company "sick" only after its entire net worth has been eroded, and it has been referred to the Board for Industrial and Financial Reconstruction (BIFR) for a decision on reorganization or liquidation. As soon as a company was registered with the BIFR, it won immediate protection from creditors' claims for at least four years. Between 1987 and 1992, the BIFR took well over two years, on average, just to reach a decision to restore or liquidate. Very few companies emerged successfully from the BIFR and, even for those that were liquidated, the legal process took over ten years on average, by which time the assets of the company were usually almost worthless.[9]

In sum, protection of creditors' rights had existed only on paper in India, and its bankruptcy process was perennially ranked among the worst in World Bank surveys on business climate. This could well explain why Indian banks have historically under-lent and invested primarily in government securities.

Though financial disclosure norms in India have traditionally been superior to those in most Asian countries, non-compliance with disclosure norms had been rampant and even the failure of auditors' reports to conform to the law attracted only nominal fines and little punitive action. The Institute of Chartered Accountants in India has rarely taken action against erring auditors.

While the 1956 Companies Act provided an excellent framework for disclosure and protection of minority shareholders, including clear instructions for maintaining and updating share registers, in practice minority shareholders had often suffered from irregularities in share transfers and registrations. In some cases non-voting preferential shares had been used by promoters to channel funds and expropriate minority shareholders. There were cases in which the rights of minority shareholders had been compromised by management's private deals in the relatively infrequent event of corporate takeovers. And corporate boards had often been largely ineffective in their monitoring role, and their independence perceived as highly questionable.

For most of the post-Independence era, then, Indian equity markets were neither liquid nor sophisticated or powerful enough to exert effective control over companies. Although listing requirements of exchanges called for some transparency, non-compliance was neither rare nor punished. All in all, minority shareholders and creditors in India had remained effectively unprotected despite the laws on the books. But this dismal regulatory environment began to change rapidly after the monumental economic reforms and major liberalization programs initiated by the Indian government in the early 1990s.

Economic Reform and Modern Corporate Governance

Liberalization of the Indian economy accelerated significantly in 1991, when the Finance Minister, Dr. Manmohan Singh—now the Prime Minister of

India—introduced measures that reduced import controls and tariffs, reduced licensing requirements for industry while opening up the energy and telecommunication sectors to the private sector, created an environment more attractive to foreign investment, and made the rupee convertible for current account transactions. Since then, India has witnessed wide-ranging changes in both laws and regulations, as well as a major transformation of its corporate sector and corporate governance landscape.

In 1991 India had only one major stock exchange—the Bombay Stock Exchange (BSE), the oldest stock exchange in Asia, established in 1875. Until 1992 the BSE was a monopoly, an association of brokers characterized by high entry costs, settlement and administrative inefficiencies, high costs of intermediation, no price-time priorities or guarantees of best execution, and manipulative practices. As a consequence, external market users often found themselves at a serious disadvantage.

The economic reforms of the early 1990s created four new institutions: the National Stock Exchange of India (NSE), the Securities and Exchange Board of India (SEBI), the National Securities Clearing Corporation (NSCC), and the National Securities Depository. Established in 1994, the NSE is a limited liability company owned by public sector financial institutions and now accounts for about two-thirds of the stock trading in India, as well as virtually all of its derivatives trading. The National Securities Clearing Corporation is the legal counterparty to net obligations of each brokerage firm, and thereby eliminates counterparty risk and the possibility of payments crises. Thanks to a rigorous "risk containment" framework involving collateral and intraday monitoring, and with the help of the National Securities Depository, the NSCC has compiled a track record of reliable settlement schedules since its inception in the mid-1990s.

But perhaps the single most important development in the field of corporate governance and investor protection in India has been the establishment of the Securities and Exchange Board of India (SEBI) in 1992 and its gradual and growing empowerment since then. SEBI has introduced a rigorous regulatory regime to ensure fairness and transparency. To improve transparency, for example, SEBI has mandated disclosure of all transactions where the total quantity of shares is more than 0.5% of the equity of the company. Immediately after the execution of a trade, brokers must disclose to the Exchange the name of the client and other trade details, and the Exchange must then disseminate this information to the general public on the same day. The resulting environment of improved transparency, fairness, and efficient regulation also allowed the BSE to become a transparent electronic limit order book market in 1996, with an efficient trading system similar to that of the NSE. And as noted earlier, the trading of equity and equity derivatives in India has skyrocketed to record levels over the last ten years.

But while established primarily to regulate and monitor stock trading, the SEBI has also played a crucial role in establishing the basic minimum ground rules of corporate conduct. Concerns about corporate governance in India were triggered in large part by a spate of crises in the early 1990s—particularly the Harshad Mehta stock market scam of 1992—followed by a series of cases in which companies allotted preferential shares to their promoters at deeply discounted prices, or simply disappeared with investors' money.[10] These concerns about corporate governance, coupled with a perceived need to open up the corporate sector to the forces of competition and globalization, gave rise to several investigations into ways to fix the corporate governance situation in India.

One of the first such efforts was the Confederation of Indian Industry's Code for Desirable Corporate Governance, which was developed by a committee chaired by Rahul Bajaj, a leading industrial magnate. The committee was formed in 1996 and submitted its guidelines in April 1998. Then the SEBI formed two committees to look into the issue of corporate governance—the first chaired by Kumar Mangalam Birla, another leading industrial magnate, and the second by Narayana Murthy, the co-chair and cofounder of Infosys.[11] The first committee submitted its report in early 2000, and the second in 2004. These two committees have helped bring about far-reaching changes in Indian corporate governance, in large part by formulating Clause 49 of Listing Agreements (discussed in more detail below).

Along with these initiatives primarily by the SEBI, the Department of Company Affairs and the Ministry of Finance of the Government of India also began contemplating improvements in corporate governance. These efforts included the establishment of a study group to operationalize the Birla Committee recommendations in 2000, the Naresh Chandra Committee on Corporate Audit and Governance in 2002, and the Expert Committee on Corporate Law (J.J. Irani Committee) in late 2004. All of these efforts were aimed at reforming the existing Companies Act of 1956 that still forms the backbone of corporate law in India.

Clause 49

The SEBI implemented the recommendations of the Birla Committee by enacting Clause 49 of the Listing Agreements. Similar in spirit and scope to the Sarbanes-Oxley (SOX) measures in the U.S., Clause 49 has clearly been a milestone in the evolution of corporate governance practices in India. As initially applied in March 2001, the requirements of Clause 49 were binding on the companies in the BSE 200 and S&P, C&X, and NIFTY stock indices, and on all companies listing thereafter.[12] The Narayana Murthy Committee worked on further refining the rules, and Clause 49 was amended in 2004.

The key mandatory features of Clause 49 regulations deal with the following: (1) composition of the board of directors; (2) the composition and functioning of the audit committee; (3) governance and disclosures regarding subsidiary companies; (4) disclosures by the company; (4) CEO/CFO certification of financial results; and (5) reporting on corporate governance as part of the annual report.

The composition and proper functioning of the board of directors was one of the key areas of focus. Clause 49 stipulates that non-executive members should comprise at least half of a board of directors. It defines an "independent" director and requires that independent directors comprise at least half of a board of directors if the chairperson is an executive director and at least a third if the chairperson is a non-executive director. It also lays down rules regarding compensation of board members, sets caps on committee memberships and chairmanships, specifies the minimum number and frequency of board meetings, and mandates certain disclosures for board members.

Clause 49 also pays special attention to the composition and functioning of the audit committee, requiring at least three members on it, with an independent chair and made up of two-thirds independent directors, including at least one "financially literate" person. The Clause also spells out the role and powers of the audit committee and specifies the minimum number and frequency of the committee meetings.

With regard to "material" non-listed subsidiary companies,[13] Clause 49 requires that at least one independent director of the holding company serve on the board of the subsidiary. The audit committee of the holding company should review the subsidiary's financial statements, particularly its investment plans. The minutes of the subsidiary's board meetings should be presented at the board meeting of the holding company, and the board members of the latter should be made aware of all "significant" transactions—those likely to exceed in value 10% of the total revenues or assets of the subsidiary—entered into by the subsidiary.

Clause 49 also requires companies to provide specific corporate disclosures of the following: (1) related party transactions;[14] (2) disclosure of accounting treatment (if deviating from Accounting Standards); (3) risk management procedures; (4) proceeds from various kinds of share issues; (5) remuneration of directors; (6) a Management Discussion and Analysis section in the annual report discussing general business conditions and outlook; and (7) background and committee memberships of new directors as well as presentations to analysts. In addition, a board committee with a non-executive chair is required to address shareholder or investor grievances. Finally, share transfer, a long-standing problem in India, must be done expeditiously.

As required in the U.S. by SOX, the CEO and CFO or their equivalents must sign off on the company's financial statements and disclosures and accept responsibility for establishing and maintaining effective internal control systems. The company is also required to provide a separate section of corporate governance in its annual report, with a detailed compliance report on corporate governance. It is also required to submit a quarterly compliance report to the stock exchange where it is listed. Finally, it must have its compliance with the mandatory specifications of Clause 49 certified by auditors or by practicing company secretaries.[15]

As stated, then, the provisions of Clause 49 closely mirror those of Sarbanes-Oxley in the U.S. In some areas, like certification compliance, the Indian requirements are even stricter than those of SOX. But there are other areas where Indian requirements are notably more lax. For example, in cases where Indian companies have boards run by non-executive chairs, the required proportion of independent directors is lower than for boards run by executive chairs.

How did the Indian stock market react to the corporate governance improvements sought by Clause 49? The response seems to have been quite positive, in contrast to the decidedly mixed reaction of U.S. markets to Sarbanes-Oxley's adoption. Bernard Black and Vikramaditya Khanna devised a clever event-study approach to measure the stock price impact of the adoption of Clause 49 by Indian companies.[16] Focusing on the May 7, 1999, announcement by SEBI of the Birla Committee's recommendations, when Clause 49 was expected to apply only to large companies, the study reports that the large companies that first adopted these measures saw their stock prices appreciate by 4% more during a two-day "event-window" (and 7% more over a five-day period) than the prices of the smaller Indian companies that were *not* expected to be required to implement the reforms.

Changes in Bank Governance

The reforms adopted since 1991 have reflected a pronounced shift from hands-on government control to market forces as the dominant instrument of corporate governance in Indian banks.[17] Competition has been encouraged by the issuance of licenses to new private banks and by giving more power and flexibility to bank managers, both in directing credit and in setting prices. The Reserve Bank of India (RBI), India's central bank, has moved away from a regulatory model of direct interference to one of governance by "prudential norms," to the point of even allowing debate about the appropriateness of specific regulations among banks. Along with these changes, market institutions have been strengthened by government actions attempting to bring greater transparency and liquidity into markets for government securities and other asset markets.

This market orientation of governance in banking has been accompanied by stronger disclosure norms and greater stress on periodic RBI surveillance. Since 1994, the Board for Financial Supervision (BFS) has been monitoring banks using the "CAMELS" approach.[18] And audit committees in banks have been required since 1995. Greater independence of public sector banks has also been a key feature of the reforms. Nominee directors from government and the

RBI are being gradually phased out, with increased emphasis on boards being elected rather than "appointed from above." More attention has also been paid to increasing professional representation on bank boards, with the expectation that the boards will have the authority and competence to manage the banks within the broad prudential norms set by the RBI.

As for the old private banks, concentrated ownership remains a widespread feature, limiting the prospects for professional excellence while failing to address the possibility of misallocating credit. But it is the governance systems in cooperative banks and non-bank financial companies that are perhaps in need of the most attention from regulators. Rural cooperative banks are frequently run as personal fiefdoms by politically powerful families, with little professional involvement and considerable channeling of credit to family businesses. While it is widely believed that the "new" private banks—those established after the reforms of the 1990s—have better management and corporate governance systems in place,[19] the recent collapse of the private Global Trust Bank and its subsequent acquisition by a public sector bank have aroused skepticism, as well as reinforcing the popular view that the government will ultimately bail out failing banks.

Finally, it is worth noting that India has one of the best banking sectors in Asia in terms of the ratio of non-performing assets. India's NPL ratio, at around 4% of total banking assets, is far below those of China (or Japan) and most other Asian and emerging markets.

Public Sector Governance in India

Public Sector Enterprises (PSEs), or what are typically referred to elsewhere as "state-owned enterprises," have played a major role in India's mixed economy and industrialization since the 1950s. The Industrial Policy Resolution of 1956 reserved the "commanding heights" of the economy for the public sector; and in the three and a half decades that have since passed, the number of central (federal) PSEs in India climbed steadily from 5 to 242—both through nationalization and the establishment of new units. In addition, there are also many smaller PSEs that are promoted and owned by different state governments.

During the period 2005–2006, the central (federal) public sector itself accounted for over 11% of India's GDP, over 27% of its industrial output, and over a third of central government receipts. Moreover, as noted earlier, PSEs account for over 20% of the market capitalization of the Bombay Stock Exchange, and five of the six Indian companies on the Fortune 500 companies in 2006 were central PSEs[20] (the only non-PSE on the list is Reliance Industries).

Although the cumulative profits of the PSEs have gone up over time, their performance has always been a concern, with close to half of the PSEs incurring losses. In the past, as these enterprises came under the purview of the government, they were often subjected to political interference and governance by rigid bureaucratic norms rather than with the aim of improving performance and profitability. An important break with this tradition occurred in 1987, with the adoption of memoranda of understanding (MoUs) between the enterprises and the government that gave greater functional autonomy to the PSEs in return for their commitment to the government to meet more demanding performance targets. MoUs specified various targets, with gross profit margin and return on capital employed generally assigned the largest weights (30% each).

By the end of 2000, 107 PSEs had signed MoUs with the government. Thanks to their adoption of MoUs, PSEs have gained increased operating autonomy and moved gradually to a "board managed corporation" model rather than reporting to government ministry officials directly. In 1997, nine large and profitable central PSEs, now referred to as the *Navratnas* (or "nine jewels"), were granted even greater autonomy than others, including the right to form joint ventures and engage in mergers and acquisitions. Since then, 97 other profitable PSEs have attained the status of *mini-Ratnas* and, with it, greater autonomy than before.

In general, Indian PSEs are gradually being separated from direct government control, with the more profitable ones gaining autonomy faster. Yet another major step in the administration of PSEs has been the constitution in 2004 of the Board for Reconstruction of PSEs (BRPSE), which now acts as the agency in charge of the reconstruction (or liquidation) of PSEs in financial distress. All of these are extremely positive developments from a corporate governance perspective.

Partial privatization (or "disinvestment," as it is called in India) of PSEs emerged as a policy objective in 1991, with the initiation of economic reforms. But disinvestment has followed an uneven path in India, with unions and leftist political parties attempting to block almost every disinvestment effort. Nevertheless, 42 central PSEs had been partially privatized by the end of March 2005. In addition, between 1999 and 2004, there were 16 "strategic sales" with transfer of control. After 2004, however, the disinvestment process effectively stalled when the national elections of May 2004 yielded a coalition government that included left and communist parties as influential members—this despite the fact that the government was headed by the Congress party and the newly elected Prime Minister, Dr. Singh, who, as already noted, was the principal architect of India's economic reforms in the early 1990s.

The Institutional Environment in India:
A Current Assessment

Figure 8.4 provides an overview of several interesting indicators of the Indian institutional environment relative to the other major emerging economies,

Brazil, China, and Russia, now popularly labeled the "BRIC" countries. The figure shows country rankings on a variety of attributes that are reported by *Doing Business 2008*, a World Bank publication,[21] and the 2007 report of Transparency International. A country rank of 1 is best, and the ranking covers 178 countries in the World Bank analyses, and 180 countries in the case of Transparency International.

Business Laws and Regulations

The Indian legal system is built on English common law and, on paper, provides one of the highest levels of investor protection in the world. India has a "shareholder rights index" of 5 (out of a maximum possible of 6), the *highest* of any country in the rankings presented by Rafael La Porta, Florencio Lòpez-de-Silanes, Andrei Shleifer, and Rob Vishny in their much cited 1998 study.[22] Equivalent to that of the U.S., U.K., Canada, Hong Kong, Pakistan, and South Africa (all English-law countries), India's ranking on this dimension was higher than that of all the other 42 countries in the study, including countries like France, Germany, Japan, and Switzerland.

In terms of creditor rights, the Indian legal system also appears to provide excellent protection for lenders, according to the La Porta et al. rankings. With no automatic stay on assets in the reorganization phase, its requirement that secured creditors are to be paid first, its restrictions on going into reorganization, and its provision for replacing management in reorganizations, India has a creditor rights index of 4 (the maximum possible), higher than that of Australia, Canada, Ireland, New Zealand, and the U.S. *Doing Business 2008* also

FIGURE 8.4

Ease of Doing Business: BRIC Country Rankings
Rankings are based on World Bank Doing Business 2008 and the 2007 Report of Transparency International. The best possible country rank is 1 and the worst possible is 178 for most of the indicators below.

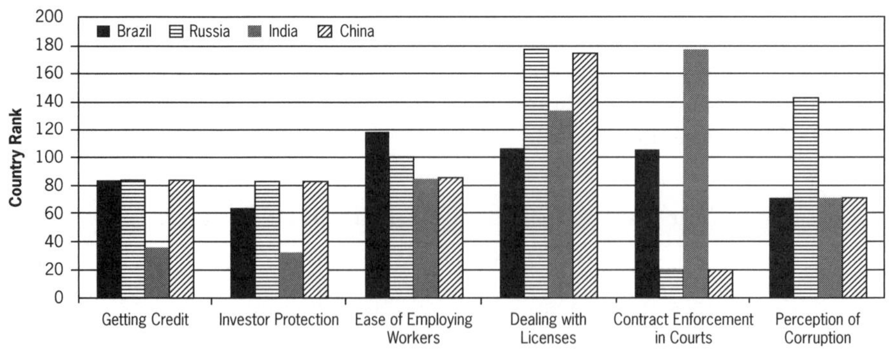

gives India a relatively high score of 6 on creditors' rights, well ahead of other major emerging economies, including Brazil (2), China (3), and Russia (3).

But when it comes to enforcement, the La Porta et al. index, constructed from figures obtained from private country risk rating agencies, suggest that the *de facto* protection of investor's rights in India lags significantly behind the *de jure* protection. India has a score of 4.17 on the "rule-of-law" index, ranking 41st out of 49 countries studied. To be sure, India gets a score of 8 out of 10 on the "efficiency of judicial system" variable, just behind the English-law average of 8.15, and higher than the overall sample average of 7.67. And India's accounting standards are also better than the sample average across all countries rated, though lagging behind all of the other English-origin countries rated.

On the matter of corruption, India has been ranked 72nd out of 180 countries in the *Corruption Perception Index 2007* published by *Transparency International.* This index is a "composite index, a poll of polls, drawing on corruption-related data from expert and business surveys" carried out by 14 sources representing 12 independent institutions, that reflects assessments of the "degree to which corruption is perceived to exist among public officials and politicians." It focuses on the public sector and on abuse of public office for private gain, for example, bribery, kickbacks in procurement, embezzlement, and the strength of anti-corruption policies. India has a corruption perception index of 3.5, with a "confidence interval" of 3.3 to 3.7. Scores from 3 to 5 are said to indicate that corruption is perceived to be a "serious challenge" while scores below 3 indicate "rampant corruption." Interestingly, Brazil and China have the same corruption perception index of 3.5, albeit with wider confidence intervals, while Russia has a much lower index of 2.3 (and a country rank of 143). By comparison, the U.S. is ranked 20th with an index of 7.6.

Red tape and regulation are among the main deterrents to business and foreign investment in India, leading to its latest overall ranking of 120 out of 178 in *Doing Business 2008,* behind China (83) and Russia (106), but slightly ahead of Brazil (122). India is ranked 111th out of 178 for the ease of starting a business, worse than Russia (50th) but better than Brazil (122nd) and China (135). India's entrepreneurs must follow, on average, 13 procedures over 33 days, which, though worse than the global average, compares favorably with the average of 13 procedures over 72 days for the other BRIC countries. Delays and costs of dealing with licenses in India are also far worse than the global average, with India ranked 134th out of 178, worse than Brazil ranked 107th, but still much better than China (175) and Russia (177).

However, India scores well on getting credit. It is ranked 36th, significantly ahead of Brazil, China, and Russia, which are all tied at 84th. India's creditors' rights score is particularly good, even though there is no credit information available from public registries, and there is a serious paucity of credit information available from private bureaus.

India is ranked 85th overall for the ease of employing workers, ahead of China (86), Russia (101), and Brazil (119). Payroll and social security taxes are 17% of salary in India, half the average of the other BRIC countries, but the costs of firing an employee are higher, at 56 weeks' salary, relative to the BRIC average of 50 weeks' salary. There is also considerable variation in labor laws across Indian states. And a study by Timothy Besley and Robin Burgess shows that, during the three-and-a-half decades before liberalization began in 1991, Indian states that followed more "pro-worker" policies experienced lower output, investment, employment, and productivity in the registered or formal sector, as well as higher urban poverty and increased informal sector output.[23]

Doing Business 2008 gives India an investor protection score of 6, ahead of each of the other BRIC countries. An extremely important aspect of investor protection in any country is securities markets regulation. Using La Porta et al.'s newer (2006) framework that evaluates the disclosure and liability requirements as well as enforcement of the regulations in national securities markets, India scores an impressive 0.92 in the index of disclosure requirements, which is the third highest after the U.S. and Singapore.[24] In the case of liability standards, India's score of 0.66 is the fifth highest, and relative to the sample mean is only 0.47. In terms of the quality of public enforcement—or the nature and powers of the supervisory authority—India's SEBI earns a score of 0.67, significantly higher than the overall sample average of 0.52 and the English-law country average of 0.62.

In comparing the regulatory powers and performance of the SEBI with those of the U.S. SEC, a 2005 study by Suchismita Bose concluded that while the scope of Indian securities laws is ambitious, there are significant problems in enforcing compliance, particularly in areas such as price manipulation and insider trading.[25] The study found, for example, that between 1999 and 2004, the SEBI took action in only 481 cases as compared to 2,789 cases by the SEC, even though the latter regulates a significantly more mature market. The SEBI took action against only 9% of the companies under its jurisdiction, while the SEC's corresponding figure was 52%. As for appeals before higher authorities, such as the Securities Appellate Tribunal or the Finance Ministry, the decisions have gone against the SEBI in 30% to 50% of cases. Though the SEBI has had some success prosecuting intermediaries, it has failed to convince the Securities Appellate Tribunal in its proceedings against corporate insiders and major market players.

With the aim of speeding up the judicial process to create higher debt recoveries and more efficient reorganizations of troubled companies, India established Debt Recovery Tribunals (DRTs) in the early 1990s and passed the Securitization and Reconstruction of Financial Assets and Enforcement of Security Interest (SARFAESI) Act in 2002. SARFAESI paved the way for the establishment of Asset Reconstruction Companies that take non-performing assets off the balance sheets of banks and recover them. The operations of these companies are restricted to asset reconstruction and securitization. SARFAESI also allows banks and financial institutions to seize the assets of a defaulting borrower that fails to respond within 60 days of a notice. Borrowers can appeal to a DRT only after the assets are seized and the Act allows the sale of seized assets.

But SARFAESI itself is by no means a complete solution to India's debt recovery problems. Thanks to distressed borrowers' right to approach the DRT, the DRAT (Debt Recovery Appellate Tribunal) and, in some cases, even a High Court, cases can easily be dragged out for three to four years, during which time the sale of the seized asset cannot take place. In the World Bank's *Ease of Doing Business Index,* India ranks 137th out of 178 in terms of ease of closing a business, and it continues to have the dubious distinction of being among the countries where it takes the "longest time to go through bankruptcy in the world" (ten years on average). Consequently, recovery rates have also been very low, below 12%, as compared to about 27% in the other BRIC countries.

At the heart of the problem is the absence of a single comprehensive and integrated policy on corporate bankruptcy in India along the lines of Chapter 11 or Chapter 7 of the U.S. bankruptcy code.[26] Overlapping jurisdictions of the High Courts, the Company Law Board, the Board for Industrial and Financial Reconstruction, and the Debt Recovery Tribunals all contribute to the delays and costs of bankruptcy.

But a solution to this problem has at least been set in motion. The Companies (Second Amendment) Act of 2002 has attempted to address this problem of overlapping jurisdictions by establishing a National Company Law Tribunal and stipulating a time-bound rehabilitation or liquidation process of less than two years. And while it is perhaps too soon to evaluate the effects of this measure and SARFAESI, public sector banks have had some notable success in recovering their loans by seizing and selling assets since the Act came into existence. The recovery rates of bad debts have risen sharply in 2005–2006 and after—on the other hand, the booming economy during this period may well be concealing a problem that remains to be addressed more effectively.

Enforcement of Corporate Governance Laws

Enforcement of corporate laws remains the soft underbelly of India's legal and corporate governance systems. The World Bank's 2004 *Reports on the Observance of Standards and Codes* (ROSC) concluded that while India observes or largely observes most of the principles, it could do better in many areas, including the use of nominee directors, the enforcement of laws and regulations pertaining to stock listing on major exchanges, insider trading, and dealing with violations of the Companies Act.[27] Some of these problems arise from unsettled questions about jurisdictional issues and powers of the SEBI.

Nevertheless, contract enforcement through the court system clearly remains a major problem in India. The *World Bank Doing Business 2008* publication ranks India virtually the worst in the world—177th out of 178—in terms of the efficiency of its judicial system in resolving commercial disputes.[28] The estimated time for contract enforcement was said to run as high as 1,420 days! But this is not surprising. Case arrears and decade-long legal battles are commonplace in India. Although it has some 10,000 courts (not counting tribunals and special courts), India has a serious shortage of judges. While the U.S. has 107 judges per million citizens, Canada over 75, Britain over 50, and Australia over 41, for India the figure is slightly over 10.[29] In April 2003, for instance, the Supreme Court of India had almost 25,000 cases pending before it.[30] In a 2004 study, Arnab Hazra and Maja Micevska reported that about 20 million cases were pending in lower courts and another 3.2 million cases in High Courts.[31] A termination dispute contested until all appeals are exhausted can take up to 20 years for disposal, while writ petitions in High Courts can take between 8 and 20 years. Almost two-thirds of pending civil cases are more than a year old, and almost a third are over three years old. Automatic appeals, extensive litigation by the government, underdeveloped alternative mechanisms of dispute resolution like arbitration, and the shortfall of judges all contribute to this unenviable state of delays in Indian courts. Since the same courts try both civil and criminal matters, and the latter get priority, economic disputes suffer even greater delays.

Legal Problems of Small and Medium-Sized Enterprises (SME) in India

The small and medium-sized enterprises (SME) sector in India has played, and continues to play, an important role in India's growth story. As in many other countries, this sector consists largely of family enterprises.

From their recent surveys of such businesses, Franklin Allen and his co-authors have concluded that small firms in India operate in a system governed almost completely by informal mechanisms based on trust, reciprocity, and reputation, with little recourse to the legal system.[32] The owners of these businesses also deal with widespread corruption. Over 80% of the firms surveyed required a license to start their businesses, and for about half of them obtaining the license was a difficult process. Government officials were most often the problem, which was usually solved through payment of bribes or by enlisting friends of government officials as negotiators. Clearly, networks and connections are critically important in negotiating with a government bureaucracy. As for conducting day-to-day business, legal concerns were said to be far less important than the unwritten codes of the informal networks in which the firms operate. In cases of default and breach of contract, the primary concern was said to be loss of reputation, followed closely by loss of property, with the fear of legal consequences being the least important concern. In fact, about half of the firms surveyed did *not* have a regular legal adviser, and less than half of those that did employed lawyers in that capacity. For mediation of a business dispute or to enforce a contract, the first choice was "mutual friends or business partners." Only 20% of the respondents mentioned going to courts as the first option, indicating that the legal system, while not completely ineffective, is clearly less cost-effective than the informal mechanisms.

The survey also provides evidence of serious credit constraints for firms in this sector, resulting in their ongoing reliance on informal finance. Relationship-based financing systems, which are characteristic of Asian countries, are generally far more important for these companies than the explicit arm's-length systems of governance and contracts observed in Western businesses.

Recent Findings about Corporate Governance in India

In the past few years, a burgeoning empirical literature has begun to document important features of corporate governance in India. We summarize some of the major findings in this section, beginning with research examining corporate board composition.

In India as in the U.S., studies have linked larger corporate boards to poor operating and stock-price performance.[33] One study showed that large company boards in India in the late 1990s were slightly smaller than those in the U.S., with 9.46 members on average in India, as compared to 11.45 in America.[34] While the percentage of inside directors was almost identical (25.38% as compared to 26% in the U.S.), Indian boards had relatively fewer independent directors (just over 54% as compared to 60% in the U.S.) and relatively more affiliated outside directors (over 20% versus 14% in the U.S.). Over 40% of the Indian companies also had a promoter on the board—and, in over 30% of the companies, the promoter also served as the chair.

As we noted at the beginning, shareholding patterns in India reveal a marked level of concentration in the hands of the "promoters," (i.e., the founding and controlling shareholders). As also reported earlier, a study by Jayati Sarkar and Subrata Sarkar reported that promoters own over 50% of a sample of almost 2,500 listed manufacturing companies.[35] As for the effect of concentrated shareholding on firm performance, an earlier study by these same authors reported that, during the period 1995–1996, holdings above 25% by directors and their relatives were associated with higher valuation of companies (while there was no clear effect below that threshold).[36]

Executive compensation in India, which was freed from strict regulation by the Companies Act of 1994, is another area of corporate governance that has received attention among researchers. In addition to retirement and other benefits and perquisites, managerial compensation in India often has two main components—salary and the performance-based bonus, or what is referred to as "commission." Based on her analysis of roughly 300 firms each year, Sonja Fagernäs reports that the average total compensation (salary plus commission) of Indian CEOs increased almost three-fold between 1998 and 2004 (from INR 2.1 million (≈$52,500) to INR 6.4 million (≈$160,000) in real terms.[37] During this period, the proportion of profit-based commission to total pay also rose steadily, from 13.4% to 25.6%; and the percentage of CEOs with commission as part of their pay package jumped from 34% to 51%. Meanwhile, executive compensation as a fraction of profits has also almost doubled, from 0.55% to 1.06%. In comparison, in 2000 average U.S. CEO compensation was 7.89% of corporate profits for companies included in the 1,500-company ExecuComp dataset.[38] CEO pay has thus clearly become more performance-based over the past decade. There is also some evidence that this increased performance-pay linkage has been influenced by the introduction of the corporate governance code or Clause 49. Fagernäs also reports that CEOs related to the founding family or directors are paid more than other CEOs.[39] She also presents evidence that the presence of directors from lending institutions lowers CEO pay while a higher percentage of independent directors on the board is associated with greater pay for performance.

Another recent study reports that, during the period 1997–2002, the average (of a sample of 462 manufacturing firms) *board* compensation in India was around INR 5.3 million (≈$132,500), with wide variation across firm size.[40] The average board compensation was INR 7.6 million (≈$190,000) for large firms and INR 2.5 million (≈$62,500) for small firms. Board compensation was also higher, on average, at INR 6.9 million ($172,500) when the CEO was related to the founding family.

Since almost two-thirds of the largest 500 Indian companies are group-affiliated, issues relating to corporate governance in business groups are naturally very important. As we noted earlier, tunneling, or "the transfer of assets and profits out of firms for the benefit of those who control them," is a major concern in business groups with pyramidal ownership structure and inter-firm cash flows.[41] A 2002 study reported finding that industry shocks result in 30% lower earnings growth for business group firms than for stand-alone firms in the same industry.[42] The study also reported that companies farther down the pyramidal structure were less affected by industry-specific shocks than those nearer the top, suggesting that positive shocks in the former are effectively buffered using the assets and cash flows of the latter, benefiting the controlling shareholders at the expense of the minority shareholders. On the other hand, Tarun Khanna and Yishay Yafeh question how such a practice would insulate them from negative shocks over longer periods of time.[43] And there is also some evidence that companies associated with business groups outperform stand-alone firms.[44]

More recently, Raja Kali and Jayati Sarkar argue that diversified business groups help increase the "opacity" of within-group fund flows, driving a broader "wedge" between control and cash flow rights and providing more opportunities for tunneling.[45] More specifically, after examining Indian companies in nearly 400 business groups during the period 2002–2004, the study reports that companies with greater ownership opacity and a smaller disparity between control and cash flow rights than those in a group's core activity were likely to be located farther away in the pyramid from the core activity—and, hence, were the most likely candidates for receiving tunneled cash flows and assets.

Using a sample of over 600 of the 1,000 largest Indian companies (in 2004), another study reported that, after controlling for other corporate governance characteristics, firm performance was negatively associated with the extent of related party transactions for group firms but positively so for stand-alone companies—a finding that adds to the circumstantial evidence on tunneling and its adverse effects.[46] The same study also showed, using a sample of over 5,000 firms for the period 2003–2005, that group companies consistently report higher levels of related party transactions than stand-alone companies—and that most related party transactions in India occur between the firm and related companies, such as joint ventures, fellow subsidiaries, and associated companies. (In the U.S., by contrast, the counterparties tend to be the firm's own management personnel.)

In addition to this tunneling problem, two cross-country studies published in 2003 have put India among the worst nations in terms of earnings opacity and management.[47] Indian accounting standards provide companies with considerable flexibility in financial reporting and differ from the International Accounting Standards (IAS) in several ways that can often make interpreting Indian financial statements relatively challenging. However, India is far from an extreme case in this matter. A 2007 analysis of international accounting policies reports that India continues to be below the median of a 49-country sample in terms of the number of deviations of its accounting code from the International Accounting Standards (India had eight deviations, as compared to a median of nine).[48]

Hostile takeovers and the market for corporate control, another potentially important force for more effective governance, have largely failed to emerge in India. Although M&A activity was very limited in India until the mid-1990s, things have picked up sharply since then.[49] And as we noted at the outset, such transactions achieved a record high in 2007. To the extent this activity continues, it should provide better managed and more valuable Indian companies with opportunities to acquire less efficient competitors. Moreover, to the extent Indian companies continue to acquire companies abroad, Indian regulators—largely resistant until now to the idea of "hostile" acquisitions, whether by foreign or local companies—may become more open to the possibility of an international market for corporate control operating within its own borders.

With regard to public sector governance, a 2005 study of 47 partial privatizations by Nandini Gupta finds that, even when control stays in government hands, such privatization has positive effects on the profitability, productivity, and investment of the privatized PSEs.[50] While Gupta attributes such changes primarily to the monitoring role of the markets, others have pointed out the difficulty of distinguishing these improvements from the disciplinary effects of the application of MoUs or "Performance Contracts" (that preceded privatization in 38 of the 47 cases).[51]

Conclusions

While on paper the Indian legal system provides one of the highest levels of investor protection in the world, the reality is different, with overburdened courts and significant corruption. Even though India has a well-functioning banking sector (with one of the lowest proportions of non-performing assets) and ranks high on the ease of getting credit, most of the country's many small and medium-sized enterprises (SME) continue to rely on relationship-based, informal control and governance mechanisms that limit financing and keep the cost of capital higher than perhaps necessary.

Moreover, even among large companies, shareholdings remain relatively concentrated, with "promoters" and family business groups continuing to dominate the corporate sector. There is significant pyramiding and tunneling among Indian business groups and, despite copious reporting requirements, evidence of earnings management. But all this is not surprising, since concentrated ownership and family control tend to be important in all countries where enforceable legal protection of minority property rights is relatively weak. In such circumstances, as economists have recognized, family-controlled businesses and relationship-based financing have the positive effects of reducing information and other transactions costs.

Most of the corporate governance problems discussed in these pages, far from being unique to India, are common in Asia and other developing economies. One of the main messages of this chapter is that corporate governance in India does not compare unfavorably with—and in many respects represents a major improvement over—the governance systems of the other major emerging economies: notably, Brazil, China, and Russia.

Moreover, despite its shortcomings in corporate governance, the Indian economy and its financial markets have started attaining impressive growth rates in recent years, and have shown an exceptionally high level of optimism. One important contributor to such optimism is India's clear commitment to maintaining and accelerating the major economic reforms and liberalization that were started in the early 1990s. Specifically, the Securities and Exchange Board of India that was established as a part of these reforms has made considerable progress in becoming a rigorous regulatory regime to ensure fairness, transparency, and good practice. And the National Stock Exchange of India, also established as part of the reforms, now functions with enough efficiency and transparency to generate the third largest number of trades in the world, just behind the NASDAQ and NYSE.

At the same time, the Indian corporate governance landscape has been changing very rapidly during the past decade, particularly with the enactment of the Sarbanes-Oxley-type measures in Clause 49 of the listing agreements, and the legal changes designed to improve the enforceability of creditors' rights. We are also seeing the rise of successful companies like Infosys that are completely free of the influence of a dominant family or group, and have made the individual shareholder their central governance focus. Thus there is strong momentum for continuing reforms that, by providing investors with better information and the promise of higher returns, should help Indian companies to sustain their remarkable growth.

Notes

1. See S. De, K. Kumar, and Pradeep K. Yadav, 2008, "Hiding Behind the Veil: Pre-Trade Transparency, Informed Trading, and Market Quality," Working Paper, Center for Analytical Finance at Indian School of Business, and the University of Oklahoma.
2. Based on 2006 data from *Prowess*.
3. See Raghuram Rajan and Luigi Zingales, "Which Capitalism? Lessons from the East Asia Crisis," *Journal of Applied Corporate Finance,* 11, Fall 1998.
4. An example of this literature is M. Bertrand, P. Mehta, and S. Mullainathan, "Ferreting Out Tunneling: An Application to Indian Business Groups," *Quarterly Journal of Economics* 117(1) 2002: 121–48.
5. As shown in figure 8.2, about 11% of Indian companies accounting for about 22% of the market capitalization are companies with largest blockholding by the central (federal) or state governments.
6. See Jayati Sarkar and Subrata Sarkar, 2005, "Multiple Board Appointments and Firm Performance in Emerging Economies: Evidence from India," Working Paper 2005–01, Indira Gandhi Institute of Development Research, Mumbai, India. See also Petia Topalova, 2004, "Overview of the Indian Corporate Sector: 1989–2002," IMF Working Paper No. 04/64.
7. See Jayati Sarkar and Subrata Sarkar, 2005, "Corporate Governance, Enforcement, and the Role of Non-Profit Organizations," Background Paper for IFMR Conference on Corporate Governance, IFMR, Chennai, India.
8. This section draws heavily on the history of Indian corporate governance by Omkar Goswami in "Corporate Governance in India," in *Taking Action against Corruption in Asia and the Pacific* (Manila: Asian Development Bank, 2002), chapter 9.
9. While SICA and BIFR still function, in recent years other avenues of reorganization like Debt Recover Tribunals and negotiated resolutions under the Securitization Act

(sometimes involving Asset Reconstruction Companies) are becoming increasingly important.

10. See Omkar Goswami, 2002, "Corporate Governance in India," in *Taking Action against Corruption in Asia and the Pacific* (Manila: Asian Development Bank), chapter 9.

11. Infosys, which is at the center of the Indian IT outsourcing success story, has been built using a widely held ownership structure rather than the traditional family-controlled Indian model. And Narayana Murthy, and his fellow co-chair at Infosys, Nandan Nilekani, have both led important corporate governance initiatives in India.

12. One year later, the requirements were extended to all companies with a paid-up capital of INR 100 million (≈ $2.5 million) or with a net worth of INR 250 million ($6.3 million) at any time in the past five years. And in March 2003, the requirements applied to all listed companies with a paid-up capital of over INR 30 million (≈ $0.75 million).

13. Defined as those with turnover/net worth exceeding 20% of a holding company's turnover or net worth.

14. In 2001, with the aim of reinforcing the effect of Clause 49, the Institute of Chartered Accountants in India (ICAI) adopted Accounting Standard (AS) 18, which requires, among other things, the reporting of related party transactions by Indian companies. Related parties include holding and subsidiary companies, key management personnel and their direct relatives, "parties with control" (which includes joint ventures and fellow subsidiaries), and other parties like promoters and employee trusts. Transactions that must be disclosed include purchase or sale of goods and assets, borrowing, lending and leasing, hiring and agency arrangements, guarantee agreements, transfer of research and development and management contracts. Adoption of this standard has been a major positive development in Indian corporate governance by bringing transparency to the dealings of Indian companies, particularly those of group-affiliates.

15. In addition to these mandatory requirements, Clause 49 also makes recommendations regarding the facilities provided a non-executive chairman, the remuneration committee, half-yearly reporting of financial performance to shareholders, progress toward unqualified financial statements, training and performance evaluation of board members, and the development of a clear "whistle blower" policy.

16. See Bernard Black and Vikramaditya Khanna, "Can Corporate Governance Reforms Increase Firms' Market Values? Evidence from India," *Journal of Empirical Legal Studies*, 4, 2007.

17. Reddy summarizes the reforms-era policies for corporate governance in Indian banks. See Y.V. Reddy, "Public Sector Banks and the Governance Challenge: The Indian Experience," *BIS Review* 25, 2002, Bank for International Settlements, Basle.

18. An acronym for Capital Adequacy, Asset Quality, Management, Earnings, Liquidity, and Systems and Controls.

19. See Rajesh Chakrabarti, 2006, *The Financial Sector in India: Emerging Issues* (with a foreword by Richard Roll) (New Delhi: Oxford University Press).

20. Indian Oil Corporation, Bharat Petroleum Corporation, Hindustan Petroleum Corporation Ltd., and Oil and Natural Gas Corporation, and State Bank of India (all listed at BSE and NSE).

21. See World Bank, 2008, *Doing Business 2008* (Washington, DC: World Bank and Oxford University Press).

22. See Rafael La Porta, Florencio Lopez-de-Silanes, Andrei Shleifer, and Rob Vishny, "Law and Finance," *Journal of Political Economy* 106, 1998: 1113–50.

23. See Timothy Besley and Robin Burgess, "Can Labor Regulation Hinder Economic Performance? Evidence from India," *Quarterly Journal of Economics,* 119, 2004: 91–134.

24. This index is described in Rafael La Porta, Florencio Lopez-de-Silanes, and Andrei Shleifer, "What Works in Securities Laws?" *Journal of Finance* 61, 2006: 1–32.

25. See Suchismita Bose, "Securities Markets Regulation: Lessons from US and Indian Experience," *Money and Finance,* Jan–June 2005: 83–124.

26. See Nimrit Kang and Nitin Nayar, "The Evolution of Corporate Bankruptcy Law in India," *Money and Finance,* Oct 3–Mar 4 2004: 37–58.

27. See World Bank, 2004, "Report on the Observance of Standards and Codes (ROSC), Corporate Governance Country Assessment: India, ROSC," World Bank–IMF, Washington, DC.

28. The supporting data were reportedly collected through study of the codes of civil procedure and other court regulations as well as surveys completed by local litigation lawyers.

29. These data are from Bibek Debroy, 1999, "Some Issues in Law Reform in India," in Jean-Jacques Dethier, ed., *Governance, Decentralization, and Reform in China, India, and Russia* (Boston: Kluwer Academic Publishers).

30. See Pravin Parekh, 2001, "Access to Justice" in "Souvenir of All India Seminar on 'Access to Justice,'" UNDP, 326–40, http://www.undp.org.in/events/AISAJ/.

31. See Arnab K. Hazra and Maja Micevska, 2004, "The Problem of Court Congestion: Evidence from Indian Lower Courts," Working Paper, University of Bonn.

32. See F. Allen, R. Chakrabarti, S. De, J. Qian, and M. Qian, 2006, "Financing Firms in India," Working Paper, The Wharton School.

33. See Saibal Ghosh, "Do Board Characteristics Affect Firm Performance? Firm-Level Evidence from India," *Applied Economic Letters* 13, 2006: 435–43.

34. See Jayati Sarkar and Subrata Sarkar, "Large Shareholder Activism in Developing Countries: Evidence from India," *International Review of Finance* 1, 2000: 161–94.

35. See Jayati Sarkar and Subrata Sarkar, 2005, "Multiple Board Appointments and Firm Performance in Emerging Economies: Evidence from India," Working Paper 2005–01, Indira Gandhi Institute of Development Research (IGIDR), Mumbai, India.

36. See Jayati Sarkar and Subrata Sarkar, "Large Shareholder Activism in Developing Countries: Evidence from India," *International Review of Finance* 1, 2000: 161–94.

37. See Sonja Fagernas, 2007, "How Do Family Ties, Boards, and Regulation Affect Pay at the Top? Evidence for Indian CEOs" Working Paper, University of Cambridge.

38. See Lucian Arye Bebchuk and Jesse M. Fried, "Executive Compensation as an Agency Problem," *The Journal of Economic Perspectives* 17(3) Summer 2003: 71–92.

39. Using a firm "fixed effects" model, she finds being related to the founding family can raise CEO pay by as much as 30% while being related to a director can cause an increase of about 10%.

40. See A. Ghosh, "Determination of Executive Compensation in an Emerging Economy: Evidence from India," *Emerging Markets Finance and Trade* 42, 2006: 66–90.

41. See S. Johnson, R. LaPorta, F. Lopez-de-Silanes, and A. Shleifer, "Tunneling," *American Economic Review* 90, 2000: 22–27.

42. See M. Bertrand, P. Mehta, and S. Mullainathan, "Ferreting Out Tunneling: An Application to Indian Business Groups," *Quarterly Journal of Economics* 117, 2002: 121–48.

43. See Tarun Khanna and Yishay Yafeh, 2005, "Business Groups in Emerging Markets: Paragons or Parasites?" Finance Working Paper No. 92/2005, European Corporate Governance Institute.

44. See Tarun Khanna and Krishna Palepu, 2000, "Emerging Market Business Groups, Foreign Investors, and Corporate Governance," in Randall Morck, ed., *Concentrated*

Ownership (National Bureau of Economic Research Conference Report, University of Chicago Press).

45. See Raja Kali and Jayati Sarkar, 2007, "Diversification and Tunneling: Evidence from Indian Business Groups," Working Paper, IGIDR.
46. See Jayashree Saha, 2006, "A Study of Related Party Transactions in Indian Corporate Sector," Draft Ph.D. dissertation, IGIDR.
47. See U. Bhattacharya, H. Daouk, and M. Welker, "The World Price of Earnings Opacity," *Accounting Review* 78, 2003: 641–78, and C. Leuz, D. Nanda, and P. Wysocki, "Earnings Management and Investor Protection: An International Comparison," *Journal of Financial Economics* 69, 2003: 505–27.
48. See Kee-Hong Bae, H. Tan, and M. Welker, 2007, "International GAAP Differences: The Impact on Foreign Analysts," Working Paper, Queen's University, Canada.
49. The number of Indian company mergers per year jumped from 30 during the period 1974–1987 to 63 between 1988–1994 to over 171 between 1994 and 2003. See Manish Agarwal and Aditya Bhattacharya, "Mergers in India—a Response to Regulatory Shocks," *Emerging Markets Finance and Trade* 42, 2006: 46–65.
50. See Nandini Gupta, "Partial Privatization and Firm Performance," *Journal of Finance* 60, 2005: 987–1015.
51. See S. Sangeetha, 2006, "Empirical Essays on Enterprise and Ownership Reforms in Public Sector Enterprises—Evidence from India," Draft Ph.D. dissertation, IGIDR. She finds that the application of MoUs or performance contracts had a positive impact on the profitability and the operational performance of PSEs.

CHAPTER 9

The Financial and Economic Lessons of Italy's Privatization Program

WILLIAM L. MEGGINSON AND
DARIO SCANNAPIECO

IN JULY 2005, the Italian Ministry of Economics and Finance executed a $4.9 billion share offering of a 9.3% stake in the electric utility company ENEL, which dropped the state's direct holdings in the company to 20%. Four months later, the state-controlled airline Alitalia launched a major reorganization—which involved splitting the company into two separate parts—along with a rights issue that raised $1.25 billion and resulted in the state's holdings dropping below 50% for the first time ever. These two transactions culminated a twelve-year privatization program comprising some 75 major deals that raised over $125 billion, the most of any country during this period.

This paper surveys Italy's massive program and draws financial and economic lessons that should prove useful to countries in Asia and the Middle East that are now embarking on their own privatization programs. By any measure, Italy's program must be considered a huge success, and a study of it offers many lessons about what a government should do. However, Italy's program has also yielded many disappointments, not least its failure to bring about the creation of truly global firms. Furthermore, while the regulatory system that has evolved in response to privatization of banks and utilities is far more effective than many dared hope at the program's inception, this remarkable system has not ensured lower prices for consumers or spurred the degree of competition in key industries that its planners first envisioned. In short, Italy's privatization program has dramatically improved the nation's economic and financial systems, without realizing the expected level of consumer benefits or transforming what once were national monopolies into truly competitive global companies.

Italian State Ownership Grows, Then Falls into Crisis

The modern Italian state is less than 150 years old, and extensive state ownership of business and finance was not part of the nation's founding ideology.

Instead, state ownership principally grew out of the need to rescue very large numbers of failing banks and industrial firms during the Great Depression. IRI, the Institute for Industrial Reconstruction *(Istituto per la Ricostruzione Industriale)*, was established by the Mussolini government in 1933 as an emergency vehicle, but was institutionalized by statute as the principal state holding company in 1937.[1] From that time onwards, the scale and scope of IRI and its sister institutions, EFIM *(Ente Partecipazionie Finanziamento Industrie Manifaturiere)*, ENI *(Ente Nazionale Idrocarburi)*, and ENEL *(Ente Nazionale per l'Energia Elettrica)*, grew steadily over the next half-century, a development that also occurred in several other European countries during the early postwar period. Italy was different in that the growth of SOEs was propelled less by ideology than by happenstance and political expediency. IRI or one of the other state enterprises was often called in to rescue an ailing company or to channel investment to a specific region. Italy also differed from other rich Western European countries in that its banking sector was almost completely state-owned.[2]

This mixed economic system worked tolerably well for five decades, and Italy's economic growth exceeded that of most other large European countries through the 1970s. However, after a decade of frenetic expansion during the 1980s, propelled by heavy state and SOE borrowing, Italy's economy and political system lurched into crisis. Throughout most of the 1980s and early 1990s, the central government's fiscal deficits averaged 10% of GDP, causing the state's debt-to-GDP ratio to rise to over 120%.[3] The uncompetitive state sector became both intolerably intrusive and financially desperate as IRI's debt levels exploded during the 1980s. By 1992, as can be seen in the graph of IRI's organizational structure presented in figure 9.1, IRI held sway over entire economic sectors. In 1991, 12 of the 20 largest Italian firms by sales (and more than one-third of the Top 50) were state owned, and state-controlled banks accounted for more than 70% of total loans and deposits. The three main holding companies employed over 500,000 workers in 1992, and almost two-thirds of IRI's workers were producing goods and services in markets sheltered by legal monopolies, dominant state demand, or exclusive state concessions.[4] Even with these protections, the SOEs were massively unprofitable.

Coinciding with this major economic crisis, Italian politics was gripped in 1992–1993 by a corruption scandal that some have described as the worst ever experienced by any Western democracy.[5] These woes came to a head during the summer of 1992, when the Italian lira (along with the British pound) was ejected from the European fixed exchange rate system—and promptly depreciated by 20% against the German mark. Given this background, it is not surprising that the general election of April 1992 was contested in an atmosphere of profound crisis. Not for the first time in democratic history, Italy's crisis proved to be a prerequisite for implementing fundamental change.

The Organizational Structure of the Istituto per la Ricostruzione Industriale (IRI) in 1992

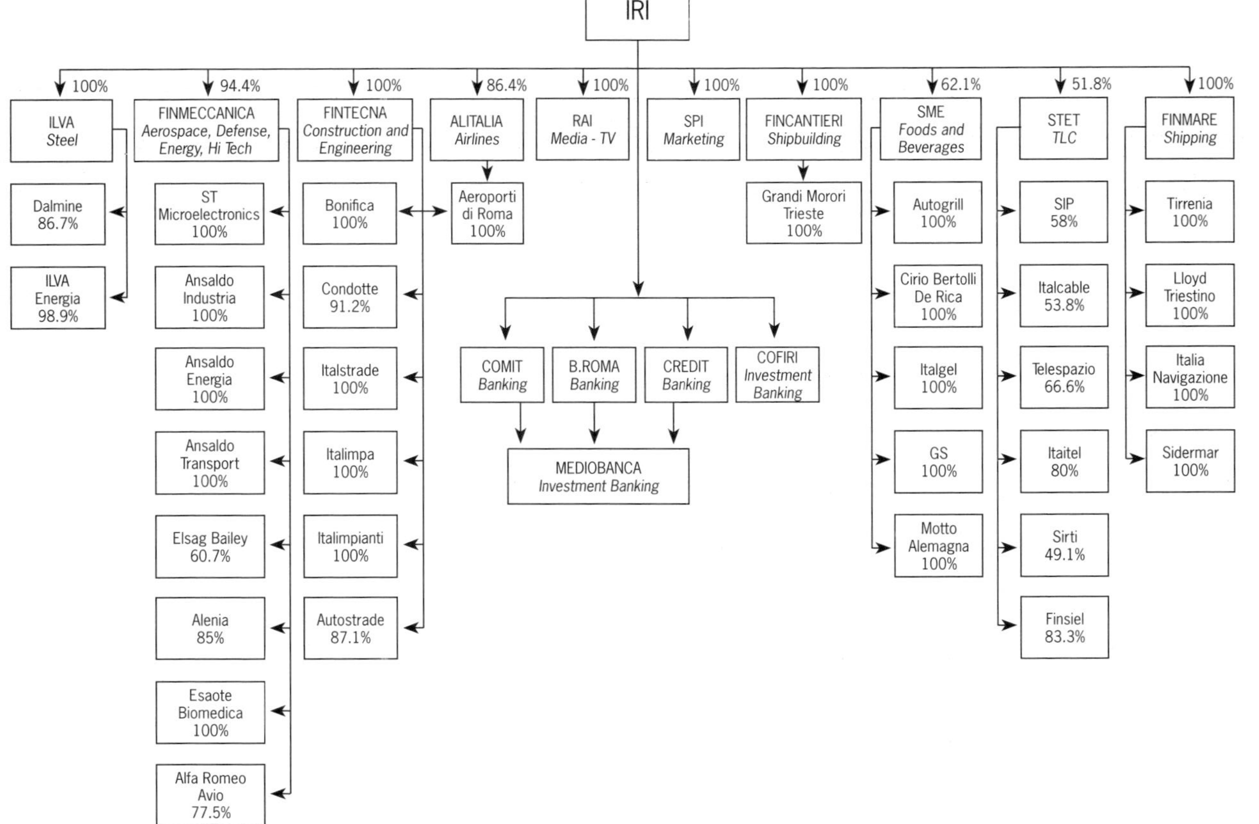

Source: Simone Bemporad and Edoardo Reviglio, 2002, "Privatization in Italy and the Role of IRI," Working Paper, Italian Ministry of Economics and Finance (Rome).

Crisis Brings Reform

The center-left government of Giuliano Amato that was elected in 1992 committed itself to a program of basic reforms centering on the privatization of state enterprises.

A committee of independent experts was established and charged with drafting a program for privatizing SOEs. The committee's proposal, spelled out in the Green Paper on State Ownership *(Libro Verde sulle Particiazioni delle Stato)* and presented to Parliament in November 1992, cited four general goals for a privatization program: (1) improve corporate efficiency; (2) increase the degree of market penetration and competition; (3) promote financial market development; and, residually, (4) increase fiscal revenues and reduce public debt.[6] Primary responsibility for first "corporatizing" and then divesting state enterprises was transferred from the highly politicized Ministry for State Holdings to the Ministry of Economics and Finance (MEF), which has spearheaded the privatization program ever since.

The years 1993–1995 witnessed the passage of a series of enabling laws. The reform measures envisioned by the *Libro Verde* were codified in Law 474 of July 1994, sometimes called the keystone legal document of Italian privatization. This legislation also explicitly (1) gave preference to the use of public share offerings as a divestment method whenever practical, (2) called for privatization of utilities to be delayed until independent regulatory authorities (IRAs) were established, and (3) allowed the government to employ golden shares and other ownership restrictions in limited circumstances where needed to protect ongoing public interests. Law 432 of October 1993 established a debt retirement fund *(Fondo per l'ammortamento dei titoli di Stato)* for all proceeds from privatization sales. The fund's purpose was to ensure that sale proceeds would be used to reduce the national debt rather than to finance recurring government spending or to fund special projects. Thanks to this flow of funds, over the coming decade the government's debt was reduced from 122% to about 110% of GDP. Finally, Law 281 of 1995 laid the framework for establishing independent regulatory authorities. These were given wide latitude to regulate markets, define tariffs and universal service obligations, and ensure access to essential facilities.

During the summer of 1993, the Italian foreign minister and the European Union's Commissioner for Competition signed a protocol obliging Italy to quantify by the end of 1993 the total indebtedness of all state enterprises that had been converted into joint stock companies. This agreement also committed Italy to reducing the indebtedness of these enterprises to levels appropriate for private commercial entities—and gave the state a strong incentive to reduce its ownership levels, since this fixed the maximum amount of its obligation for enterprise debts.

The *Comitato Privatizzazioni* Begins Life

One other legal innovation was created by the Prime Minister's Decree of June 30, which set up the Global Advisory Committee on Privatization (technically, the *Comitato Permanente di Consulenza e di Garanzia per le Privatizzazioni*) to guarantee the transparency of each privatization and to advise the ministers involved in the privatization process on the timetable, placement methods, and choice of financial advisors and underwriters.[7] The five voting members of the *Comitato* are the Director General of the Treasury and four independent outside experts, who are supported by the Treasury Department staff as needed. Fourteen outside experts have served on this committee during its 13-year existence; all have been university professors, and all but one (this chapter's first author) have been Italian citizens. The *Comitato* has been consulted on every major sale, and has never been accused of any impropriety or scandal. Intriguingly, the committee's advice is not legally binding on the government—unlike France's ad hoc Privatization Commission—but its recommendations are recorded and its advice has rarely been ignored.

Public Sales during the "Core" Privatization Period, 1994–1999

With the *Comitato Privatizzazioni* established and the key agreements and laws in place, Italy launched its massive privatization program in December 1993 with a public offering of the state's remaining 58% holding in Credito Italiano, which raised almost $1.2 billion.[8] The first six months of 1994 saw the flotation of a 30% stake in the investment bank, Istituto Mobiliare Italiano (IMI), for $1.5 billion, the sale of the state's remaining 54% stake in Banca Commerciale Italiana (BCI) for $1.7 billion, and the massive sale of a 51% stake in the insurer Istituto Nazionale de Assicurazoni (INA), which raised $3.1 billion.

These and other early share issue privatizations (SIPs) were structured, as was common practice in the financial markets at that time, as simple fixed price offerings in which the selling agency (either the MEF or IRI) set a price far in advance of the offering. Prices were therefore set without considering the results of the book-building process—that is, the collection of orders from institutional investors—performed by the investment banks executing the sale. These four sales also reflected two of the core principles motivating Italy's program: to sell financial institutions first and to employ public share offerings whenever feasible. Table 9.1 details the most important Italian privatizations from 1993 through November 2005.

The Credito Italiano, BCI, IMI, and INA offerings also set a number of patterns that were to be followed in almost all subsequent Italian SIPs. First, the *Comitato* advised on offer timing and sales methods, approved the selection of the financial advisors and underwriters, and certified that the entire process

TABLE 9.1

Major Italian Share Issue Privatizations, 1993–2005

Issue date	Company name	Industry	Stake sold (%)	Issue size (US$ millions)
Dec 93	Credito Italiano	Commercial banking	65	1,179
Feb 94	Banca Commerciale Italiana SPA	Commercial banking	54	1,700
Jan 94	Istituto Mobiliare Italiano	Commercial banking	30	1,513
Jun 94	Istituto Nazionale di Assicurazioini	Insurance	51	3,100
Nov 95	ENI	Petroleum and natural resources	15	3,907
Jun 96	Istituto Nazionale di Assicurazioini	Insurance	34	2,100
Jul 96	Istituto Mobiliare Italiano	Commercial banking	7	327
Oct 96	ENI	Petroleum and natural resources	14	5,864
May 97	Instituto San Paolo di Torino	Commercial banking	46	730
Jul 97	ENI	Petroleum and natural resources	17	7,800
Jul 97	Aeroporti di Roma	Airport management	41	315
Oct 97	Telecom Italia	Telecommunications	41	15,500
Nov 97	Banca di Roma	Commercial banking	37	1,740
Mar 98	Saipem SpA	Natural resources	26	553
May 98	Alitalia	Airline	17	450
Jun 98	ENI	Petroleum and natural resources	15	6,740
Jun 98	Finmeccanica	Manufacturing and engineering	–	1,129
Jul 98	Azienda Electrica Municipale	Electric service	49	900
Nov 98	Banca Nazionale del Lavoro	Commercial banking	85	4,600
Jun 99	Banca Monte dei Paschi di Siena	Commercial banking	24	2,093
Jul 99	ACEA SpA	Electric service	49	848
Nov 99	ENEL	Electricity production and distribution	35	18,900
Dec 99	Autostrade	Roadways	48	4,600
Jun 00	Finmeccanica	Manufacturing and engineering	45	5,360

TABLE 9.1 (*continued*)

Issue date	Company name	Industry	Stake sold (%)	Issue size (US$ millions)
Feb 01	ENI	Petroleum and natural resources	5	2,183
Dec 01	Snam Rete Gas	Natural gas distribution	–	1,800
Dec 02	Telecom Italia	Telecommunications	4	1,400
Oct 03	ENEL	Electricity production and distribution	7	2,520
Oct 04	ENEL	Electricity production and distribution	20	9,520
Jul 05	ENEL	Electricity production and distribution	9	4,900
Nov 05	Alitalia	Airline	12	1,250
			Total	**$115,521**

Source: Appendix 1 in William L. Megginson, *The Financial Economics of Privatization*, Oxford University Press, New York (2005), supplemented with data from table 1 of Bernardo Bortolotti, "Italy's Privatization Process and Its Implications for China," consultant report for the World Bank (2005).

was conducted transparently. Second, all but IMI were pure secondary issues of existing shares, where all of the proceeds flowed to the government rather than to the firm whose shares were being sold. Third, the offers were designed to promote participation by retail investors—especially firm employees— through the use of preferential share allocations, deliberate (though fairly modest) underpricing, and aggressive promotion and advertising campaigns.[9] Most large SIPs also offered retail participants "bonus" or "loyalty" shares, usually distributing one share for every ten initially purchased if the investor retained the original shares for at least three years. Fourth, the offers were oversubscribed, in some cases massively so. Finally, the fees offered to the underwriters for handling the issues were significantly below levels offered on private-sector share issues. The early SIPs required three to four months to arrange and offered banks spreads of about three.[10] These spreads were also set to decline steadily over the life of the program, so much so that the underwriters of the $4.9 billion ENEL 4 offering in July 2005 received a mere 1.26% fee. Table 9.2 describes the allocation of shares to enterprise employees, domestic retail, institutional, and foreign investors in 17 Italian share issue privatizations.

The pace and scale of Italian SIPs accelerated dramatically after 1994, beginning with the second offering of INA in January 1995 (raising $936 million)

Allocation of Shares in Major Share Issue Privatizations

Name	% of Capital Sold	Bonus Share*	Retail	-of which Domestic	Employees	US	Institutions	-of which Italy	UK & Ireland	Europe	US	Rest of World
Credito Italiano	58.10	3.30	62.17	91.00	9.00	0.00	37.82					
Banca Commerciale Italiana SPA	54.30	3.00	61.00	89.00	11.00	0.00	39.00					
IMI 1	27.90	1.13	82.00	66.00	40.00	31.00	18.00	83.00	0.00	0.00	17.00	0.00
ENI 1	14.70	0.07	55.42	52.00	9.00	40.00	44.58	66.00	34.00[1]	0.00	0.00	[1]
ENI 2	15.82	0.75	68.52	71.00	10.00	19.00	31.48	32.00	35.00	0.00	0.00	32.00
IMI 3	6.94	0.00	0.00	–	–	–	100.00	45.00	19.00	27.00	6.00	4.00
Banca di Roma	36.50	0.00	79.50	92.00	8.00	0.00	20.50					
ENI 3	17.60	1.53	75.14	75.00	6.00	19.00	24.85	46.00	31.00	0.00	0.00	23.00
Istituto Bancario San Paolo di Torino	3.36	1.47	48.00	83.00	17.00	0.00	52.00	100[2]	0.00	0.00	0.00	[2]
BNL	68.27	2.11	59.40	91.00	9.00	0.00	40.60	39.00	0.00	0.00	11.00	50.00
ENI 4	14.83	1.10	84.52	88.00	5.00	7.00	15.48	54.00	35.00	0.00	0.00	11.00
Autostrade Spa	56.00	4.10	79.10	100.00	-	0.00	10.20					
ENEL 1	31.74	1.00	68.49	93.00	7.00	1.00	31.51	41.00	14.00	30.00	10.00	5.00
TI 1	42.10	1.95	87.11	85.00	11.00	4.00	12.89	33.00	15.00	0.00	20.00	33.00
ENI 5	5.00	–	0.00	–	–	–	100.00					
TI 2	3.00	–	0.00	–	–	–	100.00	16.00	48.00	14.00	18.00	4.00
ENEL 2	6.60	–	0.00	–	–	–	100.00	6.00	46.00	26.00	20.00	2.00
ENEL 3	18.90	0.40	40.50	95.70	4.30		59.50	23.00	28.00		18.00	31.00
ENEL 4	9.40	0.20	43.50	95.50	4.50		56.50	35.00	36.00		10.00	19.00
Mean	**27.22**	**1.54**	**53.55**	**83.00**	**12.00**	**8.00**	**45.82**	**43.00**	**0.22**	**8.00**	**8.00**	**19.00**

Source: *Ministry of the Economy and Finance*, presented as table 7 in Bernardo Bortolotti, "Italy's Privatization Process and Its Implications for China," consultant report for the World Bank (2005).

1. UK+Rest of World

2. Italy+Rest of World

*as a percentage of stock capital

Note: These data include the green-shoe.

and the first major sale of an industrial company, the $3.9 billion IPO of the national oil and gas company, ENI, in November 1995. Over the next two years, three progressively larger, secondary offerings of ENI raised a further $20.4 billion. A second, $2.1 billion tranche of INA was sold in June 1996 through a complex recapitalization that included a large convertible bond offering. Following a 1997 merger between the two largest state-owned telecommunications companies, the government sold most of its 45% stake in the newly christened Telecom Italia in a colossal (and highly successful) $15.5 billion public offering. This European record for offering size was to last two years, only to be eclipsed by the largest IPO (in dollar terms) in world history, the $18.9 billion initial offering of a 34.5% stake in the electric utility company ENEL. This single offering attracted 3.8 million individual investors.

Other major sales of this frenetic 1995–1999 period were the $1.7 billion offer of Banca di Roma (November 1997), the $4.6 billion secondary offering of Banca Nazionale del Lavoro (BNL) (November 1998), the $4.6 billion offering of the roadway operator Autostrade, and the sale of a 24% stake in Banca Monte dei Paschi di Siena—which was founded in 1458—for $2.09 billion. In December 1999, the state exited the banking sector entirely with the private sale of its 100% holdings in Medicredito Centrale.[11] Privatization sales that year raised proceeds equal to 2.3% of Italy's GDP.[12]

Share Sales Methods Become More Efficient

As the SIP program evolved, so did the offering methods employed. As noted, the first sales were simple fixed-price offers, but the Treasury introduced the marketed block trade technique with its second offering of IMI in June 1996. The Treasury employed the open-price placement method six months later for the second Eni tranche.[13] From the late 1990s onward, American-style bookbuilding methods were being employed in most large SIPs, but with a distinctly political twist.[14] Unlike book-built private-sector offerings, the privatization share issues launched by the Italian government (and most others) involved book building for an institutional tranche only. The pricing and demand data gleaned during this process were then used to set the price for both the institutional tranche and the much larger domestic retail tranche.[15] A series of indicative prices was typically set as the offering process unfolded, with a final maximum price being set the weekend before the offering was to be placed. Most of the later issues also were subject to a 15% Green Shoe option that underwriters could exercise in the event of strong demand.

The early practice of selling sizeable stakes in firms being privatized to presumably more stable "core" shareholders (usually banks and industrial firms) was soon discarded, though the impulse to retain Italian control over divested firms never disappeared. Golden shares, which give the government the right to veto major asset sales or other decisions that might affect public order, safety, or the provision of essential services, were employed in four cases: ENI, ENEL, Telecom Italia, and Finmeccanica.[16] After broadly defined golden shares were ruled illegal by the EU Court of Justice in 2002, the scope of Italy's golden shares was duly narrowed, but otherwise remained in place.[17] Additionally, five privatized companies were cross-listed in the United States, either through direct listings or as Level III American Depositary Receipts.

While most Italian state enterprises were privatized via public share offering, there have also been several important private sales. One of the first was the September 1995 direct sale of a controlling 56.2% stake in Aeroporti di Roma (ADR) to an investor group for $262 million. The remaining state holdings in ADR were divested through a $327 million public offering two years later. A similar strategy was used to privatize the roadway operator, Autostrade. A 30% stake was sold to an Italian investor group for $2.5 billion in October 1999, and an additional 56% stake was divested through a $3.8 billion public offering two months later.

Sales Drop Sharply after March 2000—and Methods Change

The worldwide drop in stock market values that began in March 2000 also had a dramatic impact on Italy's privatization program. After exceeding $25 billion in 1999, sales revenue dropped to less than $6 billion in 2000—and even further over the next two years. The final large public offer of the "core" period of Italy's privatization program was the June 2000 seasoned offering of a 54% stake in the aerospace and defense company Finmeccanica, which raised $5.4 billion. The new center-right government that was elected in 2001 promised to restart the privatization program (and appointed the current members of the *Comitato Privatizzazioni*), but was hamstrung by the sharp drop in the value of all European equity markets. Faced with uninviting public market valuations, the government turned to private sales and to direct share placements with institutional investors through accelerated seasoned equity offerings.[18] The Treasury executed its first accelerated transaction in February 2001, when it raised almost $2.2 billion through an accelerated book-built offering (ABO) of a 5% stake in ENI—then a second in December 2002, the $1.38 billion accelerated book-building of its residual 3.5% holding in Telecom Italia.[19] Both of these accelerated deals closed within 24 hours, and both were considered successes. However, the third such deal most certainly was not. Immediately after the $2.52 billion ABO of ENEL was announced in October 2003, the stock price dropped sharply, forcing the government to halt temporarily all further public sales.

Fortunately, the private market remained open, and in July 2003 the government executed its largest ever private sale of the entire equity capital of a company. After a long and competitive evaluation process, which saw an original dozen interested parties whittled down to three actual bidders, the Treasury sold the tobacco manufacturer *Ente Tabacchi Italiano* (ETI) to British-American Tobacco Company for $2.6 billion through a sealed-bid auction.[20]

By late 2004, the public market had reopened enough to sell a third tranche of ENEL. In a replay of the immense and highly promoted public offerings of the late 1990s, the Treasury and its bankers raised $9.52 billion through an oversubscribed secondary offering. This complex sale included preferential share allocations to loyal original shareholders and new domestic retail investors, plus large tranches reserved for Italian, European, and U.S. institutions. For the first time, there was also a special Japanese tranche, which proved so popular that it will likely become a fixture in all future sales. ENEL's shares performed very well after this offering—not least because the company promised to pay a series of special dividends, including one using the proceeds from the $15.5 billion sale, finalized in June 2005, of its Wind mobile phone subsidiary to a consortium headed by Egypt's Orascom. One month later, the Treasury sold a fourth tranche of ENEL for $4.9 billion in another traditional, and successful, fully marketed public offering.

The final major privatization of the Italian program (thus far) was the restructuring and recapitalization of the national airline, Alitalia, which closed in November 2005. Alitalia had been financially distressed and losing market share for over a decade, and had received a series of "onetime" capital infusions from various Italian governments. In 2004, however, the European Union made clear that no further state aid would be allowed. Faced with extinction, the company and its unions agreed to a radical restructuring plan put forth by its new CEO in early 2005 that called for the company to be split into two parts—an airline, Alitalia Fly, and a ground service group, Alitalia Servizi. The plan also called for some 10% of Alitalia's workforce to be laid off, and for the proceeds of a €1.05 billion ($1.25 billion) rights offering to be used to finance the restructuring. This plan was approved by the EU on the condition that the Italian government promised to reduce its stake in the company to less than 50%, which the Treasury accomplished by subscribing to less than its full allocation of the rights offering. After the offering closed, Alitalia became a majority-private company for the first time in its history.

Italy's privatization program has been in suspended animation since the Alitalia rights offering closed in November 2005. It was hoped that the April 2006 general election would provide a clear indication of whether the program would be re-energized as part of a new economic reform agenda.

As it turned out, the election was a virtual tie, with the center-left commanding a slim majority in both houses of Parliament (especially the Senate). At this writing, the new government has taken charge, but it is unclear whether any new Italian privatization sales will be launched any time soon. On the other hand, it is a fact that since 1992 Italy has experienced ten different governments (both center-left and center-right), and the privatization process has never been stopped—only slowed by adverse market conditions.

Has Italy's Privatization Program Been Successful?

The Italian privatization program has evolved much more rapidly, completely, and transparently than anyone imagined possible in 1994, yet a full assessment of the program's success must examine its impact along four dimensions. First, has privatization improved the financial and operating performance of divested firms? Second, has the program achieved its stated goal of developing Italy's financial markets and improving the health and stability of the nation's banking system? Third, have the asset sales and the accompanying financial reforms improved Italy's historically poor system of corporate governance and promoted the emergence of large, globally competitive public companies? Finally, have the privatizations and accompanying legal and regulatory reforms promoted competition, lowered prices to consumers, and spurred new entry into previously closed markets? We briefly answer each of these questions below, and then close with a summary of the lessons Italy's massive privatization program can offer to governments contemplating the launch of such a program in their own countries.

The Financial and Operating Performance of Privatized Firms

The most complete empirical analysis of the effect of privatization on the performance of divested Italian firms is provided by Andrea Goldstein.[21] Using a pre-versus-post-privatization comparison methodology developed in part by one of the current authors,[22] Goldstein tested a sample of 25 divested companies for whether the average profitability, efficiency, investment, output, leverage, and tax-payment ratios had changed during the three years following privatization. Using both "raw" and matched-firm-adjusted tests for performance change, he finds a modest, statistically insignificant, increase in profitability. Efficiency generally, but again insignificantly, declines after privatization, while output increases significantly on an unadjusted basis. The unadjusted long-term debt-to-equity ratios of privatized companies increase significantly; but once the general increase in leverage of Italian private-sector firms is accounted for, the leverage ratios of divested firms decline significantly. The propensity of companies to pay taxes does not change significantly after privatization, nor does the average current ratio of these firms. In fact, the only striking and unambiguous performance improvement documented by Goldstein is a significant increase in capital investment spending.

Riccardo Gallo also analyzes the impact of privatization on the financial and operating performance of a sample of divested companies, but he studies 14 companies that were sold by auction to either multinational corporations (six firms) or to Italian companies (eight).[23] He documents significant declines in staffing, and significant improvements in productivity and, especially, profitability for the acquired companies, with much greater improvements occurring in those firms acquired by Italian private companies. He also finds that the leverage ratios of the divested SOEs decline significantly and dramatically after they are acquired.

On balance, it seems that privatization indeed improved the financial and operating performance of divested companies. However, the improvements were less general and less dramatic than those documented in most other countries.[24]

Privatization's Impact on the Italian Capital Markets and Banking System

While privatization appears to have had only a minor impact on the performance of individual companies, it has had a massive impact on the capitalization and trading volume of Italy's stock and bond markets. Figures 9.2 and 9.3, respectively, describe the profound increase in total value and liquidity of the main Italian bourses, particularly the Borsa Italiana (formerly the Milan Stock Exchange). Total market capitalization grew from less than $150 billion in 1992 to over $770 billion at year-end 2000. Values then fell sharply over the next two years, before rebounding strongly from 2003 onward.[25] At year-end 2005, the Borsa Italiana's capitalization reached a new record in dollars, almost $800 billion, though it remains below the 2000 peak measured in euros. Capitalization as a percentage of GDP tripled (to 54%) between 1992 and 2000, while the number of listed companies increased by one-third. Trading volume increased more than fifty-fold between 1992 and 2005, rising from $27 billion to $1.3 *trillion,* and the turnover ratio rose eight-fold over this same period.

Privatized companies accounted for much of the increase in capitalization and liquidity detailed above. By 2002, partly and fully divested companies accounted for 41% of capitalization and 33% of trading volume.[26] These same firms accounted for 60% of total floating capitalization in 2002. Privatization also promoted sharp increases in the fraction of the population that owns shares and in the value of household equity ownership. By 2000, direct equity ownership represented 27% of the total asset value of Italian households, which rises to 41% when indirect holdings in mutual and pension funds are factored in.

Privatizing the banks also dramatically improved their safety and stability. Bortolotti shows that the average loan-loss ratio for large Italian banks declined

FIGURE 9.2

Italian Stock Market Capitalization, 1990–2005

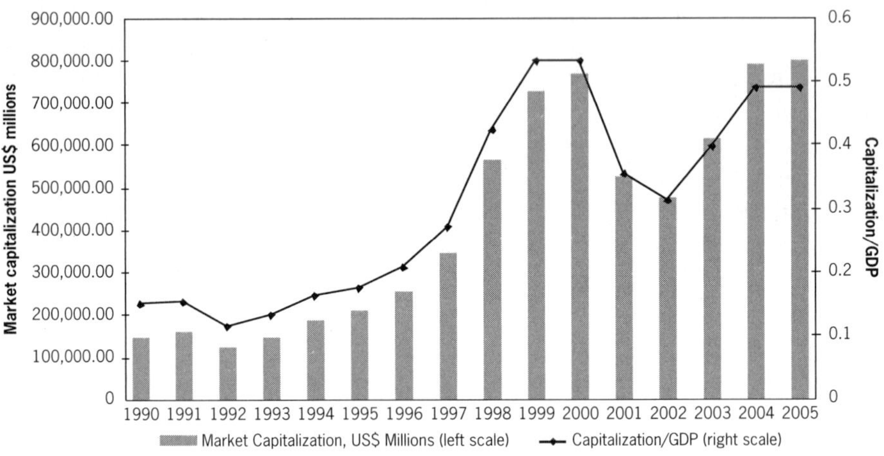

FIGURE 9.3

Italian Stock Market Trading Volume, 1990–2005

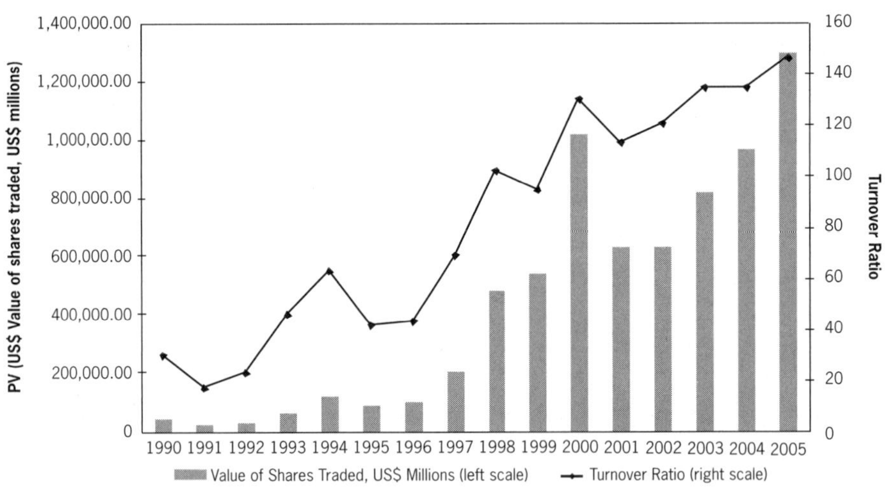

from over 11% in 1992 to less than 5% a decade later.[27] In summary, in perhaps its most unambiguously positive effect, privatization has dramatically increased the size and efficiency of Italy's stock markets and has transformed the safety and stability of the nation's banking system.

Privatization's Impact on Corporate Governance

Italy's massive share issue privatization necessitated drastic improvements in the country's previously woeful corporate governance. The 1998 Draghi Law codified existing statutes and was also designed to improve disclosure by means of restrictive regulation of shareholder agreements (the traditional method of maintaining tight insider control of Italian business) and of takeover bids.[28] Trading and governance became much more transparent, and the stock exchange regulator CONSOB was given greater authority and resources. Bernardo Bortolotti and Domenico Siniscalco (2004) estimate that these changes led to a three-point increase in Italy's LLSV (1998) shareholders' rights index between 1992 and 2000.[29]

On the other hand, Italian corporate governance remains imperfect, especially in practice. Ownership remains highly concentrated; in 2001, the largest shareholder still owned an average 42% of the typical publicly listed company.[30] Minority shareholders' rights are routinely and often flagrantly ignored. Perhaps most ominously, far fewer large, globally competitive firms have developed than could reasonably have been expected, which is a severe national problem because this leads to a trading structure that puts Italy in direct competition with low-wage emerging markets.

Privatization's Impact on Competition and Prices

Certainly the most disappointing aspect of Italy's privatization program is the limited impact it has had on competition, pricing, and consumer choice in key service sectors. There have been significant improvements, particularly in telecommunications and energy. Fixed-line telecom prices dropped by some 30% after Telecom Italia's privatization and implementation of the EU Telecom Directive in 1998. Additionally, electricity markets have been massively restructured as a result of a 1999 Legislative Decree (the Bersani Decree), and accounting separation of generation and distribution has been imposed on ENEL. In 2005, ENEL sold its transmission business.[31] The natural gas and electricity markets have also been liberalized as a result of privatization and deregulation.

On the other hand, ENEL and ENI retain commanding positions in their relative markets and energy prices remain higher than elsewhere in the EU. In fairness, this partly results from a penalizing fuel mix in the electricity generation business (following a public referendum in 1987, Italy has ceased nuclear energy production), the lack of infrastructures to import natural gas in this sector, and high taxation on all energy products. Furthermore, entire sectors remain dominated by entrenched incumbents and prices have generally not fallen as much as they should have. This partly reflects a more general failure of deregulation and market-opening throughout continental Europe, but has also been exacerbated by political reluctance to force open protected markets and promote entry, particularly if that entry might be achieved by foreign companies. Despite 12 years of reform and privatization, Italy remains a high-cost place to do business, particularly with respect to those services that are so vital to the competitiveness of a modern, export-oriented economy.

Lessons of Italy's Privatization Program

Numerous governments in Asia, Africa, and the Persian Gulf have either already launched or are contemplating major new privatization programs. What lessons can Italy's program offer them? We offer five. The first lesson is that privatization works, but only yields decisive benefits if the divestment program is properly designed and sequenced. Italy's experience also suggests that a sense of crisis can help rally popular support for a reform program, but this is neither a necessary nor sufficient condition for launching such a program.

Second, a government should privatize its state-owned banks and other financial institutions first, and as quickly as is economically and politically feasible. Commercial banks are vital (and often the only) suppliers of credit to—and disciplinarians of—private sector firms. When governments have retained control of banks while privatizing other industries, the results have usually been disastrous. In Eastern Europe and Latin America, enduring state ownership of banks has resulted in widespread bankruptcies, recapitalizations and, ultimately, near-complete foreign ownership of the banking sector.

Third, governments should emphasize share issue privatizations over asset sales, and seize this unique opportunity to develop stock markets and promote effective corporate governance. A complete system of corporate governance—laws, regulatory bodies, and self-regulating institutions—should be constructed before large-scale divestments begin, and special care should be taken to protect the interests of unsophisticated retail investors, who will be attracted to stock market investing for the first time. The systems developed should also be consistent with national traditions and practices rather than being imported *en masse* from abroad. Governments should also be willing to significantly underprice privatization IPOs, particularly early in the program, in order to build a base of investors willing to purchase seasoned offerings and later PIPOs. This is often a difficult political case to make, since reformers are criticized for "selling the family silver cheaply," but it can usually be finessed by preferentially allocating underpriced shares to SOE employees and domestic retail investors.

Fourth, governments should consider creating local versions of the *Comitato Privatizzazioni* to advise the government on sales techniques, and to ensure transparency and fairness. Professors and experienced professionals are the most logical candidates for staffing these committees of experts, particularly those who have an international reputation. In addition to local academics, virtually every nation can draw on a diaspora of accomplished citizens, including executives of multinational corporations and tenured faculty in prestigious Western universities.

Finally, governments should promote competition wherever possible—and set up powerful and independent regulatory agencies *before* divesting powerful incumbents. Global experience shows that enlightened and informed regulation, adopted in advance, can solve many of the problems that arise naturally from privatization of utilities, offer a stable regulatory system to investors, and ensure that the benefits that result from private ownership are shared by all.

Notes

We wish to thank Martin Serreqi for his invaluable contribution in researching and collecting data for this project, and Bernardo Bortolotti for his comments on preliminary drafts. All remaining errors are the authors' alone.

1. Much of this section is based on the historical discussion in pages 2–7 of Simone Bemporad and Edoardo Reviglio, "Privatization in Italy and the Role of IRI." Working paper, Italian Ministry of Economics and Finance (2002).
2. In addition to being state-owned, the state banks were also politicized, as documented in Paolo Sapienza, "The Effects of Government Ownership on Bank Lending," *Journal of Financial Economics* 72 (2003), pp. 357–384.
3. The financial problems of Italy's state-owned enterprises and banks during the early 1990s are described in pages 10–12 of Bernardo Bortolotti, "Italy's Privatization Process and Its Implications for China," Consultant report for the World Bank (2005). Additionally, Bertero and Rondi (2000) document that Italian state-owned enterprises did become subject to hard budget constraints for the first time during the 1980s, as the state's financial condition deteriorated. See Elisabetta Bertero and Laura Rondi, "Financial Pressure and the Behavior of Public Enterprises Under Soft and Hard Budget Constraints: Evidence from Italian Panel Data," *Journal of Public Economics* 75 (January 2000), pp. 73–98.
4. These statistics are from Andrea Goldstein, "Privatization in Italy, 1993–2002: Goals, Institutions, Outcomes, and Outstanding Issues." CESifo Working paper, Munich (2003).
5. Bemporad and Reviglio (2002), cited earlier, p. 2.
6. See Bortolotti (2005), p. 11, and Goldstein (2003), p. 4, both cited earlier.
7. Descriptions of the decree establishing the Comitato, and analyses of its duties, are presented in Goldstein (2003), p. 5.
8. The proceeds values of share offerings used throughout this chapter (including table 9.1) are from appendix 1 of William Megginson, *The Financial Economics of Privatization,* Oxford University Press, New York (2005). The appendix values are based on contemporary news reports in (principally) the *Financial Times,* and these values are generally larger than those reported by the Italian MEF, as presented in Goldstein (2003) and Bortolotti (2005).
9. Macchiati (1999), quoted in table 6 of Bortolotti (2005), finds that the average (median) underpricing of six Italian fixed-price privatization IPOs [PIPOs] was 15.0% (15.4%), and was 0.9% (1.2%) for nine fixed-price seasoned offers. See A. Macchiati,

"Breve Storia delle Privatizzazioni in Italia: 1992–1999. Ovvero: Si Poteva fare Meglio?" *Mercato, Concorrenza, Regole,* 3: 1999, ed. Il Mulino. This contrasts favorably with the 34.1% average (12.4% median) initial return for 242 global privatization IPOs, and the 9.4% (3.3%) for seasoned SIPs, documented in Steven L. Jones, William L. Megginson, Robert C. Nash, and Jeffry M. Netter, "Share Issue Privatizations as Financial Means to Political and Economic Ends," *Journal of Financial Economics* 53 (August 1999), pp. 217–253.
10. See Bemporad and Reviglio (2002), p. 19, cited earlier.
11. See Bemporad and Reviglio (2002), p. 13, cited earlier.
12. See Dario Scannapieco, "Indagine Conoscitiva sulle Politiche di Privatizzazione in Italia," Presentation at the Financial Management Association European meeting, Siena (2005). Other years when privatization revenues exceeded 1% of GDP include 1997 (2.0%), 2003 (1.3%), and 1998 (1.1%).
13. See Bemporad and Reviglio (2002), p. 13, cited earlier.
14. Ljungqvist, Jenkinson, and Wilhelm (2003) show that the use of book-building in IPOs was spreading around the world during the late 1990s. See Alexander Ljungqvist, Tim Jenkinson and William J. Wilhelm, Jr., "Global Integration in Primary Equity Markets: The Role of U.S. Banks and U.S. Investors," *Review of Financial Studies* 16 (Spring 2003), pp. 630–699.
15. See Bortolotti (2005), pp. 20–22, and Bemporad and Reviglio (2002), pp. 20–21, both cited earlier.
16. See Bortolotti (2005), p. 22, cited earlier.
17. The evolution of European golden shares is described and analyzed in Mara Faccio and Bernardo Bortolotti, "Reluctant Privatization," Working paper, Vanderbilt University (2006).
18. The three principal types of accelerated underwritings—accelerated book-built offerings (ABO), block trades (BT), and bought deals (BD)—employed around the world are described and analyzed in Bernardo Bortolotti, William L. Megginson, and Scott Smart, "The Rise of Accelerated Seasoned Equity Underwritings," Working paper, University of Oklahoma (2006).
19. See Massimo Pappone and Giacomo Ciampolini, "European Privatizations: From Marketed Offerings to Accelerated Transactions—and Back! The ENEL Case," *Privatization Barometer Newsletter* No. 2 (January 2005), pp. 22–28.
20. The auction process used for ETI and other private sales is described generically in Bemporad and Reviglio (2002), pp. 20–22. While advising on the ETI offer itself, the authors personally drew on the auction design principles described in Paul Klemperer, "What Really Matters in Auction Design," *Journal of Economic Perspectives* 16 (Winter 2002), pp. 169–189.
21. See Goldstein (2003), p. 9 and tables 6 and 7, cited earlier.
22. See William Megginson, Robert Nash, and Matthias van Randenborgh, "The Financial and Operating Performance of Newly Privatized Firms: An International Empirical Analysis," *Journal of Finance* 49 (June 1994), pp. 403–452.
23. See Riccardo Gallo, "The Economic and Structural Effects of Privatization on Enterprises in Italy," Presentation at the Financial Management Association European meeting, Siena (June 2005).
24. The empirical evidence on privatization's impact is summarized in William Megginson and Jeffry Netter, "From State to Market: A Survey of Empirical Studies on Privatization," *Journal of Economic Literature* 39 (June 2001), pp. 321–389.
25. Most of the values presented in this section are from Bortolotti (2005), pp. 32–35, cited earlier.

26. See Bortolotti (2005), p. 33, cited earlier. The impact of privatization on trading volume is lower than for capitalization primarily because the state still retains large chunks of several of the biggest companies, which reduces their free float.
27. See Bortolotti (2005), figure 8, cited earlier.
28. See Goldstein (2003), p. 12, cited earlier.
29. See Bernardo Bortolotti and Domenico Siniscalco, *The Challenges of Privatization: An International Analysis,* Oxford University Press (2004). The LLSV index is developed in Rafael La Porta, Florencio López-de-Silanes, Andrei Shleifer, and Robert W. Vishny, "Law and Finance," *Journal of Political Economy* 106 (December 1998), pp. 1113–1150.
30. Much of the data presented in this section is from Goldstein (2003), pp. 12–14, cited earlier.
31. The figures presented in this section are drawn principally from Bortolotti (2005), pp. 29–31, and Goldstein (2003), pp. 26–27, both cited earlier.

CHAPTER 10

Changes in Korean Corporate Governance

A Response to Crisis

E. HAN KIM AND WOOCHAN KIM

A DECADE HAS PASSED since the outbreak of the Korean financial crisis in November 1997. One of the fundamental causes of the crisis was widespread corporate value destruction, especially among the family-controlled business groups known as "chaebol." Before the crisis, these business groups routinely pursued growth and market share at the expense of profitability and shareholder value. For some of the chaebol, size added to their political influence, which could be used to tilt the playing field in their favor. Being bigger also meant better access to external financing and lower borrowing costs, thanks in part to the "too big to fail" legacy.

But another important factor driving this value-destroying growth were the so-called private benefits of controlling a larger corporate empire to the controlling shareholders, typically referred to in Korea as the "owners." In addition to the consumption of perks, the chaebol's "owners" commonly used "tunneling" and "asset-grabbing" schemes to transfer corporate value from their minority shareholders.

As we discuss in more detail below, one important factor motivating and enabling the chaebol to expropriate their minority shareholders has been the substantial gap between their "cash flow rights"—that is, their percentage claim on dividends and earnings—and their voting, or "control," rights. While the cash flow rights of the controlling chaebol families have often been relatively small—about 20% on average—their control rights have been near absolute thanks to a web of complex cross holdings among affiliated firms. Such disproportionate control rights, together with various legal and socio-political impediments to shareholder activism, have also made the chaebol immune to the threat of hostile takeovers. Thus, as we argue in the pages that follow, the chaebol have largely avoided the disciplining forces of capital and corporate control markets, even as their distorted incentives have resulted in unprofitable growth, diversification, and massive destruction of value.

In a study (involving one of the present writers) that was commissioned by the Korea Stock Exchange prior to the 1997 financial crisis, the authors calculated the economic value added (EVA) produced by 570 non-financial Korea Stock Exchange companies in each year from 1992 through 1996.[1] After adding up the annual EVAs for each company over this five-year period, the authors concluded that only about 27% of the companies created or maintained shareholder value. In other words, nearly three-quarters of Korean companies destroyed value by failing to generate sufficient operating profits to cover their capital costs over the five-year period preceding the crisis.

While this unchecked value destruction was reducing shareholder wealth and shrinking the value of its economy, Korea should have experienced substantial depreciation of its currency during the run-up to the crisis. However, the government maintained the value of the won at artificially high levels until it ran out of foreign reserves in November 1997. When lack of reserves forced the government to let the exchange rate float freely, the currency's value immediately plummeted. The won-dollar exchange rate more than doubled, rising from 964.4 to 1,964.8, during the two months from the beginning of November through December 24.

The currency crisis coincided with a presidential election, and the ruling party was swept from office. The new administration proposed a number of reform measures, targeting primarily chaebol ownership and its governance structure. But, at this point, the crash in currency value was followed by a sharp increase in interest rates resulting from the tight monetary policy prescribed by the International Monetary Fund (IMF). The immediate result was that unemployment skyrocketed and GDP dropped sharply.

The crash of its currency was more than a financial blow to Korean citizens. The loss of Korean economic independence to foreign powers represented by the IMF was a public humiliation, an assault on the national psyche. Citizens lost faith in their leaders, questioning their authority and credibility. And in response to this national crisis of confidence, Korea suddenly exhibited the political will to make major governance reforms, an uncommon event in democracies.[2]

The reform measures announced by the new administration were a mix of market-based solutions and government intervention. The government-engineered, large-scale swaps of business units among the largest chaebol—the so-called big deals that were designed to force each chaebol to specialize in its core business—failed miserably, with serious unwanted side effects. This was not surprising since the new government played the role of corporate matchmaker rather than allowing market forces to restructure the corporate portfolios. And as this experience demonstrated once again, politicians and government bureaucrats have neither the incentive nor the expertise to allocate resources to their highest-valued uses and users.

At the same time, however, new laws and regulations designed to increase corporate transparency, oversight, and accountability were put in place. And the effects of these laws and regulations on the quality of governance of Korean corporations have been unmistakably positive. Among this package of reforms, one major contributor to improved governance has been the lowering of barriers to foreign ownership of Korean companies. By the end of 2006, foreign ownership of listed Korean companies amounted to about 37%, up from just 13% in 1996. And in addition to the growing pressure for better governance from foreign investors, strong grass-roots reform movements have sprung up. Several newly formed non-governmental organizations (NGOs) have pressed for increased corporate transparency and accountability, particularly in the largest chaebol. After witnessing the collapse of large chaebol once believed to be too big to fail, the Korean business community has shown a heightened awareness of the importance of increasing shareholder value as a strategy for national competitiveness and long-term corporate survival. And in recent years, such awareness has led to a number of voluntary as well as mandated reforms in Korean corporate governance.

In this chapter, we describe these reforms while assessing the current state of corporate governance in Korea. In so doing, we divide the subject of corporate governance into three broad categories—ownership structure, internal governance mechanisms, and external monitors—and discuss each in turn.

The Chaebol and "Emperor-Like" Management

How well a company is governed is largely determined by various implicit and explicit contracts among the stakeholders of the firm—management, employees, investors, directors, and so forth—and the effectiveness with which the contracts are enforced. Such contracts differ among companies in terms of the degree of alignment between managerial and shareholder interests, the priority given to shareholder value by the board of directors, and the level of voluntary disclosure for external financing. The ability of corporate stakeholders to monitor and enforce such contracts depends on laws and regulations governing timely and accurate disclosure, managerial and board accountability, board independence, and protection of minority shareholders. It also depends on the extent of social and political acceptance of the concept of shareholder value maximization.

Before the crisis of 1997, neither the chaebol ownership structure nor Korean legal institutions encouraged effective corporate governance. In 1996, the controlling shareholders of the large chaebol owned an average of 23% of the outstanding shares, but effectively controlled 68% of the votes through various forms of cross- and circular-holdings in subsidiaries and related firms.[3] Such disproportionate control gave the chaebol owners the power to appoint the top managements and boards of their affiliated firms. Also important were the financing practices of chaebol affiliates, which have typically relied on the "internal capital markets" created by the conglomeration of numerous affiliated and related firms. Given this supply of internal funding, chaebol-affiliated firms have been able to avoid the disclosure necessary to obtain external financing, as well as the discipline—including the possibility of takeover—that comes with relying on outside equity capital.

Before the crisis, Korean laws and regulations were largely ineffective in protecting minority shareholders, ensuring timely and accurate disclosures, and preventing insider trading. Even the media, which are expected to expose corporate scandals and bad governance practices, were often captives of the chaebol, either through their direct ownership or their power to withhold advertising expenditures. For example, Samsung Group, Korea's largest chaebol, owned *ChoongAng Daily,* one of the two most widely subscribed newspapers. The Federation of Korean Industries, the lobbying organization for the chaebol and other large corporations, owns the *Korea Economic Daily,* one of the leading business newspapers in Korea. Other possible external sources of shareholder protection, such as institutional investors or activist block holders seeking value-increasing changes or encouraging takeover bids, were virtually non-existent.

In sum, before the crisis, the chaebol owners encountered few obstacles to practicing what Koreans call *hwangje kyungyoung,* or "emperor-like management."

An Overview of the Changes

Much has changed in Korean corporate governance during the ten years that have passed since the crisis. In a 2005 working paper, a group of four academics (including one of the present writers) developed a Korea Corporate Governance Index (KCGI) that is based on evaluation of five attributes of corporate governance: shareholder rights; board structure; board procedures; disclosure; and ownership parity.[4] Changes in the KCGI, together with the performance of the Korean stock market and a wealth of "anecdotal evidence," suggest a dramatic increase in the quality of Korean corporate governance during the post-crisis period. Between 1998 and 2004, the last year these data have been compiled, the KCGI for large listed Korean corporations (those with book asset values greater than about $2 billion) jumped from 30.78 to 69.64 (out of a possible 100).[5]

One important contributor to the increase in Korea's governance index has been the emergence of large (non-chaebol) industrial corporations that have been recently privatized, including POSCO, now the world's third largest steel producer; KT, Korea's largest telecom provider; and KT&G, Korea's largest tobacco company. The other major group showing notable improvements in the quality of governance is Korean banks with large infusions of foreign capital, including Hana, Kookmin, and Shinhan. In most of these groups of companies, a majority of the outstanding shares are held by foreign investors.[6] All are run by professional—that is, non-family—managers under a great deal of public scrutiny. And since all these companies are listed on foreign stock exchanges that require financial statements prepared in conformity with either U.S., GAAP, or IFRS, they provide far more disclosure than typical chaebol-affiliated firms.[7]

To illustrate the kind of changes that have taken place in the past decade, let's take a closer look at the governance system of POSCO, which is the second largest Korean corporation in terms of market capitalization (in the $50 to $60 billion range during the second half of 2007). We chose POSCO for a number of reasons. One, it was the first Korean company to list on the New York Stock Exchange, a step the firm took in 1994. Second, and perhaps even more telling, Warren Buffett had accumulated a 4% stake in the firm by the end of 2006, citing the firm's strong governance system. Third and last, one of the authors of this chapter has served as an independent director of POSCO since 2002, and is currently the firm's non-executive chairman.

Given POSCO's position as the first Korean firm to list on the NYSE, the list we provide below of the most important features of its governance system reflects NYSE listing requirements as well as the requirements of Sarbanes-Oxley:

- The company is governed by a board of 15 people, including six executive "insiders" and nine independent outside directors.

- The CEO does not chair the board.

- The audit committee consists entirely of outside independent directors, two of whom are financial experts.

- The current public auditing firm was chosen through an open bidding process.

- The company complies fully with the internal control system required by the U.S. Sarbanes-Oxley Act.

- The bylaws allow cumulative voting, greatly increasing the ability of minority shareholders to elect their own representatives to the board.

- The company has no explicit anti-takeover devices in place and no golden parachutes for its executives.[8]

Together, these features not only surpass global standard requirements, they also represent advances over most major American companies, where poison pills are common and the majority of CEOs continue to serve as their board chairmen.

POSCO's system appears to be working for its non-investor stakeholders as well as its shareholders. Its stock price more than quadrupled during the past five years, and its leadership in corporate responsibility is widely recognized. As just one example, a recent issue of *BusinessWeek Japan* (November 7, 2007) recognized POSCO as one of the 30 most socially responsible, "sustainable" companies in the world.

Of course, POSCO is not the only company in Korea with good governance. In addition to the banks and newly privatized firms mentioned earlier, at least a dozen other companies (including SK Telecom, LG Telecom, and KTF) are widely regarded as effectively managed, well-governed companies—indeed, on a par with the best-governed U.S. companies. But, as suggested, these companies present a striking contrast to the majority of Korean firms affiliated with the chaebol, where the quality of governance systems is highly variable and the propensity to reform unclear.

Back to the Chaebol Problem: Ownership Structure

The core of the chaebol's governance problem lies in its ownership structure. It is typically a web of complex cross-shareholdings, often involving a number of circular shareholdings with no clear holding company. In December 2004, the Korean Fair Trade Commission (KFTC) began to disclose the intra-group ownership structures of the chaebol, and opened a website solely designated for such purpose in July 2007.[9]

Our analysis of this data shows that during the period 1997–2005, the average percentage of shares owned by the controlling shareholder (family) was only 22%, while effectively exercising control over 69% of the voting rights through cross- and circular-holdings.[10] In other words, the average gap between cash flow rights and control rights for chaebol-affiliated firms was close to 50%! (Figure 10.1 shows the difference between the cash flow and control rights for the ten largest chaebol in Korea as of April 2004.)

A large disparity between cash flow rights and control rights is a warning signal, an indication of the strength of the controlling shareholders' incentives to transfer wealth from their minority shareholders. When a controlling shareholder owns 22% of the outstanding shares, for example, diverting $100 worth of corporate assets for private uses provides the shareholder with a net gain of $78. And a large disparity makes it easier to divert assets. In 2006 the People's Solidarity for Participatory Democracy (PSPD), the leading shareholder activist group in Korea, documented 70 cases of "tunneling"—that is, the transfer of public corporate assets at below-market prices to other, often private, family-owned entities—by chaebol owners during the period 1995–2005.[11] Of the 70 cases, 30

Control-Ownership Disparity of the Top 10 Chaebol (as of April 2004)

Size is determined by the book value of total assets. Control rights are the sum of cash flow rights and disparity. Figure 10.1A shows size-weighted averages of firm-level measures within each group, and Figure 10.1B shows equal-weighted averages of firm-level measures within each group. Because smaller firms tend to have larger disparities, group-level disparities are higher using equal weightings.

A: Size-Weighted Averages

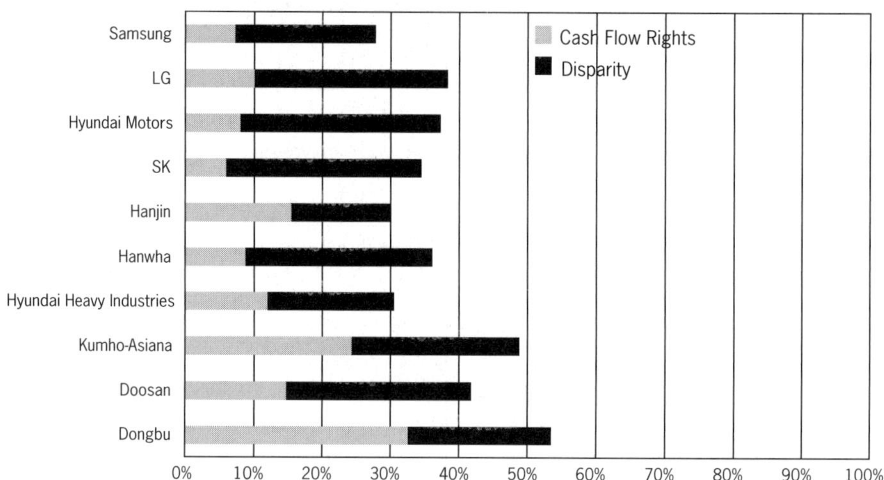

B: Equal-Weighted Averages

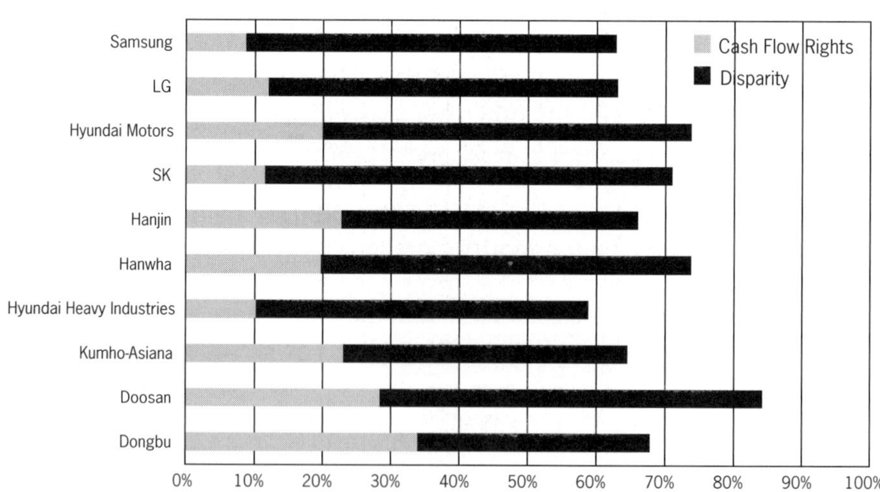

were classified as appropriating valuable corporate opportunities; 20 as illegal securities transactions, such as selling securities to family members at a discounted price; and the remaining 20 as illegal related-party transactions.[12] What's more, a 2007 report by another NGO, Solidarity for Economic Reform (SER), identified information technology subsidiaries established within chaebol as a favorite tunneling tool, shifting wealth from public companies to privately owned family firms.[13]

An alternative to the typical chaebol ownership structure is a holding company format, a corporate organizational structure not permitted in Korea until 1999. That year, in an effort to ease the restructuring process for distressed chaebol after the financial crisis, the government started to allow holding company structures through a revision of the Monopoly Regulation and Fair Trade Act. In 2003, LG Group, the second largest chaebol at the time, was the first among the large chaebol to convert into a holding company. LG was soon followed by other large chaebol, including SK, the energy, chemical, and telecom conglomerate, and CJ Corporation, with major investments in food processing, retail, and entertainment. Figure 10.2 provides a diagram of the LG Group ownership structure before and after its conversion to a holding company structure, illustrating that the holding company structure makes the ownership structure less complicated and less opaque. A holding company also effectively eliminates the "chairman's office"—the center of group control, with no legal status and hence no accountability.[14]

The Current State of Korean Corporate Governance

We now discuss in more detail how Korean corporate governance has evolved in terms of internal governance, and then describe the growing presence of external governance monitors and active investors with the ability to bring about corporate change.

Internal Mechanisms

There are two major internal corporate mechanisms for achieving effective corporate governance: (1) the alignment of executive compensation and managerial incentives with shareholder value; and (2) oversight and control by the board of directors. And let's begin with managerial pay and incentives.

Better Incentives. The most common way to align managerial incentives with shareholder value maximization is performance-based pay, which can be linked either to stock prices and/or measures of operating profitability. Before the 1997 crisis, merit-based compensation was largely shunned by Korean companies, whether affiliated with chaebol or not, and executives and employees at all levels were paid almost entirely on the basis of rank and seniority. When profits were

Ownership Structure of LG Group before and after Its Conversion to a Holding Company Structure. Before Transformation (December 2000)

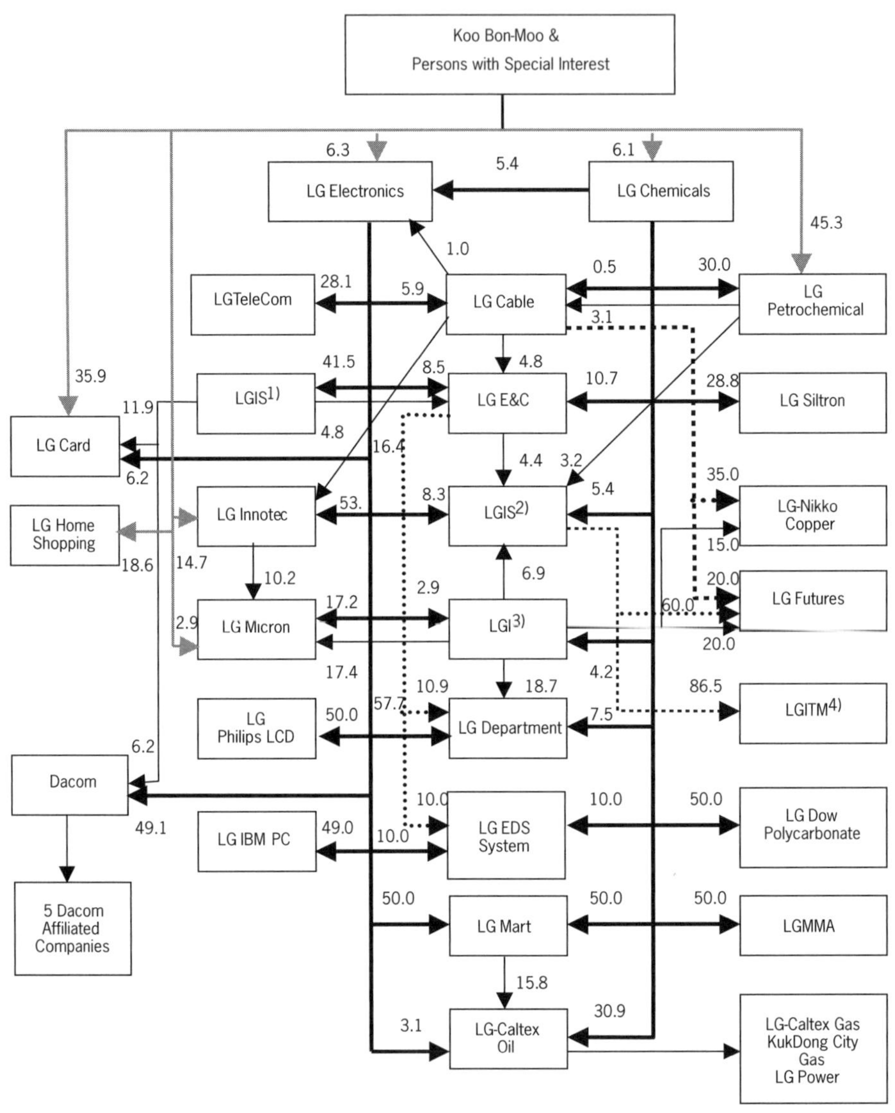

Source: Joo-Young Lee, Simpler Ownership Structure for LG Group, Center for Good Corporate Governance Issue Report (February 12, 2003).

1. LGIS: LG Industrial Systems.
2. LGIS: LG Investment & Securities.
3. LGI: LG International Corp.
4. LGITM: LG Investment Trust Management.

After Transformation (February 2003)

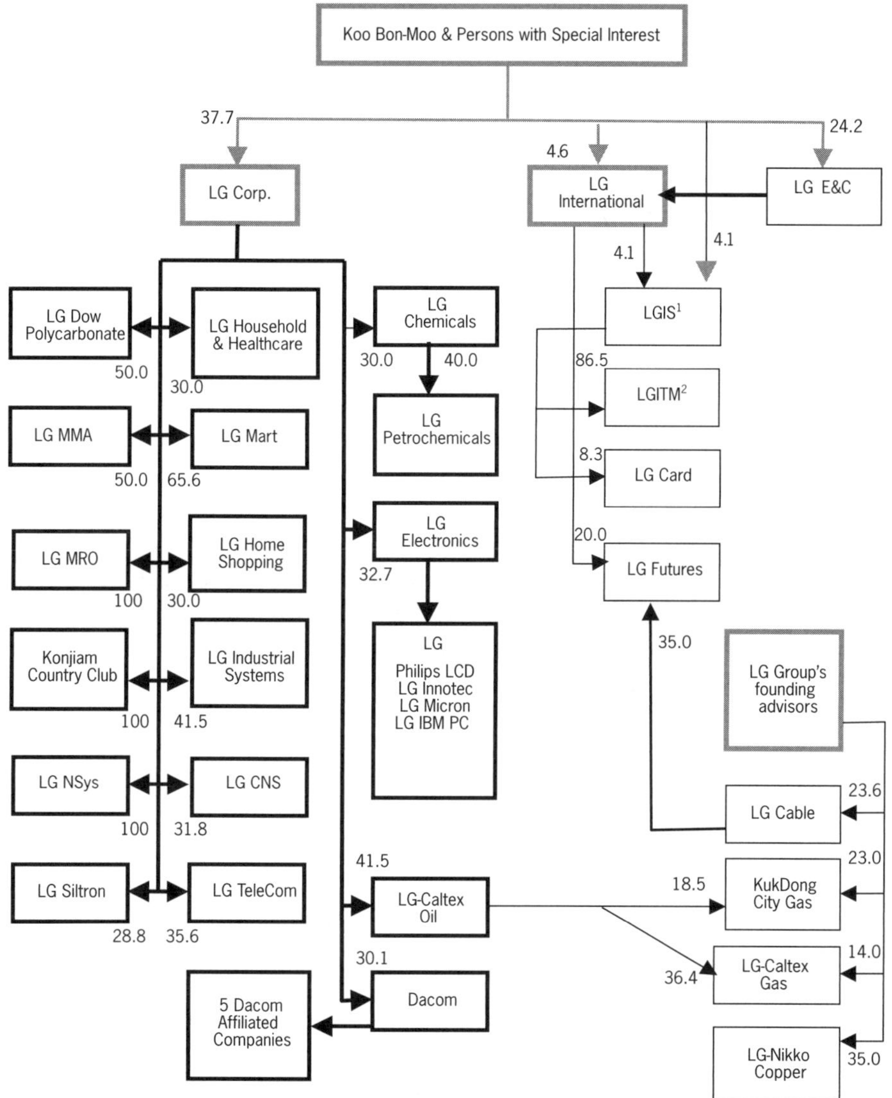

Source: Joo-Young Lee, Simpler Ownership Structure for LG Group, Center for Good Corporate Governance Issue Report (February 12, 2003).
1. LGIS: LG Industrial Systems.
2. LGITM: LG Investment Trust Management.

higher, employees received higher bonuses, but the amount of the individual bonuses depended largely on rank and seniority rather than performance. The only way an employee could be rewarded for superior performance was to get promoted faster than others, but early promotions were uncommon.

Although such pay practices clearly reflected the country's Confucian cultural heritage, with its emphasis on hierarchy and group harmony, they were also consistent with the chaebol owners' private incentives. If company executives were instead intent on maximizing shareholder value in order to increase their own rewards, they would be less inclined to initiate, or cooperate with, tunneling schemes designed to shift profits and valuable assets out of their companies.

As the financial crisis led to numerous bankruptcies, including that of the Daewoo Group, the second largest chaebol at the time of default in 1999, the Korean business community became increasingly aware of the need to increase shareholder value for long-term survival and competitiveness.

And, as a direct consequence, the Korean seniority-based, egalitarian compensation system came under heavy criticism. Companies gradually began to adopt some form of performance-based pay linked to reported earnings or other accounting-based measures of profit, EVA, and/or their stock prices. Stock options were introduced in 1997[15]—and by October 2005, 139 listed companies (over 20% of the 657 firms then listed on the Korean Stock Exchange) had granted stock options to their executives.[16] Also worth noting, Korean companies have been required to expense executive stock options using the Black and Scholes formula since January, 2004. And there have been no Korean option "back dating" scandals like those in the U.S., perhaps reflecting Korean firms' greater consciousness of the *costs* associated with granting options.

One study of 246 Korean listed companies over the period of 1998–2001 (involving one of the present writers) reported that, for the entire sample (both chaebol-affiliated and otherwise), managerial compensation was significantly related to stock market performance, and that the sensitivity of pay to stock performance was comparable to that in the U.S. and Japan.[17] More interestingly, this linkage between Korean pay and performance was driven entirely by the non-chaebol companies, with no significant relation observed for chaebol-affiliated firms. The appointment of top executives in chaebol-affiliated firms has generally been the prerogative of the chaebol owners, who are not likely to encourage firm value maximization when they intend to pursue tunneling and other forms of private benefits of control.

Better Monitors Another important change to Korean internal corporate governance has been the introduction of independent outside directors. Immediately after the crisis, regulations were put into effect requiring that at least one-quarter of the board members of all listed companies be independent outside

SK Telecom and Its Outside Directors

Actions taken by outside directors of SK Telecom in 2003 illustrate the benefits of truly independent directors. In February 2003, prosecutors uncovered an accounting fraud of 1.5 trillion won (roughly $1.5 billion) at SK Global, a distribution and logistics company and a member firm of SK Group (the third largest chaebol at that time). On May 19, creditor banks disclosed their due diligence report revealing that SK Global's book value of equity had negative 4.4 trillion won. Soon thereafter, SK Group pledged group-wide financial support for SK Global, which included a debt-to-equity swap and a promise to improve SK Global's yearly EBITDA from 279 billion to 436 billion won.

The support plan had to be approved by the board of each member firm. The actions taken by the boards of the two flagship companies of the group, SK Corporation (an energy and chemical company) and SK Telecom (a wireless telecom company), contrasted sharply. The board of SK Corporation approved the plan; the board of SK Telecom rejected it. The two boards were differentiated by the true independence of SK Telecom's outside directors from management and the controlling Chey family. In particular, two outside directors of SK Telecom were elected in March 1998 at the recommendation of minority shareholders. The two directors believed that the group support plan to rescue SK Global was harmful to SK Telecom's shareholders and persuaded the majority of outside directors to vote against the plan. (SK Telecom's articles of incorporation require approval by a majority of outside directors of related-party transactions exceeding 10 billion won.)

Although SK Telecom's refusal to join the group-wide support plan did not prevent the creditor banks from restructuring their debts and bailing out SK Global, SK Telecom was freed from the group-wide risk originating from SK Global. During the three-day window surrounding SK Telecom board's decision to reject the group support plan, its share price jumped by 8%—and foreign ownership of the stock increased from 39.23% to 41 .45%.

directors. In 2001, the required percentage of independent directors was increased to 50% for companies with a book value of assets exceeding 2 trillion won (about $2 billion). At least two studies have shown that the larger companies that were required to increase their percentage of independent directors also experienced significant share price increases when the reforms were announced in the second half of 1999.[18] The same studies also reported that those companies afterward reported greater increases in profits, fewer asset sales to related parties (i.e., tunneling), and more frequent board meetings with higher attendance rates than a control group of smaller companies not required to increase the percentage of independent directors. In sum, the requirement for more independent outside directors on the board seems to have had positive effects on the quality of governance, providing better protection for minority shareholders.

Skeptics, of course, question the actual degree of independence of outside directors, pointing out that many nominally independent directors in fact have past ties to the firm or chaebol owners—former executives, current and former executives of a related firm or creditor bank, and lawyers with past or present business ties. A recent report by the SER concludes that almost 20% of the independent directors of 211 chaebol-affiliated publicly listed firms had past or present ties to the firm on whose board they serve.[19] To look at the brighter side, however, this finding also means that over 80% of the board members are fairly independent. Skeptics also criticize corporate boards for rubber-stamping management proposals, pointing to relatively low rejection rates of management proposals by the boards. The business community responds to this charge by attributing the low rejection rates to management's careful preparation and prior consultation with their boards.

We believe there is an element of truth in both sides of this argument. For an illustration of how independent directors can and have made a difference in a Korean company, see the story of SK Telecom in the text box on page 207.

External Governance Mechanisms

The independence of outside directors and their willingness to take assertive action against management have also been questioned in the U.S. But, at least until recently, there has been one important difference between the U.S. and Korea in this regard. When U.S. boards fail to take proper actions against poorly performing management, activist institutional investors or block holders often call for disciplinary actions by the board that are aimed at increasing shareholder value. Sometimes these actions succeed, often with help from the media. But when such external pressures fail in the U.S., the market for corporate control provides a solution by making the underperforming firms the targets of hostile takeover bids. Before the 1997 crisis, these external forces were not in place in Korea. Since the crisis, however, the legal and institutional environments in Korea have changed substantially, and a number of players have emerged as key external monitors and "enforcers."

For external monitors to function properly, they need access to information and enforceable rules that ensure transparency and accountability. Korea has undertaken several important reforms with this end in mind. In 2004 it enacted its own version of Sarbanes-Oxley. The Korean version of SOX and related regulations require, among other things, certification of periodic financial reports by the CEO and the CFO, and a change in auditors after six continuous years of engagement. In 2007 the Financial Supervisory Commission (FSC) also announced a plan for the gradual adoption of the International Financial Reporting Standards (IFRS), with all listed firms having to conform to IFRS by 2011.

To give bite to these new regulations, Korea recently introduced a law permitting securities class action suits. The law applies to all publicly traded companies that are found guilty of false disclosure in their company prospectus or quarterly, semi-annual, or annual reports—and to companies convicted of insider trading, market manipulation, or negligent external audits.

Derivative suits are another potentially important deterrent and legal tool for external monitors that have been used in Korea with considerable effectiveness. According to a 2007 SER study, 17 of the 40 suits filed and adjudicated during the past ten years (1997–2006) were decided for the plaintiffs.[20] Among the best-known of these cases were suits filed against the managements of Korea First Bank in 1997, Samsung Electronics in 1998, and LG Chemical in 2003. In particular, the suit against Samsung Electronics was a wake-up call for all directors serving on the boards of chaebol-affiliated firms. Because Samsung Electronics' directors were not covered by D&O insurance, the directors and Chairman Kun-Hee Lee, the controlling shareholder of Samsung Group, had to pay almost 20 billion won (about $20 million) to the company out of their own pockets. Korean subscriptions to D&O insurance surged soon after the district court verdict in December 2001.

In Korea, potentially effective external monitors and enforcers include shareholder activist NGOs (non-profit, non-government organizations), institutional investors, foreign block holders, and the media.

NGOs, which are typically funded by membership fees, have played an unusually important role in promoting corporate governance reform in post-crisis Korea. The best-known are PSPD and SER. These two NGOs have filed most of the derivative suits against chaebol-affiliated firms for malfeasance, and played a major role in prodding the Korean government to enact various reform measures and prosecute controlling shareholders for white-collar crimes.

In 2006, one of the founders of PSPD helped to create an activist governance fund, the Korea Corporate Governance Fund (KCGF), which is managed by Lazard Asset Management LLC based in New York.[21] The fund is more commonly known as the Jang Hasung Fund, named after the shareholder activist who now advises it. The fund targets small-to-medium-sized companies listed on the Korea Stock Exchange, engages in a dialogue with management with the aim of improving governance practices and increasing shareholder value, and takes hostile action if management response is deemed inadequate.

To the extent we can judge from the market's initial response, the fund's activities appear to be good news for shareholders. A 2007 study shows that the stock prices of companies targeted by KCGF increased significantly on the announcement of the targeting.[22] Moreover, even firms *not* targeted by KCGF experienced positive stock price reactions at the announcement of KCGF's acquisition of target company shares, with greater price jumps for non-target firms with lower quality of governance as measured by a governance index produced by Korea Corporate Governance Service (KCGS). To cite one dramatic example, in August 2006 when KCGF announced that it was buying 5% of its first target, Dae-Han Synthetic Fiber, the company's stock price, as shown in figure 10.3, jumped by over 200% in about a month's time.

Another institutional investor with large potential to improve Korean corporate governance is the National Pension Fund (NPF). In December 2005, the NPF management committee included in its statement of proxy voting princi-

FIGURE 10.3

Share Price Impact of the Activist Korea Corporate Governance Fund

This figure shows the share price movements of Dae Han Synthetic Fiber Co., Ltd., around the announcement that it became the very first target of the activist Korea Corporate Governance Fund (KCGF). KCGF disclosed its 5% ownership on August 23, 2006. The share price of Dae Han and the Korea Stock Price Composite Index KOSPI) are normalized to 100 as of August 22, 2006.

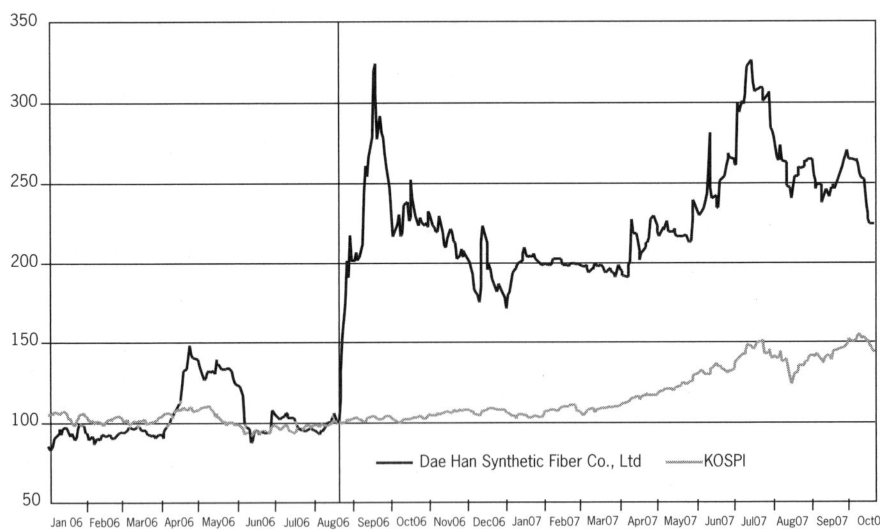

ples and guidelines a clear declaration that proxy voting should be carried out for the sole purpose of enhancing long-term shareholder value. The NPF has also committed to disclosing its votes no more than 14 business days after a shareholders' meeting, allowing outsiders to monitor whether the NPF is actually living up to its principles and guidelines. Part of the promise comes from the realization that the amount of assets under management by the NPF— about $240 billion based on the exchange rate as of September 2007—represents almost 20% of the Korean stock market's total capitalization of $1.2 trillion. With its current investment in domestic equity of $37 billion, the NPF's impact on Korean corporate governance could exceed the combined effect of CalPERS and other U.S. public pension funds in strengthening the accountability of U.S. management and boards.

Although there have been many M&A transactions in Korea since the 1997 crisis, hostile takeover bids against underperforming management have been relatively rare. The external pressure on companies exerted by the Korean market for corporate control stems mainly from activist foreign block holders. Two of the most notable cases have been a proxy fight by Sovereign Asset Management against the management of SK Corporation and the attempt by Icahn Partners, jointly with Steel Partners, to break up KT&G. Although Sovereign lost the proxy fight, its actions contributed to an increase in the share price of SK Corporation of more than 500% over a 16-month period. To win the proxy fight, the management of SK Corporation had to promise major improvements in transparency and governance—promises it kept by revamping its board structure, improving governance practices, and converting to a holding company structure. In the case of KT&G, although the attempt to break up the firm was unsuccessful, the dissidents won a proxy fight against management and secured a board seat.

Additionally, a 2007 study involving one of the current authors provides strong evidence of the important role of foreign block holders in improving Korean corporate governance.[23] Since March 2005 all block holders in Korean companies with more than 5% ownership have been required to state whether they intend to be "passive" or "active" investors, and to declare any changes in their intent over time. The study shows that when foreign block holders announce they are switching their position from passive to active, the stock prices of those companies increase significantly, anticipating the holders' attempts to take more active roles in firm management and governance. And when the anticipated level of future activism is high, as indicated by the number of areas in which the block holder intends to engage actively, stock prices increase by 6% on average.

Finally, the Korean media have become more active monitors of large corporations. The traditional media now openly report corporate scandals and malfeasance committed by the largest and most powerful chaebol. The catalyst for this change has been the Internet. With high-speed broadband connection reaching almost 90% of Korean households at the end of 2006, Korea is one of the most Internet-connected countries in the world. Numerous Internet-based news organizations and websites have sprung up since the crisis and, with few ties to big business, they are not afraid to expose corporate wrongdoing. Because most young people rely heavily on such Internet-based news, the traditional media have little choice but to report corporate problems.

Although Korean corporations now face increased external pressure to practice good governance, some of the pressures are still emerging. For example, securities class action suits against companies with book values of assets below 2 trillion won (again, about $2 billion) were not permitted until January, 2007. Furthermore, the legal hurdles to file class action and derivative suits are much higher than those in the U.S. In addition, a backlash against the Korean reform movement led opponents of full disclosure to argue successfully in 2006 that 129 of the 200 disclosure items are unnecessary for minority shareholder protection, scaling back mandatory disclosure. In response, the SER has maintained that 86 of these 129 deleted items could provide valuable protection for minority shareholders.

Another cloud over the future of Korean corporate governance is being cast by the intensity of the current debate over anti-takeover measures. Korea up to this point has not permitted poison pills, dual class shares, or golden shares—all powerful anti-takeover devices limiting the ability of the market for corporate control to discipline poorly governed companies. However, big business lobbying groups argue that such protective devices are necessary for management to focus their full attention and energy on long-term business planning. Yet another anti-takeover measure under consideration is passage of an act similar to the U.S. Exxon-Florio Act that protects American companies from a foreign takeover for national security concerns.

So far there is no clear consensus on any of these anti-takeover measures in Korea. Even government agencies disagree. For example, the Ministry of Finance and Economy has taken a firmly pro-market position, stating that any anti-takeover measures are harmful to the economy. On the other hand, the Ministry of Commerce, Energy, and Industry has taken a more sympathetic view of business lobbying efforts to introduce these anti-takeover devices.

Concluding Remarks

In this chapter we describe the evolution of Korean corporate governance since the 1997 financial crisis. Any such discussion inevitably involves the chaebol because of their dominant role in the economy. The chaebol are widely credited with helping lead the backward Korean economy of the 1960s into its current position as the eleventh largest economy in the world. At the same time, however, they are blamed—and rightly so—for much of the corporate value destruction leading to the financial crisis. Accordingly, many governance reform measures triggered by the crisis have targeted chaebol.

Although some reform measures have been unsuccessful or had undesirable side effects, their overall impact has been positive. Most notable are improved corporate transparency, better alignment of managerial incentives with shareholder value, greater managerial accountability, and more effective oversight by the board. External monitors and enforcers of good governance, largely nonexistent before the crisis, have emerged to play important roles in improving Korean corporate governance.

The best governance practices in Korea today can be seen mainly in three kinds of corporations: (1) newly privatized companies; (2) large corporations run by professional management; and (3) banks with substantial equity ownership in the hands of foreign investors. The governance practices of many of these companies meet the global standard. At the other end of the spectrum, however, are many large chaebol-affiliated or family-run firms that refuse to change and circumvent regulatory reform measures. Also worth noting is that such resistance to change has not been without consequences for the controlling shareholders, several of whom have gone to jail for white-collar crimes, often linked to bad governance.

Having said this, there are also marked differences in governance practices among the chaebol. Some have transformed their web of cross- and circular-shareholdings into holding company structures, making their ownership clearer and less complicated. Some of the flagship companies affiliated with these chaebol now have governance practices that are on a par with those of well-governed U.S. companies. But many others continue to resist change and actively lobby against reforms.

It appears that some of these lobbying efforts are working. Not only does the political will for governance reform appear to be losing momentum, there also are signs of a growing backlash against reforms recently implemented. Although the recent reduction in the number of mandatory disclosure items is troubling, more disturbing is the current push to allow American-style anti-takeover devices, which, if successful, would clearly weaken the disciplinary effect of the market for corporate control.

What will Korean corporate governance look like in the future? As in the U.S. and throughout the world, some companies will practice good governance while others will not.[24] At this point, however, it is difficult to predict whether the average quality of Korean governance will continue to improve. With the reform movement losing its momentum, vested interest groups may succeed in eroding some of the gains already made. Much of the outcome will eventually depend on swings in socio-political moods, as well as on the globalization of trade. Because the Korean economy is so closely linked to foreign trade and capital, continued globalization will provide pressure for further improvement in corporate governance through both product and capital markets. Unfortunately, globalization appears to be on the defensive everywhere, even in the U.S, the self-proclaimed champion of free trade. This negative political climate surrounding globalization is the major threat to the future of Korean corporate governance.

Notes

We are deeply indebted to Don Chew for helpful comments and suggestions.

1. EVA is calculated as net operating profits after taxes minus a charge for the cost of capital equal to WACC multiplied by total capital. See E. Han Kim, Myeong Kyun Kim, and Jaekyung Yi, "Economic Value Added (EVA) of the Listed Companies," The Korea Stock Exchange Report 9801, February 1998 (in Korean).

2. For a more detailed description of the causes of the financial crisis and the type of restructuring measures undertaken by the new administration, See E. Han Kim, "Globalization of Capital Markets and the Asian Financial Crisis," *Journal of Applied Corporate Finance,* Vol. 11, Fall 1998, pp. 30–39.

3. In classifying chaebol as "large," we used the designation of the Korea Fair Trade Commission. The numbers are equally weighted averages of individual firm level cash flow rights and control rights. Group-level disparity, which is computed by size-weighted averages of firm-level numbers within the same group, is smaller because larger firms tend to have smaller disparities. The controlling shareholder's cash flow rights and control rights at the group level are 16% and 34%, respectively. We include non-listed firms in our calculation.

4. The KCGI was compiled and presented by Bernard S. Black, Woochan Kim, Ha Sung Jang, and Kyung-Suh Park in their working paper, "Does Corporate Governance Affect Firms' Market Value? Times Series Evidence from Korea," European Corporate Governance Institute Finance Working Paper No. 103, 2005. The numbers reported above represent updates of the indices presented in the original version.

5. For smaller listed firms with book value of assets less than 2 trillion won (about $2 billion), the increase in KCGI was less dramatic, increasing from 22.96 in 1998 to 38.58 in 2003. These companies are subject to looser regulatory requirements concerning board composition and inter-corporate investment. However, because regulations on inter-corporate investment apply at the group level, member firms of a group with a size exceeding 5 trillion won (the threshold has been relaxed in recent years) are subject to the more stringent regulations even if they are very small.

6. As of December 10, 2007, foreign ownership of POSCO shares was 49%, while foreign ownership of KT, which is subject to an upper ceiling of 50%, was 46%. The foreign ownership for the remaining four firms was well over 50%.

7. POSCO, KT, Kookmin, and Shinhan are listed on the New York Stock Exchange, Hana on the London Stock Exchange, and KT&G on the Luxemburg Stock Exchange.

8. POSCO does, however, have mutual shareholdings with a number of other companies (e.g., Nippon Steel Corporation and Hyundai Heavy Industries). Although these inter-firm share investments represent strategic alliances, they could be used to thwart hostile takeover attempts if the strategic partners decided to vote with POSCO management.

9. http://groupopni.ftc.go.kr.

10. These numbers are based at the individual firm level.

11. People's Solidarity for Participatory Democracy, "Report on the Tunneling Activities of 38 Chaebol Families," 2006 (in Korean).

12. An example is LG Chemical's sale in 1999 of its LG Petrochemical shares to LG group family members at a heavily discounted price. In 2002, LG Petrochem was listed and the family members earned combined profits of approximately $200 million on the transaction. This case of self-dealing later resulted in a derivative suit that was won by the plaintiffs in 2006, with no appeal by LG family members.

13. Solidarity for Economic Reform, "Why Are Chaebol Families Fond of IT Firms?" Economic Reform Report No. 05, 2007 (in Korean).

14. Because affiliated firms cannot hold the shares of a parent company in a holding company structure, there is no disparity between cash flow rights and control rights in the parent company. For the affiliated firms, however, the disparity did not decrease noticeably because the parent's ownership of affiliated firms can be as low as 20%. Since the controlling family directly holds shares only in the parent company and two layers of pyramidal structure are allowed, the companies at the bottom of the control chain can have large disparities between cash flow and control rights.

15. Turbotek, a non-listed venture firm, was the first to introduce stock options to attract and motivate skilled workers.

16. Korea Listed Companies Association, "Stock Option Grants among Listed Firms," Press Release, October 2005 (in Korean).

17. Takao Kato, Woochan Kim, and Ju Ho Lee, "Executive Compensation, Firm Performance, and Chaebol in Korea: Evidence from New Panel Data," *Pacific-Basin Finance Journal,* Vol. 15, 2007, pp. 36–55.

18. See Bernard S. Black and Woochan Kim, "The Effect of Board Structure on Firm Value: A Multiple Identification Strategies Approach Using Korean Data," European Corporate Governance Institute Finance Working Paper No. 179, 2007; and Jongmoo Choi, Sae Won Park, and Sean Sehyun Yoo, "The Value of Outside Directors: Evidence from Corporate Governance Reform from Korea," *Journal of Financial and Quantitative Analysis,* Vol. 42, No. 4, 941–962.

19. Solidarity for Economic Reform, "The Independence of Outside Directors," Economic Reform Report No. 2007–06 (in Korean).

20. Solidarity for Economic Reform, "Shareholder Derivative Suit Since 1997," Economic Reform Report No. 09, 2007 (in Korean).

21. In the interest of full disclosure, the second author of this chapter is a member of SER's Policy Advisory Committee and of a group that serves as a consultant to KCGF.

22. See Jung Yong Choi, Dong Wook Lee, and Kyung-Suh Park, "Corporate Governance and Firm Value: Endogeneity-Free Evidence from Korea," mimeo, 2007.

23. See Woochan Kim, Woojin Kim, and KapSok Kwon, "Value of Shareholder Activism: Evidence from the Switchers," mimeo, 2007.

24. There are wide within-country variations in the quality of corporate governance among companies in emerging markets. For a discussion of firm-level determinants of the quality of governance and the effect of governance on firm valuation, see Art Durnev and E. Han Kim, "To Steal or Not to Steal: Firm Attributes, Legal Environment, and Valuation," *Journal of Finance,* Vol. 60, June, 2005, pp. 1461–1493, and Art Durnev and E. Han Kim, "Explaining Differences in the Quality of Governance among Companies: Evidence from Emerging Markets," *Journal of Applied Corporate Finance,* Vol. 19, Winter 2007, pp. 16–24.

CHAPTER 11

The Ownership Structure, Governance, and Performance of French Companies

Corporate Control and the Politics of Finance

PÉTER HARBULA

*We cannot all be kings, it is not well that there should be many
masters, one man must be supreme, one king to whom the son of
scheming Saturn has given the sceptre of sovereignty over you all.*
—Homer, *Iliad*, Book II, translated by Samuel Butler

IN FRANCE, as in most countries in continental Europe, the concept of corporate governance as a means of promoting shareholder value was not really taken in earnest until the early 1990s. The growth of interest in value-oriented governance at the beginning of the last decade can be traced to the wave of financial scandals and general economic turmoil in those years, a combination that was again in evidence at the start of the new millennium. In this sense, the French focus on corporate governance can be viewed as a response to crisis. But even if the crisis that gave rise to it has largely receded, the governance of listed companies remains very much at the center of economic concern and debate in France today.

In typical public companies in the U.S. and U.K., ownership tends to be dispersed among many shareholders with relatively small holdings and limited voting power, thus resulting in a separation of ownership from control. But for most listed French companies, and for companies in other continental European countries as well, ownership tends to be more concentrated, with a single shareholder group (often the founding family) exercising effective control. Such concentration of ownership and interest is generally understood to have important benefits. Most important, it limits the "agency costs"—the loss of efficiency and value from the tendency of professional managers without significant ownership stakes to pursue goals other than value maximization—associated with raising equity from a dispersed shareholder base. On the other hand, the presence of a controlling shareholder creates the clear potential for another kind of agency problem: the possibility that controlling shareholders will consume "private benefits" that come at the expense of minority shareholders.[1] Controlling shareholders—particularly those with voting rights that are proportionately greater than their rights to corporate cash flows and dividends—sometimes use their influence to receive excessive compensation for services, tailor company policies to their personal preferences, or otherwise dilute the value of the minority shareholders.

This chapter begins with the assumption that the goal of corporate governance is to ensure that companies aim to maximize their value to (all of) the firm's shareholders.[2] The relative effectiveness in creating value of the different ownership types—those dominated by a controlling shareholder versus those with a dispersed shareholder base—will depend on the extent to which the benefits of concentrated ownership in terms of control over management outweigh the costs stemming from the potential for expropriating minority shareholders.

The first theoretical studies of the link between corporate ownership structure and performance and value, which were published in the early 1980s, suggested that large (controlling) shareholdings tend to be associated with lower levels of efficiency, profit, and value.[3] The underperformance of such companies, particularly family-owned firms, was attributed to managerial entrenchment and the possible expropriation of minority (or at least passive) shareholders. A more recent theoretical study concluded that, although the increased scrutiny of management provided by controlling shareholders may help reduce the waste of resources, such oversight also limits management initiative and creativity.[4] Yet another study argued that although controlling shareholders should have a positive impact on earnings quality, the lower liquidity of the shares should have the overall effect of reducing firm value.[5]

Within the past ten years, however, a number of empirical studies have presented controlling shareholders in a more favorable light. For example, in a widely cited study of international corporate governance, a 1998 article by Raphael La Porta, Florencio Lopez-de-Silanes, and Andrei Shleifer reported that in countries other than the U.S. and U.K., most corporations have a controlling, or "reference," shareholder, such as a family, another corporation, or the State. The main explanation provided by La Porta et al. is that, in countries with relatively little protection of minority shareholders, inside owners intent on raising outside capital for their enterprises must retain significant ownership stakes to persuade outside investors to commit their capital to the firm (an argument that is also made by René Stulz in chapter 6).[6]

What's more, we now have some persuasive evidence of the value added by controlling shareholders in U.S. companies. For example, a 2003 study of U.S. family-owned companies during the period 1992–1999 reported that such firms earned average returns on assets (EBITDA/Total Assets) that were 6.6% higher than the ROAs of non-family firms. The study also reported, however, that the margin of superiority was greatest when family ownership reaches a peak of about 32%, after which point it progressively declines (though still remaining positive) as proportional ownership increases.[7] Perhaps even more surprising, the same study reported evidence of family control in over 35% of S&P 500 industrial companies, and family ownership of nearly 18% of the outstanding equity in such family-controlled firms.[8]

Those readers who were unaware of the prevalence of family ownership and control in the U.S. may be equally surprised by recent changes in the ownership of French companies. Thanks to the progressive internationalization of the French economy and stock exchange during the past ten years or so, the extensive network of corporate cross-holdings that once bound together the largest French companies has begun to dissolve. As a consequence, listed French companies today exhibit a striking diversity of ownership structure—one that ranges from the more conventional, predominantly State- or family-owned enterprises to companies with dispersed shareholder bases that often include significant blocks held by foreign institutional investors. This variation in turn provides an opportunity for researchers like me to investigate the correlation between corporate ownership structure and performance and value.

In this chapter, I summarize the findings of my recent study of the ownership structure and operating performance of 150 large, publicly traded French companies during the 20-year period 1986–2005. Using EVA and CFROI as measures of performance and value creation, my research shows that, as in the case of U.S. family-owned companies, operating performance improves with increases in the concentration of ownership up to a certain point—around 30%—and then falls off as ownership becomes even more concentrated. I also examined the effect of having multiple classes of stock with different voting rights. Like previous work that identifies a large premium for voting stock as an indicator of ineffective corporate governance, my findings point to major agency problems within companies that continue to have "hard-core" corporate shareholders. But perhaps most important, my study presents clear evidence of extensive change in French corporate ownership structure and improvements in governance during the past 20 years.

Development and Evolution of French Corporate Ownership Structure

The origins of the current French corporate governance system can be traced to the French government's attempt to restore the economy after World War II. At that time, a number of significant enterprises were nationalized to strengthen the presence of the State in key sectors and create "national champions" that could compete with foreign companies.

In 1982, after an almost decade-long period of economic stagnation, the goals of the nationalization program were reformulated as the following three: (1) restore national ownership of key assets; (2) "jumpstart" a new cycle of economic growth with the help of a national industrial policy; and (3) encourage a new civic role for enterprises.

Starting in 1986, however, economic policy took a sharp turn away from state ownership and toward free enterprise. A new political regime launched a privatization program made up of 65 companies. From 1986 to 1988, CGE (now Alcatel), Saint-Gobain, Société Générale, Matra, Paribas, and Suez (or TF1) were privatized through initial public offerings. Since the State was no longer financing their industrial projects, the companies raised equity on the financial markets, often through the issuance of non-voting shares.

The same political coalition was responsible for a second burst of privatizations that began in 1993. During the next four years, eight large French groups—Seita, Renault, BNP, Rhône-Poulenc, Elf, UAP, Usinor, Péchiney—were either partly or fully privatized. By the end of 1994, only three French industries—telecommunications, energy, and transport—continued to be dominated by the public sector.

During the privatization process, only a limited portion of equity shares was reserved for specific shareholders such as mutual funds and workers. The bulk of the shares in such public offerings was purchased by other domestic companies, often still state-owned themselves and waiting to be privatized. Foreign shareholdings were rare, owing largely to the relatively underdeveloped state of French capital markets. And French households, unlike their Anglo-Saxon counterparts, had little experience with, and showed little interest in, acquiring shares. As a result, the main groups that were being privatized became not just the sellers, but also major buyers and owners in the privatization process.

In other words, the companies acquired shares in one another, forming a network of cross-holdings. Such networks provided a number of attractions for management and regulators. Perhaps most important, by "locking up" a significant portion of the capital, such cross-holdings made hostile takeovers very difficult if not impossible. This system is referred to as *"noyau dur,"* or what is rendered in English as "hard-core" ownership. In theory, the justification for providing management such protection from capital market forces is to encourage it to take the long view, and in so doing take fuller account of the interests of the firm's non-investor stakeholders. But whether management can be relied on to use such protection to create long-term value is at best a doubtful proposition—one that I present evidence on later.

The hard-core system is bound together by more than just a network of cross-holdings. It is composed of companies run by professional managers and overseen by board members who have been bred into a common tradition, in many cases through training at the "Grandes Écoles." Such tradition and training have in turn worked to preserve a "high-level" union of business and political interests.[9]

The resulting distinctive French corporate governance model, in which the shareholders of many different companies are linked in a web of cross ownership, is a model of *de facto* control by management in which shareholders have very little voice or influence. Moreover, the fact that many of the directors of such hard-core companies are also directors or managers of other such firms results in an even larger concentration of influence and control, as

FIGURE 11.1

Cross-Holdings in the French Corporate Governance Structure (% as of December 1997)

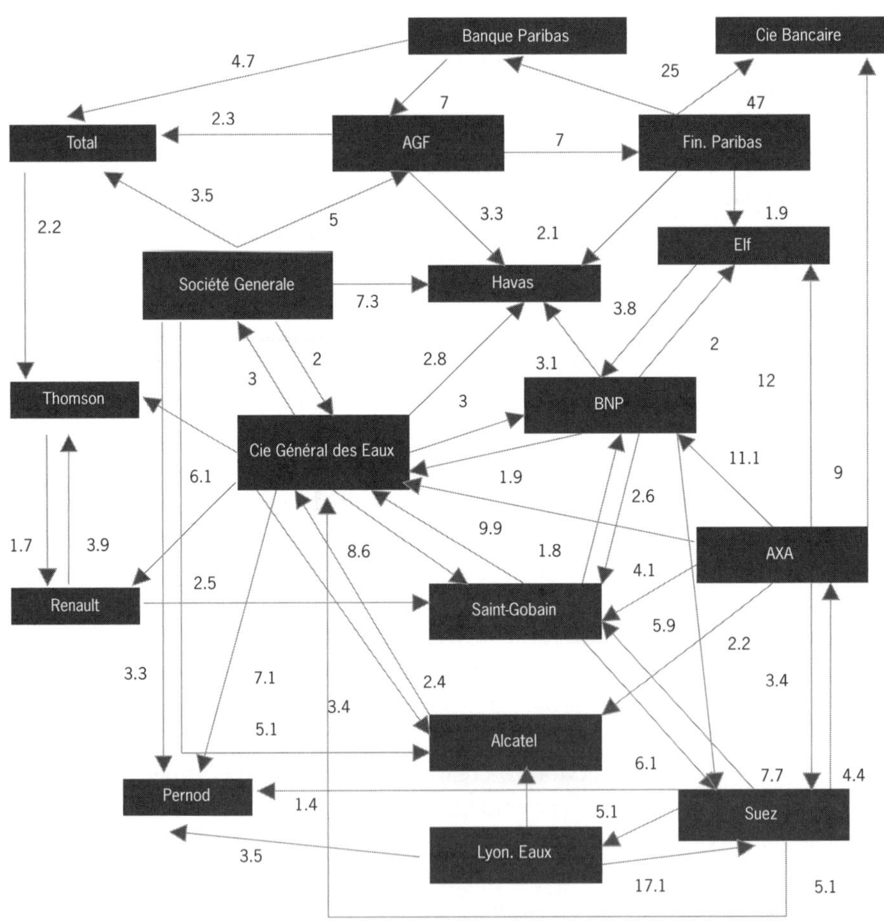

well as corporate boards distinguished mainly by their willingness to defer to management.[10]

In sum, the hard-core ownership structure resulting from corporate cross-holdings that dominated the French corporate landscape a decade ago can be viewed as a network of tacit corporate alliances that put effective control in the hands of management. The ownership stakes of the corporate allies in any one firm rarely constituted a voting majority; and as one moved beyond the hard-core, the remaining minority shareholders tended to be highly diffused and have minimal participation in corporate decision-making. Share ownership by foreign institutions was much less common in those years.

Figure 11.1 illustrates the cross-holdings of the CAC 40 companies in 1997. The figure does not provide a complete picture, but rather a "slice," of the network—one that I was able to reconstruct from the limited information available at that time (including previous research).

But if one then looks at table 11.1, which shows cross-holdings from 1995 to 2003, there is a perceptible trend away from cross ownership. Starting in the mid-1990s, the growing presence of international mutual funds in the shareholder bases of the largest French companies put pressure on managements to narrow the corporate focus and raise returns on the capital employed. Along with such changes, the top executives of many of these companies committed to reduce or even eliminate their cross-holdings in other companies.[11]

TABLE 11.1

Cross-Holdings between the CAC 40 Companies as of December 1995 and December 2003

Number of Cross-Holdings	1995	1997	1999	2001	2003
0–1	12	13	19	26	29
2–5	16	17	13	10	8
5–10	6	5	5	2	1
10+	6	5	3	2	2
Total	**40**	**40**	**40**	**40**	**40**

Average Size of the Cross-Holding	1995	1997	1999	2001	2003
Less than 2%	3	3	10	22	20
2%–5%	10	9	18	10	16
5%–10%	23	25	10	7	4
More than 10%	4	3	2	1	0
Total	**40**	**40**	**40**	**40**	**40**

Value Creation and Corporate Performance: Does the Shareholder Matter?

But is there any evidence that this evolution of the ownership structures of French corporations has increased efficiency and benefited shareholders?

With the aim of identifying the effects of corporate ownership structures on operating performance and value, I examined the performance of a sample of 150 French nonfinancial companies over the period 1986–2005. Although total shareholder return is likely to be a variable of great interest to investors, it is not the only way of measuring a company's performance over a given time period. The intent of my study was to provide an operating focus on value creation by using two well-known and widely accepted measures of periodic corporate performance: EVA[12] and CFROI.[13]

I divided my sample of 150 companies into two categories (with further subdivisions as noted below):[14]

- Ninety-nine companies with *reference* shareholders deemed to have exclusive control, *de jure or de facto,* over critical managerial decisions. Companies were considered as part of the reference shareholder group if the major shareholder held at least 20% of the voting rights. For the purpose of the analysis, I considered not only single shareholders but also known and announced coalitions of significant shareholders. I also identified a subsample of 55 companies with "large" reference shareholders (those with ownership stakes larger than 50%).

- Fifty-one companies with a diffuse shareholder base that, although lacking a 20% shareholder (or shareholder coalition), often includes institutional as well as individual investors. From this group I also carved out a subset of 25 companies with a hard-core ownership structure. A 15% stake held jointly by a small group of companies was considered sufficient for classification within this subcategory, provided there was no other major shareholder with an equivalent or larger voting stake.

As reported in table 11.2, the 99 French companies with reference shareholders produced notably higher EVAs and CFROIs than the 51 firms with diffuse ownership, suggesting that controlling shareholders can play an important monitoring and disciplinary role in large companies. (My analysis of shareholder returns also pointed in the same direction, but the results were less conclusive.) On the other hand, as can be seen in table 11.3, when I removed the 25 hard-core companies from my sample, the underperformance of the remaining 26 companies with diffuse ownership largely disappeared.

In addition, the 55 companies with "large" reference shareholders underperformed the overall sample for all selected measures. This finding suggests

TABLE 11.2

Value Creation and Performance for 150 French Firms between 1986 and 2005*

	Corporations with a Reference Shareholder Structure versus the Overall Sample	Corporations with a Diffused Ownership Structure versus the Overall Sample
Shareholder Return		
Average	2.3%	−4.5%
Median	2.2%	−4.1%
Number of firms on average	99	51
EVA™		
Average	5.5%	−10.4%
Median	7.0%	−13.6%
Number of firms on average	99	51
CFROI™		
Average	2.2%	−8.1%
Median	2.1%	−9.0%
Number of firms	93	57

* EVA™ performance is measured every year and the firms are categorized into one of the categories for each year. CFROI™ is computed over the observation period and firms are categorized to one category only (based upon the category they were attributable for most of the observed period).

that, beyond a certain level of ownership, the greater possibility for expropriation of minority holders outweighs the potential advantages of better monitoring and control.

In conclusion, the companies with hard-core corporate shareholders were the clear underperformers in my sample. The same can be argued to a lesser extent about companies with large reference shareholders, especially when the ownership stake is well above 50%. Thus, my findings provide no support for the claim that the insulation from market forces provided management by cross-holdings allows for a more effective, longer-term investment strategy. And the underperformance of firms with single majority owners contains the strong suggestion that too much concentration of ownership is also suboptimal.

Signs of Progress

In an additional effort to see the extent to which the failings of the hard-core companies were dragging down the performance of firms with diffuse ownership,

TABLE 11.3

Value Creation and Performance for Diffused Ownership French Firms between 1986 and 2005*

Versus Overall Sample Average	Hard-Core Governed Firms	Non Hard-Core Governed Diffused Ownership Structure Firms	Reference Shareholder	Large Reference Shareholder
Shareholder Return				
Average	−5.8%	−3.0%	6.1%	−0.9%
Median	−6.9%	−1.6%	8.7%	−3.0%
Number of firms on average	25	26	44	55
EVA™				
Average	−27.4%	6.0%	7.7%	3.6%
Median	−36.3%	8.5%	9.8%	4.8%
Number of firms on average	25	26	44	55
CFROI™				
Average	−31.7%	5.5%	8.7%	−5.2%
Median	−32.0%	4.6%	10.2%	−7.7%
Number of firms	21	36	39	54

*EVA™ performance is measured every year and the firms are categorized into one of the categories for each year CFROI™ is computed over the observation period and firms are categorized to one category only (based upon the category they were attributable for most of the observed period).

I also attempted to see whether these performance measures changed over the 20-year period of my study. For the entire sample of 150 companies, as well as for each of the three subsets of companies described, I compared the average shareholder return, EVA, and CFROI during the first 10-year period (1986–1995) to averages for the second period (1996–2005).

As reported in table 11.4, there were significant improvements in performance for all groups. Part of this improvement can be attributed to the favorable macroeconomic conditions of the late 1990s. But the main explanation is the gradual dissolution of the hard-core governance system, as reflected in the dramatic increase in the operating returns of the hard-core sample of companies.[15]

Such changes, as suggested earlier, can be viewed as responses by French managers and their boards to growing pressure from overseas institutional shareholders to create value by focusing on core businesses. Take the case of Alcatel. In 1990, it was a recently privatized conglomerate with interests in mechanics, energy, naval construction (activities that were later spun off under the

TABLE 11.4

Performance Improvement in the Sample 1986–1995 versus 1996–2005

Versus Average Sample Results	Reference Shareholder	Large Reference Shareholder	Diffused Ownership	"Hard-Core" Governed
Shareholder Return 1986–1995	−8.9%	−9.2%	−12.2%	−14.5%
Shareholder Return 1996–2005	+7.3%	+13.2%	+11.5%	+8.9%
EVA 1986–1995	−9.2%	−9.1%	−12.5%	−14.5%
EVA 1996–2005	+8.4%	+12.9%	+9.8%	+19.4%
CFROI 1986–1995	−7.5%	−8.5%	−7.7%	−12.3%
CFROI 1996–2005	+8.4%	+11.0%	+8.9%	+15.1%

name Alsthom), publishing, book editing (Générale Occidentale), electric construction (Cegelec), and cables (Nexans), among others. By early 2000, the company had become a "pure play" in telecom OEM, achieved in part through a series of divestitures and acquisitions (DSC, Xylan, Packet Engines, Spatial Technologies and, most recently, Lucent). A similar path was taken by Suez, which divested its financial services and media businesses to become a pure utility. The evolution of these two companies since the mid-1990s is representative of the general improvement in French corporate governance and performance.

Dissolution of the Hard-Core Governance Model

The role in the French economy of the hard-core governance model "installed" during the privatization of many previously State-owned French companies has progressively declined. As one telling piece of evidence, consider that when Marceau Investissement launched a hostile takeover for Société Générale (SG) in 1988, SG's core shareholders formed an alliance that blocked the offer. By contrast, when Pechiney was threatened with takeover by Alcan in 2003, essentially the same hard-core shareholder group (including BNP Paribas, AGF [itself controlled by the German Allianz] and Caisse des Dépôts et des Consignations [CDC])[16] did not resist. The difference in the outcome of the two cases can be attributed, at least in part, to the fact that the U.S. mutual funds families Fidelity and Franklin held about 12% of Pechiney's stock while the hard-core had little more than 13% of the voting rights.

Moreover, the change in Pechiney's ownership structure during the last two decades reflects the progressive internationalization of the French economy and stock market. Whereas only about 10% of the shares of French companies were held by foreigners in 1988, by the end of 2003 this percentage was close to 44%.[17]

Is There an Optimal Level of Ownership Concentration?

Although the above analysis suggests the limitations of "hard-core" ownership and corporate cross-holdings as a governance model, it does not offer much insight into the question raised at the beginning of this chapter: Does the presence of a controlling shareholder lead to more effective corporate governance and greater efficiency than the "market-based" controls that are supposed to discipline companies with diffuse ownership? And if so, does corporate performance and value appear to vary directly (that is, in pretty much linear fashion) with increases in the concentration of ownership? Or to put it another way, do companies with a 50% controlling shareholder systematically outperform those with a 25% shareholder?

In a pioneering 1985 study of ownership concentration and value in U.S. companies, Harold Demsetz and Ken Lehn argued that different kinds of businesses (say, high-tech vs. low-tech, start-up vs. mature) with different investment requirements should lend themselves to different kinds of ownership structures. To the extent this is so, as Demsetz and Lehn went on to argue, we should not expect to find any clear relationship between ownership structure and value.[18] And in a follow-up study in 2001, Demsetz and Belen Villalonga found that, after controlling for differences in the types of U.S. companies that have concentrated holdings, such companies performed more or less the same as firms with dispersed ownership.[19]

On the other hand, as noted earlier, Anderson and Reeb's 2003 study of U.S. family-controlled public companies reported systematically higher operating returns for firms with larger percentage family holdings. But, as also mentioned earlier, the performance margin of superiority over non-family firms reaches a peak at around 30% ownership, after which it falls progressively lower (though never completely disappears).

This result for U.S. family firms is similar to what I found when exploring the relationship between ownership concentration and value in my sample of large French companies. I measured ownership concentration as the percentage of voting rights (which, in France, often differs significantly from rights to cash flows and dividends) held by the largest shareholder or coalition of shareholders.

My findings, as depicted graphically in figure 11.2, show two distinct groups of high-performance companies. One group (at the left end of the distribution) is characterized by highly diffuse ownership (with no shareholder owning more than 5–10% of the voting rights) while the second group has controlling shareholders whose percentage ownership clusters around 25%. Companies with large (greater than 50%) controlling shareholders underperformed the sample average somewhat while there was significant underperformance by the hard-core sample of firms.

CFROI, EVA, and Shareholder Structure

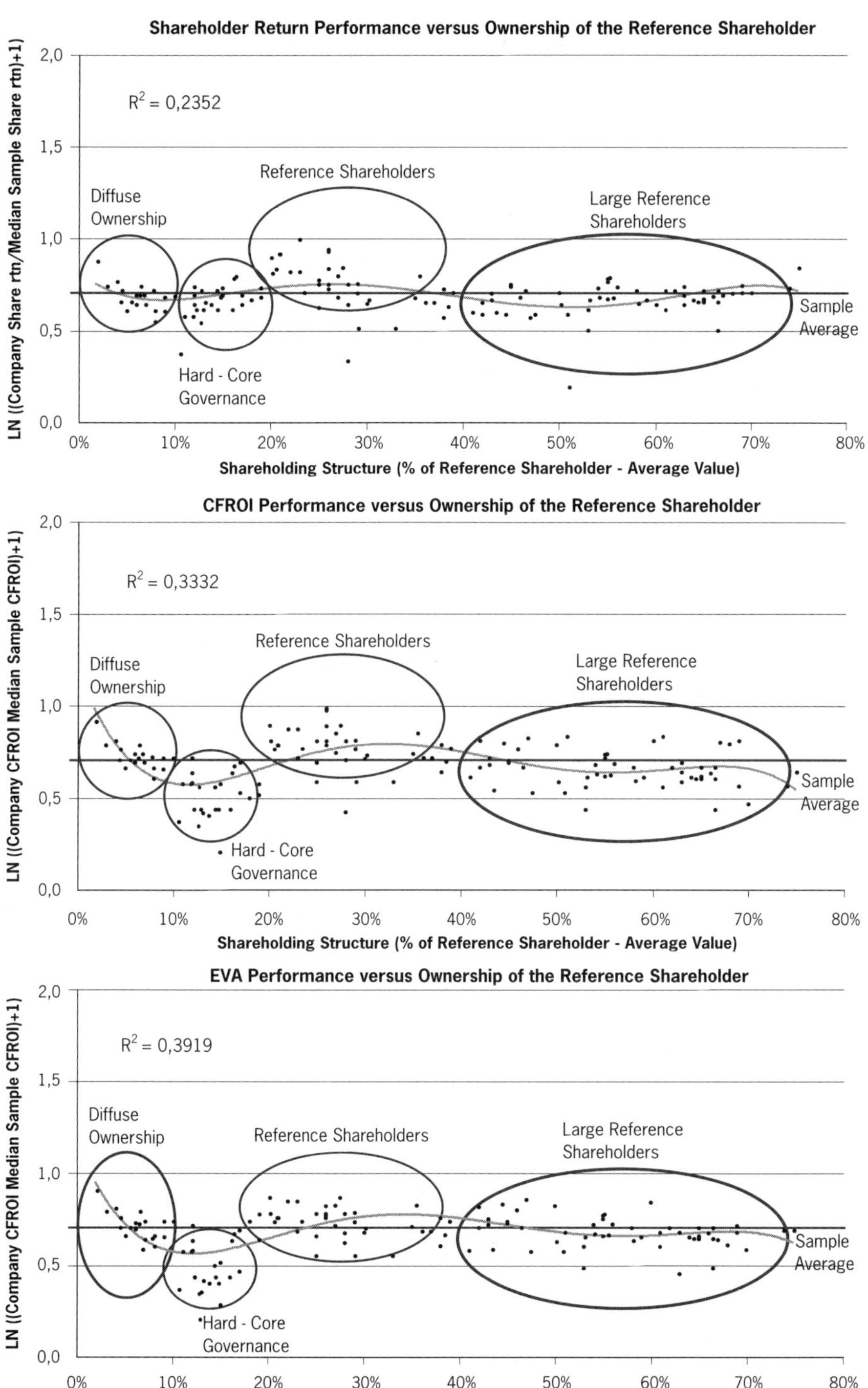

The Family Role in French Corporations

The shareholding structure of the companies observed in this study was influenced to a large extent by the presence of family-founded or family-owned companies. At least one-third of the companies I investigated had a founder, or his or her family, as its largest shareholder. The influence is the most important for the reference and large-reference type companies, but there is also evidence of founder or family influence in a number of diffusely owned companies (see table 11.5). Some examples of the latter are Accor, Danone, and Capgemini.

What would explain such findings? Some would argue that the companies at the left end of the distribution are likely to have an abundance of promising growth opportunities, and hence the greatest demand for the liquidity and risk-bearing capacity provided by a broadly diversified shareholder base.[20] In addition, the potential threat of a takeover could push management to optimize the performance of the companies. But the superior performance of such companies may also have much to do with the skill and quality of their management teams. A number of the companies in this sample are run by influential CEOs with a reputation for maintaining effective control over operations, much as controlling shareholders are reported to do. Companies like Air Liquide and Accor (until the middle of the 1990s) are good examples of such firms.

But if companies with promising growth opportunities and large funding requirements are more likely to have a dispersed ownership base, more mature

TABLE 11.5

Shareholding Structures between 1986 and 2005*

	Diffused Ownership Structure	"Hard-Core" Ownership Structure	Large Reference Shareholder	Reference Shareholder Structure	Total
State	4	5	2	8	19
Family/Founder	7		27	28	62
French Corporation	2	8	6	8	24
Foreign Corporation	2	1	3	3	9
Employees/ Management	3	2	2	2	9
French Financial Institution	4	8	2	4	18
Foreign Financial Institution	4	1	2	2	9
Total	**26**	**25**	**44**	**55**	**150**

*Average values for the entire observed period.

companies, with less dependence on outside capital, are likely to benefit from concentration of ownership, at least up to a point—and my research, as well as that of others, suggests an optimal range centering around 25%. While this level of control is clearly large enough to rule out the possibility of a hostile takeover, it is also arguably small enough to allow for extensive trading and liquidity, along with some degree of influence by capital markets and perhaps even the possibility of a hostile takeover. But, as ownership (and, perhaps more important, voting rights) begin to exceed the 30% level, the controlling shareholder's main intent is more likely to be viewed by investors as the preservation of long-term control, with less focus on value maximization as the overriding objective and a reduced probability of takeover or eventual sale to outsiders.[21]

Thus, one clear message of figure 11.2 is the suggestion that, in companies where controlling shareholders have an overwhelming majority of the voting rights, the private benefits accruing to such shareholders are likely to outweigh the shared benefits from the monitoring and control of management provided by committed, long-term owners.[22] The other main message, perhaps equally clear, is the tendency of the hard-core ownership structure to produce underperformance, thereby reducing the values of both the companies that invest in other firms, and the firms that receive such "protection." Although this system has long been defended as providing management with the freedom to take the long view, my results suggest that the long-term payoff rarely materializes.[23]

The Message from Voting Premiums

The effect of ownership structure on performance and value can also sometimes be detected by looking at another variable: the premium that voting shares command relative to non-voting shares (see Figure 11.3).[24] The size of this premium is often viewed as a proxy for the quality of corporate governance, with low premiums construed as evidence of well-functioning governance systems.[25] A number of studies have found that voting premiums are higher in countries with poor shareholder protection.[26] For example, in civil law countries such as Italy and France, the value of control is generally higher than in common law countries like the U.S. and U.K (see figure 11.4).

What makes this issue of special interest in the case of France is the ability of many French companies, during the privatization process of the late 1980s and early 1990s, to raise equity from the capital markets using *non-voting stock*. Since the middle of the 1990s, most of these non-voting stocks have been withdrawn from the markets.

When companies issue non-voting shares, the value of such shares must be discounted to reflect investors' expectation that controlling shareholders will use their disproportionately high voting rights to consume private benefits and transfer value from minority holders. Such wealth transfers can take a variety

FIGURE 11.3

Voting Premium and Shareholder Structure

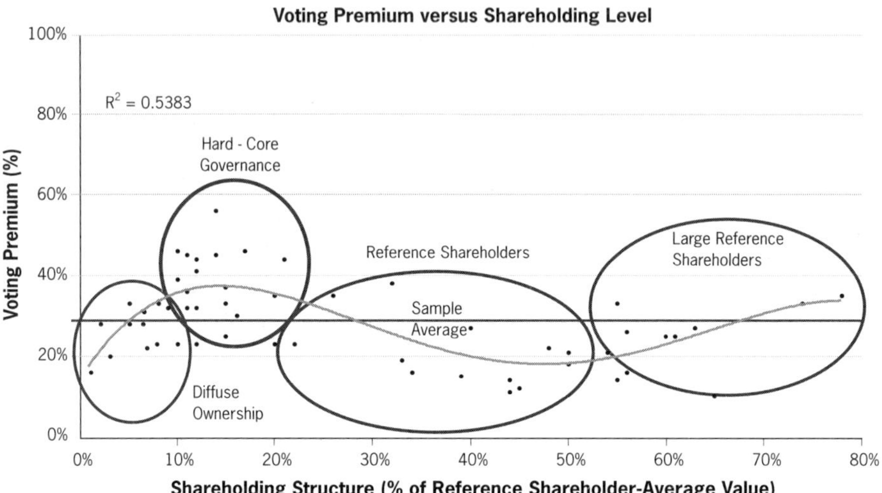

of forms, from perks to spending on uneconomic pet projects. But, in cases where such transfers are particularly egregious, the largest gap between voting and non-voting shares is likely to arise in the event that voting shares are used to block—or otherwise influence the outcome of—a transaction that would transfer corporate control.

For that reason, in analyzing the voting premium in French companies, my study did not examine the stock prices of voting and non-voting shares under "normal" trading conditions. I focused instead on the gap between voting and non-voting shares during 57 "squeeze-out" transactions in which the minority shareholders of French companies were offered a "control value" for their shares (in accordance with French stock exchange regulations).[27]

As shown in table 11.6, the voting premium decreased significantly during the 18-year period (1988–2005) I examined. Also consistent with the trends in "value creation" described earlier, I found that the hard-core companies within the sample exhibited above-average voting premiums during the entire period (see figure 11.3)—and that firms with large reference shareholders also had higher average premiums than those of the overall sample.

Concluding Remarks

The ownership structure and governance of French corporations has long been characterized by a peculiar mix of insider and outsider control. In contrast to

International Comparison of the Voting Premium

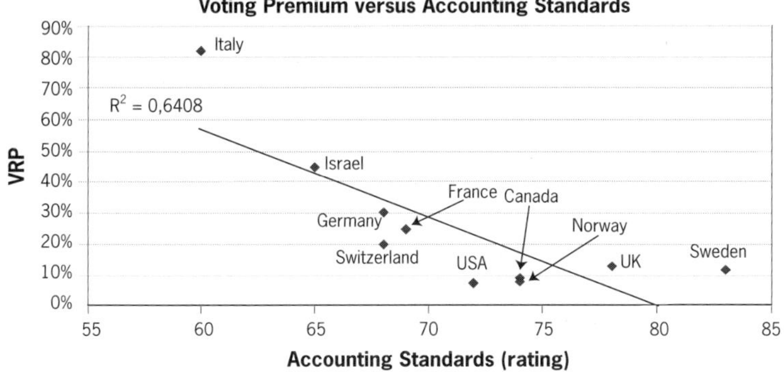

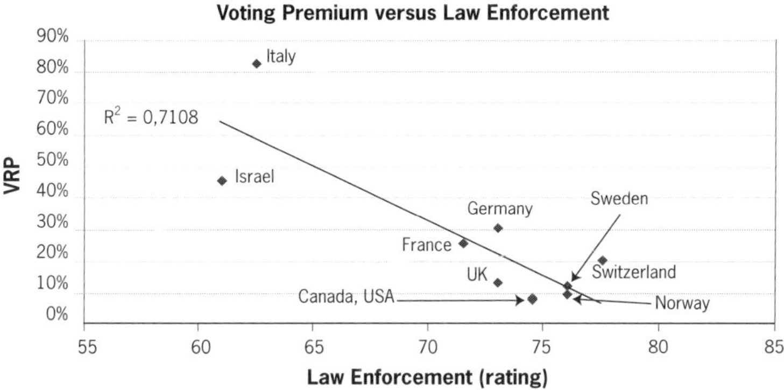

* La Porta et al. (1998, 1999, 2000) and Muus (1998).

Analysis of the Evolution of the Voting Premium between 1988 and 2005

	Overall Sample	Diffused Ownership Structure	"Hard-Core" Ownership Structure	Large Reference Shareholder Structure	Reference Shareholder Structure
	Premium Level	Premium Level	Premium Level	Premium Level	Premium Level
Average	28.6%	28.0%	32.1%	28.2%	20.2%
Median	25.3%	23.8%	30.8%	22.5%	20.0%
Time analysis (average values)					
1988–1995	39.4%	39.7%	40.8%	39.9%	34.9%
1996–2005	24.2%	22.5%	30.8%	21.2%	17.2%
Transaction number	57	17	18	17	5

the more dispersed ownership of publicly traded companies in the U.S. and U.K., the vast majority of listed French companies continue to have large (in many cases controlling) shareholders that include founders or founding families, the French government, or other corporations.

But with the progressive internationalization of the French economy and stock exchange during the past decade, the extensive networks of corporate cross-holdings that once bound together the largest French companies have started to unravel. As a result, listed French companies today exhibit a wide range of ownership structures that encompasses not only large State- and family-controlled enterprises, but a growing number of widely held firms in which foreign institutional investors have major holdings.

Attesting to the value of concentrated ownership, my study of 150 large listed French companies suggests that, in the past 20 years, companies with controlling shareholders have outperformed their counterparts with fragmented ownership. But concentration of ownership appears to add value only up to a certain point. In a finding similar to those produced by studies of U.S. family-owned companies, my study also presents evidence that corporate performance improves with increases in the controlling shareholder's percentage ownership stake, reaching peak levels at around 25–30% ownership and then falling thereafter. The suggestion here is that, up until that point, the stronger incentives to monitor corporate performance provided by greater ownership outweigh the temptation to expropriate value from minority shareholders, while still preserving some degree of liquidity (and possibility of intervention by "outsiders").

The clear underperformers in my sample were those large companies with significant corporate ("hard-core") shareholders but no single controlling shareholder. But, as my study also suggests, one of the major accomplishments of French corporate governance in the last decade or so has been the progressive dismantling of the hard-core ownership and governance structure. Such change has been brought about not only by pressure from foreign institutional investors, but by major governance reform initiatives involving French public authorities and corporate executives.[28]

Whether the changes in the ownership structure and governance of French companies described in this study have major long-run benefits for the economy can be determined only by future research. By insulating many French companies from the competitive rigor of market capitalism, the "hard-core" governance system arguably allowed some of these firms to become internationally competitive in their respective industries. Yet the fact remains that, for much of the past 20 years, these companies have provided inadequate returns for their shareholders.

But, to return to the main message of this study, the most reliable protection of minority (or passive) shareholders may well be provided by a mix of significant internal shareholdings with some opportunity for external market influence. And this principle may well apply to the U.S. "market-based" governance system. Much of the value added by private equity in the U.S. and elsewhere can be attributed to the strengthening of incentives accomplished by concentrating ownership. But even in the case of large U.S. public companies, a recent (as yet unpublished) study provides suggestive evidence that insider holdings are far larger than has been recognized.[29] In short, even the most market-oriented governance systems may have always relied, at least to some degree, on the monitoring activity of large, committed owners.

APPENDIX: THE SHAREHOLDER RETURN, EVA AND CFROI MODELS

The sample for my study consisted of 150 listed French nonfinancial firms from the "Premier Marché" and the "Second Marché." The series started in 1986 and ended in 2005. Each firm included in the sample provided information for at least 15 of the 20 years between 1986 and 2005.

The ownership structure, shareholder returns, and operating performance (as measured by EVA) of these firms were examined each year during this period. For the shareholder return and EVA approach, all firms were classified into a category of ownership structure every year. For the CFROI approach, firms were assigned the category based on their ownership structure during the majority of the period.

Shareholder returns were computed by measuring the capital gain plus the dividend income received during the holding period less paid-in capital increases.

EVA was computed as the difference between operating profits less the cost of all capital charges on the capital employed to produce those earnings. The EVA analysis is based on the "EVA ratio," which was based upon the calculated NOPAT and the average capital employed ("CE") for the year. The cost of capital (c) was defined as the weighted average cost of capital and computed using the average market capitalization for the year for the weight of equity and the average level of net financial[30] debt for the weight of debt. The EVA ratio is defined as:

$$\frac{NOPAT_n - c_a \frac{(CE_{a-1} + CE_a)}{2}}{\frac{(CE_{n-1} + CE_n)}{2}}$$

The CFROI model is rooted in the DCF principles and uses an internal rate of return (IRR) approach. As in the case of EVA, in the CFROI model, the income measure is the operating cash flow available for distribution to both debt
```
```

and equity holders. The CFROI rate is therefore the IRR, for which the following equation holds:

$$\frac{\text{NOPAT}_n - c_a \dfrac{(\text{CE}_{a-1} + \text{CE}_a)}{2}}{\dfrac{(\text{CE}_{n-1} + \text{CE}_n)}{2}}$$

where GCE_o is the level of gross capital employed at the beginning period and GCE_n is the released gross capital employed at the end of the estimated lifetime.

The Profit & Loss and Balance Sheet elements were obtained from Bloomberg and annual reports (*Onesource.com* and company web sites). Share quotes were used from Bloomberg, Fininfo, and through the courtesy of Euronext NV. The CAPM model was used for computing the required rate of return for all companies. The risk-free rates and the equity risk premiums were obtained through Dimson-Marsh-Stanton (2004) while the yearly beta factor was derived from Bloomberg data.

Notes

This chapter is based upon a chapter of the author's PhD dissertation at the Paris II Assas University. The views expressed herein reflect only those of the author. I would like to thank the editors of the Journal of Applied Corporate Finance, my wife, Olena Tokar, and Matthew Thumas for their assistance.

1. La Porta et al. (1999) suggested that the problem of the separation of ownership and control in large firms is mainly the potential expropriation of minority interests by large controlling shareholders. Their study shows that, except in the U.S. and U.K., the largest companies tend to have large shareholders, such as founding families, the State, or other corporations, and controlling shareholders often have control rights in excess of their cash flow rights. Full citations of all articles referenced in the text or notes can be found at the end of the chapter.
2. The goal of value maximization should not be interpreted, as it often is, as neglect of a company's non-investor stakeholders. Companies should make value-increasing (or value-preserving) "investments" in all of the firm's key stakeholders, groups such as employees, customers, suppliers, and, in cases where important, federal and local governments.
3. As studied by, among others, Fama and Jensen (1983) and Demsetz (1983).
4. Burkart, Gromb, and Panunzi (1997).
5. Bolton and Von Thadden (1998).
6. La Porta, Lopez de Silanes, and Shleifer (1998).
7. Similar performance by family-owned firms has been reported by a number of other studies, including Barontini and Caprio (2006), Draho and McVey (2005), and Chang and Hertzel (2004). In addition to the evidence suggesting that ownership structures can become too concentrated, recent research also suggests that companies where voting rights are disproportionately larger than cash flow rights tend to underperform. For example, the study by Lemmon and Lins (2003) of the impact of the ownership structure on corporate values during the Asian stock market crisis of 1998

found significant underperformance by companies with pyramid-like shareholding structures.

8. Anderson and Reeb, *Journal of Finance* (2003). Moreover, a *Business Week* study published in the same year reported that, over the ten-year period 1993–2002, family companies produced an average annual return to shareholders of 15.6%, as compared to 11.2% for non-family firms. See J. Weber, L. Lavelle, T. Lowry, W. Zellner, and A. Barrett, "Family, Inc." *BusinessWeek* (Nov. 2003).

9. The system has been aptly described by Prowse (1995) as dominated by "revolving door" bureaucrats who share common political roots or education and are therefore willing to become part of the network and strengthen this interaction between the parties.

10. The large groups in France are characterized by overrepresentation by executives originating from the ENA (Management School for the top-level French State bureaucracy) and other "Grandes Écoles." In 1999, 27 top executives of the CAC40 were from the ENA or Polytechnique. Although cumulative board membership has been largely limited under the new laws and regulations adopted in 2002 (Loi sur la Nouvelle Réglementation Economique), at the end of 2003, 22% of board directors were still holding 44% of the CAC40 board seats.

11. This evolution of the French corporate structure is described in detail in Bancel (1995), Belin-Meunier (1997), Chabanas and Vergeau (1996), Charreaux (1997), and Harbula (1999).

12. Stewart (1991).

13. Madden (1998, 1999).

14. The figures represent the average number of companies in each category during the observation period. Ownership stakes refer to voting rights.

15. As noted, the hard-core system was facilitated by the network of cross-holdings and board members with common training and overlapping interests. But that system has also changed significantly since the mid-1990s. For example, in 1997, only 8% of the board members were independent. This ratio increased to 24% in 2000 and 39% in 2004. Similarly, in 1996 about 50% of the board members were graduates of one of the "Grandes Écoles," as compared to only about 33% in 2004. (Source: Korn Ferry International Annual Board of Directors Study and the author's research).

16. This non-listed and fully State-owned bank has a key role in expressing the will of the French government and still owns significant stakes in many leading French companies, but rarely more than 5%.

17. According to the research performed by Georgeson Inc., as reported in *Le Monde,* July 29, 2003.

18. Demsetz and Lehn (1985).

19. Researchers found contradictory results on this topic in general: Demsetz and Villalonga (2001) tested for the joint determination of ownership and performance and concluded that there was no relationship, as compared to Anderson and Reeb (2003), who reported contradictory results with an outperformance of family-owned businesses and an optimal shareholding level of approximately 30%.

20. The significance of the shareholder criterion for determining value creation was tested through a series of regression equations. The inclusion of the shareholding criteria increased the significance of the regression equations (adj. R^2 ranges from 50% to 55% depending on the measurement type, whereas it is closer to 30% to 35% if the shareholder criteria are excluded). Thus the hypothesis that ownership stake and performance are "jointly determined" was rejected by the X^2 tests.

21. Several other factors were included in the overall analysis to control for factors such as size, asset turnover ratio, indebtedness return on capital, and share price liquidity.

The results indicate that industry-specific distortions were not driving the sample results. Share-price liquidity proved a significant explanatory factor of the performance measurement analysis, underlining the hypothesis that a large controlling stake, in addition to private benefits, may also lead to a decrease in value because of lack of liquidity, as suggested by Grossman and Hart (1980, 1986).

22. These situations may be helped somewhat by changes in national law and regulatory policies designed to provide outside (particularly foreign) investors with greater protection and the promise of better governance. But, until the beginning of the new millennium, French policy had clearly lagged behind that of Anglo-Saxon countries in this respect.

23. This generalization should not be interpreted as applying to all shareholder coalitions.

24. Most corporations follow the one-share-one-vote principle. Whenever this rule is violated, the direct relationship between residual income rights (dividends or cash flows) and residual control rights (i.e., voting power) is broken, and shareholder control over management is reduced. Grossman and Hart (1988) or Harris and Raviv (1988) extensively analyzed and demonstrated the optimality of the one-share-one-vote system from the perspective of the separation of cash-flow (dividends) and voting rights.

25. See Zingales (1994, 1995).

26. Modigliani and Perotti (2000).

27. See Hanouna et al. (2001), who argue that when examining voting premium from a minority position, what really matters is the difference between the premium paid to minority shareholders and to blockholders in a control transfer.

28. As reflected in the Viénot reports of 1995 and 1999, which were sponsored by the French union of employers, CNPF/MEDEF.

29. See Clifford Holderness (2006).

30. For the purpose of the analysis, net financial debt is defined as long-term financial debt plus the current portion of financial debt less cash and cash-equivalent marketable securities.

References

Anderson, R., and Reeb, D., 2003, "Founding-Family Ownership and Firm Performance: Evidence from the S&P 500," *Journal of Finance,* Vol. 58, 3, 1301–1327.

Bancel, F., 1995, "Le Processus de Privatisation: la Spécificité Française," in *Les privatisations* (Paris, La documentation française).

Barontini, R., and Caprio, R., 2006, "The Effect of Family Control on Firm Value and Performance: Evidence from Continental Europe," *European Financial Management,* Vol. 12, 5, 689–723.

Belin-Meunier, C., 1997, "Les holdings comme outil de gouvernement d'entreprises," in *Le gouvernement d'entreprises* (Paris, Economica).

Bolton, P., and von Thadden, E., 1998, "Liquidity and Control: A Dynamic Theory of Corporate Ownership Structure." *Journal of Institutional and Theoretical Economies,* Vol. 154.

Burkart, M., Gromb, D., and Panunzi, F., 1997, "Large Shareholders, Monitoring, and the Value of the Firm," *Quarterly Journal of Economics,* Vol. 112.

Chabanas, N., and Vergeau, E., 1996, "Nationalisations et Privatisations depuis 50 ans," *Les notes bleues de Bercy,* Paris, No. 87.

Chang, S., and Hertzel, M., 2004, "Equity Ownership and Firm Value: Evidence from Targeted Stock Repurchases," *The Financial Review,* Vol. 39, 3, 289-407.

Charreaux, G., 1997, "Vers une Théorie du Gouvernement d'entreprises," in *Le gouvernement d'entreprises* (Paris, Economica).

Demsetz, H., 1983, "The Structure of Ownership and the Theory of the Firm," *Journal of Law & Economics,* Vol. 26, 2, 375–390.

Demsetz, H., and Lehn, K., 1985, "The Structure of Corporate Ownership: Causes and Consequences," *Journal of Political Economy,* Vol. 93.

Demsetz, H., and Villalonga, B., 2001, "Ownership Structure and Corporate Performance," *Journal of Corporate Finance,* Vol. 7.

Dimson, E., Marsh, P., and Staunton, M., 2004, *The Triumph of the Optimists: 101 Years of Global Investment Returns* (Princeton, Princeton University Press).

Draho, J., and McVey, H., 2005, "U.S. Family-Run Companies—They May Be Better Than You Think," *Journal of Applied Corporate Finance,* Vol. 17, 4, 134–143.

Ehrhardt, O., and Nowak, E., 2003, Private Benefits and Minority Shareholder Expropriation, Humboldt University and University of Southern Switzerland Lugano, Working Paper.

Fama, E., and Jensen, M., 1983, "Separation of Ownership and Control," *Journal of Law and Finance,* Vol. 26.

Grossman, J., and Hart, O., 1980, "Takeover Bids and the Free Riding Problem and the Theory of the Corporation," *Bell Journal of Economics,* Vol. 11.

Grossman, J., and Hart, O., 1986, "The Costs and Benefits of Ownership: A Theory of Vertical and Lateral Integration," *Journal of Political Economy,* Vol. 94.

Grossman, J., and Hart, O., 1988, "One Share–One Vote and the Market for Corporate Control," *Journal of Financial Economics,* Vol. 20.

Hanouna, P., Sarin, A., and Shapiro, A., 2001, Value of Corporate Control: Some International Evidence, University of Southern California Marshall School of Business, Working Paper.

Harbula, P., 1999, "Ownership and Enterprise Structure in France," *Közgazdasági Szemle* (Economic Review), Budapest.

Harbula, P., 2004, "Ownership Structure and Corporate Governance in France," PhD dissertation, University of Paris II Assas.

Harris, M., and Raviv, A., 1988, "Corporate Governance: Voting Rights and Majority Rules," *Journal of Financial Economics,* Vol. 20.

Holderness, C., 2006, "The Myth of Diffuse U.S. Corporate Ownership," *Review of Financial Studies.*

Jensen, M., and Meckling, W., 1976, "The Theory of the Firm: Managerial Behavior, Agency Costs, and Ownership Structure," *Journal of Financial Economics,* Vol. 3.

La Porta, R., Lopez de Silanes, F., and Shleifer, A., 1998, "Law and Finance," *Journal of Political Economy,* Vol. 53.

La Porta, R., Lopez de Silanes, F., and Shleifer, A., 1999, "Corporate Ownership Around the World," *Journal of Finance,* Vol. 54.

La Porta, R., Lopez de Silanes, F., Shleifer, A., and Vishny, R., 2000, "Investor Protection and Corporate Governance," *Journal of Financial Economics,* 58.

Lemmon, M., and Lins, K., 2003, "Ownership Structure, Corporate Governance, and Firm Value: Evidence from the East Asian Financial Crisis," *Journal of Finance,* Vol. 58, 4, 1445–1468.

Madden, B., 1998, "The CFROI Valuation Model," *Journal of Investing,* Vol. 7, 1, 31–45. Madden, B., 1999, *CFROI Valuation: A Total System Approach to Valuing a Firm* (London, Butterworth-Heinemann).

Modigliani, F., and Perotti, E., 2000, Security versus Bank Finance: The Importance of a Proper Enforcement of Legal Rules, MIT, Working Paper.

Muus, K., 1998, Non-Voting Shares in France: An Empirical Analysis of the Voting Premium, University of Frankfurt, Working Paper No. 22.

Prowse, S., 1995, "Corporate Governance in an International Perspective," *Financial Markets, Institutions and Instruments,* Vol. 4.

Stewart, G. B., III, 1991, *The Quest for Value* (New York, HarperCollins).

Zingales, L., 1994, "The Value of the Voting Right: A Study of the Milan Stock Exchange Experience," *Review of Financial Studies,* Vol. 7.

Zingales, L., 1995, "What Determines the Value of Corporate Votes?" *Quarterly Journal of Economics,* Vol. 110, 4, 1047–1073.

CHAPTER 12

Corporate Ownership and Control in the U.K., Germany, and France

JULIAN FRANKS AND COLIN MAYER

DIFFERENCES AMONG NATIONAL FINANCIAL SYSTEMS have been a subject of continuing debate for well over a century. The primary distinction drawn by economists has been that between "bank-based" and "market-based" systems.[1] In the stylized description of bank-based systems, companies raise most of their external finance from banks that have close, long-term relationships with their corporate customers. By contrast, the market-based systems of the U.K. and the U.S. are characterized by arm's-length relationships between corporations and investors, who are said to be concerned primarily about short-term returns.

While these distinctions cannot be dismissed, they have proved to be difficult to formulate with much precision. Empirical evidence does not provide grounds for the sharp distinction that would have been expected if there were fundamental differences in the structure and operation of national economies. Nevertheless, there is one area in which there are clear differences in the structure and conduct of economies that are deep-rooted and open to quite precise quantification. These differences concern the ownership and control of corporations.

In their 1932 classic, *The Modern Corporation and Private Property*, Adolph Berle and Gardiner Means warned that the growing dispersion of ownership of U.S. stocks was giving rise to a potentially value-reducing separation of ownership and control.[2] In 1976, the general argument of Berle and Means was given a more rigorous formulation by Michael Jensen and William Meckling in their theory of "agency costs."[3] Agency costs, loosely speaking, are reductions in value resulting from the separation of ownership from control in public corporations. Pointing to a roughly tenfold decline in the percentage of managerial stock ownership of large U.S. public companies between the 1930s and the 1980s, Jensen argued that dispersed ownership was leading to major inefficiencies in U.S. companies, particularly in the form of widespread conglomeration.

In this view, the rise of hostile takeovers and LBOs in the 1980s was a value-increasing response by U.S. capital markets—one that reduced agency costs by removing inefficient managers and, especially in the case of LBOs, concentrating corporate ownership.[4]

However, a study by Harold Demsetz and Kenneth Lehn has argued that concentrated ownership is likely to have had significant costs as well as benefits.[5] That is, besides providing stronger incentives to maximize value, concentrated ownership can impose costs in two ways: (1) by forcing managers and other inside shareholders to bear excessive company-specific risks—risks that could be borne at lower cost by well-diversified outside stockholders; and (2) by allowing inside owners to capture private benefits at the expense of minority or outside owners. In the view of Demsetz and Lehn, ownership patterns should reflect a tradeoff between the incentive benefits of concentrated ownership and the expected costs arising from excessive concentration of risk and the potential for expropriating minority holders.

In this chapter, after a brief summary of existing theories of corporate ownership and control, we describe patterns of ownership in France, Germany, and the U.K. We also review the evidence (much of it our own) on the operation of the market for corporate control in the U.K. and Germany. As we conclude, none of the existing theories offers a completely satisfying explanation of the differences between the *insider* ownership systems of Germany and France, on the one hand, and the *outsider* systems of the U.S. and the U.K. on the other. Nevertheless, given the durability of the two systems, both appear to have devised effective ways of disciplining poor managers and otherwise promoting efficiency.

Theories of Ownership and Control

There are two strands of literature that are relevant to this discussion. The first concerns the determinants of corporate ownership, and the second focuses on the operation of the market for corporate control.

With regard to ownership there are three classes of models. The first is the industrial economics literature on vertical relationships—for example, those between manufacturers and their suppliers. This class of models seeks to explain the tendency of upstream and downstream firms to own each other (or to remain independent companies) in terms of the "externalities" that may exist between the parties.[6] For example, upstream firms will not always take full account of the interests of downstream firms in the prices that they charge and the way in which they treat their purchasers. In such a case, joint ownership may be required to "internalize this externality" in the absence of suitable contractual alternatives.

A second, related, class of literature on ownership argues that transaction costs may make transactions through markets more costly than internal activities within the firm.[7] It may be difficult or costly to write the contracts necessary to undertake transactions between firms through the marketplace. Discouraging "opportunistic" breaches of implicit contracts may be accomplished more effectively inside the firm than through the marketplace.

A third literature on ownership is concerned with the effect of incomplete contracts on the incentives that firms have to make long-term, highly specialized investments—the kind of investments that would have little value if transferred beyond the context of the particular firm.[8] Joint or vertical ownership is viewed as a means of encouraging such "firm-specific" investments by guaranteeing that important parties will honor their implicit commitments to projects involving joint effort (for example, those involving suppliers and manufacturers).

According to this theory, one would expect to see joint ownership where (1) it is difficult to use contracts to avoid expropriation of subsequent returns; (2) there is a high degree of "complementarity" between the assets of the two firms; and (3) one of the assets or one of the owners of the assets is particularly important to the other party and should therefore become the owner of both the assets. These theories suggest that we would expect patterns of ownership to reflect complementarities in production.

The second major strand of literature is concerned with corporate control. Separation of ownership and control in outsider systems like the U.S. and the U.K. has prompted the rise and refinement of a number of mechanisms designed to limit the agency problems with dispersed ownership.[9] Such mechanisms include monitoring and control by non-executive (or "outside") directors, pay-for-performance management incentive systems, and a market for corporate control.

Most financial economists' attention to date has focused on the operation of the corporate control market or, in popular parlance, the takeover market. In the standard conception of this market, corporate raiders identify companies that are not being managed so as to maximize shareholder value. Raiders launch bids for controlling ownership that, if successful, give them the right to bring about value-increasing changes in strategy and, in many cases, top management.

Patterns of Ownership in France, Germany, and the U.K.

The stereotypical description of the structure of corporate sectors runs as follows: There are a large number of small companies that are privately owned by individuals, families, and partners; and there are a much smaller number of large companies that are quoted (or "publicly traded") on the stock market and owned by a large number of individual shareholders. Complicating this pattern somewhat, a significant fraction of the shares of quoted companies are owned by institutional investors—in particular, pension funds, life insurance firms, and mutual funds.

Corporate Ownership in the U.K. The above description fits the U.K. reasonably well. There are over 2,000 U.K. companies quoted on the stock market out of a total population of around 500,000 firms. Almost 80% of the largest 700 companies are quoted on the stock market, and the value of companies quoted on the stock market is around 81% of the GDP. Approximately two-thirds of the equity of quoted U.K. companies is held by institutions.

But this pattern of ownership is by no means universal; on the contrary, it appears to be the exception rather than the rule. Although the U.S. has more quoted companies than the U.K., in most other countries the number of quoted companies is far lower. In Germany, for example, there are fewer than 700 quoted companies and in France less than 500 (see figure 12.1). In both countries, the value of quoted companies amounts to only 25% of GDP (figure 12.2). In short, quoted companies in Germany and France account for a much smaller fraction of total national corporate activity than those in the U.K. and the U.S.

In the U.K. and the U.S., moreover, ownership is widely dispersed among a large number of institutions or individuals. Most of the equity of quoted U.K. companies is held by institutions, but no one institution owns very much of any one company. In the U.S., the largest category of shareholders is individuals.

In most of continental Europe, however, ownership is much more concentrated. Consider the ownership pattern revealed in figure 12.3, which shows the

FIGURE 12.1

Comparison of the French, German, U.K., and U.S. Capital Markets in 1990 and 1991: Number of Domestic Listed Companies on Stock Markets

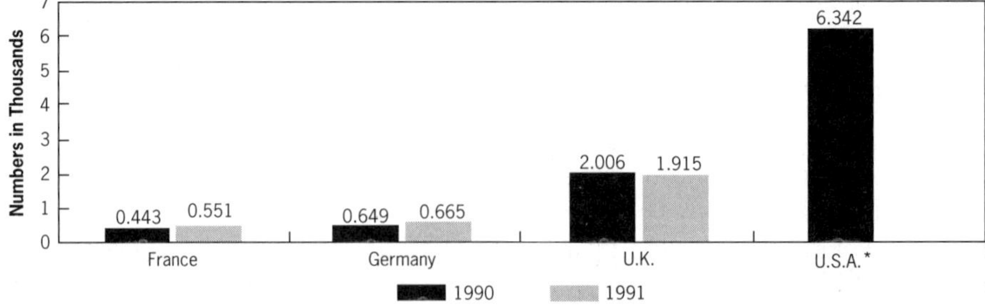

* U.S.A.=NASDAQ+NYSE.

FIGURE 12.2

Comparison of the French, German, U.K., and U.S. Capital Markets in 1990 and 1991: Market Capitalization of Domestic Equity as a Percentage of GDP

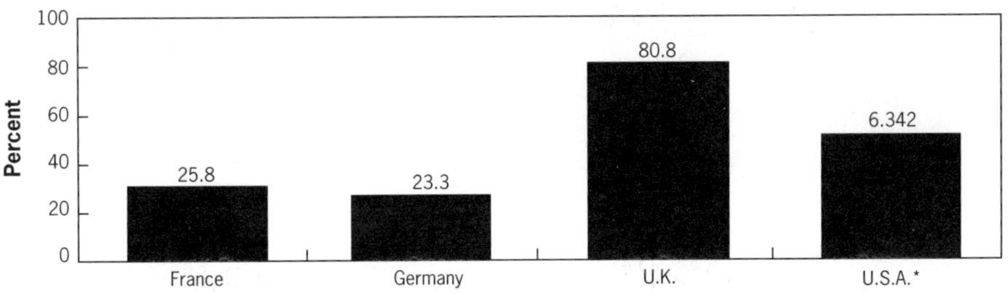

* U.S.A.=NASDAQ+NYSE.

FIGURE 12.3

Percent of Ownership of a Sample of French, German, and U.K Quoted Companies (Percent)

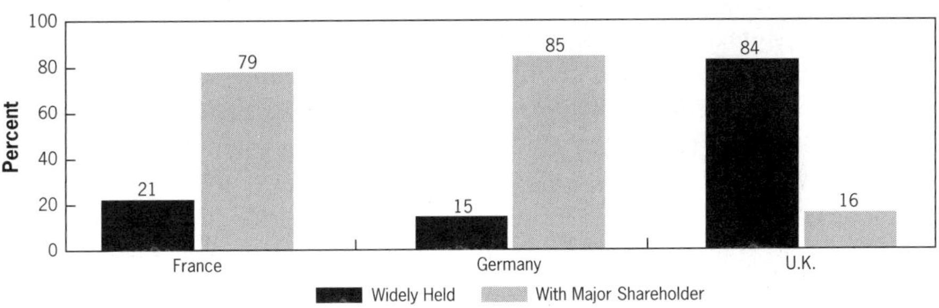

percentage of (approximately) the largest 170 quoted companies in France, Germany, and the U.K with a single large (at least 25%) shareholder. In only 16% of the U.K. companies did a single shareholder own more than 25% of the shares. By contrast, in nearly 85% of the German firms there was at least one shareholder owning more than 25%; and almost 80% of the French companies had at least one shareholder with more than 25% ownership. In short, concentration of ownership is much greater in corporations based outside the U.K. and the U.S.[10]

Corporate Ownership in Germany and France. In France and Germany, by far the single largest group of shareholders is the corporate sector itself. Figure 12.4 breaks down large share stakes in 171 large quoted German companies by

FIGURE 12.4

Percentage of Companies with Share Stakes in Excess of 25% in 171 German Industrial and Commercial Quoted Companies in 1990

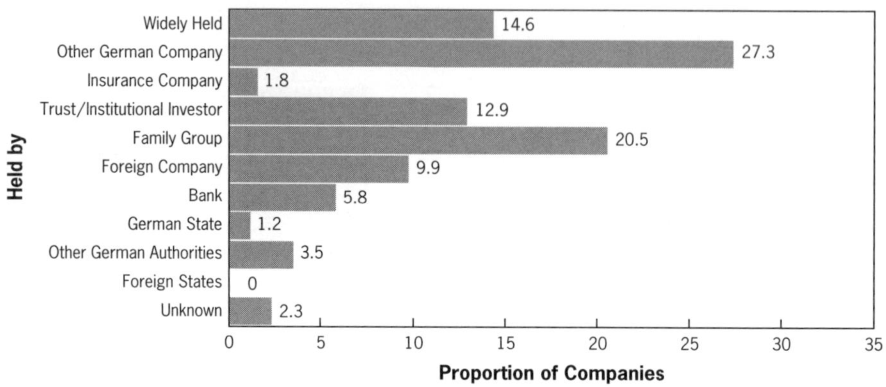

different groups of investors—banks, investment institutions, companies, government, and so forth. It reveals that a majority of the large share stakes are held by companies. The next largest group is families, followed by trusts, institutional investors, and foreign companies.

Although there is a commonly held view that banks control corporate Germany, banks actually come far down the list of large stakeholders. Nevertheless, the control exerted by banks is significantly greater than their direct equity holdings would suggest. As holders of the bearer shares owned by their customers, they are able to exercise proxy votes on behalf of dispersed shareholders. (And, since all the companies studied here are quoted, at least a portion of the shares are widely held.)

Figure 12.5 provides more detail on the ownership of the 171 large German companies analyzed in figure 12.4. As shown in figure 12.5A, trusts and institutional investors are sometimes large shareholders in German companies. However, their share stakes are rarely majority holdings. The same holds for banks (figure 12.5B): there are some large share stakes but rarely majority holdings. This contrasts with the pattern of family ownership. In almost one-third of the cases, families appear to be majority holders of German companies (figure 12.5C).

In examining these figures, one should keep in mind that they refer to the *largest* German companies. Thus, in contrast to our earlier description of the U.K. ownership structure, large-block family ownership is a highly representative feature of the largest enterprises in Germany. This raises the interesting question (to which we return later) of how and why German (and French)

Proportion of Disclosed Stakes by Size of Stakes in 171 German Industrial and Commercial Quoted Companies in 1990

PANEL A. HELD BY TRUSTS/INSTITUTIONAL INVESTORS (NO. OF STAKES = 54)

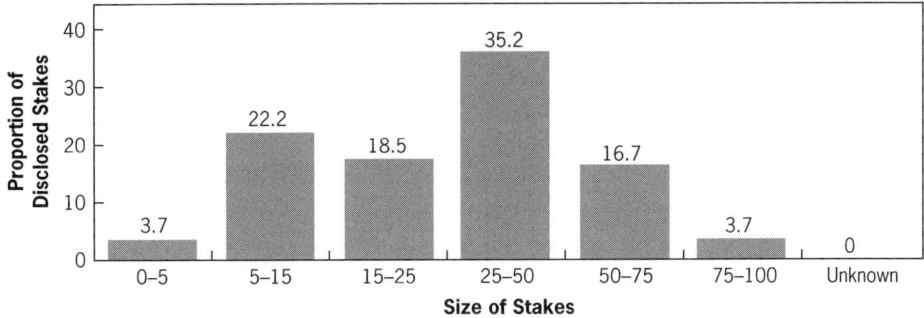

PANEL B. HELD BY BANKS (NO. OF STAKES = 39)

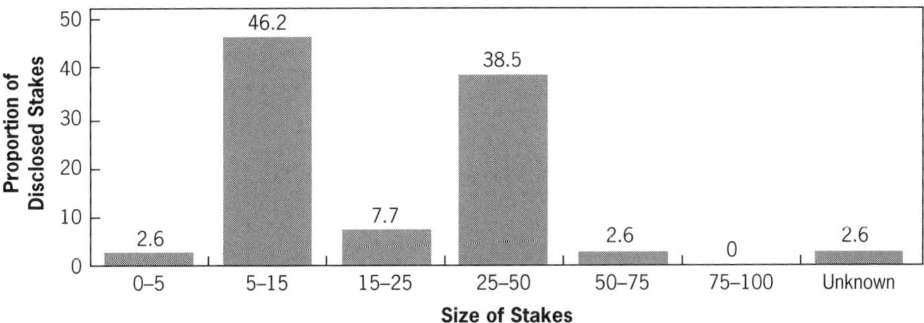

PANEL C. HELD BY FAMILY GROUPS (NO. OF STAKES = 58)

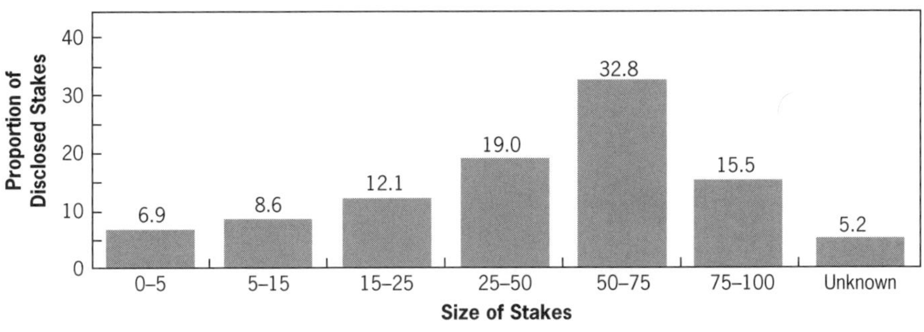

PANEL D. HELD BY OTHER GERMAN COMPANIES (NO. OF STAKES = 80)

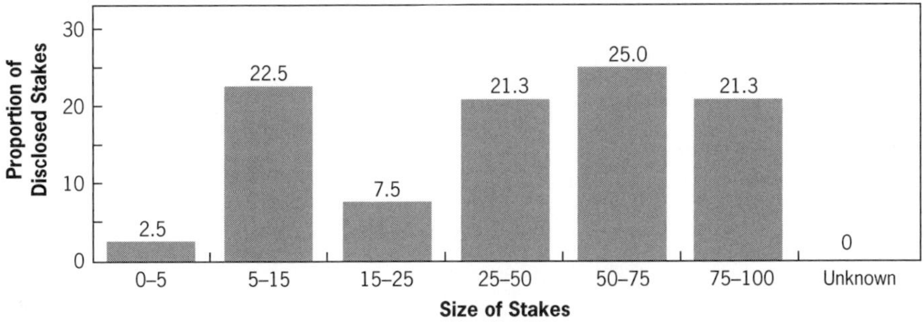

families play a much more significant role in corporate ownership than, say, their U.K. counterparts.

The other group that emerges as having majority shareholdings in Germany is the German corporate sector (figure 12.5D). Not only do German companies have many and large stakeholdings in other German firms, but also these inter-corporate shareholdings are often majority ones. What makes such corporate equity stakes in other firms especially noteworthy is that these are all quoted companies, not just subsidiaries of other companies.

In sum, then, while German banks do have quite large share stakes, they are rarely majority shareholders. The pattern for insurance companies, trust, and institutional investors is very similar—some large but rarely majority shareholdings. The two dominant investor groups in German companies are families and other German firms.

A remarkably similar pattern emerges for France. First, as noted above, the proportion of large stakeholdings in total is about the same as in Germany. Figure 12.6 summarizes the ownership distribution for 155 large quoted French

FIGURE 12.6

Share Stakes in Excess of 25% in 155 French Industrial and Commercial Quoted Companies in 1990

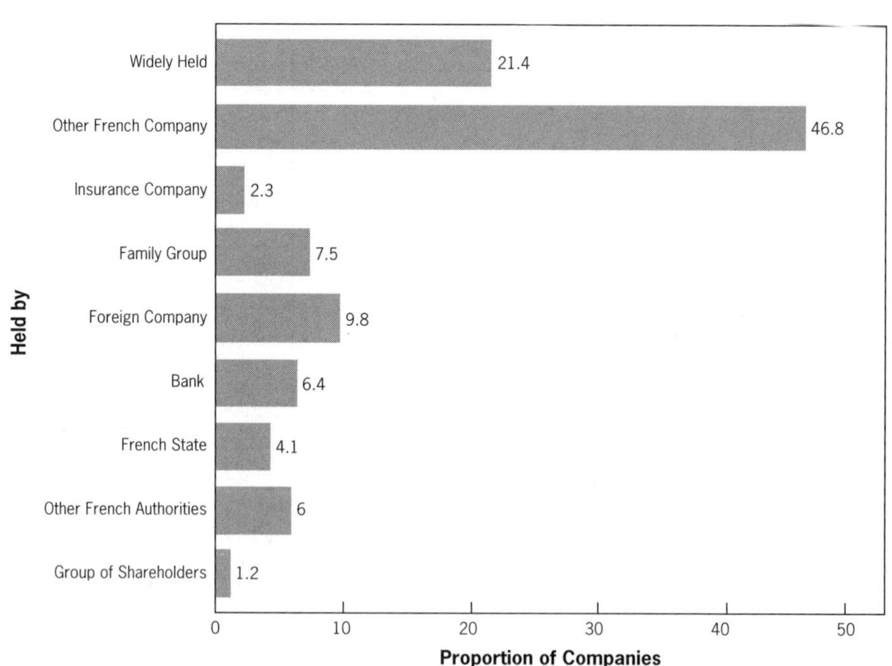

companies. As in the case of Germany, a majority of these stakes are held by other companies. Other large stakeholders in French firms are foreign companies, families, and banks.

Further detail on the ownership of these 155 French companies is provided in figure 12.7. As we saw in the case of Germany, there are some large stakes held by insurance companies but these are rarely majority holdings (figure 12.7A). Banks have some large minority shareholdings, often in excess of 25% (figure 12.7B). But, as in Germany, it is French families (figure 12.7C) and other French companies that have the largest proportion of majority shareholdings (figures 12.7C and 12.7D).

There is, however, one notable difference between France and Germany, and that is the comparative importance of state ownership of large companies. As shown in figure 12.8, share stakes by the state are more prevalent and tend to be larger in France than in Germany.

Four Cases of German and French Corporate Structure. The ownership patterns of individual firms reveal a number of characteristics that are hidden in the aggregate data. Figures 12.9, 12.10, and 12.11 show the ownership structures of three prominent and representative German companies—Renk AG, Kromschroder AG, and Metallgesellschaft AG. Figure 12.12 describes the ownership of the French water company, Degrémont.

What can we learn from these exhibits? First, they show the extent of equity holdings of corporations in each other's shares. These investments are frequently in quoted companies and are often by firms in a related or the same industry. Figure 12.9, for example, shows a large holding by MAN AG, a large German engineering company that produces buses, lorries, and machines, in Renk AG, another mechanical engineering company. Ruhrgas (shown in figure 12.10) is a gas company that owns Elster, another gas company.

Second, the other corporate owners are frequently *not* trading partners. For example, the gas company Elster holds Kromschroder, a precision mechanics and optics company.

Third, banks and insurance companies often emerge higher up in the ownership tree. For example, partnerships between Allianz, which is a German insurance company, and German banks show up in a number of large corporations. Allianz and Deutsche Bank between them have a controlling interest in the holding company of Metallgesellschaft (figure 12.11). Allianz, Allianz's life insurance company, and Commerzbank have a controlling interest in a holding company that has a large stake in MAN. And, as shown in figure 12.12, Compagnie Financière de Suez, Credit Lyonnaise, and UAP all have significant holdings in Société Lyonnaise des Eaux-Dumex, which in turn owns Degrémont.

Thus, institutional owners play a prominent role in all three countries. But, whereas institutional ownership is highly dispersed in the U.K., it is highly

Stakes Held in 155 French Industrial and Commercial Quoted Companies in 1990

PANEL A. HELD BY INSURANCE COMPANIES (NO. OF STAKES = 27)

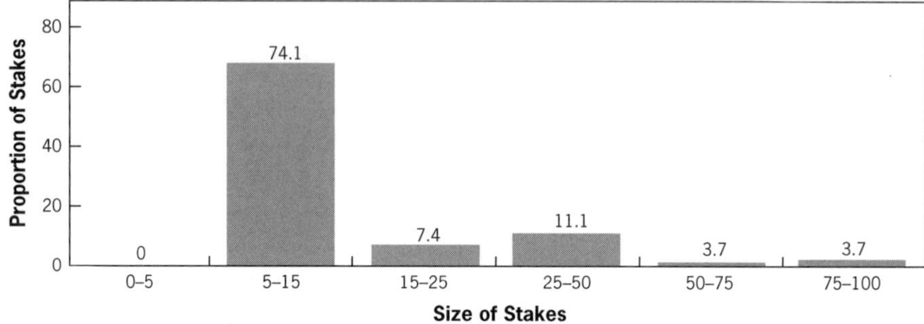

PANEL B. HELD BY BANKS (NO. OF STAKES = 21)

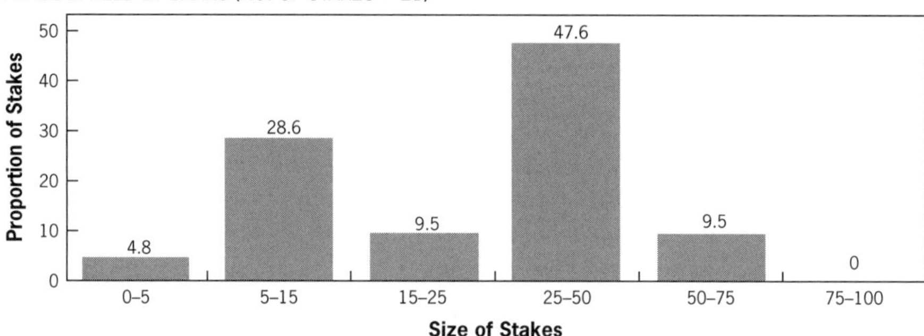

PANEL C. HELD BY FAMILY GROUPS (NO. OF STAKES = 33)

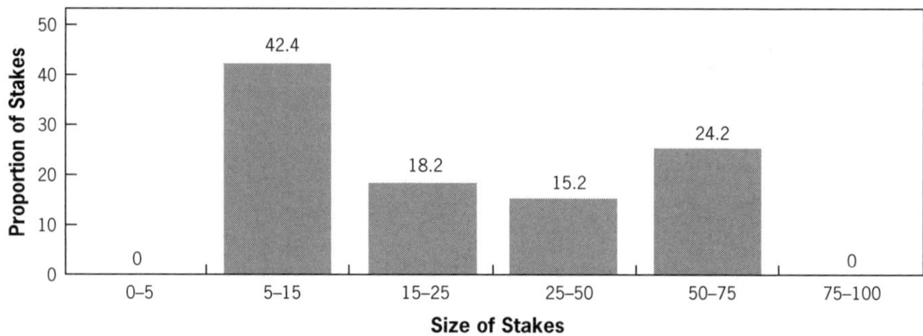

PANEL D. HELD BY OTHER FRENCH COMPANIES (NO. OF STAKES = 149)

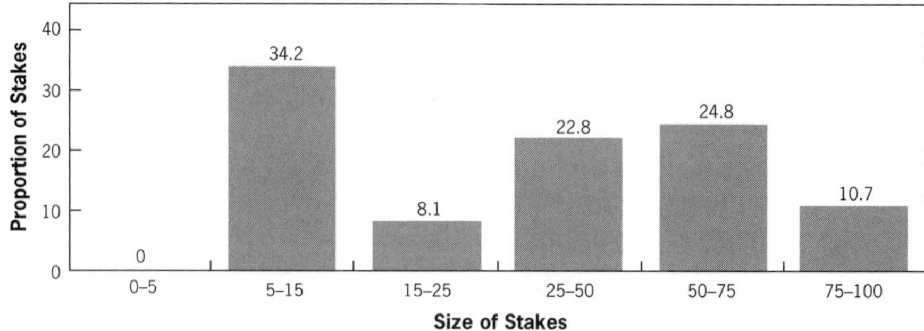

FIGURE 12.8

Proportion of Disclosed Stakes Held by the State in Germany[a] and France[b]

PANEL A. GERMANY (NO. OF STAKES = 4)

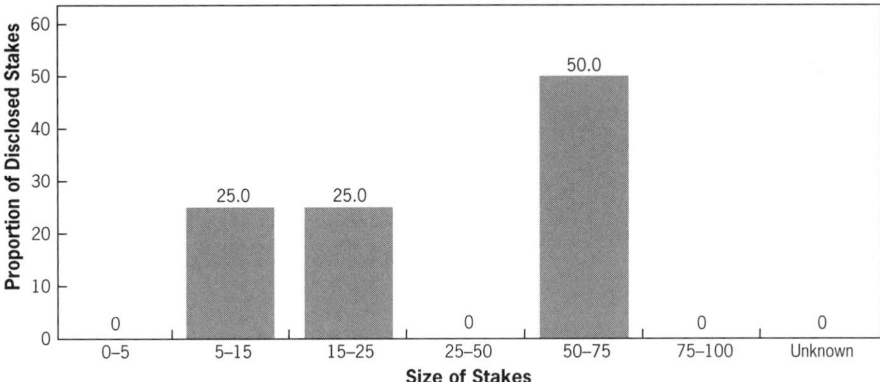

PANEL B. FRANCE (NO. OF STAKES = 10)

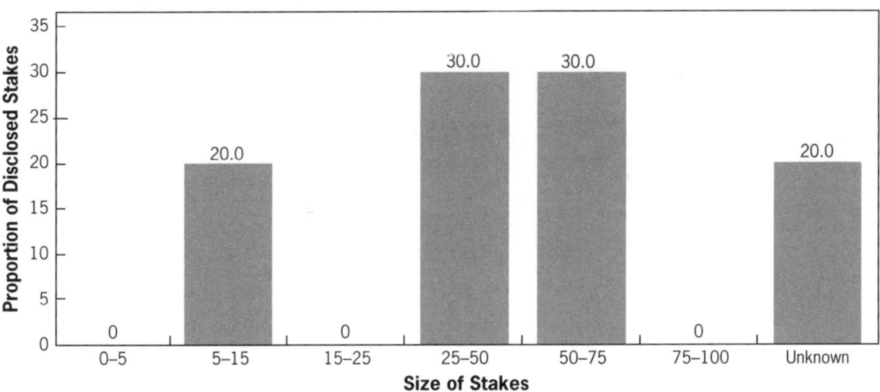

a. In 171 German industrial and commercial quoted companies.
b. In 155 French industrial and commercial quoted companies.

concentrated in France and Germany. And, as the above illustrations further suggest, the corporate governance role of outside shareholders in France and Germany is even less significant than the small number of quoted companies in these countries would suggest. For, even in those cases in which companies are quoted on the stock market, controlling shareholdings often reside with other companies.

Therefore, as we noted earlier, the German and French corporate governance systems are perhaps best described as *insider* systems (see figure 12.13). Insider systems are those in which the corporate sector has controlling interests

Ownership Structure of Renk AG

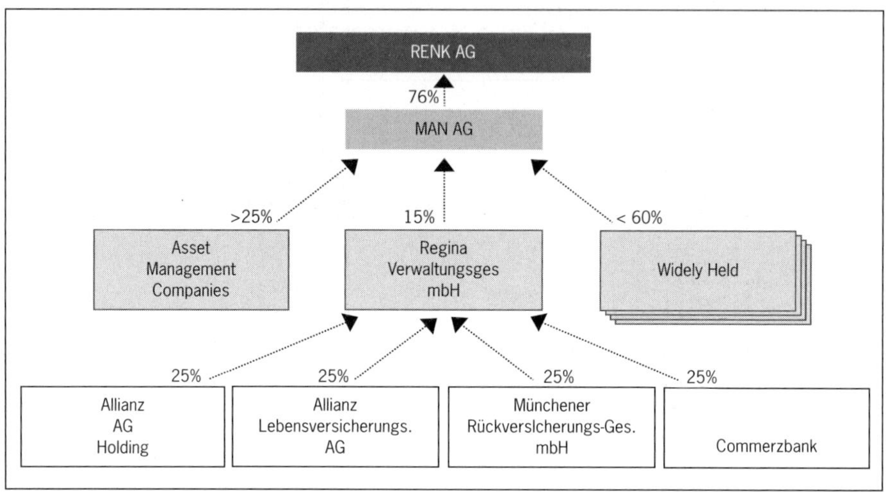

Ownership Structure of G. Kromschröder AG

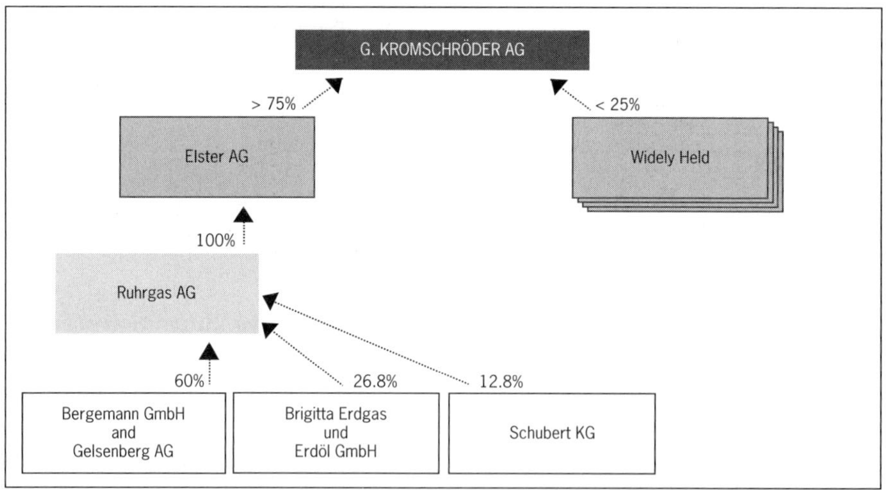

Ownership Structure of Metallgesellschaft AG

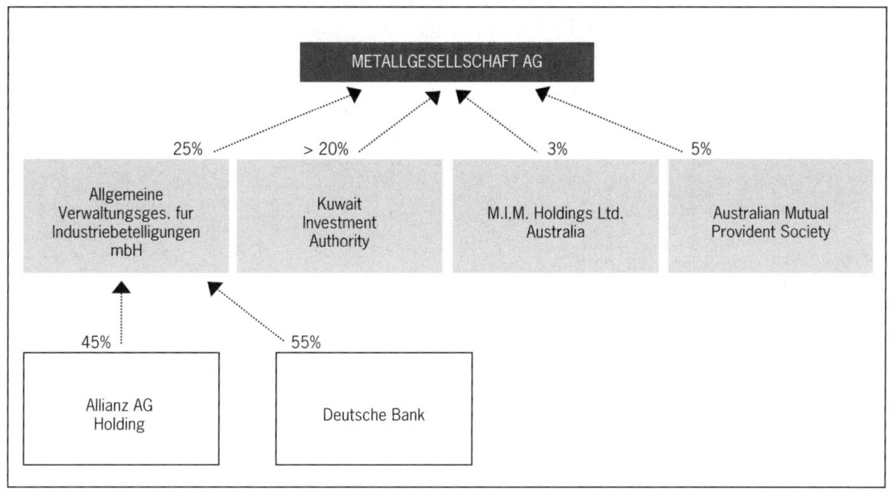

Ownership Structure of Degrémont

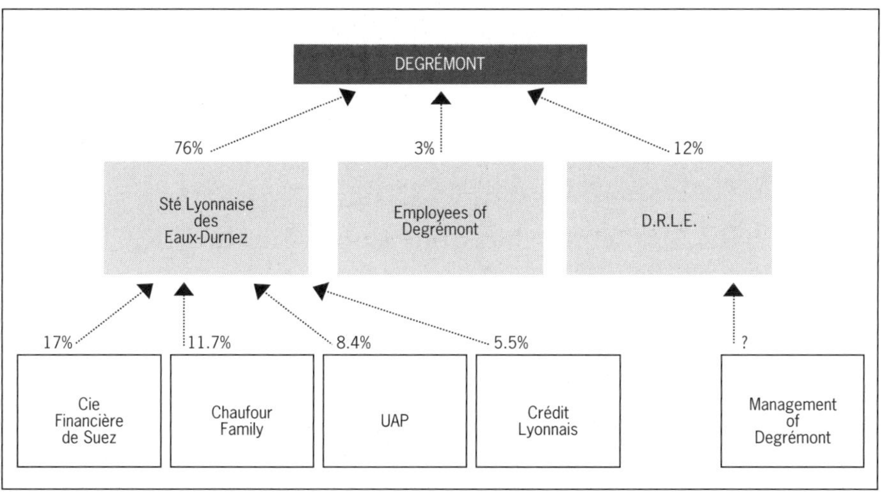

Corporate Control Systems

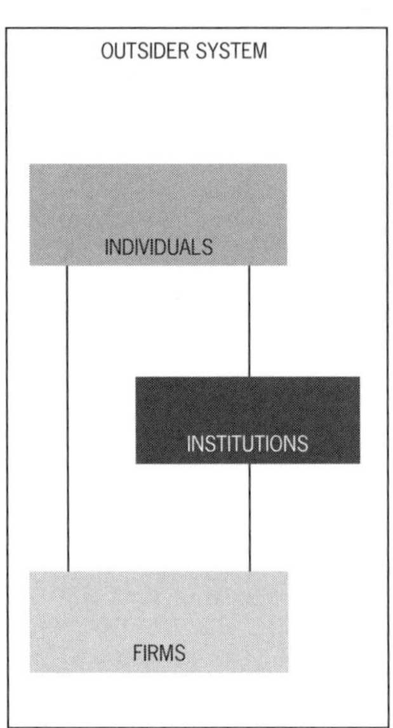

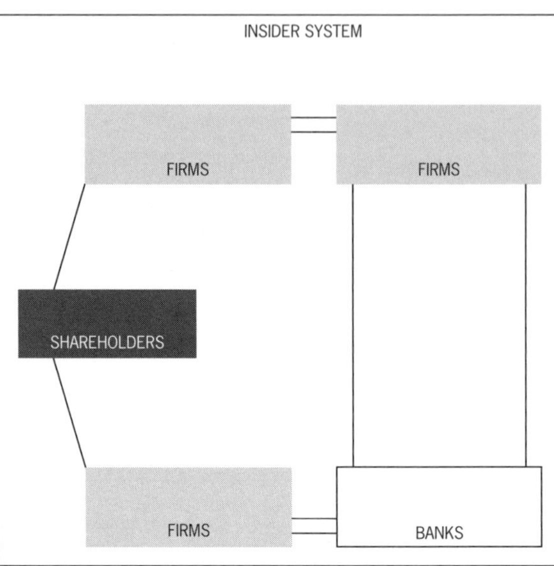

in itself and in which outside investors, while participating in equity returns through the stock market, are not able to exert much control. By contrast, the U.K. and the U.S. are *outsider* systems of corporate control, in which there are few controlling shareholdings (what controlling blocks do exist are rarely associated with the corporate sector itself). And, as we discuss below, these differences in ownership systems give rise to very different forms of corporate control.

The Market for Corporate Control in the U.K.

The takeover market is active in the U.K. During the merger waves at the beginning of the 1970s and the end of the 1980s, as much as 4% of the total U.K. capital stock was acquired by takeover (or merger) in one year.[11] Furthermore, it has been estimated that about 25% of takeovers in the 1980s were "hostile" in the sense of being rejected initially by the incumbent management.[12] Of those bids that were hostile in nature, approximately one-half were successfully completed.

There are two empirical studies of takeovers that have attempted to distinguish takeovers designed to correct past managerial failure from those that were not. In a 1991 study of the U.S. market, Kenneth Martin and John McConnell investigated the disciplinary role of corporate takeovers in the U.S. over the period 1958 to 1984, using a sample of 253 successful tender offers. They classified a takeover as "disciplinary" if there was any change in the CEO of the target firm. Their study, somewhat surprisingly, reported no difference in bid premiums associated with disciplinary and non-disciplinary takeovers and only moderate evidence of differences in the share price performance of targets of disciplinary and non-disciplinary bids prior to takeover.

In a study published in 1995, we reported similar results for a sample of 80 contested bids in the U.K. in 1985 and 1986.[13] We found that for a range of financial variables, including share price returns, dividends, and cash flow rates of return, the performance of targets of hostile bids in the six years prior to a bid was not statistically distinguishable from that of samples of either accepted bids or non-merging firms. In fact, the dividend performance of targets of both friendly and hostile bids was *appreciably better than* that of firms in the lowest deciles of share performance. Whereas poorly performing firms frequently reduced their dividends, targets of hostile and friendly bids rarely reduced their dividends in the two years prior to a bid.[14]

We also repeated our analysis of U.K. firms using Martin and McConnell's definition of managerial failure as replacement of top management. But, again, we found little evidence that managerial control changes in takeovers were a response to poor financial performance. The past performance of acquired firms where managers were replaced was not significantly worse than the performance of those targets in which top managers were retained.

All these results question the common association of markets for corporate control with the correction of managerial failure. Nevertheless, even in the absence of poor pre-merger performance, we did find evidence of considerable restructuring after takeovers. More precisely, we found that levels of asset disposals and restructurings were significantly higher in cases where bids were either hostile or followed by managerial control changes. Furthermore, we found that managerial dismissals were much higher in hostile than in friendly bids. Indeed, nearly 80% of executive directors either resigned or were dismissed within two years of a successful hostile bid.

In sum, then, while the market for corporate control does not appear to be associated with the correction of managerial failure as measured by past corporate performance (which we henceforth refer to as *ex post failure*), it does give rise to substantial corporate restructurings in the form of asset disposals and executive dismissals (*ex ante failure*). One possible interpretation of these results is that hostile bids can occur, even in the absence of any evidence of poor past performance, in the expectation that the acquiring firm will implement a new and more valuable policy in the future (an explanation that would fall under the classification of *ex ante failure*). In support of this argument, we found in the previously mentioned study of takeovers that hostile bidders paid much larger premiums over market than friendly acquirers, which is consistent with higher expected benefits from the planned restructurings of targets of hostile bids.[15]

The Market for Corporate Control in Germany

In another study, we found that during the 1980s the total number of mergers in Germany was only about one-half of those in the U.K.[16] More significantly, in contrast to the active market in corporate control in the U.K., there have been just four recorded cases of hostile takeovers in Germany since World War II, and three of those four have occurred within the last six years.

Several explanations have been suggested for the low level of hostile takeovers in Germany. The first focuses on the dominant position of banks resulting from owning corporate equity and sitting on the supervisory boards of many quoted German companies. As noted earlier, German banks' holdings of equity are a quite modest proportion of the total, but they exercise considerable control by virtue of their ability to vote in proxy contests the bearer shares they hold in custody for customers.

The second explanation is that voting right limitations prevent predators from acquiring controlling interests in firms. German companies frequently pass resolutions at shareholders' meetings limiting the voting right of any one shareholder to a maximum of 5%, 10%, or 15% of total votes, irrespective of the size of the shareholding. The justification for such voting restrictions is that, in the absence of a U.K.-style takeover code, they protect minority shareholders from predators who, after acquiring a controlling interest, attempt to dilute the value of the minority's investments.

The third explanation is that it may prove difficult to remove members of the supervisory board and thereby gain control of a company, even when a majority of the shares are tendered. The supervisory board comprises representatives of employees as well as shareholders. For an AG (public limited company), 50% of the board is composed of employee representatives, who by tradition vote with the incumbent management.

Case studies of hostile takeovers in Germany provide evidence of the effectiveness of these institutional features as barriers to takeover.[17] The unwelcome bid by Pirelli for Continental, Germany's largest tire manufacturer, was launched in September 1990. During the course of the bid, substantial share stakes were acquired by allies of the two parties: Italmobiliare, Mediobanca, and Sopaf in the Pirelli camp; BMW, Daimler-Benz, and Volkswagen in the Continental camp. These share stakes were in large part acquired from individual investors and investment institutions.

At the time of the Pirelli bid, there was a 5% limitation on the voting rights that could be exercised by any one shareholder. Prior to launching the bid, Pirelli attempted to have the 5% limitation removed so as not to dilute the voting rights of its own (and its partners') holdings. A motion for removal of the restriction was passed at a shareholders' meeting in March 1991, thereby paving the way for Pirelli to launch a tender bid for Continental. Nevertheless, the removal was delayed (and never implemented) due to a court action by shareholders objecting to rule violations of minority interests.

The Continental case illustrates that voting right restrictions can introduce a two-stage procedure into German takeovers. In the first stage, predators solicit the support of small shareholders to have voting right limitations removed. In the second stage, a normal tender can be launched. The Continental case suggests that the first stage can represent a significant, though not necessarily insurmountable, barrier to takeover.

Although the management board of Continental was resolutely opposed to the merger, the supervisory board showed itself more willing to explore merger possibilities with Pirelli. This difference in approach resulted in the dismissal of the chairman of the management board in May 1991. He was replaced by a chairman who was more sympathetic to merger discussions.

The Continental case suggests that neither proxy votes nor voting right restrictions are absolute defenses against hostile takeovers, though the latter certainly slows down the process. Furthermore, the supervisory board may remove members of the management board, though this is less easy to achieve than in the U.K.

The main impediment, however, to an Anglo-American market for corporate control is the ownership structure of German companies. In the Continental case, there was no major shareholder who owned a stake of 25% or more, thus allowing Pirelli and its partners to build large holdings. Two other hostile takeovers in Germany—that of Feldmühle Nobel and the bid by Krupp for Hoesch—were also for firms in the small set of German companies with dispersed shareholdings. In the latter case, Krupp was able to amass a stake of 24.9% without the knowledge of Hoesch or the investment banking community. The purchase of this stake took more than five months to complete, involved purchases on the German, London, and Swiss stock exchanges, and was a crucial tactic in gaining control. Without such a stake, a merger would have proved unlikely or impossible, since all previous attempts at friendly mergers in the industry had failed.

Where ownership is concentrated, direct control is effectively exercised by boards. This is reflected in a close association between ownership and representation on supervisory boards, in particular in the all-important position of chairman. In the small proportion of companies where ownership is dispersed, bank representation on supervisory boards is more in evidence.

This suggests that, in widely held companies, proxy votes and voting restrictions together permit banks to exercise effective control through board representation.

A Discussion of the Evidence

The evidence presented above on national differences between corporate ownership and control can be summarized by the following observations:

1. There are marked differences in the ownership structures of similar companies in different countries.

2. Inter-corporate holdings of companies are very significant in some countries but not others.

3. Large shareholdings by families are of much greater importance in some countries than others.

4. Markets for corporate control are little in evidence in countries with concentrated ownership.

5. Even where companies are widely held, markets for corporate control are seriously restricted in some countries.

6. Bank control is associated primarily with widely held companies where the market for corporate control is restricted.

7. There is little association of the market for corporate control with poor past performance (or *ex post failure*).

8. Corporate control transactions such as takeovers lead to substantial restructuring and management changes (which can be interpreted as evidence of *ex ante failure*).

How well do the theories of ownership and the market for corporate control square with these observations? The answer is not well at all; they leave a large number of unresolved issues.

First, it would not be expected that the broadly similar production technologies that are employed in different countries would give rise to the marked variations in ownership patterns recorded in this chapter. Moreover, it is difficult to imagine that there are sufficient differences in production complementarities across countries to explain much larger inter-corporate holdings in some countries than in others.

Second, the large family holdings in France and Germany suggest that families in those countries either (1) possess greater managerial skills or (2) derive larger "private" benefits from control (larger at least in relation to the value they could realize by selling their controlling interest) than their English and American counterparts. It is possible that regulation may create greater private benefits in some countries, for example, by being more permissive toward insider trading or providing less protection of minority interests.[18] In this respect, regulation may have important consequences for the structure of corporate organization.

Third, if markets for corporate control improve corporate efficiency, why are they largely absent in some countries? For example, it is very difficult to understand why markets for corporate control in Germany are restricted by bank intermediation *even* in cases of widely held companies where there are weak incentives for shareholders to exert control directly.

On the other hand, if the market for corporate control really does work to correct managerial failure, the puzzle posed by the U.K. is why there is so little evidence of poor pre-bid performance. And, in the absence of poor pre-bid performance, why is there so much restructuring after the takeover?

In this sense, then, current theories of ownership and control fail to provide adequate explanations for the ownership structure and operation of either U.K. or Continental European capital markets. For example, there is clearly more to the determination of ownership in the U.K., Germany, and France than complementarity in production. Moreover, the market for corporate control does not appear to perform its assumed function of correcting managerial failure—or not at least the kind of failure that manifests itself in substandard operating and shareholder returns.

One might suggest that dispersed public ownership, because of its efficiencies in risk-bearing and the liquidity of public markets, is better suited to providing capital for large-scale corporate expansions. But this ignores the reality that even companies with concentrated share ownership can raise external equity while retaining control through either the issuance of dual class shares or the "pyramiding" of inter-corporate holdings (as illustrated earlier in the case of several German and French companies).[19] It also ignores the fact that active secondary markets can be (and are) organized in shares other than those that are part of the controlling block.[20]

Concentrated ownership, as suggested by Demsetz and Lehn, is likely to occur for one or both of the following reasons: (1) the greater potential for owners to exercise control over managers increases the value of the enterprise (relative to the value it would command under dispersed ownership), or (2) there are "private" benefits to owners of exercising control—that is, benefits that do not accrue to (and may even come at the expense of) minority stockholders. Both of these factors are likely to explain the extent of family ownership in Germany and France. Concentrated ownership allows investors to exert *direct* control, which is presumably much less costly than the indirect control exerted by takeover markets (especially given restrictions on takeovers in Continental markets). And the private, perhaps even non-monetary, benefits of owning a large enterprise (which may include greater powers to keep minority shareholders at bay) may well be larger in France and Germany than in the U.S. or the U.K.

Nevertheless, the differences in the extent of family ownership of public corporations among these nations remain a puzzle. Unless the relative costs of direct and indirect control can be shown to vary greatly among countries, or unless families in different countries attach very different values to private benefits, the diverse forms of ownership cannot be readily explained.

The hypothesis we offer is that the different patterns of ownership across countries are associated with different forms of corporate control that allow for different kinds of correction. Large share stakes and concentrated ownership are likely to be more effective in responding to *ex post* managerial failures (poor past performance), in large part (as we will argue below) because of the "information and agency costs" that confront dispersed shareholders. And there is at least one piece of supporting evidence for this argument: In a study (with a colleague), we found that those companies in the bottom decile of corporate performance were far more likely to replace their managers than those with dispersed ownership.[21] By contrast, dispersed ownership seems to be more effective in correcting *ex ante failure*—that is, in bringing about valuable restructuring and management changes in cases where financial performance has been adequate, but managers have failed to maximize value.

At first sight, this argument would appear to suggest that national systems with dispersed ownership will tend to achieve more efficient resource allocations than those with concentrated ownership. Nevertheless, there is a problem presented by dispersed ownership—namely, the inability of a large number of small shareholders to make "commitments" to other key corporate stakeholders such as employees and suppliers.

A simple example illustrates the point. Consider a company with 100,000 shareholders each owning one share in a firm. An alternative prospect, for example, a proposed acquisition, emerges. A sale of a majority of shares results in a change in corporate policy to the detriment of existing stakeholders (suppliers, purchasers, and employees). Individually, shareholders base their decision to sell purely on the price that they are offered since the action of any one shareholder has no effect on policy. In addition, the loss sustained by stakeholders in the event of a change in policy cannot be attributed to the actions of any one shareholder. In contrast, large shareholders know that if they sell their shares, they will affect corporate policy to the detriment of stakeholders. Their decisions will be affected by the loss of their reputation as well as the price for their shares.

According to this description, the key distinction between corporate systems concerns the degree of anonymity of shareholders. To a much greater extent than in the U.S. or the U.K., the Continental system allows a large number of small investors to buy and sell shares without having any effect on control. At the same time, large investors such as families or other companies—those who are likely to have the best information about the firm's long-run prospects—effectively guarantee the ability of the firm to make good on strategic commitments.

On the other hand, the advantage of dispersed ownership is that outside shareholders who are not bound by prior commitments are more likely to seek the highest value control group *at any point in time.* Thus, dispersed share ownership achieves value maximization, at least over the short run, although possibly at the expense of valuable long-term relationships with other stakeholders.[22]

It is in this sense, then, that the U.K. and the U.S. financial markets may be considered "short-term." Dispersed shareholders cannot commit to the same extent as concentrated owners and cannot therefore sustain the same set of prior relations. This kind of short-termism thus does not represent a mispricing of securities or excessive trading of shares, but is rather a direct result of the structure of ownership. And if the short-term orientation of dispersed shareholders limits their ability to commit to key corporate stakeholders, it also provides a potentially valuable flexibility (an ability to reduce operating leverage, if you will, by converting fixed into variable costs). For this reason, in cases where little investment is required of other stakeholders, or relationships can be sustained through explicit contracting, dispersed share ownership may well lead to more efficient allocation of resources than a concentrated ownership burdened by commitments.[23]

Moreover, while it is possible to provide a rationale for high levels of concentration of ownership, majority (or large minority) inter-corporate ownership remains very hard to explain. Indeed, the main puzzle presented by the Continental ownership structure is this: Where control is retained within the corporate sector through large corporate shareholdings and corporate representatives who serve on supervisory boards, management is likely to enjoy a high degree of protection from external influences. Managerial failure will not be corrected, either directly by large outside shareholders such as families or indirectly by takeovers, as in economies with dispersed share ownership. Thus, one plausible view of the insider system holds that the complex web of inter-corporate holdings in France and Germany is designed, not to promote efficiency, but to perpetuate control within the corporate sector itself.

Conclusions

There are pronounced differences in the ownership patterns of corporate sectors across countries. The U.K. and the U.S. have large quoted sectors with share ownership dispersed across a large number of investors. (In the U.K. the dominant shareholding group is institutional investors; in the U.S. it is individual investors.)

In contrast, France and Germany have small quoted sectors. Perhaps more significant, even the largest quoted companies in France and Germany typically have at least one shareholder owning more than 25% of the equity and, in many cases, even a majority shareholding. Such large shareholdings tend to be held either by the founding family or by other corporations. In this sense, both France and Germany can be seen as having "insider systems" of corporate ownership, as contrasted with the "outsider systems" of the U.K. and the U.S.

The different ownership systems are associated with very different forms of corporate control. There is an active market for corporate control in the U.K. and the U.S., but very little in the way of a market for corporate control in France and Germany. In the case of Germany, even in the comparatively small widely held component of the quoted sector, the market for corporate control is impeded by proxy votes and voting right restrictions that effectively confer more power on banks than on the concentrated ownership segment.

Some economists have suggested that complementarities in production can make vertical relationships (including inter-corporate block holdings) a cost-effective way of reducing transaction costs or "completing" incomplete contracts. Nevertheless, the patterns of inter-corporate ownership we observe in France and Germany do not appear to be particularly closely associated with trading relationships. And, in further contradiction of this theory, similar companies have quite different ownership structures in the U.K., on the one hand, and France and Germany on the other.

In theory, the market for corporate control should be closely associated with the correction of managerial failure. In practice, however, there is very little evidence of a relation between the incidence of hostile takeovers and poor corporate performance. The performance of targets of hostile takeovers in the U.K. is close to that of the average quoted company. At the same time, however, hostile takeovers do result in considerable restructuring and managerial turnover. This can be construed as evidence that targets, while performing up to averages, were failing to *maximize* shareholder value.

The different patterns of ownership in the U.K. and in France and Germany create different incentives and corporate control mechanisms. Concentrated ownership would seem to encourage longer-term relationships between the company and its investors. But, while perhaps better suited to some corporate activities with longer-term payoffs, concentrated ownership could also lead to costly delays in undertaking necessary corrective action, particularly if the owners receive non-monetary benefits from owning and running a business. And although widely dispersed ownership may increase the likelihood that corrective action will be sought prematurely (that is, in cases where the firm is suffering a temporary downturn and outsiders rush to sell their shares), the presence of well-diversified public owners may also be more appropriate for riskier ventures requiring large amounts of new capital investment.

In short, different forms of ownership would appear to be suited to promoting different types of activity. Concentrated ownership may be necessary where investment by other stakeholders is important and cannot be promoted contractually, but dispersed ownership will be advantageous where little investment is required by non-investor stakeholders or where adequate contracts can be written that protect their interests. What is finally very hard to explain, however, is the high level of inter-corporate holdings in the French and particularly the German systems. Such holdings, while possibly achieving some coordination benefits, are also likely to create insider systems that are largely immune to necessary corrective intervention by outside investors.

Notes

1. For interesting examples of this, see F. Allen and D. Gale, "A Welfare Comparison of the German and US Financial Systems," CEPR-Fundacion BBV Conference, April 1994; and J. Edwards and K. Fischer, *Banks, Finance and Investment in Germany* (Cambridge: Cambridge University Press, 1994).
2. A. Berle and G. Means, *The Modern Corporation and Private Property* (New York: Macmillan, 1932).
3. For the original formulation of agency theory, see M. Jensen and W. Meckling, "Theory of the Firm: Managerial Behavior, Agency Costs and Ownership Structure," *Journal of Financial Economics*, No. 3 (1976).
4. See M. Jensen, "The Agency Costs of Free Cash Flow: Corporate Finance and Takeovers," *American Economic Review* 76 (May 1986); and M. Jensen, "The Eclipse of the Public Corporation," *Harvard Business Review* (1989).
5. H. Demsetz and K. Lehn, "The Structure of Corporate Ownership: Causes and Consequences," *Journal of Political Economy*, 93 (1985), 1155–77.
6. See, for example, A. Dixit, "Vertical Integration in a Monopolistically Competitive Industry," *International Journal of Industrial Organization*, 1 (1983), 63–78; M. Salinger, "Vertical Merger and Market Foreclosure," *Quarterly Journal of Economics*, 103 (1988), 345–56; and W. Waterson, "Vertical Integration, Variable Proportions and Oligopoly," *Economic Journal*, 92 (1982), 129–44.
7. See, for example, R. Coase, "The Nature of the Firm," *Economica* 4 (1937), 386–405; O. Williamson, *Markets and Hierarchies: Analysis and Anti-Trust Implications* (New York: Free Press, 1975); O. Williamson, *The Economic Institutions of Capitalism* (New York: Free Press, 1985); and M. Aoki, B. Gustafsson, and O. Williamson, *The Firm as a Nexus of Treaties* (London: European Sage, 1988).
8. See, for example, B. Klein, R. Crawford, and A. Alchian, "Vertical Integration, Appropriable Rents, and the Competitive Contracting Process," *Journal of Law and Economics*, 21 (1978), 297–326; S. Grossman and O. Hart, "The Cost and Benefits of Ownership: A Theory of Vertical and Lateral Integration," *Journal of Political Economy*, 94 (1986), 691–719; O. Hart and J. Moore, "Property Rights and the Nature of the Firm," *Journal of Political Economy*, 98 (1990), 1119–58.
9. See H. Manne, "Mergers and the Market for Corporate Control," *Journal of Political Economy* (1965), 110–20; and A. Alchian and H. Demsetz, "Production, Information Costs and Economic Organization," *American Economic Review*, 62 (1972), 777–95;

and E. Fama and M. Jensen, "Separation of Ownership and Control," *Journal of Law and Economics,* No. 26 (1983).

10. For a comparison of ownership in Japan and the U.S. that makes a similar observation, see S. Prowse, "The Structure of Corporate Ownership in Japan," *Journal of Finance,* 47 (1992), 1121–40. In the case of Japan, the largest group of shareholders is financial institutions.

11. See our article, "Corporate Ownership and Corporate Control: A Study of France, Germany and the UK," *Economic Policy* (1990).

12. T. Jenkinson and C. Mayer, *Hostile Takeovers* (London: Macmillan, 1994).

13. J. Franks and C. Mayer, "Hostile Takeovers and the Correction of Managerial Failure," *Journal of Financial Economics,* 40 (1996), 162–81.

14. Although it appears inconsistent with standard explanations of the control market, such a finding is consistent with Jensen's free cash flow theory of takeovers, in which companies with excess capital tend to overinvest. See Jensen (1986), cited earlier.

15. J. Franks and C. Mayer, "Corporate Control: A Synthesis of the International Evidence," mimeo.

16. J. Franks and C. Mayer, see [13].

17. Ibid.

18. And differences in estate taxes may lead to differences in ownership; for example, many large family interests in U.S. companies are reportedly sold to pay estate taxes.

19. For a defense of the economic efficiency of the pyramid ownership structure, see Brian Kantor, "Shareholders as Agents and Principals: The Case for South Africa's Corporate Governance System," *Journal of Applied Corporate Finance,* 8, No. 1 (Spring 1995).

20. For a paper arguing that this may be an important source of information for structuring incentives for management, see B. Holmstrom and J. Tirole, "Market Liquidity and Performance Monitoring," *Journal of Political Economy,* 101 (1993), 678–709.

21. J. Franks, C. Mayer, and C. Renneboog, "The Ownership and Control of Poorly Performing Companies in the U.K.," working paper (1995).

22. This provides the basis for the Shleifer and Summers assertion that shareholders are unable to make commitments to other stakeholders and employ managers to do this on their behalf. The observation here is that through concentrated ownership some financial systems permit investors to make commitments. (See A. Shleifer and L. Summers, "Breaches of Trust in Hostile Takeovers," in *Corporate Takeovers: Causes and Consequences,* ed. Alan Auerbach [University of Chicago Press for National Bureau of Economic Research, 1988].)

23. Franks and Mayer (1996), cited above, emphasize another distinguishing feature of insider and outsider systems and that is the importance of committees. Control in insider systems is exercised by committees that can reflect the interests of parties who, for credit constraint reasons, are underrepresented in ownership stakes. In Germany, stakeholder representation on boards is in part dictated by legal considerations.

PART IV

The Role of Active Investors

CHAPTER 13

London Business School Roundtable on Shareholder Activism in the U.K.

CENTER FOR CORPORATE GOVERNANCE, LONDON, FEBRUARY 9, 2006

Laura Tyson: Good evening, I'm Laura Tyson, Dean of the London Business School, and it's my pleasure to welcome you to this event. We have a very important topic: shareholder activism in the U.K. I also want to note that this is the inaugural event for the new London Business School Center for Corporate Governance. I've worked very hard with many people in this room—particularly with the inspired leadership of Professor Julian Franks and Paul Coombes—to launch this Center, which has been made possible by generous support from Oracle, Freshfields, and Prudential. Let me also mention that tonight's event is being offered through a partnership of our new Center with the European Corporate Governance Institute and the *Journal of Applied Corporate Finance*, which is a publication of Morgan Stanley.

So we have some great sponsors and a great topic. Our program tonight has two parts. In the first, Julian Franks and Marco Becht will provide an overview of the findings of an independent study—conducted by Julian, Marco, Colin Mayer, and Stefano Rossi—that documents the success of a venture into shareholder activism by a U.K. pension fund. Starting in 1998, the U.K. investment firm Hermes, which manages assets on behalf of the BT Pension Scheme, created a Focus Fund whose mission has been to identify underperforming companies, communicate problem areas and recommended solutions to their managements and boards, and then work with the companies to bring about the proposed changes. The actions of the Fund appear to have been remarkably successful, both in bringing about change and in increasing share values. And after Julian and Marco summarize the study's findings, we will get an insider's view of the Hermes's success story from David Pitt-Watson, who ran the Hermes Focus Fund from 2002 to 2004.

As someone who serves on several corporate boards, I find the idea that direct shareholder involvement with managements and boards can lead to improvements in corporate performance and increases in value to be a very exciting

> The idea that direct shareholder involvement with managements and boards can lead to improvements in corporate performance and increases in value is a very exciting one—and it's one that raises an important set of questions for all of us to consider in the various roles that we play.
>
> **Laura Tyson**

one—and it's one that raises an important set of questions for all of us to consider in the various roles that we play. In the second part of our program tonight, Professor Colin Mayer of Oxford University, another of the study's co-authors, will discuss the implications of the study's findings with four distinguished practitioners: Alastair Ross Goobey, a former Chief Executive of Hermes as well as a former Chairman of the International Corporate Governance Network; Sir Victor Blank, Chairman of both GUS and Trinity Mirror; Anita Skipper, Head of the Morley Fund's Corporate Governance group; and Brian Magnus, Co-head of Morgan Stanley's U.K. Investment Banking division.

So I think we can look forward to a very exciting seminar. And since I have agreed to serve as the chair for the first half of this event, it will be my job to introduce the speakers and make sure that we stay roughly on time. But before we get into the main part of our event, we will hear a few words from Juan Rada, who is a Senior Vice President of Oracle and runs the company's Applications and Industries business in Europe, the Middle East, and Africa. Oracle's vision and support played an important role in getting our Corporate Governance Center off the ground. From 1989 to 1992, Juan was dean of IMD, the highly regarded business school in Lausanne, Switzerland.

Juan Rada: Thank you very much, Laura. I want to start by explaining to you why an information company like Oracle is supporting the launch of the London Business School's Center for Corporate Governance. Oracle is not generally known for doing such things. But the explanation is fairly simple: Much of the work of corporate governance by managements and boards today depends on the use of large information systems. Large companies have massive amounts of data that are gathered piecemeal and then brought together using different systems that are organized in different ways by different people in different countries with different currencies. It is a big challenge to integrate all these systems and data in a way that enables companies to produce financial statements that CEOs and CFOs can feel confident in signing off on.

As my comments are meant to suggest, the information management infrastructure is a critical part of a company's ability to meet the requirements of effective corporate governance. The ultimate goal of corporate governance is to build the trust of all corporate constituencies—and by that I mean not just shareholders, but customers, employees, suppliers, and banks and other creditors. A reliable information system that functions as part of an effective governance system is essential to inspiring such trust. And yet this issue has not been covered well, or indeed at all, in the governance literature. Oracle's motive for supporting the London Business School in establishing this Center is to contribute to a better understanding of the relationship between information infrastructure and effective corporate governance.

Today's session is devoted to a clinical study of the methods and accomplishments of one very large and very active investor—and I agree with Laura that this is a very important topic. But, as this Center develops and continues to do more research, I look forward to the day when we will have clinical studies in the area of IT infrastructure and corporate governance. This would represent a major improvement over the current situation, where governance problems are not typically revealed by IT systems, but come to light mainly after the fact through forensic audits. Thank you very much.

Tyson: Thanks, Juan. Now we'll hear from Antonio Borges, who is Chairman of the European Corporate Governance Institute. Tony was also the Dean of INSEAD from 1993 to 2000, and today serves as an International Advisor to Goldman Sachs and sits on the boards of a number of American and European companies and foundations.

Antonio Borges: Thank you very much, Laura, and good evening everyone. This is a very important day, and it's a great pleasure to be here. Let me start by thanking the London Business School for hosting this event, and by praising Laura Tyson for her vision in encouraging the launch of this new Center.

I have known Laura for many years. I met her when she was chair of the Clinton Administration's Council of Economic Advisers in the mid-1990s. Now she is the leader of the business school I viewed as my most formidable competitor when I was the Dean at INSEAD. Over the years I've had the opportunity to observe and admire her leadership skills. We have recently learned that Laura is going back to the U.S., where I'm sure she will pursue an extraordinary career. For those of us associated with INSEAD, this might be perceived as a great opportunity. But we also know that there's nothing better for your organization than to have a strong competitor—and for that reason alone I think we all stand to lose by her departure.

When we look back at Laura's tenure as dean of LBS, I feel confident that we will remember this day as one of the high points. The creation of the Center for Corporate Governance here at the London Business School is very promising. Corporate governance has emerged as one of the crucial issues of our time.

It is of enormous interest to corporate executives, to investors and the markets, and to policy makers. Yet it is full of misconceptions and false premises that need to be dispelled. So if there is one thing that's desperately needed in this area, it is good independent research. And I think all of us who have an interest in the field will look at the creation of this Center as a promising step in that direction.

Let me also say a word about the topic of today's session. Shareholder activism is about the direct role of shareholders in the governance of corporations. It is one of the most provocative and controversial topics in corporate governance, especially in the U.S., where shareholders are not supposed to have any private contact with managers or board members. Board members of U.S. companies are told that if they talk to any shareholders, they've got to talk to *all of them at the same time.* There must be no hint of privileged information between the management and any shareholder, large or small.

But in continental Europe, it's very different. There is often frequent communication between management and large shareholders, who also tend to be the controlling shareholders. Controlling shareholders are very much in favor of so-called active ownership; in fact, they believe that they add a lot of value to their corporations through that activism. And there is a good deal of evidence that supports this statement. But there is also a downside to these relationships: When a group of outside shareholders—for example, hedge funds—decides to impose a particular solution on a venerable institution like the Deutsche Börse, the activists are liable to be called names like "locusts." They are not so welcome anymore.

And this attitude toward outsiders is true to some extent even here in Britain, which I believe to have the best corporate governance model and the highest corporate governance standards in the world. Even here in the U.K., there is still perceived to be a need for greater involvement by shareholders, and there is a great deal of debate about the role of institutional investors in that context.

So the topic tonight could not be more timely. And I think we will have the privilege of listening to some of the best experts in this area. Thank you.

Part One: The Study

Tyson: Thanks, Tony. Now let me introduce Julian Franks, the person who, along with Paul Coombes, has been most responsible for the creation of the new LBS Center for Corporate Governance. Julian is Professor of Finance at the London Business School and former Director of the school's Institute of Finance and Accounting. He is also an accomplished corporate finance and governance scholar, with many published papers on the ownership and control of public corporations in the U.S., the U.K., and continental Europe.

Julian, can you give us a brief overview of your study and its findings?

Our intuition—and it is just intuition at this point—is that shareholder activism may be a more cost-effective means of bringing about change at underperforming companies than hostile takeovers. It would be nice to have a sample of such firms where changes in top management and restructurings were brought about by both of these different means—and then we could compare the returns.

Julian Franks

Julian Franks: Thank you very much, Laura. And let me welcome you again to what, as Laura told you, is the inaugural event of our Center for Corporate Governance. The focus of our session is a case study of investor activism in the U.K. that has been conducted by four academics, including myself, who represent four different universities. And let me introduce my three co-authors on the study: Marco Becht, who will give this presentation with me, is Professor of Finance and Economics at Université Libre de Bruxelles as well as Executive Director of the European Corporate Governance Institute. Colin Mayer, besides being my co-author on numerous studies of corporate ownership and governance, is the Peter Moores Professor of Management Studies—and soon to become the Dean—at Oxford University's Said School of Business. And Stefano Rossi, who did his Ph.D. at LBS, is now an Assistant Professor at the Stockholm School of Economics. And now let's hear from Marco.

We think our study has produced persuasive initial evidence that shareholder activism can produce changes in corporate behavior that lead to significant returns for shareholders.

Marco Becht

Marco Becht: Before Julian tells you what we found, let me say a word about why I think our findings are important. Most corporate finance scholars, not to mention many corporate executives and investors, have long been skeptical about the value of shareholder activism. In their view, such actions have been at best ineffective and at worst disruptive, giving rise to shortsighted decision-making. What evidence scholars have produced to date on the effectiveness of activism—mainly studies of pension fund activism in the U.S.—has been inconclusive, showing no clear effect on shareholder returns or benefit to shareholders. Law and economics scholars in the U.S. have pointed to the U.S. legal and institutional environment as putting up major obstacles to activist investors. At the same time, two of those scholars, Bernard Black and Jack Coffee, have argued that the U.K.'s legal and cultural environment may provide the ideal conditions for shareholder activism, making the U.K. a "laboratory" for research on activism.

Our intent here tonight is to announce—and then invite you to discuss with us—the first set of findings of what we intend to be an ongoing independent study of shareholder activism in the U.K. And before I go farther, let me say that we think our study has produced persuasive initial evidence that such activism can produce changes in corporate behavior that generate significant returns for shareholders.

Our study focuses on the activities of a single fund, the Hermes U.K. Focus Fund. Starting in 1998, the Fund has taken large positions in companies that are fundamentally sound but whose shares have underperformed the market as a result of problems with strategy, governance, or financial structure—companies where the Fund's managers believe that their own involvement can be the catalyst for change and improved performance.

We were given access to Hermes's own records of its dealings with companies, including letters, memos, minutes, presentations, transcripts and recordings of telephone conversations, client reports, and the staff's personal notes and recollections. Over the period we studied—from 1998 to 2004—the Fund took positions in the stocks of 41 companies. The average holding period for the positions was almost two years.

We also found that, in 30 of these 41 cases, the Fund's managers decided to "engage with" the companies, but not to do so in 8 other cases—in some cases because change was brought about by means outside Hermes's influence before it chose to act. In the remaining 3 cases, the Fund was still holding the positions without having engaged the companies' management. Moreover, in the 30 cases where the fund approached the companies, the engagements were characterized as "collaborative" in 10 cases, "confrontational" in 10 others, "very confrontational" in 2 instances, and "mixed" in the remaining 10. The average holding periods for the stocks where there was engagement was considerably longer than the sample average—and the holding period was even longer, in fact almost three years, in the cases that were deemed to be "confrontational."

With that, let me turn this back to Julian, who will take you through the main results.

Franks: We classified the objectives of each of the engagements under three headings: (1) changes in management and the board; (2) changes in financial policies—mainly increased payouts and more disciplined capital spending; and (3) restructurings—designed for the most part to achieve greater focus by selling assets outside the core businesses. Engagements with the companies were conducted for the most part using behind-the-scenes methods of contacting managements, boards, and other shareholders, and only rarely at public shareholder meetings or through other public channels.

Our first major finding is that the Hermes Focus Fund succeeded in accomplishing its desired outcomes in the large majority of cases. For example, changing the CEO was an objective in roughly half the companies. And as things turned out, the number of CEO changes among the 41 firms exceeded half the sample, indicating that CEO dismissals occurred even in cases where it was not one of the Fund's objectives. Dismissal of the chairman was achieved in a large majority of the cases where it was a goal. And so were desired changes in financial policy, particularly increases in cash payouts and greater discipline in capital spending. The Fund was somewhat less successful in bringing about restructurings, with greater focus on the core business achieved in just over half the companies where it was proposed.

But that now brings us to the critical question addressed by our study: What, if any, effects did such changes have on shareholder returns? Using the methods of the standard event study, we examined the performance of the 41 stocks in response to public announcements of the desired board changes, increased payouts, and major restructurings. On average, there was a significant positive reaction by the stocks. Moreover, we determined that the shareholder gains from these events alone accounted for a very large fraction—perhaps as much as 90%—of the outperformance of the Fund. Using the jargon of today's portfolio managers, we might say that the "alpha" generated by the Fund can be attributed largely to shareholder activism.

We also posed the question whether collaborative engagements tended to produce higher returns than confrontational engagements—and the answer is that both forms of engagement appear about equally productive.

Now, having summarized our findings, let me give you some caveats in interpreting the results of a study of this kind. First, of course, the findings apply to one fund only, and we may want to be a bit cautious in generalizing from a sample of one about the economy-wide effect of activism in the U.K. Second, although the positive market reactions suggest that investors expect corporate performance to improve, we also want to know whether the expected improvements will materialize—and that's a question we expect to answer in the continuation of this study over the next few years. A third question has to do with the durability or permanence of these effects: Even if the expected improvements come to pass, will managements and boards continue to be more vigilant and responsive in the future?

And there's a fourth question: Is this kind of shareholder activism a lower-cost alternative to other forms of market discipline, notably hostile takeovers? Our intuition—and it is just intuition at this point—is that activism may be a more cost-effective means of bringing about change. But there is evidence on both sides of this debate. So my question is: Are there other forms of activism that are less expensive, but capable of providing the same returns? In a horse race, would activism prove more effective than hostile takeovers and private equity, or be better than relying on non-executive directors to intervene, when things go wrong?

To decide this question, it would be nice to have a sample of underperforming firms where changes in top management and restructurings were brought about by different means—say, private equity, hostile takeovers, and investor activism—and then we could compare the returns in those cases to those we found. Several years ago, Colin Mayer and I wrote a book on underperforming companies in the U.K. And after investigating which kinds of companies restructured and which did not, we found that the key was whether the companies needed capital. Those companies that didn't need new capital to stay afloat simply continued to underperform; there were no notable changes in management or improvements. But where we saw major improvements, there was also an infusion of new capital, and generally new investors and a new management team.

Now one has to wonder about the state of a governance system where companies can continue to underperform as long as they have a supply of capital. That is not a sign of a completely well-functioning governance system—one that operates to protect shareholder value. And this begs the question of the relative efficiency of the hostile takeover market. My own sense is that hostile takeovers are a very costly solution. They may end up increasing value, but they clearly impose social as well as economic costs that might be better avoided. And I think shareholder activism is a very promising alternative mechanism. At the very least, the kind of activism described in our study adds another valuable instrument to the market, one that supplements takeovers and private equity as a way of improving the performance of underperforming companies.

And let me close with what I think is a rather tantalizing question. Along with Bernie Black and Jack Coffee, let me ask: Is it possible that the U.K. today has a more efficient governance system than the United States? Thank you very much.

The Hermes Fund

Tyson: Thank you, Julian, for that account of this very careful and impressive research effort. And I agree that the results are both significant and very encouraging.

Now let's hear from David Pitt-Watson, the Chief Executive of Hermes Focus Asset Management. David heads a team of over 50 people who are responsible for shareholder engagement, corporate governance, and voting in all of the 3,000 companies in which Hermes's clients invest worldwide. From 2002 to 2004, he ran the U.K. Focus Fund, whose operations are the subject of the study, with responsibility for all its operations, including its engagements with underperforming companies. I should also add that David played an essential role in the study by agreeing to open the Fund's books to a group of independent researchers, and I think we should applaud him for doing it.

Michael Jensen argued that most companies that didn't need new equity would have higher values in the hands of private equity investors—people who actually sit on the boards of companies and monitor their performance—than under the oversight of the average listed company's board of directors. When we reflected on this, we were struck by the thought that the BT Pension Scheme, the biggest pension fund in the U.K., wasn't really carrying out its duty as an owner.

David Pitt-Watson

David Pitt-Watson: Thanks, Laura. Let me start by saying that, if you're running a fund, having an academic study done on you is rather like one of those operations on your stomach with a local anesthetic where you get to see in a mirror what's actually taking place. When Marco, Julian, Colin, and Stefano were doing their work, we sometimes found ourselves turning around and saying, "My goodness! Why did we allow them to slice us up in the first place?" But I want to thank them for the extraordinary professionalism with which they carried out their task. I also want to thank all of the people who have been involved in the Fund, especially Alastair Ross Goobey, the former CEO of Hermes, who had the idea to establish such a fund and who will speak on the panel that follows; Bob Monks, who came from the U.S. to help get things going; Peter Butler, who was the first to run the fund and provided the energy and drive to get it going; Steve Brown, its first Investment Director, who provided wisdom and experience; and, most particularly, the British Telecom Pension Scheme, which is the owner of Hermes and its Focus Fund, and was the first institutional investor in the world brave enough to establish such a venture. As Laura mentioned, I ran the fund from 2002 to 2004. There are now over 50 people within Hermes who are involved in one way or another in our steward-ship and engagement programs, all of whom have had something to do with its success.

And I'm quite proud of what we've done. But, to continue my earlier analogy, if you've seen a bit of your own body opened up for a surgical procedure, you know it's not an entirely comfortable process. To give you a better idea of what the surgeons were investigating, let me tell you what we thought we were doing when we set up our Focus Fund inside Hermes.

In setting up this fund, we were acting on behalf of the owner of Hermes, which as I mentioned is the British Telecom Pension Scheme. It's a pension scheme—in the U.S. you would call it a pension *fund*—that owns about half of one percent of the shares in the U.K. and whose U.K. equity investments are diversified across about 800 different companies. And we were trying to behave as if we took share ownership seriously. We want to be share*owners,* not just shareholders. It is one of our first principles that companies that have active and engaged shareowners are more likely to succeed in the long run than those that are allowed to do whatever their managements choose. Thus we are believers in the famous saying of the old Scottish economist Adam Smith about joint stock companies: "The directors, being managers of other people's money rather than their own, it cannot be expected that they would watch over it with the same anxious vigilance with which owners watch over their own. Negligence and profusion therefore must always prevail, more or less, in the management of the affairs of such a company."

Well, Adam Smith may have been a cynical old Scot. But I also think that, as we cast our eyes across the corporate landscape in the U.K. and the U.S., we will find no shortage of evidence of negligence and waste. In some cases, it's conscious, in others it's not. But whatever the cause, we as owners *can* do something about it.

Most people's initial reaction to this statement is to ask, "But is that not what most investment institutions do? Don't the big funds spend most of their time as investors trying to be good owners?" My answer is that a lot of institutional investors do some really terrific things. There are investors in this audience whose work in engaging companies and their managements is clearly to be applauded. But engaging companies is not the primary objective of most investment funds.

First of all, most fund managers have little incentive to intervene in companies to try and improve their performance. They're usually paid according to funds under management; and because they're paid a very small fraction of the funds under management, they benefit little from their own efforts to improve companies. So they tend to "free ride" on the efforts of others. They either wait for somebody else to improve the performance or they sell the shares. Tom

Jones, when he was head of investment at CitiBank, was pretty honest about it. He said he got paid for picking well-run companies at reasonable prices, not for shareholder activism. He didn't try to fix companies when something went wrong; he just sold the shares. To make things worse, some fund managers—particularly those whose institutions do other business with the underperforming firm—also face conflicts of interest that tend to discourage them from expressing dissatisfaction with a management team.

Warren Buffett described the behavior of most institutional investors as "gin rummy" capitalism. Most investors keep their winners and discard their losers, as if they were playing a game of cards. When they discover the company's not behaving the way they want, they sell the shares. And I think that that behavior goes a long way in explaining Julian and Colin's finding that companies that don't need more capital often continue to underperform for long periods without intervention, whereas those that have to go back to their shareholders for new funds are better disciplined.

And Adam Smith, by the way, was not the only economist who doubted whether the public corporation with dispersed owners was a workable institution. Michael Jensen, who spoke at a meeting of the ECGI a few weeks ago, wrote a number of papers in the 1980s suggesting that private equity was going to end up owning a large fraction of publicly traded corporations. Jensen's argument, in brief, was that most companies that didn't need a lot of new equity to fund their investments would have higher values in the hands of private equity investors—people who actually sit on the boards of companies and monitor their performance—than under the oversight of the average listed company's board of directors.

When we reflected on these arguments, we were struck by the thought that the BT Pension Scheme, the biggest pension fund in the U.K., wasn't really carrying out its duty as an owner—wasn't doing enough for the pensioners who rely on company profits to pay the pensions. Now, it's true that there had been some positive developments during the 1990s. There were a number of movements, starting with Adrian Cadbury's report, to strengthen corporate governance in the U.K. And there were some individuals within fund management companies, such as Huw Jones at the Pru, who tried to behave as owners. Other groups, like PIRC, actually monitored whether or not Cadbury was being put into practice and having a significant effect. It was against this background that, in 1997, the decision to start an activist group at Hermes was taken by Alastair Ross Goobey, then Hermes's Chief Executive. This initiative began with Alastair's hiring of Peter Butler. He said to Peter, "Look, we've got 3,000 companies here. Would you care to improve them for us?!"

So we had one person to monitor 3,000 companies—and I think he was allowed to hire an assistant. It may have been revolutionary in the mid-1990s, but clearly it was not enough. And it raises the question, "How do you manage to provide a market incentive for owners to behave like owners, to try and check any negligence and profusion that may be taking place?" That's what we were aiming to accomplish with our Focus Fund. We thought we had found a way to increase our own profit by helping to improve companies.

So we decided to invest in companies where we felt there were things taking place that—whether for good reasons or bad—were clearly not in the shareholders' interest. Our aim was to bring about constructive change in underperforming companies in ways that benefited long-term shareholders, including the beneficiaries of the British Telecom Pension Scheme, with their billions invested in equities. But unlike many shareholder activists—particularly those you may have read about in the U.S.—our approach was to operate privately, behind the scenes and away from the attention of the press. We thought this would lead to a more productive discussion with managements and boards. We also found ourselves working with other funds with common goals, and the cooperation and support of these funds have contributed greatly to the success of our efforts.

One of the first changes we made when setting up our Focus Fund was to change our own incentives. A deal was negotiated whereby Hermes earned success fees that varied with the extent to which our fund outperformed the average fund manager. That new incentive structure helped Peter Butler to hire a set of resources for active investing that is unlike any other large institution's anywhere in the world. Our Focus Funds currently employ three former company chief executives. We also have strategic consultants, investment bankers, and accountants. And we have an impressive number of very senior fund managers. The aim is to make investments in companies, change their behavior, and so create value. So that's what we've been trying to do.

Have we been successful? It was the purpose of the study to answer that question. I think it is telling us the following: "Look, you've done a good job of identifying the kinds of changes that needed to be triggered to increase value. You've helped to make those changes happen, given the number that you said you wanted and the number that actually took place. And the positive market reactions to those events suggest that such changes have ended up contributing heavily to the successful performance of our Funds."

I'm very comfortable with all those statements. But I would also point out that shareholder activism is absolutely not a license to print money. If anyone decides they want to do this sort of thing, they had better understand the kind of skills and resources that are required to do it well. They should understand that, from quarter-to-quarter and year-to-year, your performance can be buffeted by the stock market. Finally, they should also recognize that, if everybody decides that they want to become activist investors—and I hope we haven't encouraged them to do this—we will in fact reduce the opportunities for the kind of arbitrage that has allowed our fund to be successful. Our feeling has long been and continues to be that underperforming companies are seriously undervalued; but if active investing becomes a pervasive activity, the gap between actual and potential values will shrink.

Equally, as we think about the agenda for the LBS Center for Corporate Governance, we shouldn't view shareholder activism as a complete solution. In fact, activism is only part of pension funds' efforts to ensure that companies are managed in the shareholders' interest. In addition to our Focus Funds, we have a small corporate governance unit called Equity Ownership Services. When people ask me, "What's the difference between what the two groups do?," I often use another medical analogy. I tell them, "Our Focus Funds are like dentists, with companies for patients. When we find patients who have problems with their teeth, we drill them—and sometimes we take them out and put in new ones. But our EOS group provides prevention rather than a cure; it's putting fluoride in the water or encouraging people to brush their teeth so they don't get bad teeth in the first place."

So, helping companies get the right governance systems and structures is a very important part of our effort to keep our returns high. The accomplishments of our Focus Funds have been very specific, very targeted. They've been concentrated in a group of about 40 companies over the past eight years where we saw at least 20% upside potential from getting involved. But our success with these 40 companies answers only part of the question that Alastair asked about our ability to improve 3,000 companies worldwide. And while I'm clearly delighted with the outcome of this study of our activism, there are some other, bigger questions that we need to be asking.

Some 30 years ago I studied for two degrees: one in politics and one in business. When you study politics, you spend a lot of time thinking about the rules and institutions that make for a civil society, whether it's in America or France or Britain. And you try to understand how the institutions all interact, and how they contribute to both efficiency and effective government. But when you do an MBA, there is very little discussion of corporate governance and the institutions that are part of it. We need to start to think very seriously about what kinds of structures—whether they're found in continental Europe or the U.S. or the U.K.—give rise to companies that are producing value for all their constituencies. And it's always important to keep in mind that many corporate share owners are insurance companies and pension funds whose beneficiaries are millions upon millions of people representing all levels of wealth.

And I'd like to suggest that there are a number of conditions that we should be trying to create. One is that we need boards of directors to be more accountable to their shareholders. In America, for example, I think there is a serious gap in accountability that stems from how directors get onto boards and whom they feel they're responsible to. We need to spread accountability.

But if we're going to have accountability, we need to have responsible owners as well. Shareholder activism can accomplish some of that, but it must be activism that is practiced in an appropriate and sensible way—one that is likely to produce a constructive response by the companies. And, as you can probably tell from this statement, I don't believe the kind of shareholder activism that is done by most hedge funds will prove to be nearly as successful in making improvements in long-run performance. Again, we need responsible, committed owners, not traders.

We also need measures of company success that are considerably better than those we have just now. Earnings per share and profit growth are entirely inadequate measures of a company's strategic health. And we need independent monitors to report on these measures of their success. But even if we get the measures and the monitors, and even if we get the responsible shareholders and accountable companies, there is another, still bigger thing that all of us inside and outside this room need to be seeking. When you study political science, you come to understand that the main reason most people obey laws is not because they fear being arrested; it's because they agree, at least implicitly, that the laws are just and that the principle of law is essential to a civil society. For companies that are owned in large part by our pension funds, there will be a similarly fundamental agenda. It is that companies and their boards of directors must be constantly looking to their shareholders and seeking to serve their long-term interests. I'm very encouraged by the success of our Hermes Focus Funds in making improvements in some companies and in producing higher returns for the pensioners of BT Telecom. The LBS study has shown that we as owners have been able to improve company performance. But it's only a small part of the agenda of corporate governance. It's a promising start, but it's only a start.

Many billions of pounds of sustainable growth are possible if we get the agenda right. So I commend the work of the LBS Center for Corporate Governance in discovering how this can best be done.

Tyson: Thanks, David, for sharing your story. And that brings us to the end of the first part of this program. The second part will be moderated by Professor Colin Mayer of Oxford's Said Business School. Colin, as I mentioned, will become Dean of the School in the fall.

Part Two: More Perspectives on U.K. Shareholder Activism

Colin Mayer: Thanks, Laura. Up to this point, we have heard a summary of the findings of an independent academic study of shareholder activism as practiced by one U.K. fund—the Hermes U.K. Focus Fund. And we have just heard a former Managing Director of that Fund give his account of the Fund's begin-

One of the most striking insights from our study is how much of the activism involves direct engagement—not through meetings and shareholders' resolutions, but through direct communication with the boards of companies. In contrast to the traditional shareholder recourse of selling or mounting futile protests at shareholder meetings, this is the loud and clear voice of investors being heard and heeded.

Colin Mayer

nings, accomplishments, and remaining challenges. For the second half of this program, we have invited four well-known practitioners to give us their views on the merits or otherwise of shareholder activism and the associated institutions. We have just been told that activism can improve corporate performance and raise shareholder value by fairly substantial amounts. We want to find out, among other things, whether our panel of distinguished speakers agrees with that assessment.

My plan is to divide this session into three parts. First, we will address the question of how much activism goes on in the U.K. and what forms it takes—how representative, for example, is the Hermes case? Second, I want to ask whether shareholder activism generally tends to be beneficial, and whether there are sometimes significant negative effects. Third and last is the policy question: If we think that activism is by and large a good thing, do we think there should be more of it? And if so, how can we encourage it? Should it come from advocating institutional involvement? Should it come from government or changes in the law?

But before I ask each of our four panel members to address these questions, let me tell you a bit about them.

Alastair Ross Goobey, besides being a Senior Advisor to Morgan Stanley International, is the Senior Independent Director of GCap Media, the U.K.'s largest commercial radio group, and Chairman of its Remuneration Committee. From 2002 until July 2005, Alastair was Chairman of the International Corporate Governance Network. And as David mentioned, he was Chief Executive of Hermes Pensions Management from 1993 to 2001. In addition to his work on several corporate boards, he serves as a Governor of the Wellcome Trust, the largest U.K. charity, which funds bioscience research at a rate of some $800 million a year.

I'm greatly encouraged by the results that Julian and his team have produced—and I think the results are correct. We were able to show our trustees that our interventions were adding enough value to their portfolios to justify the cost of such activism. And our initial successes allowed for the expansion that has resulted in the much larger scope and returns produced by Hermes' current Focus Funds.

Alastair Ross Goobey

Sir Victor Blank is Chairman of Trinity Mirror, a position he has held since 1999, as well as Chairman of GUS, since July 2000. He is also Chairman Designate of Lloyds TSB Group. From 1985 to 1996, Victor was Chairman and Chief Executive of Charterhouse, one of the first houses to be involved in the U.K. development capital and private equity markets during their first big growth spurt in the '80s. He is actively involved in a number of charitable organizations, serving as Chairman of Wellbeing of Women and UJS/Hillel. I should also mention that Victor is the co-author of a textbook *Takeovers and Mergers*.

Institutional investors today are continuously engaging managements and boards in a dialogue or debate on strategic issues, operating issues, and governance issues. It's a debate as to whether management has the right strategy and objectives, and whether boards are doing a good job of overseeing management's progress in meeting its goals. And to the extent the debate has been a satisfactory one, shareholders are achieving their aims through a reasonably civilized and constructive process.

Sir Victor Blank

Anita Skipper is Head of Corporate Governance at Morley Fund Management, where she is part of their foreign engagement team. She is a member of several corporate governance committees, including the Association of British Insurers' Investment Committee and Share Schemes Panel, and the International Corporate Governance Network's committee on global governance principles. Anita is also a founding member and current chair of the Global Institutional

The trend in the last few years for U.K. institutional shareholders has been toward greater collaboration with companies as well as other shareholders. Our governance group at Morley are very much in touch—in fact almost on a daily basis—with the companies we're invested in. And this regular exchange of information can only be a good thing for both the companies and their shareholders.

Anita Skipper

Governance Network, an informal group of global investors who meet regularly to consider current global governance issues.

Brian Magnus is a Managing Director and Co-head of U.K. Investment Banking at Morgan Stanley. Brian has been involved in many of the largest and most complex M&A deals in the U.K. in recent years, including MSREF / Canary Wharf, Pernod / Allied Domecq, Deutsche Post / Exel, and the defense of Marks & Spencer. Before joining Morgan Stanley, Brian worked in the corporate finance division of Schroders.

The Extent and Forms of Shareholder Activism

Mayer: So let's begin with the first question about the extent and kinds of activism in the U.K. And let's start with Alastair Ross Goobey. Alastair, as a member of the European Corporate Governance Forum and the former chairman of the International Corporate Governance Network, there are few people who are better qualified than you to talk on this subject. What can you tell us about the current state of investor activism in the U.K.?

Ross Goobey: Thank you very much, Colin.

How much shareholder activism is now done in the U.K.? Quite a lot. There are a lot of people in the audience here—some of whom have already been mentioned—who are part of this effort. I can see Huw Jones, who runs the governance and engagement area at M&G. I also see Peter Montagnon, who is head of shareholder matters for the Association of British Insurers. And here at the table with us is Anita Skipper, who has run the Morley Fund's corporate governance activities since the early '90s.

So there's quite a lot going on here. But the great problem has always been lack of resource. As David just told you, just before we started our Focus Fund at Hermes in 1998, we were responsible for managing a large index of companies on behalf of our owner, the BT Pension Scheme. And because we had decided to make most of our U.K. core equity investments an index fund, we had no way to add value to their portfolios against the benchmark. The only way we could hope to improve their returns was to raise the absolute return of the companies—and that meant trying to improve their performance.

So, in 1997, following the lead of people like Anita, we started identifying underperforming companies where we thought we could make a difference. Some of the companies we focused on were pretty much basket cases when we found them, and we got them to make some changes of the kind Julian's told us about. We were successful enough that my trustees said to me, "We want you to do more of this." And when I said, "Can we have some more people?," they replied, "Well, hold on a minute. We're spending all of the money and everybody else is getting a free ride."

This is a problem I have run across at many of the institutions I've talked to, both as chairman of the ICGN and as an adviser to Morgan Stanley. When you talk to people about governance, they tend to say, "Adding another person on governance and activism won't add a single basis point to my performance. And that's what I get paid on and that's how I grow my business."

David mentioned that today there are more than 50 people at Hermes who are involved in governance and activism in one way or another. That is at least five times more than any other institution in the world. And it is very difficult to justify; it is hard to demonstrate the payoff from such an investment. We thought we could prove that we were adding value. But it was very difficult to prove in a way that would convince outsiders and skeptics. For that reason alone, I think David is to be applauded for having authorized the study by a team of independent academics.

I'm also greatly encouraged by the results that Julian and his team have produced—and I think the results are correct. As I said, we were able to show our trustees that our interventions were adding enough value to their portfolios to justify the cost of such activism. And our initial successes allowed for the expansion that has resulted in the much larger scope and returns produced by Hermes's current Focus Funds.

But the Hermes experience notwithstanding, most institutions in the U.K. are faced with the catch-22 I mentioned earlier. It's very expensive to do properly, as David said. And that's why Julian's question about the cost-effectiveness of the different governance mechanisms is right on the mark. We need to learn more about whether activism is cheaper than alternatives such as takeovers and private equity. My experience suggests to me that if there is a cheaper, more reliable way of improving performance than our kind of activism, I haven't run across it.

But, to come back to where I started, activism is very expensive if you're doing it properly. You need all kinds of resources and skills. And we collectively need to find a way to overcome the free rider problem that is keeping so many institutions on the sidelines. Cooperative action by people like the Association of British Insurers and the National Association of Pension Funds is helpful. But there's always somebody who has to do the donkeywork, the legwork—and that's expensive. And unless investors find ways to get some revenue from this activity, it's not easy to see who's going to do the job of monitoring and fixing the hundreds of companies in the U.K., and the thousands of companies around the world, that are failing to realize their potential.

Mayer: Thanks, Alastair. Now let's hear from Brian Magnus, who is co-head of U.K. investment banking at Morgan Stanley. Brian, how much and what kinds of investor activism are you seeing?

Although a constructive force on the whole, there is a real downside to shareholder activism, or at least a note of caution that needs to be sounded. What is sometimes forgotten is that it is management's job to formulate strategy, announce what it intends to do, and persuade the market that it's right. It is not the job of management to listen to what the market says it should do and then follow without questioning.

Brian Magnus

Magnus: As both Julian and Alastair pointed out, shareholder activism goes way beyond the letter writing and kinds of engagement with management that are the subject of this study on the Hermes's fund. We at Morgan Stanley don't see much of this activity. What we have seen, however, is an explosion in the amount of pressure put on boards through public campaigns, be it through the press or through the actions of hedge funds. There has been an enormous increase in that kind of activity and pressure in the last three years.

What has also taken place in the last three years is a major increase in the ownership of U.K. companies by U.S. investors, global value funds, and hedge funds. If you look at how the ownership of the FTSE 100 has changed in the last three years, you'll see a huge shift into U.S. value funds, which take major positions in big companies they see as undervalued. There has also been a huge increase in the ownership positions and trading volume of hedge funds. Both of these groups are much more vocal and active in the U.K. than the traditional long-only funds.

So, again, there's been a very large increase in the amount of pressure put on corporate managements and boards. And while I think most of this activity is constructive, a force for good, I have a few reservations. Most investors invest in companies where they have chosen the company and the management to use the assets to carry out a given strategy. And I think the arrangement is based on a degree of trust that requires, as David said, the right governance structure to enable the trust to work. There is trust between the investor and the management to let the management get on with it, up to a point. Activism thus plays the role of a safety net. But when it becomes more than a safety net, I think it could become somewhat destructive—but I'm getting ahead of your question here, Colin, so let me stop with that.

Mayer: Thank you, Brian. Now let's hear from Victor Blank, who is chairman of Trinity Mirror and GUS. Victor, how do you view the kinds of activism that Alastair was overseeing at Hermes and the more public, perhaps less collaborative, kinds just described by Brian Magnus?

Blank: I'm not convinced there's a simple yes or no answer that does justice to your question. On the one hand, traditional institutional investors have put in place a set of governance rules and processes that I think have led to significant improvements in the way some companies are run. Perhaps even more important, they have made managements and directors much more conscious of their obligations to serve their shareholders.

The present forms of engagement are much more sophisticated, as well as more regular and consistently applied, than they were in the past. Institutional investors today are more or less continuously engaging managements and boards in a dialogue or debate on strategic issues, operating issues, and governance issues. It's a debate as to whether management has the right strategy and objectives, and whether boards are doing a good job of overseeing management's progress in meeting its goals. And to the extent that debate has been a satisfactory one—and my guess is that in many cases it has—shareholders are achieving their aims and getting satisfaction through a reasonably civilized and constructive process.

But along with this process there has also been an increased amount of activity by hedge funds, which are proving more difficult for managements and boards to deal with. The hedge funds are by and large highly sophisticated and intelligent investors, but they tend to have a fairly short investment horizon and to press for quick change. And their approach is creating a considerable amount of tension, not all of which is healthy. The hedge fund approach is very different from the traditional relationship between U.K. institutions and corporate managements—and I think it also differs in degree if not in kind from the Hermes approach discussed tonight—and I'm far from convinced that it's the value-maximizing approach for most companies.

So, in answer to the question, I think the number and intensity of engagements is growing. And while I endorse the process of debate that investors like Hermes are helping to promote, I'm troubled by some of the more extreme kinds of activism pursued by hedge funds.

Mayer: Thank you. Now, let's hear from Anita Skipper, who is head of corporate governance at Morley and part of their foreign engagement team.

Skipper: There is clearly far more shareholder activism happening at the moment than five or ten years ago, and there is involvement by investors of all kinds and at all levels. From my vantage point, it starts with voting against resolutions at shareholders' meetings. In addition to more active voting, there's also been a lot more engagements of managements and boards in recent years, especially post-Higgs. Shareholder contacts with non-executive directors in particular are much more acceptable today than in the past, and they happen on a much more regular basis. And with the emergence of the hedge funds, the existence of such directors has become much more precarious. It's even more important now that managements and boards try to attract—and then keep in touch with and retain—their loyal shareholders, the ones who are going to be there for the long term. This way, if problems do arise, the relationship between the board and investors can help the company work through them.

Our approach is to invest in well-run companies, but also to be aware of the risks. And when we see things going wrong that we think can be fixed, that's when we consider an engagement. In situations like that, we will often work with Hermes in helping to bring about change. We have worked with them on a great number of cases, and I think our collaborations have been rather successful. My own experience suggests that when shareholders work together, they stand a much greater chance of influencing companies to do what they want them to do.

And I think the trend in the last few years has been toward greater collaboration with companies as well as other shareholders. Our governance group at Morley is very much in touch—in fact almost on a daily basis—with the companies that we're invested in. And in my view, this regular exchange of information can only be a good thing for both companies and their shareholders.

Mayer: Thanks, Anita. Your last comment begs the following question: Most of us believe that better corporate governance is a good thing, and we also tend to think that transparency is also a good thing. But do those two propositions taken together imply that institutional investors should publicly disclose their governance activities with regard to specific companies?

Ross Goobey: In principle at least, I'm in favor of transparency in these matters. When I was at Hermes, we never had a problem discussing with other shareholders the propositions that we had put on the table and finding out why they liked them or were opposed.

But is that transparency? Obviously you should—and indeed you must—disclose your policies and what you've been doing to your clients. But whether the world at large should have this information is a different question. The great danger is that it becomes a captive of single-issue lobby groups, which can be a major distraction. For example, we disclosed the remuneration of my colleagues who were running the Focus Funds—and of course that didn't necessarily redound to our advantage in terms of PR. But what we did was a lot better than saying, "We refuse to disclose the information," which would have been disastrous.

So, although we're always urging companies to be transparent, I'm agnostic about the value of *complete* transparency. As David mentioned earlier, we try to keep our discussions with management away from the press. And there are other arguments for restricting certain kinds of information, especially when the information can become part of a political process.

Skipper: There's some proposed legislation that reflects the ongoing debate about the fundamental purpose of the corporation: Is management's sole responsibility to its shareholders, or are there other stakeholders whose interests need to be considered, and perhaps even given a primacy equal to the shareholders'? The single-issue lobby groups you mention tend to believe that boards should be less concerned about serving shareholders than protecting other constituencies, such as labor or the environment or local communities. And the number and power of these lobbies is another important reason for our kind of shareholder activism. The danger is that they will dilute management's focus. It's part of our job to provide managements with a continuous reminder that their primary responsibility is to their owners.

But having said that, let me also concede that advocates of corporate social responsibility play an important role in the political process. They are alerting companies to problems and issues that will arise in the next 10 or 20 years and that will need to be addressed. Companies that want to remain in business have to satisfy all their major stakeholders—employees, suppliers, regulators, local governments, and communities. The challenge for management is to do it in such a way that maximizes returns for shareholders.

Ross Goobey: I think this question about the responsibility of boards and directors to other corporate stakeholders, and its potential to dilute their commitment to shareholders, is a bit of a chimera. There's much less here than meets the eye. As David will tell you, Hermes has a statement of investment principles that urges companies to provide high long-term returns for their shareholders by managing effectively their relationships with employees, customers, and suppliers—and to act in the interests of society as a whole.

Now, in continental Europe, some corporate codes actually equate the interests of other stakeholders with those of the shareholders. In the U.K., though, it's quite clear, even in this bill, that stakeholder interests are subordinate to the shareholders'. And that to me is the most important thing; that is, while you are obliged to take account of the interests of other stakeholders, the bill does not disturb the idea—firmly established in our common law—that management's *primary* responsibility is the pursuit of long-term shareholder returns.

Is Activism Always a Good Thing?

Mayer: Let's now move on to the second of our three questions: Is shareholder activism always a good thing, or are there undesirable consequences that in some cases can outweigh the benefits?

Skipper: Some forms of shareholder activism are almost always likely to be beneficial. And I think the approach taken by Hermes provides a good illustration. It's a highly professional operation with lots of competent people who proceed in a disciplined, responsible, and reasonably patient manner. But I'm not sure the same can be said of many of the hedge funds that have emerged in recent years. In such cases, there's always the potential for a destructive conflict that can lead to both shortsighted decisions and the unwillingness of qualified people to serve on boards. I'm not saying that's what is actually happening. But it is cause for concern. And that's why I think it's good for corporate boards and managements to know that, in addition to all the hedge funds they read about in the newspaper, there are activists like the Hermes Fund that are willing to work with them in a fairly collaborative spirit.

So, I would say that activism as a whole is clearly a positive force. And it's something that is also evolving, growing a better platform. We all have a duty to consider what that platform should be, and perhaps get involved in bringing it about.

Blank: I think there are two distinct questions here. We have had a number of initiatives aimed at improving corporate governance that started in the early '90s with the Cadbury Commission, and such activities have continued into this decade. We have also had an increasing number of engagements of corporate managements and boards by institutional shareholders, including the Hermes Fund, to help ensure proper governance. And the first question is, has this kind of activism been good for performance?

Overall I think such developments have had a positive effect on performance. It has also been very good for the relationship between managers and the owners of the businesses. Somebody earlier mentioned that managers and boards needed to have more accountability, and I think that the system unquestionably has greater accountability as a consequence.

But what about the more aggressive, less collaborative forms of activism that seem to pit shareholders in a sense *against* the board or the management? In that case, I think the answer is less clear. I was especially puzzled by the research finding that Hermes engaged with the non-executive directors in only half the cases where it intervened. The chairmen and chief executives all have a vested interest in maintaining the status quo. And without knowing much about the specifics of the Hermes's approach, I would have thought it would be very important to engage the non-executives—those people who are appointed by the investors to look after their interests—and persuade *them* to make the necessary changes.

Ross Goobey: One benefit of shareholder activism, which my friend William Claxton-Smith is fond of pointing out, are the so-called positive externalities associated with these kinds of engagements. That is, the benefits of activism come from improvements not only in the companies that are engaged, but in those that are fearful of being engaged. Just the thought of being subjected to shareholder pressure is, at least in some instances, enough to bring about change.

Magnus: That's an important point—one that really gets to the core of whether shareholder activism is good, effective in making companies more accountable to the shareholders. I too think the answer to that question is yes.

If boards think that they can do nothing and preside over perpetual decline, they will eventually be put to task. But, at the same time, I think there is a real downside to investor activism, or at least an important qualification or note of caution that needs to be sounded.

What is sometimes forgotten in the current debate over shareholder activism is that, at the end of the day, it is the job of the management to formulate strategy, announce what it intends to do, and persuade the market that it's right. It is not the job of management to listen to what the market says it should do and then follow without questioning.

In June of 2004, a number of hedge funds had bought stakes amounting to about 35% ownership of Marks & Spencer, and these funds were pressuring top management to open the books to Philip Green, who had proposed an indicative offer of £4 per share. The funds couldn't understand why management wasn't prepared to let that happen. They said, "We are the shareholders. We demand that you do it." And Stewart Rose, the CEO, responded, "You may represent the owners, or at least some of the owners. But I am the management, and I believe that in the long term this company will be worth significantly more than £4." And their response to this was, "Well, if we get to 50.1%, then will you listen?" And Stewart said, "Not necessarily—not if I still think it's worth significantly more than £4. My job is to serve the *long-term* interests of my shareholders."

So there was no sale, and the shares today are trading at about £5. And the lesson here is that the proposals of activist shareholders—and particularly those of hedge funds—can prove to be shortsighted.

Mayer: Does anyone want to say a word on behalf of hedge funds, or are they generally to be avoided?

Ross Goobey: It's important to be careful when generalizing about hedge funds because they come in so many varieties and take so many different approaches. We know that many hedge funds take short positions in stocks, and most charge higher fees than traditional long-only funds—both of which practices, of course, immediately arouse suspicion. What seems to be less well known is that, like the Hermes Focus Fund, many hedge funds have relatively concentrated portfolios—that is, large stakes in relatively few stocks—and many also have relatively long holding periods, again like the Hermes Fund. So, many hedge funds are long-term, value-based investors that are interested in bringing about the same kinds of changes. On the other hand, there are many other funds that go for the quick turn; it's slash-and-burn and out. But that's fine, too. It's important to remember that even these kinds of hedge funds can build their positions only if other shareholders—who are also presumably "short-term" or at least "disloyal" shareholders—are willing to sell their stock to them.

Going back to Brian's case, though, if enough other shareholders had agreed with the hedge funds that the company was worth only £4, they could have achieved their 50.1% stake, called an Extraordinary General Meeting, and forced off the rest of the board. That's what being a shareholder entitles you to, at least in this country. If you happen to own shares in or make a bid for a German company, you might find yourself being viewed as "locusts."

But, again, I think there is plenty of room for all kinds of investors. And I think hedge funds in general play an important—and on the whole constructive—part in the overall governance process. Many of them are natural allies of Hermes.

But, to come back to a point that was made very early in this discussion, any sort of activism or engagement represents a failure of governance. It means that internal governance controls and process have been allowed to slip to the point where outside intervention is required. And I think what Victor said is true—namely, that boards of directors are increasingly serving the long-term interests of shareholders by taking a very active role in making sure that corporate strategy and capital structures and payout policies are the right ones. Board members are waking up to the fact that, if companies fail to take such steps on their own, some outsider will knock on their door and say, "If you're not going to make this change, we'll make a fuss until you do it, or somebody else comes in and does it for you."

Active investors like Hermes are thus the second line of defense for shareholders. The first line is the board of directors and the management team itself. And, as Brian's example suggests, they get the first chance to set things right. We want them to do the work for us. It's only after they've clearly failed that shareholder activism comes into play.

Encouraging More Activism

Mayer: Now let's take the third of our three questions: Should there be more shareholder activism? If so, how do we make it happen? Does it require a change in the law or some action on the part of government?

Ross Goobey: Well, I can think of one problem that could benefit from some attention. As David mentioned earlier, investors inside an organization with corporate clients often have a conflict of interest. If you're operating a fund inside a large investment or commercial bank, it doesn't necessarily benefit your bank as a whole if you start complaining about the lousy governance at some of your investment banking clients. And that means that shareholder activism is likely to come mainly from institutions, such as state and local government pension plans, that do not have corporate clients.

In the States, there has been a change in the rules that govern the trustees of mutual funds that directs them to uphold the interests of their shareholders—those people who, after all, are the funds' clients. And that's where the pressure should come from—from the clients. In the case of Hermes, as David mentioned, Hermes is the fund manager, not the shareholder. The shareholder is the BT pension scheme—or it's the Royal Mail pension scheme. The pension scheme trustees are the responsible owners of these shares.

What this means is that fund managers like Hermes are agents in what amounts to a *double* principal-agent problem. That is, both fund managers and the managers of companies are agents for the shareholders—people who are supposed to do the bidding of shareholders, but whose interests diverge from the shareholders' in more or less subtle ways. And it's the responsibility of the funds' trustees, as representatives of the principals or owners, to instruct their agents and ensure that they are serving the owners' interests.

In the U.K., there's no legal or structural impediment to this kind of activity. In fact, people like Will Claxton-Smith, whom I mentioned earlier, spend much of their time advising funds on such governance issues. But there are a lot of obstacles to this kind of oversight in the States, which is why this new rule looks promising.

Mayer: Alastair has just suggested that the growth of hedge funds is on balance a positive development. Do you agree with that, Brian?

Magnus: Yes, I do. I think the growth of hedge funds has been one of the best things that could have happened in terms of activism functioning as a safety net to prevent underperformance. I think the main reason hedge funds came about was investors' dissatisfaction with the returns from passive investing.

At the same time, it's not clear to me that such activism needs to be carried to greater extremes. As I said earlier, the combination of hedge funds and activism by more traditional investors is now exerting a tremendous amount of pressure on U.K. corporate boards and managements. And I think we've reached the point where there is enough pressure to ensure that at most a small minority of companies can continue to underperform while their boards fail to respond to the external signals for change.

Mayer: Victor, what's your assessment? Do we need more activism, or have we reached the optimal point?

Blank: I would like to see shareholder engagements with companies focus more on strategy and operations than they do now. In the past, and for good reasons, the main focus of most of the engagements was on the chairman's remuneration. I'm not saying that that's irrelevant, but it certainly isn't the most important decision affecting a company's future performance and value. And I think that investors with a good understanding of a company's operations and strategy would be in a much better position to suggest changes and, when necessary, to intervene.

I can give you examples from my own experience where I found a shareholder engagement to be less than productive. GUS, one of the companies I chair, owns a company called Burberry. Some of our shareholders came to us recently and said, "We don't think Burberry fits your strategy. We think you should get rid of it." We could have sold it for several hundred million pounds, but we didn't. We thought that, by investing in the business, we could turn it into something much more valuable. And we have done just that: We turned a business that we could then have sold for a few hundred million pounds into one that today is worth perhaps as much as £2 billion.

So, we felt that the institutional investors did not really understand the potential in our business. Was it our fault for not explaining it to them? To some extent maybe it was. But I also think they bear part of the blame for not doing their homework, for not working hard enough to understand our business, its requirements and its potential.

Now I can also think of many cases where corporate boards have sat down, listened to what the shareholders were saying, and then recognized, for example, that the company's configuration of businesses was not working, was clearly failing to maximize value. In such cases, the boards have generally gone along with the shareholders' recommendations. And these to me are examples of positive, constructive engagements by shareholder activists.

But, in other cases, the board listens and then correctly determines that shareholders don't really understand the business or the strategy. And that's why I feel that if the engagements probed more deeply by focusing much more on the strategic and operating issues, there'd be less need for activism, and the activists themselves would be better received by managements and boards.

Mayer: Anita, how can we encourage more activism and engagement?

Skipper: Well, I agree with Victor that engagements would be more constructive and better received if shareholders knew more about the business. On the other hand, I don't think shareholders can ever know as much about the business as management does—nor can the board, for that matter. And I think it's the responsibility of shareholders, and of the non-executive directors, to challenge companies when things don't appear to be going to plan. Even if the challenges reflect misunderstanding in some cases, it's important that the challenge take place just so management knows that someone is watching. It's that kind of challenge that pushes people to make better decisions.

What I would really like to see is the non-execs providing the challenge on the board. And I would also like them to engage with the shareholders and to tell them what it is the board is doing on their behalf. If this became a regular part of their job, there would be very little need for activism. Because actually none of us really wants to become active; it's only as a last resort, when all else has failed, that we get active.

Closing Thoughts

Mayer: That has the sound of an ending, so let me just briefly wrap up.

David Pitt-Watson very astutely described the study that we just discussed as like being operated on under a microscope. One conclusion that I think emerges pretty clearly from our examination is that shareholder activism is an important weapon in the armory of corporate governance instruments that are available to institutions and other investors. As such, it should be seen along-side other so-called control mechanisms such as takeovers, shareholder resolutions, non-executive directors, and remuneration, which could all play an important role in encouraging good management and good performance. Is it better than these other forms? We're not sure. Is it different? Unquestionably yes. Is it important? Almost certainly.

I think one of the most striking insights from the study is how much of the activism involves direct engagement—not through meetings and shareholders' resolutions, but through direct communication with the boards of companies. In contrast to the traditional shareholder recourse of selling or mounting futile protests at shareholder meetings, this is the loud and clear voice of investors being heard and heeded. And I believe that it has a vital role to play in governance of a board, and that we're very likely to see much more of it in the years to come. Thank you all for participating and for making this evening such a success.

CHAPTER 14

Leveraged Buyouts in the U.K. and Continental Europe

Retrospect and Prospect

MIKE WRIGHT, LUC RENNEBOOG, TOMAS SIMONS, AND LOUISE SCHOLES

BUYOUT MARKETS IN THE U.K. and continental Europe have developed substantially over the past 25 years. The European market appears to be entering its third period of significant growth, following the waves of buyouts during the latter halves of the 1980s and 1990s. In recent years, successive records have been set in terms of both individual deal size and the total market value of transactions in a given year. In 1997, for example, the U.K. market broke the £10 billion barrier for the first time. Only three years later, in 2000, more than £20 billion worth of deals were completed. The first European deal larger than £3 billion, the buyout of MEPC by Leconport, was completed in 2000. And 2004 saw the closing of the 20,000th transaction in the combined U.K.-European buyout market since the late 1970s, when the first recognizably "modern" LBOs appeared in the U.S. and U.K.

With a few notable exceptions such as France and the Netherlands, buyout markets in continental Europe did not materialize in earnest until around 1996. As can be seen in Panel A of table 14.1, the growth in the number of buyout deals in the U.K. and continental Europe from 1996 through 2005 has been steady if unspectacular (with the weak European stock markets of 2000–2004 appearing to have dampened activity). Although the U.K. has by far the most active of these markets, there has also been considerable buyout activity in France, Germany, Italy, Spain, and the Netherlands. Panel B shows a more striking evolution in terms of value: From 1996 through 2005), the combined value of all buyouts in Europe rose more than fivefold and broke through the Euro 100 billion mark in 2005.

In the U.K. at least, the buyout market has become a significant part of the takeover market, accounting for half of all acquisitions by value in 2005, as compared to less than 20% two decades earlier. U.K. buyouts have also consistently produced the highest rates of return for investors among all the various sectors of the overall private equity (PE) market, which includes early-stage

TABLE 14.1

Number and Value of Buyouts/Buy-Ins in Continental Europe (CE) and U.K., 1996–2005

Panel A: Number of Buyouts/Buy-Ins

Country Name	1996	1997	1998	1999	2000	2001	2002	2003	2004	2005
Austria	6	7	5	4	13	7	18	12	14	9
Belgium	11	10	19	16	19	25	24	20	37	28
Denmark	14	16	13	18	18	12	18	12	14	30
Finland	25	32	16	19	15	23	29	28	27	32
France	115	139	150	148	131	126	124	141	157	227
Germany	73	99	80	52	66	91	107	105	111	122
Ireland	9	9	15	9	12	16	20	14	11	6
Italy	24	25	32	43	30	17	38	44	42	45
Netherlands	56	61	75	66	79	60	62	74	72	82
Norway	7	6	4	8	7	9	12	16	13	16
Portugal	5	3	5	6	5	1	6	5	3	5
Spain	13	23	37	30	28	36	42	52	34	50
Sweden	16	20	23	32	25	49	25	24	39	38
Switzerland	53	65	51	56	54	50	36	31	32	28
Total (CE)	**427**	**515**	**525**	**507**	**502**	**522**	**561**	**578**	**606**	**718**
U.K.	**646**	**709**	**691**	**656**	**621**	**642**	**638**	**711**	**703**	**687**
Total (Including U.K.)	**1,073**	**1,224**	**1,216**	**1,163**	**1,123**	**1,164**	**1,199**	**1,289**	**1,309**	**1,405**

(continued)

TABLE 14.1 (*continued*)

Panel B: Value of Buyouts/Buy-Ins (€m)

Country Name	1996	1997	1998	1999	2000	2001	2002	2003	2004	2005
Austria	72	128	95	680	734	47	154	303	88	28
Belgium	147	414	820	2,595	337	1,744	517	1,448	2,266	4,057
Denmark	411	263	267	2,173	1,313	500	1,391	848	260	7,060
Finland	724	440	560	1,085	675	1,047	480	1,039	977	2,044
France	2,189	5,275	6,198	8,387	6,503	6,387	15,557	8,772	11,489	20,714
Germany	1,704	3,538	5,265	4,629	15,084	7,229	8,143	11,908	17,915	11,727
Ireland	116	119	244	1,475	259	5,021	4,930	747	970	770
Italy	1,146	3,121	673	2,756	2,555	1,002	3,428	7,773	3,013	17,512
Netherlands	1,001	1,059	3,528	2,906	1,856	4,433	1,870	4,958	7,612	10,256
Norway	315	180	22	225	1,004	1,370	142	308	455	426
Portugal	158	64	83	206	83	2	26	54	8	76
Spain	227	374	859	1,715	941	1,528	2,069	934	2,274	9,391
Sweden	700	1375	928	2,926	3,169	3,005	1,116	2,226	1,701	4,702
Switzerland	1,316	2,426	1,347	1,013	1,772	715	2,766	864	1,570	563
Total (CE)	**10,226**	**18,776**	**20,889**	**32,771**	**36,285**	**34,030**	**42,589**	**42,182**	**50,598**	**89,326**
UK	**12,555**	**17,114**	**23,273**	**26,864**	**38,349**	**31,343**	**24,844**	**23,570**	**30,144**	**35,406**
Total (Including U.K.)	**22,781**	**35,890**	**44,162**	**59,635**	**74,634**	**65,373**	**67,433**	**65,752**	**80,742**	**124,732**

Source: CMBOR/Barclays Private Equity/Deloitte.

and later-stage venture capital (VC) as well as buyouts. But for all its successes in the past ten years, the U.K. buyout market in particular now faces a number of formidable challenges—notably, finding new deals at attractive prices while competing with new market entrants, devising lower-cost ways to fund deals, and effecting timely exits capable of producing targeted rates of return.

In this chapter, we provide a backward look at market developments for buyouts in the U.K. and continental Europe and then consider the prospects for such markets. Because the U.K. is the most developed buyout market in Europe, we start with an overview of the research on all major aspects and stages of the buyout life cycle, including fund-raising, deal sourcing, deal structuring, offer premiums, exit mechanisms, and returns. Then, after noting the salient features of the largest buyout markets in continental Europe, we conclude with a brief discussion of the challenges confronting the buyout market as a whole.

The U.K. Buyout Market

The development of the U.K. buyout market into its present state can be viewed as taking place in five distinct phases.[1] Although there have been buyout-like deals stretching back to the 19th century, the first phase of the modern buyout market in the U.K. began in the early 1980s (see figure 14.1), roughly the same time as the U.S. market got its start. During the deep recession in the U.K. in 1979–1982, many of the first deals involved failed companies or firms restructuring to avoid failure. The relaxing in 1981 of the prohibition on companies providing financial assistance—specifically, security for the debt used—to purchase their own shares reduced the barriers faced by lenders in funding stock buybacks. And the introduction of a secondary tier stock market in 1980 (the Unlisted Securities Market) opened up possibilities for realizing exit gains from smaller buyouts.

The second phase in the development of the U.K. buyout market saw the rapid market growth from the mid-1980s to the end of the decade. The buyouts transacted during this period were increasingly the result of corporate refocusing strategies, and a first peak in the value of deals was reached in 1989. Such transactions, which generally included the existing management and were thus dubbed "management buyouts" (or MBOs), offered an alternative disposal route to a trade sale to a third party.

MBOs were especially attractive in cases where the selling company wanted a speedy low-profile sale or where there were few external bidders for the business. In addition to the many MBOs, the late 1980s saw large numbers of "management buy-ins" (MBIs), transactions in which private equity firms (or, in some cases, institutional investors) brought in their own management teams to run the purchased businesses. The advent of specialist private equity and mezzanine funds, along with entry by U.S. banks starting in the mid-1980s, helped fund the development of MBIs as well as MBOs.

FIGURE 14.1

U.K. Buyouts/Buy-Ins, 1980–2005

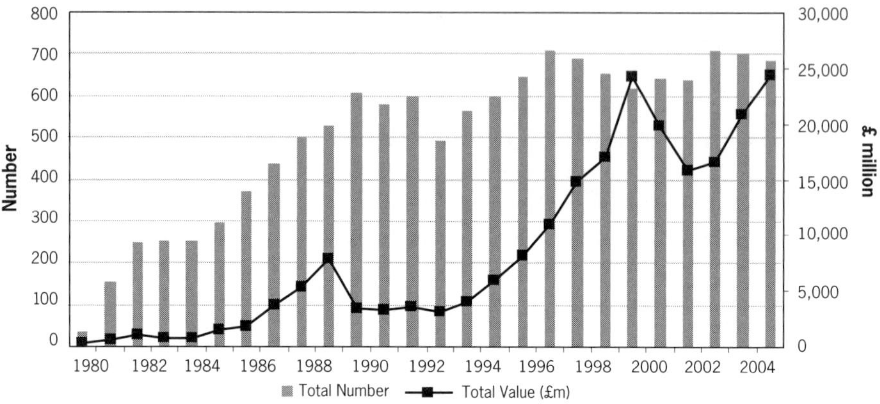

The third phase of U.K. buyout development, which began with the recession of the early 1990s, involved the restructuring of many of the largest transactions of the previous phase along with a return to the smaller buyouts that characterized the first half of the 1980s. As in the U.S., both the number and value of U.K. MBIs fell sharply as it became clear that many of the highly leveraged deals completed during the late 1980s—often premised on major asset sales—were having problems servicing their debt. The recession exacerbated these problems and made turnarounds longer and more difficult. Many foreign banks abandoned the buyout market, and those banks that remained active tightened their terms and covenants. Both private equity and debt providers were heavily involved in restructuring the problem cases in their portfolios, and some of the latter disbanded their lending teams that specialized in buyout-type transactions.

The end of the recession in 1994 saw the emergence of a fourth phase of U.K. buyout activity—one that saw rapid growth in total transaction value, which reached a new peak in 2000. At the same time, though, a focus by private equity investors on larger transactions kept the total *number* of buyouts from exceeding their "local" peak of just over 700 in 1997 until six years later in 2003. Along with a modest contraction in the number of deals in 1998 and 1999, the years after 2000 saw a sharp plunge in the total value of new deals in the wake of the collapse of the dot.com boom and its repercussions.

But a major resurgence in the value of the U.K. buyout market began in 2004, the start of the current phase five. In 2005, there were a record-high 49 buyouts with purchase prices in excess of £100 million, and the total value of deals also set a new record of £24.2 billion. But a preliminary look at statistics in the first half of 2006 suggests a slow start to the year, raising questions about challenges to the market to which we return below. (For a more detailed overview of the major events in the evolution of the U.K. buyout market over the past 20 years, see table 14.2.)

Raising Funds

Fund-raising in the U.K. has increased significantly over time and recently jumped to a record high of £18.6 billion ($24 billion) in 2005. During the period 2000–2003, the total amount raised by buyout funds in both the U.K. and continental Europe exceeded the amount invested in each year. But as can be seen in table 14.3, this trend was reversed in 2004, when the amounts invested exceeded funds raised by a considerable margin.

In the U.K., the trend among buyout firms has been to raise fewer, larger funds, each with more capital than the last. While persuaded of the attractions of private equity as an asset class, institutional investors in the U.K. (pension funds, mutual funds, and insurance companies) have indicated that they are likely to reduce their investments in all types of private equity in the future. At the same time, they also say that their investments specifically in buyouts will grow in importance as a percentage of their total commitment to private equity. By contrast, evidence from continental Europe indicates the intent of institutional investors to increase their commitments to investment in all forms of private equity, including buyouts.

In addition to the funds raised and invested within Europe, in recent years U.S. private equity firms have become much more prominent investors in European buyout markets. The investment in U.K. firms by U.S. private equity funds increased from £1.6 billion in 1999 to £5.3 billion in 2005 (figure 14.2). Among the explanations offered for such international expansion by U.S. PE firms are the increased competitiveness of the U.S. buyout market and hence declining returns on U.S. deals; the reduced appetite of institutional investors for early-stage funds since the end of the dot.com era; and greater opportunities for restructuring in the U.K. and, especially, continental Europe.

The hedge funds that have recently emerged in the U.K. are now providing an additional source of investment funds in the buyout market. In the last year or so, hedge fund returns have not been as high as those of buyout funds and, last year, presumably as a result, more money went into private equity than into hedge funds. Hedge fund managers are now pushing into less liquid markets, such as taking controlling positions in mid-cap stocks, which is the traditional territory of private equity firms. Increased competition for traditional private equity players has also come from new entrants such as government-sponsored operators like Dubai International, family offices, and wealthy entrepreneurs. In the first quarter of 2006, such relatively new investor groups led 33% of all transactions over £100 million, as compared

TABLE 14.2

Management Buyouts 1986–2006: Major Highlights

	U.K.	Continental Europe
1986	Emergence of bought deals and U.S. banks; First going private buyouts involving recommended offers (Gomme, Raybeck). First over £250 million U.K. Buyout Fund.	CMBOR begins to record the deals across CE in earnest. There were 167 buyouts with a combined value of €1 billion. First PTP recorded in France and Sweden.
1987	Emergence of large buyouts and growth of going private; Privatization buyouts record market share (10.3%) and deal volume (32) but receivership buyouts record low at 0.6%; Strong growth in Western European market. 100th buyout flotation.	First investment in CE firms by U.S. financiers (in France and Spain).
1988	First mezzanine debt fund; buy-ins exceed 100 deals and £1 billion value in a year for the first time; peak year for subsequent buy-in failure.	First PTP in Denmark and the Netherlands. Market value exceeds €5 billion for first time. Beginning of first market boom due to rapid growth in the number and types of financiers and major growth in management buy-ins.
1989	Emergence of hostile LBOs and unbundling; Record total deal value £7.5 billion. First £2 billion transaction (Isosceles). First 500 MBIs; Record MBO trade sales; almost £1 billion raised for U.K. buyout specific funds.	First investment in German buyout by U.S. financier. First use of mezzanine by 3i (investment in Lignotock in Germany).
1990	Collapse of large highly leveraged deal market; resurgence of smaller buyouts and those from receivership; record total buyout/buy-in deals volume (597) and of buyouts (486). U.K. interest rates at their highest.	Deal numbers peak for the first time at 413. Europe-wide recession closes in.
1991	Buyouts from receivership record 19.3% of deals; record failures of buyouts/buy-ins at 124.	A relatively quiet year for the buyout market with deals numbers falling compared to previous years to 336 and value falling similarly to €5.5 billion.
1992	Buyouts and Buy-in account for record 57% of all takeovers and 35% of their value; Emergence of Eastern European Buyouts.	First PTP in Germany. Surge in buyouts in Germany due privatizations by Treuhandanstalt post reunification. Basel I implemented in G-10 countries (risk management in banking). First secondary buyout recorded by CMBOR.

Year		
1993	500th buyout recorded by CMBOR; buyouts from receivership decline from earlier peak; buyouts from U.K. parents reach record low of 39%; 200th buyout flotation.	Second highest number of privatizations across Europe.
1994	Emergence of Serial Buyout/Buy-in Entrepreneurs. All-time privatization buyouts exceed 200. First 1,000 MBIs; record buyout fund-raising; record flotations of buyouts/buy-ins at 48.	The number of buyouts from foreign parent divestments peaked for the first time at 74; those from privatizations fell from the year before but remained a significant source.
1995	Emergence of Investor Buyouts (IBOs); buy-ins account for a record 36% of the buyout/buy-in market; buyouts of privately held/family businesses at record 40% of market; record trade sales of buyouts/buy-ins at 95; 10,000 buyouts recorded by CMBOR. The Alternative Investment Market (AIM) was introduced.	SWX (Switzerland), the world's first fully automated stock exchange, comes into operation.
1996	Total buyout market at £7.8 billion exceeds previous 1989 record. Buy-ins rise to a record 55% of total M&A. Rise of secondary buyouts and a new record for exits.	The end of a Europe-wide recession leads to the second market boom and the buyout market begins to take off again. Market value exceeds €10 billion for the first time.
1997	Another record year beats the £10 billion barrier. Exits down with flotations only two-thirds of previous year. New trend of privately sourced deals exceed U.K. divestments. Continental buyout market receives increasing focus.	Neuer Market launched in Germany for smaller companies. Geberit Beteiligungs was Switzerland's largest buyout (€1.3 billion). Deal numbers across CE exceed 500 for first time.
1998	Growth of IBOs and MBIs lead the third successive record market value year at £14.5 billion. PTPs responsible for 20% of value. Trade sales reach record high, but flotations continue to fall.	Tecnologistica (Italy) was the first tertiary buyout in CE. Deal value exceeds €20 billion for first time. The second highest number of buyouts from family firms is recorded. MBIs become a major feature of market. Andritz largest buyout in Austria (€481 million).
1999	Buyouts over £100 million reach record numbers to boost value to another record £16.8 billion. PTPs account for a quarter of market value; deals under £5 million drop by a third. Exits slow, particularly flotations. Emergence of U.S. fund interest.	
2000	At £23.9 billion market is more than four times 1995 value, but with a depressed number of smaller and mid-market deals. Family/private deals lowest since 1986. PTPs smash previous record. Receivership show largest increase in exits. 15,000 buyouts recorded by CMBOR. First £3bn deal (MEPC/Leconport, £3.5 billion).	Dyno Nobel was Norway's biggest buyout (€680 million). Alfa Laval was Sweden's largest buyout (€1.6 billion). Euronext formed in September in order to take advantage of the harmonization of the European Union financial markets.

(continued)

TABLE 14.2 (*continued*)

	U.K.	Continental Europe
2001	Value falls 20% to £19.2 billion as mega deals disappear and PTPs slow. Big drop in trade sales emphasize exit difficulties but funds raised boom to an even higher amount.	Eircom Ireland's largest buyout (€4.8 billion). Cognis Holland's biggest buyout (€2.5 billion). Basel II deliberations begin. Kabel Deutschland CEs largest secondary (€2.1 billion).
2002	Further fall in volume, value down another 20%. Large deals and PTPs disappearing. Buyouts still account for nearly half of M&A activity. Trade sales continue to drop, but receiverships and secondary buyouts increasing.	Neuer Markt closes after losing 95% of its value in 2.5 years. Legrand was largest buyout in France (€5.1 billion). Telediffusion de France was largest privatization (€2.4 billion). Number of buyouts from the high-technology sectors at their highest.
2003	Buyout market stabilizes: 6% increase in value; 8% increase in volume. PTPs highest for three years. Exits still flat but secondary buyouts almost equal to trade sales.	There were more buyouts originating from the business services sector than in any other year.
2004	Year ends strongly with second-highest-ever value of £20.1 billion. Mega deals bounce back with 47 above £100 million. Record exits largely due to secondary buyouts. Fund-raising lowest since 1996. 20,000 buyouts recorded by CMBOR.	Record value of buyouts in Germany (€17.9 billion). Celanese was largest ever German buyout (€3.1 billion). CBR first German buyout over €1 billion. Deal value across CE exceeds €50 billion for first time.
2005	Another strong year with highest-ever value at £24.2 billion. Buyouts over £100 million a record 49. Highest number of exits with secondary buyouts highest recorded. First buyout financed by Hedge Fund.	There were 694 buyouts with a combined value of €88.7 billion. Record number of buyouts in Germany (113). SBS Broadcasting Belgium's largest buyout (€2.1 billion). Wind Telecommunications was Italy's largest buyout (€12.1 billion). Amadeus was Spain's largest buyout (€4.3 billion). Sanitec was Finland's biggest deal (€1 billion). Frans Bonhomme and Eau Ecarlate (both France) were the first quatemary buyouts. Highest number of buyouts from family firms.
2006	Slow start, especially in deal value.	TDC of Denmark becomes largest ever buyout in the whole of Europe including the U.K. (€13 billion).

Source: CMBOR/Barclays Private Equity/Deloitte.

TABLE 14.3

European Buyout Funds Raised and Invested (€m)

	2000	2001	2002	2003	2004
Funds Raised	24,347	21,541	18,255	20,661	17,787
(of which U.K.)	(12,265)	(14,286)	(12,323)	(13,732)	(7,975)
Funds Invested	14,406	10,945	16,917	18,438	25,743
(of which U.K.)	(6,871)	(3,863)	(7,519)	(9,446)	(15,128)

Source: EVCA.
U.K. in parentheses.

FIGURE 14.2

U.S.-Based Buyout Funds Invested, 1999–2005 (£Billion)

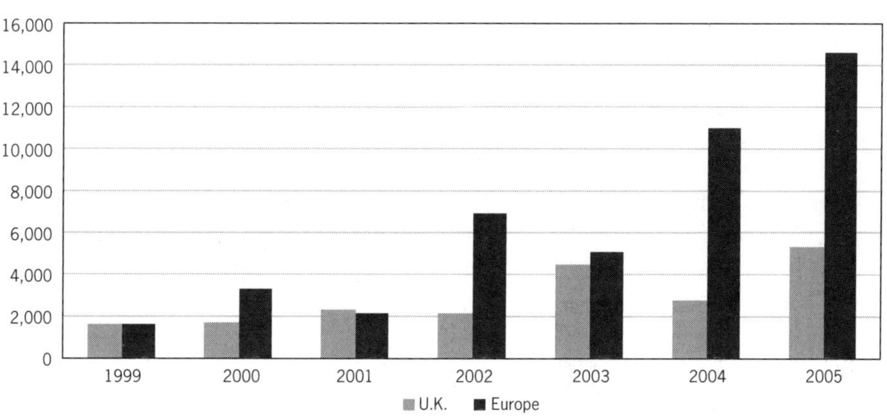

Source: CMBOR/Barclays Private Equity/Deloitte.

to only 8% of these larger deals during the whole of 2005, and none at all in 2001.

Sourcing Deals

There are a number of common sources of management buyouts. As can be seen in figure 14.3, the main source of U.K. buyouts has been divestments of divisions or subsidiaries by listed U.K. companies. Such divestment-induced buyouts were especially prevalent in the late 1980s, when large U.K. conglomerates were frequently selling off noncore activities. This phenomenon was less in evidence in the second half of the 1990s, when buyouts were equally likely to come from sales of family-owned and other private companies.

FIGURE 14.3

Sources of U.K. Management Buyouts/Buy-Ins (Volume %)

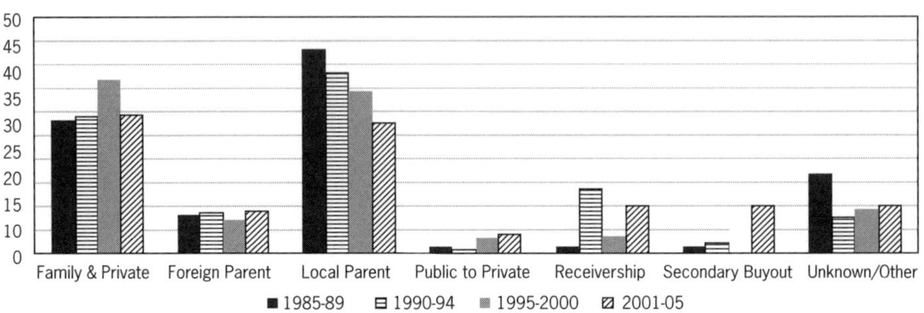

Source: CMBOR/Barclays Private Equity/Deloitte.

Another important source of U.K. buyouts was the state-sector privatizations that gathered pace during the second half of the 1980s, leading to a sharp increase in *management-employee* buyouts (not broken out in figure 14.3). In such cases, the specific skills of the incumbent management and employees were presumably believed to be key to the value of the business.

As already noted, the late 1980s also saw a wave of management buy-ins, in which PE firms sought to match experienced entrepreneurial outside managers with underperforming businesses in cases where poor internal management made a management buyout or a trade sale infeasible. The first buyouts of U.K.-listed companies, known as public-to-private transactions (PTPs), also took place during the second half of the 1980s, in some cases in response to hostile bids. And in 1989, a U.K. PE firm actually made a hostile bid for a listed public company (Gateway) (and won!)—the first of its kind in U.K. history.

Then, during the recession of the early 1990s, buyout acquirers benefited from a steady deal flow at a time when reductions in corporate profits led to divestments and limited the ability of established groups to make further acquisitions. In the second half of the 1990s, the pressure to maximize shareholder returns in corporate divestiture programs meant that the incumbent managers of subsidiaries were no longer seen as the preferred bidder, especially in larger transactions. This period saw the rise of *investor-driven* buyout acquisitions of subsidiaries, notably the so-called institutional buyout (IBO).[2] Additionally, as mentioned earlier, publicly listed family firms (as well as those in private hands) were a main source of buyout investments, reflecting the need of founding owners for successors and wealth diversification, as well as a greater effort by intermediaries and financiers to target these kinds of companies, given the increasing difficulties with divestment cases.

A Privatization Success Story

Inmarsat, the U.K. mobile satellite communications company, came into being as an intergovernmental organization (IGO) in 1979 to provide global safety and other communications for the maritime community. Starting with a customer base of 900 ships in the early 1980s, it then grew rapidly to offer similar services to other users on land and in the air, until in 1999 it became the first IGO to be transformed into a private company.

Apax and Permira bought the company in December 2003 for £921 million. Their strategy was to continue to develop the company into the world's leading mobile satellite communications company by continuing with plans to launch the Inmarsat-4 satellites and the next generation of high-speed data and voice services—the Broadband Global Area Network (BGAN) service. The company was successfully floated on the London Stock Exchange in June 2005 for a market capitalization of £1,120 million. Inmarsat now supports links for phone, fax, and data communications to more than 287,000 ship, vehicle, aircraft, and other mobile users and its BGAN service is now accessible across 85% of the world's landmass and to 98% of the population.

Since the late 1990s, the major changes in the relative prominence of different deal types have been the growth in importance of both secondary buyouts and public-to-private buyouts (PTPs), and the shift of attention to larger deals caused by the severe challenges in exiting smaller deals. Although private equity providers had previously been reluctant to purchase companies from each other, the pressure for existing PE firms to obtain an exit due to the limited life of their funds helped them overcome their reluctance. Much of the impetus for private equity providers to buy portfolio companies from other financial investors has come from the difficulties in finding attractive deals from other sources as corporate restructuring programs passed their peak and auctions pushed up prices. In fact, over a third of the total U.K. market value of buyouts is now accounted for by secondary buyouts. There were 91 such buyouts in 2005, as compared to just 29 in 1995.

PTPs have developed over the life cycle of the market's growth, starting somewhat later than general activity in 1985 and showing a marked resurgence during the second half of the 1990s. Due to the high costs and risks associated with such deals, the first PTPs were relatively small and invariably involved incumbent management. But, as the process became better understood and those initial deals were successfully completed, there was a growing tendency towards investor-led or institutional buyouts (IBOs) of larger public companies.

FIGURE 14.4

PTP Numbers and Values as Share of Total Market

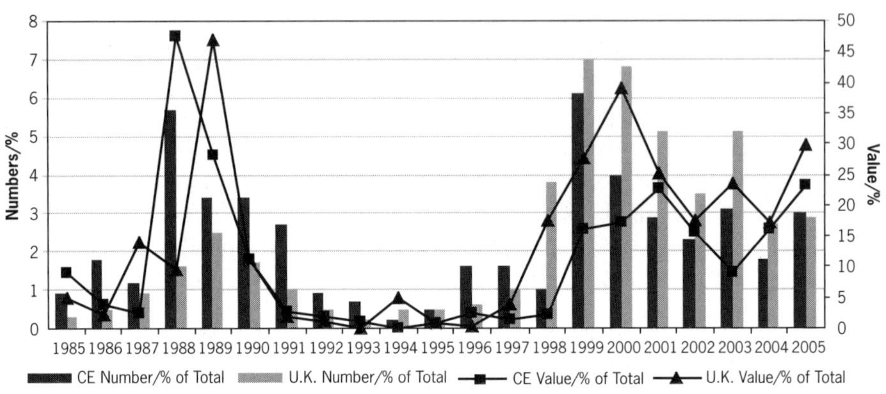

Source: CMBOR/Barclays Private Equity/Deloitte.

This suggests that the opportunities to restructure listed corporations by taking them private may be greater than once thought. Both in terms of volumes and values, PTPs have been far more important in recent years than in the top deal years of the 1980s, reaching a peak in 1999–2000, and then easing before recovering in value terms in 2005 (figure 14.4). The continental European trend has been similar.

The Financial Structure of Buyouts

In contrast to the U.S. experience, where buyouts represented a continuously large fraction of total private equity investing throughout the 1980s, U.K. buyouts during the 1980s started small and became increasingly important relative to the overall private equity market.[3] One major contributor to the rise of the U.K. market was the significant entry by U.S. banks into the U.K. market, which boosted the provision of senior debt and mezzanine finance. At the same time, a number of new specialist funds for investment in buyouts were launched in the U.K. Although domestic U.K. lenders were initially reluctant to become involved in transactions where asset sell-offs were necessary to repay debt, such an approach, after successful applications by U.S. buyers, gradually became an accepted feature of the larger end of the U.K. market.

As deal size increased from the mid-1990s, so did financial innovation. Most important for the development of the larger end of the buyout market was the emergence, in March 1997, of a European subordinated high-yield debt market that was willing to fund buyouts. The initial demand for larger amounts of financing in the larger U.K. buyouts could not be met with traditional senior debt or privately placed mezzanine. As a consequence, larger U.K. buyouts before 1997 resorted to the U.S. high-yield bond market. But, from 1997 onwards, U.K. financial institutions became at first willing and then eager to invest in high-yield, non-amortizing senior debt instruments.[4] Such instruments enabled buyout financiers to operate with highly leveraged capital structures but without creating foreign exchange risks. The securitization of such leveraged loans, already popular in the U.S. buyout market, also gained momentum in the U.K. and continental Europe during this period.

The proportion of debt in U.K. buyouts has varied considerably over the past 20 years. While the percentage of debt in buyout deals peaked in the late 1980s in the U.K. and sharply declined in the early 1990s, the recent decline in interest rates has been associated with a relative increase in leverage ratios. In the average deal transacted in 2005, debt represented 51% of the purchase price (figure 14.5).

The number of equity, mezzanine, and debt providers that participate in any one buyout has also changed over time. In the early years (1985–1989), when the market was immature, broad syndication was more common. The top ten buyouts during this period were funded by, on average, ten equity providers, eleven debt providers, and two mezzanine providers. These high numbers reflected the desire to spread the risks of the relatively smaller, less experienced fund providers that comprised the market at the time. But, as the U.K. buyout market has matured, the number of providers involved in buyouts has fallen. For example, in the ten largest buyouts over the period 2001–2005, there were, on average, three equity providers, four debt providers, and one mezzanine

FIGURE 14.5

Average Deal Structures and U.K. Interest Rates

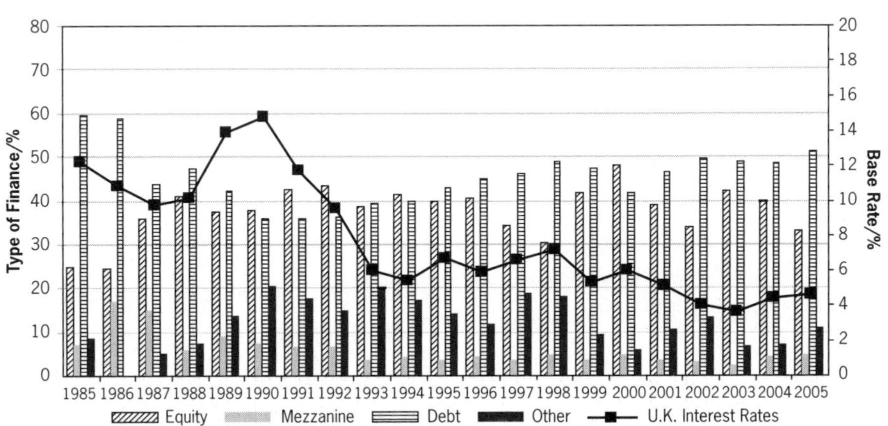

Source: CMBOR/Barclays Private Equity/Deloitte.

provider. But even so, as the deals keep getting larger, so does the number of equity providers that makes up the consortia.

Buyout Bids and Probable Sources of Value Added

To gain control of a buyout target, investors usually pay a premium over its going-concern market value. While this premium cannot generally be observed for private companies, studies of PTP transactions have shown large abnormal gains for the selling shareholders when an LBO is announced.[5] The premium is traditionally calculated as the difference between the last price traded before the delisting and the pre-announcement price of the firm. The pre-announcement price is usually taken some weeks (or months) prior to the first announcement to control for market "anticipation," which may drive prices upwards following insider trading or trading on rumors.

As reported in table 14.4, a reasonable estimate of the average premiums paid to selling shareholders in LBOs is around 45%. Our recent study of U.K. PTPs during the period 1997–2003 found an average premium of 41% (with the pre-announcement price measured one month prior to the announcement). The average share price reaction on the day of the PTP announcements was a positive 30%.[6]

TABLE 14.4

Premiums Paid above Market Price to Take a Firm Private: U.S. and U.K. Studies Compared

Study	Sample Period/ Country	Type of Deal	Obs.	Premium	Event Window	CAAR
DeAngelo, DeAngelo and Rice (1984)	1973–80 U.S.	ALL	72	56.3%	-1,0 days -10,10 days	22.27%*** 28.05%***
Lowenstein (1986)	1979–84 U.S.	MBO	28	56.0%	N.A.	N.A.
Torabzadeh and Bertin (1987)	1982–85 U.S.	ALL	48	N.A.	-1,0 months -1,1 months	18.64%*** 20.57%***
Lehn and Poulsen (1989)	1980–87 U.S.	ALL	244	36.1%	-1,1 days -10,10 days	16.30%*** 19.90%***
Amihud (1989)	1983–86 U.S.	MBO	15	42.9%	-20,0 days	19.60%***
Kaplan (1989a)	1980–85 U.S.	MBO	76	42.3%	-40,60 days	26.00%***
Marais, Schipper and Smith (1989)	1974–85 U.S.	ALL	80	N.A.	0,1 days -69,1 days	13.00%*** 22.00%***

(continued)

TABLE 14.4 (*continued*)

Study	Sample Period/ Country	Type of Deal	Obs.	Premium	Event Window	CAAR
Asquith and Wizman (1990)	1980–88 U.S.	ALL	47	37.9%	N.A.	N.A.
Slovin, Sushka and Bendeck (1991)	1980–88 U.S.	ALL	128	N.A.	-1,0 days -15,15 days	17.35%[***] 24.86%[***]
Lee (1992)	1973–89 U.S.	MBO	114	N.A.	-1,0 days -69,0 days	14.90%[***] 22.40%[***]
Frankfurter and Gunay (1992)	1979–84 U.S.	MBO	110	N.A.	-50,50 days -1,0 days	27.32%[***] 17.24%[***]
Travlos and Cornett (1993)	1975–83 U.S.	ALL	56	41.9%	-1,0 days -10,10 days	16.20%[***] 19.24%[***]
Lee, Rosenstein, Rangan and Davidson (1992)	1983–89 U.S.	MBO	50	N.A.	-1,0 days -5,0 days	17.84%[***] 20.96%[***]
Harlow and Howe (1993)	1980–89 U.S.	ALL	121	44.9%	N.A.	N.A.
Easterwood, Singer, Seth and Lang (1994)	1978–88 U.S.	MBO	184	32.9%	N.A.	N.A.
Van de Gucht and Moore (1998)	1980–92 U.S.	ALL	187	N.A.	-1,1 days -10,10 days	15.60%[***] 20.20%[***]
Goh, Gombola, Liu and Chou (2002)	1980–96 U.S.	ALL	323	N.A.	-20,1 days 0,1 days	21.31%[***] 12.68%[***]
Weir, Laing and Wright (2003)	1998–2000 U.K.	ALL	95	44.9%	N.A.	N.A.
Renneboog, Simons and Wright (2006)	1997–03 U.K.	ALL	177	41.0%	-1,0 days -5,5 days -40,40 days	22.68%[***] 25.53%[***] 29.28%[***]

Source: Renneboog and Simons (2005)
Note: ***, **, * stand for statistically significant at the 1, 5 and 10% level, respectively. ALL=all going private deals. MBO=MBO deals only.

How can the private equity buyers in such deals feel comfortable offering 30–40% premiums, especially when their own investors are looking for returns on the order of 15–25% per annum? A number of arguments have been offered to explain such large anticipated gains.[7] While there are some similarities between U.S. and U.K. sources of value creation in LBOs, there are also some important differences.

Consistent with most studies of U.S. LBOs, studies of pre-transaction shareholders in the U.K. PTPs suggest that part of the value created by taking *public companies* private may be attributable to the market's undervaluation of the firm.[8] But the most important source of value creation in PTPs—and presumably in buyouts and private equity of all kinds—is likely to be the strengthening of managerial incentives and more intensive monitoring and participation by large investors. The operating managers in such companies are typically either given or asked to purchase significant amounts of stock or options. And the fact that the private firm's board of directors is made up of its largest investors suggests a much more vigorous and effective monitoring process. Lending additional support to this argument, studies of U.K. PTPs show that companies with outside blockholders reap *smaller* benefits from going private. This is consistent with the idea that in firms monitored by this type of outside shareholder, there is less scope for operating performance improvements following the PTP transaction.[9]

In contrast to studies of U.S. LBOs, studies of U.K. PTPs also suggest that the reduction of the corporate tax bill potentially accomplished by high leverage is not a significant motive to take a listed company private. Nor do U.K. deals appear designed to manage a corporate free cash flow problem—a conclusion reached by most studies of U.S. buyouts as well. But there is some evidence that the costs of maintaining a listing could be motivating some companies to go private. What's more, since the indirect costs of a listing—in the form, say, of management time spent on investor relations—are almost certainly much higher than the direct costs, it may be worth focusing more attention on this motive.

PTPs have also been used as a means of purchasing financially distressed companies. But our own recent study shows that, in a sample of 182 U.K. PTPs transacted during the period 1997–2003, only five firms were in financial distress before the transaction and required concessions from their banks for the continuation of their operations.[10]

But, even when free of the complications of financial distress, PTPs are costly to undertake and the risk that a bid will fail is significant. In the U.K., private equity bidders for listed companies often use "irrevocable commitments"—legally binding promises to sell made by major shareholders before the offer is made public—both to ensure the success of a PTP proposal and to discourage a bidding contest that would potentially reduce their returns from the investment.[11] Irrevocable commitments are widely used in U.K. PTPs: 23.40% of a sample of 155 PTPs completed in the period 1998–2003 gained up to 20% irrevocables, and some 60% achieved at least 50% support from shareholders prior to the bid announcement.[12] This approach is likely to be especially effective in cases where the incumbent management holds significant stakes and existing institutional shareholders are locked in to holding shares in the company.[13]

Exit Mechanisms and Returns from Buyout Investments

Studies of the longevity of buyouts suggests that private equity firms are under significant pressure to achieve their target returns and hence work towards a timely exit.[14] As a consequence, besides more intense monitoring of their portfolio companies, PE firms are also likely to use exit-related equity-ratchets on management's equity stakes. As can be seen in figure 14.6, the most common type of exit has varied somewhat over the life of the U.K. buyout market. Sales to corporate buyers, or "trade sales" as they are typically called, have generally been the most common form of exit in the U.K., accounting for about a third of all exits during the recessionary period 1990–1994 (when receivership was an even more common end) and for close to 50% during the latter half of the 1990s.

For the largest, most successful buyout portfolio companies, however, the most popular choice is likely to be an initial public offering (IPO). This was the choice in roughly a third of the exits in the second half of the 1980s. But since then, the percentage of exits through IPOs has fallen sharply, from about 10% in the 1990s to 5% during the last five years.

The total value of exits reached a record of £18 billion in 2004 and remained high at £22 billion in 2005. This is more than three times the total value of exits that took place a decade earlier.

Secondary buyouts—sales of portfolio firms from one PE firm to another—have gained in importance since their start in the early 1990s, and they now account for almost a third of all exits. A number of factors have contributed to financial investors' decisions to sell their portfolio firms to other PE firms. Chief among them are (1) difficulties in exiting buyouts through IPOs; (2) the reduced acquisition appetite of corporations (especially for smaller deals), which appear increasingly intent on achieving greater focus; and (3) the need for private equity firms to exit from deals when their funds are nearing the

FIGURE 14.6

Exits of U.K. Buyouts and Buy-Ins (%)

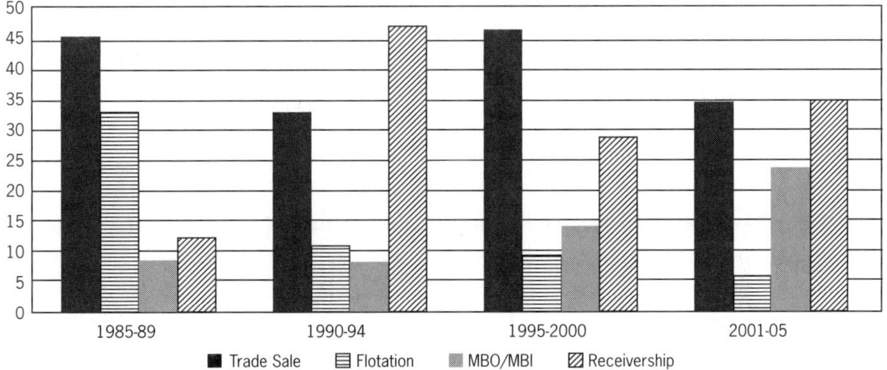

Source: CMBOR/Barclays Private Equity/Deloitte.

The Case of Bols: Creating Value through Trade Sales

Bols, founded in Amsterdam in 1575, had become the Bols Royal Distilleries division of Dutch food group Royal Bols Wessanen NV by the time it was sold to CVC Capital Partners Ltd. in 1998 for €185 million. That move marked the end of a five-year effort to combine Wessanen foods with Bols drinks. Under the CVC umbrella, Bols bought the Metaxa and Asbach brands in 1999 from Diageo PLC, the world's biggest liquor company, which at the time was slimming its huge portfolio to focus on a core group of nine global brands. France's second largest liquor and wine company, Remy Cointreau S.A., wanting to participate in industry consolidation, agreed to buy Bols Royal Distilleries for €510 million in August 2000 just two years after the buyout.

ends of their contractual lives. The record levels of U.K. exit values in 2004 and 2005 were driven largely by major exits through secondary buyouts.

An increasing number of buyouts have had several subsequent private equity owners (sometimes referred to as "tertiary" or "quaternary" buyouts). At the end of 2005, a total of 41 companies had gone through at least three buyouts. Such companies tend to be mid-sized cash generators in mature sectors that can be easily releveraged.

Performance of IPOs. Studies show that IPOs of U.K. buyouts result in positive and highly significant first-day returns to IPO buyers. MBOs that are (at least) partly controlled by private equity firms tend to be more underpriced than MBOs without private equity investors.[15] However, there is no difference in the long-run, post-IPO performance of either type of MBO.

Venture-backed MBOs in the U.K. tend to go public at an earlier stage than their non-venture-backed counterparts. PTP MBOs in the U.K. that are backed by more reputable private equity firms tend to exit through IPO earlier and to perform better than those backed by less prestigious private equity firms.[16]

Returns. Private equity returns have been declining in recent years, which is not surprising considering the negative trend in the stock market over the period 2000–2004, the higher competition for deals, and the prevalence of auctions. But even so, the fund-level data published by national venture capital associations and the European Venture Capital Association (EVCA) consis-

> ## The Case of Sirona Dental Systems: A Tertiary Buyout
>
> Sirona Dental Systems, headquartered in Bensheim, Germany, manufactures dental equipment for clinics and dental laboratories worldwide and has been the subject of three buyouts. The first took place in 1997, when the company was bought by Permira from Siemens for €460 million. In 2003, EQT Partners bought the company from Permira for €418 million. Finally, in 2005, the company was sold as a secondary buyout to Madison Dearborn Partners for €800 million, with debt provided by JP Morgan. Sirona had performed well with EQT and a strong European business plan had been implemented. With Madison Dearborn at the helm, they aim to focus on the U.S. market and further develop their global strategy.

tently show that the internal rates of return (IRRs) on buyout funds outperform the two other main categories of private equity funds: early-stage and all-stage venture capital funds.

A study (involving one of the current writers) using firm-level data on 321 exited buyouts in the U.K. during the period 1995–2004 found that the average buyout company earned an IRR of 22.2% on its total enterprise value (debt plus equity) and an average IRR on its equity of 70.5%.[17] IPO exits, as expected, outperformed trade sales and secondary buyouts. Larger buyouts—those with an initial transaction value above £100 million—had greater returns than medium-sized or smaller buyouts. The study further provides evidence that the monitoring and incentive effects associated with larger managerial equity stakes are a major contributor to the increases in enterprise value. (But, interestingly enough, this effect reverses when management controls the *majority* of the equity, a phenomenon limited to very small buyouts that fall below the target size range of most financial sponsors.) In the average U.K. buyout, the study also finds that leverage and interest coverage are also positively related to the rates of return and value increases.

Refinancings and Partial Sales. In recent years, with the traditional forms of exit proving somewhat difficult, refinancings and partial sales have become a popular way for private equity houses to cash out part of their investments while at the same time keeping control of their portfolio companies. There are two common methods of exiting through refinancing. First, the private equity house can refinance a business they own by having it borrow more and then paying themselves special dividends from the borrowings. Alternatively, the

TABLE 14.5

Total Value Realized for U.K. Buyouts/Buy-Ins

Year	Total Value Realized (£m)	Total (Percent) Exit Value	Total Value (%) Refinance	Total Value (%) Partial Exit
1997	6801	87%	12%	1%
1998	6283	70%	28%	2%
1999	8471	77%	12%	11%
2000	16736	59%	25%	16%
2001	18179	47%	23%	30%
2002	17587	62%	21%	17%
2003	13417	66%	19%	15%
2004	34258	53%	30%	17%
2005	40533	54%	31%	15%

Source: CMBOR/Barclays Private Equity/Deloitte.

A German Case of Partial Sale

The Moeller Group, headquartered in Bonn, is one of Germany's largest and longest-established privately owned industrial and buildings electronic component producers. After the company suffered a downturn in performance in 2000–2002, it was bought in 2003 for €49 million by Advent International, which aimed to use the buyout structure to create a platform for successful growth and enhanced competitiveness. The existing management team was joined by two new board members from Advent and a restructuring plan was implemented. Advent turned an underperforming business into a profitable one in about two years and partially exited their investment by selling a 75% stake to Doughty Hanson in 2005, in a secondary buyout, for €1.1 billion.

PE firm can sell some of its property assets to a third party (for example, to an insurance company), lease back the property, and transfer the proceeds from the sale to the PE firm in the form of a dividend. In 2005, the total refinancings accounted for almost a third of the total value realized in the U.K., as compared to a little over a tenth in 1997 (see table 14.5).

A partial sale of the portfolio company provides another means of realizing part of the initial investment without losing control. These sales made up just under a third of the total value realized in the U.K. in 2001, when the value

FIGURE 14.7

Buyouts as a Percentage of GDP

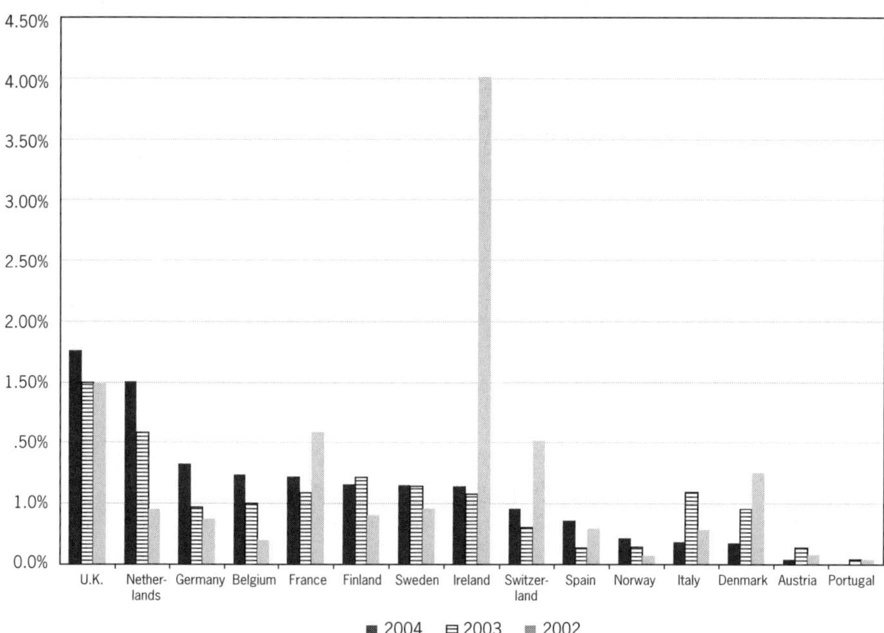

Source: CMBOR/Barclays Private Equity/Deloitte.

of the FTSE 100 fell sharply, but have since become less popular and now account for less than 10% of the total.

Financial distress represents, of course, a forced exit. Over the last 20 years, there have been 12,267 U.K. buyouts, of which 1,431, or about 12%, have so far entered protection from creditors.[18] The high leverage in LBOs means that financial default will occur sooner, and with greater frequency. And for this reason, we would expect significantly higher recovery rates for creditors. In U.K. buyouts that defaulted, secured creditors recovered on average about 60% of their investment. And, as happened in the U.S., many of these companies were eventually restructured and sold as going concerns.[19]

Buyouts in Continental Europe

Despite the growth in U.K. and continental European markets noted earlier, the maturity of the different buyout markets varies markedly. One common indicator of the relative maturity of buyout market is the ratio of the value of buyout transactions to a country's GDP. As can be seen in figure 14.7, the U.K.

and the Netherlands have the largest buyout markets as a proportion (about 1.5%) of their GDP, while the French and German markets appear to be about half that size. Spain and Italy have relatively undeveloped buyout markets, representing only about 0.5% of GDP.

Table 14.6 compares the factors influencing the development of private equity-backed buyouts in four different markets that are representative of the different stages of maturity observed in European private equity markets. As mentioned above, the U.K. represents the most mature market, with France closely following. Germany represents the less developed, though large, European PE economies, and CEE is representative of the undeveloped, emerging markets.

As summarized in Panel A of table 14.6, there are important differences among countries in terms of the supply of buyout opportunities. For example, in the U.K. most opportunities have come from the restructuring of diversified groups, with going private transactions becoming more important only in recent years. In France, by contrast, the marked growth in buyouts has been driven mainly by succession and portfolio reorganization issues in the large number of both listed and unlisted family-controlled companies. But even so, divestments by French corporations, in response to growing competitive pressures and an increasing focus on corporate governance and shareholder value, have recently become a major part of the French private equity market.

By contrast, in countries like Germany, Spain, and Italy, the reluctance of founders of small and medium-sized firms to sell to private equity firms—or to cede control at all—has restricted market growth. As a result, divestments and secondary deals have been the most important sources of buyouts in these countries. In CEE, the transition from communism has been the main source of opportunities as many state-owned firms were privatized, though these volumes have steadily declined in recent years. The overall continental European market for PTP transactions is still small, in part because these countries have far fewer listed companies in the first place. Culture may also play a role in this, with managers in some countries apparently expressing such pride in their listings that they refuse to even consider going private.

Panel B of table 14.6 attempts to summarize aspects of the "demand" side of the buyout market, particularly cross-country differences in attitudes to entrepreneurial risk and the willingness of managements to undertake buyouts. The most notable finding here is that U.K. managers appear much more inclined to take risks than managers in continental European countries. The most important exception to this generalization is France, where the recent growth in buyouts seems to have been fueled in part by a more entrepreneur-

TABLE 14.6

Comparison of Factors Affecting MBO Market Development in Europe

Panel A: Supply of Opportunities

	U.K.	France	Germany	CEE
Need to deal with family succession problems	Moderate need	High need	High need	Low need
Need to restructure diversified groups	Established patterns throughout period	Became established in 1990s	Becoming established from mid-1990s	Increasingly established in early 2000s
Need to privatize state-owned companies	Well-established program from 1980s; now complete	Less extensive than U.K.	Former GDR apart, relatively little	Bulk of privatizations completed
Scope for 'going-private' transactions	Large stock market; few initial deals now significant	Steady flow but often family control issues	Relatively small number quoted companies	Many candidates; specific opportunities must grow
Development stage of M&A markets	Highly developed	Relatively active	Becoming active	Relatively active

Panel B: Demand for Private Equity

	U.K.	France	Germany	CEE
Attitude to entrepreneurial risk	Was very positive from early 1980s	Moderate	Traditionally low, changing slowly	Positive and growing
Willingness of managers to buy	High	Moderate	Starting to develop	High, but lacking financial means

(continued)

TABLE 14.6 (continued)

Panel C: Infrastructure to Complete Deals

	U.K.	France	Germany	CEE
Private equity and venture capital market	Grew rapidly from early 1980s	Grew from late 1980s but many small players	Traditionally small & not MBO orientated	Small but developing
Supply of debt	High	High	Tradition of high leverage	Low but growing
Intermediaries network	Highly developed	Moderately developed	Fragmented	Highly developed
Favorability of legal framework	Favorable	Favorable	Moderately favorable	Favorable
Favorability of taxation regime	Favorable	Favorable	Reforms in progress	Moving to favorable with EU reforms

Panel D: Realization of Gains

	U.K.	France	Germany	CEE
Stock markets	Receptive to private equity cos. from mid-1980s; now more difficult	Development of 2nd market	New issues sparse; secondary tier market closed	Growing domestic capital pool and appetite
Trade sales	Highly active	Becoming more active especially for partial sales	M&A market developing	Highly active
Secondary buyouts/ restructuring	Increasing interest	Favored route	Possible route	Possible exit route

Source: CMBOR/Barclays Private Equity/Deloitte.

Profiting from Divestment

In March 2002, CDC Equity Capital acquired Européenne de Stationnement, France's second largest car park operator, as part of a €100m ($88.4m) buyout from Groupe Fabricom, a construction subsidiary of French water utility Suez Lyonnais des Eaux. Européenne de Stationnement was sold to CDC along with Cabinet Villa, the second largest residential property management company in Paris, with a real estate portfolio valued at roughly €20m. Xavier Thoumieux, a partner at CDC Equity Capital responsible for the deal, planned to sell the real estate portfolio and develop Cabinet Villa before selling it on to another financial sponsor or strategic partner. Both Européenne de Stationnement and Cabinet Villa generate strong cash flow and yield attractive contracts. In France, the markets for both car park operators and property management have yet to be consolidated and provide good buyout opportunities for financial buyers.

ial culture. In contrast, the willingness of German managers to undertake buyouts has traditionally been low, but this appears to be changing as a high number of corporate restructurings reduces the security of managerial tenure.

The "infrastructure" for doing buyout deals also differs significantly across countries. As can be seen in Panel C, the U.K. has more developed private equity and debt markets, better intermediary networks, and more favorable legal and taxation frameworks. Nevertheless, changes are under way in the other countries to improve their institutional and regulatory infrastructure. The French private equity industry grew rapidly from the mid-1980s, with law firms playing a particularly important role in the diffusion of the buyout concept. The infrastructure to complete German deals was for a long time less than favorable—few intermediaries, an underdeveloped private equity market, and high rates of taxation. Many of these restrictions did not begin to ease until the mid-1990s, when, for example, the country's punitive capital gains tax regime relating to share disposals began to be relaxed.

Finally, we considered cross-country differences in exit routes and their importance to private equity firms in realizing the value of their buyout investments. As summarized in Panel D of figure 14.6, there are notable differences among countries in the extent to which stock markets facilitate IPOs of buyout companies. One must begin by recognizing that even highly developed stock markets provide limited exit opportunities for all but the larger, fastest-growing businesses. At the same time, as many corporations complete their restructuring and markets become more concentrated and global, the corporate

> ## The Case of Autobahn Tank & Rast
>
> The secondary buyout of Autobahn Tank & Rast by Terra Firma for €1.1 billion was announced in 2004. For more than 50 years, Autobahn Tank & Rast has operated a network of filling stations, and service and catering sites throughout Germany. The company had performed well under Allianz Capital Partners and Apax Partners, which funded the €961 million first buyout in 1998, and planned to realize their investment through an IPO on the Frankfurt stock exchange. But since the IPO would only have given shareholders a 40% exit, the selling PE firms chose the secondary buyout by Terra Firma, which provided a 100% exit.

M&A market provides less scope for the trade sale as an exit route, especially for smaller deals. As a result, secondary buyouts and buy-in transactions have become a popular exit route for PE buyout investments in the U.K. market; and they are likely to become increasingly important in other markets as they mature, particularly as companies seek exits when both the stock and M&A markets are weak. In France, although the development of the Second Marché and the Nouveau Marché enlarged the possibility for the realization of value in buyout investments, partial sales have provided a frequent exit route for investors.

Prospects and Challenges

In this section, we present the challenges and prospects now facing the European private equity sector. We focus on the most pressing issues at the moment, including challenges in fund-raising, deal sourcing, structuring, bidding, and exit.

Fund-raising: What Are the Implications of the Current Fund Overhang?

Private equity fund-raising has reached record levels in the last five years, but the investment of funds has not kept pace. As a result, Europe is currently endowed with a fund overhang estimated at roughly $40 billion;[20] and the general sentiment, shared by practitioners and academics alike, is that too much capital is chasing too few deals. With rising entry multiples, and many new entrants in the private equity industry in the last few years, this suggests the need for rationalization of the playing field and some consolidation of the industry.

Deal-Sourcing: How Will Private Equity Firms Source Their Deals in the Future?

Data on buyouts of subsidiaries and parent-to-parent sales suggest that divestment activity by U.K. corporations has passed its peak. But, as corporations continue to make acquisitions, opportunities for divestment buyouts are likely to remain—for example, in cases where post-acquisition integration issues are not adequately addressed, or senior managers fail to provide compelling incentives for the management of the new subsidiaries or divisions. Also, there still seems to be ample potential for restructuring larger corporations in continental Europe.

In the U.K. as well as continental Europe, there also continue to be large numbers of family-owned firms, many with aging founders and little active succession planning.[21] A central issue in such firms is the founder's expectation of future involvement with the business, which can play a major role in the negotiation of the deal. Owners of private businesses in the U.K. seem in general to be more willing both to sell and to cut their ties with their firms than their counterparts in continental Europe.

The entry of hedge funds into the continental European buyout market poses a competitive challenge to private equity firms in terms of deal sourcing. The expectation is that hedge funds' investments may trigger restructuring and focus on cost reduction over the relatively shorter term. To the extent this turns out to be correct, it raises doubt about hedge funds' ability to build the longer-run "growth" value of the LBOs they invest in. Questions are also being raised about how hedge funds will behave when one of their LBO companies becomes financially distressed. Will they walk away or focus mainly on generating fees (at the expense of total value) when participating in recapitalizations? The presence of hedge funds thus also has implications for the approach adopted by existing debt providers in the market.

Our expectation is that different types of hedge funds will emerge with different mandates and a focus on different types of buyouts. Securitization likely will become more prevalent, and its impact on the future buyout market could be far-reaching in terms of the size of deals that will be possible.

Deal Structuring: What Further Innovations Can PE Firms Make in Buyout Structuring and Financing?

The majority of hedge funds active in the leveraged buyout market have focused so far on providing subordinated debt, such as second-lien and mezzanine debt, and payment-in-kind securities (PIKs). Thus, they may represent more serious competition for providers of mezzanine and junior debt than for the private equity funds themselves. The emergence of alternative private equity providers at the top end of the market may bring more innovative and more flexible players with a lower cost of capital, but it remains to be seen whether they have the skills to generate the gains achieved by private equity firms.

The resurgence of club deals has enabled syndicates of private equity firms to bid for very large buyouts that would otherwise be too risky to fund on their own. In addition to this risk-spreading rationale, they may also bring together the diverse specialist skills required to restructure and regenerate a particular deal.[22] However, club deals pose a number of potential problems.[23] Limited partners seeking to diversify their investments in private equity may be concerned when the different funds in which they invest are part of the same syndicate to complete a particular deal. Despite the presence of "drag along," "come along," and "tag along" provisions, coordination may be problematical when restructuring is required. Where these syndicates involve partners who are highly experienced players in the market, the potential for tensions when egos clash about strategy and restructuring seems clear.

The emergence of second-lien bonds and loans, typically with fewer covenants than first-lien debt but sharing collateral with senior debt providers, introduces the possibility of longer maturities and more attractive interest rates. But such debt instruments may have the disadvantages of limiting future finance options by creating conflicts of interest between first- and second-lien providers. In Europe, second-lien loans in buyouts are typically mezzanine debt.[24]

Buyout Bid: Will Bidding Conditions for Private Equity Firms Change?

Given the greater prevalence of auctions, record levels of fund-raising, and difficulties in identifying attractive new deals, it seems unlikely that PE firms will be able to acquire control of target companies at lower bid premiums than those observed to date. This fact, combined with the current high market valuations and entry multiples, as well as the institutionalized pressure on PE firms to invest, raises the important question of how buyout financiers will be able to generate sufficiently high returns to satisfy their investors three to ten years from now.

Facing limits on the further use of leverage as a value-creation mechanism as well as pressure to generate high exit returns over the short to medium term, PE firms will have to make their buyout operations even more efficient. As a consequence, private equity firms will increasingly have to distinguish themselves through their operating capabilities and, perhaps, industry specialization.

Exit: What Further Challenges Does the Advent of the Secondary Buyout Pose?

The recent record growth in secondary buyouts may help management to remain independent while enabling private equity firms to obtain at least a partial exit. For the incoming investors, even though management has a proven track record, a major question needs to be answered: will managers be buyers or sellers in the deal? This raises a further number of issues. First, when the management team is seeking to increase their equity stake, there may be a corresponding reduction in control by the private equity firm. This may be problematical if it means that management is able to embark on risky growth strategies with little monitoring. When managements are able to realize significant gains, motivating them to perform in the subsequent deal may also be difficult.

A final, unresolved issue about secondary buyouts concerns the possibility that limited partners will be asked by private equity firms to invest again in the same deal through a subsequent fund, and presumably at a higher price than the first time around. While exit from the first buyout allows the realization of capital gains, limited partners may take some convincing that further significant capital gains will be forthcoming.

Conclusions

During the past two decades, European buyout markets have continuously adapted to changing conditions, including challenges relating to deal sourcing, the entry of new players, and the generation of returns. Competition for larger buyouts has forced prices higher, but with record amounts of capital raised in 2005, it seems that large deal flow will continue to grow over the coming years. With strong buying power at the disposal of specialized venture capital, private equity firms, and hedge funds, and with the growth of club buyouts, it may only be a matter of time before we see very large firms—even FTSE 100 companies—being taken private.

With the higher profile of the private equity asset class enabling buyout funds to attract the best managers to run the target companies, banks have been more willing to gear up deals and even refinance them after a short period of time. Although this strategy involves significant risks—and growing concerns about the near-term performance of European economies and trends in interest rates are beginning to raise questions about the degree of leverage in buyout deals—there is also potential for commensurately higher returns.

The U.K. market has become quite mature and has one of the highest proportions of buyout values to GDP. If this remains at around 1.5 to 2%, as it has for the last several years, the buyout market should grow at least in line with the U.K. economy. Elsewhere in Europe, pressures on larger corporations to restructure will likely lead to increased deal activity, notably divestments. The growing number of large secondary buyouts provides valuable liquidity for the buyout market at a time when exits have become difficult. Trade sale opportunities appear to be growing once again and stock markets have become more encouraging, which should help allay building concerns of institutional investors about the recycling of capital seen in recent years.

Notes

1. M. Wright, B. Chiplin, K. Robbie, and M. Albrighton, "The Development of an Organizational Innovation: Management Buyouts in the U.K., 1980–1997," *Business History* 42 (2000), 137–184.
2. A related development was the growth of leveraged build-ups (LBUs), an initial buyout-type transaction to which further companies are added through a process of acquisition.
3. Accounting for more than half of U.K. PE investments since 1987.
4. As a reaction to the ruling environment of low nominal yields and the dampening of volatility in traditional asset classes.
5. Michael C. Jensen, "The Modern Industrial Revolution, Exit, and the Failure of Internal Control Systems," *Journal of Finance* 48 (1993), 831–880.
6. L. Renneboog, T. Simons, and M. Wright, "Leveraged Public to Private Transactions in the UK," Working Paper ECGI and Tilburg University, 2005.
7. For an overview see L. Renneboog and T. Simons, "Public to Private Transactions: Motives, Trends, Theories and Empirical Literature on LBOs, MBOs, MBIs, and IBOs," Discussion Paper, Tilburg University, 2005.
8. Especially since the 1990s, both the statements of CEOs of firms going private and the deterioration of PTP firms' share prices relative to those of comparable firms that remain public suggest that an important driver of U.K. PTP deals is the incumbent management's belief that the market has undervalued the company's prospects. C. Weir, D. Laing, and M. Wright, "Incentive Effects, Monitoring Mechanisms, and the Threat from the Market for Corporate Control: An Analysis of the Factors Affecting Public to Private Transactions in the UK," *Journal of Business Finance and Accounting* 32 (2005a), 909–944; C. Weir, D. Laing, and M. Wright, "Undervaluation, Private Information, Agency Costs, and the Decision to Go Private," *Applied Financial Economics* 15 (2005b), 947–961.
9. Evidence also shows that, before they go private, PTPs have higher concentrations of insider ownership, on average, and tend to separate the functions of CEO and Chair of the board more often (as suggested by the Combined Code). Weir et al., ibid.
10. In three of these five cases, the banks had actually announced that they were terminating their investments, thus forcing these firms to seek a new lifeline. Since the bidders in these transactions have to supply the company with additional funds and assume a high risk of failure, they usually pay a discount to the going-concern market value. For example, starting in 1995 Industrial Control Services underwent a major restructuring and a new management team consolidated the firm's technological position after 1997. Nevertheless, the financial position continued to deteriorate as the firm was too small to function in a market dominated by large competitors. The man-

agement could not rely on the continuing support of the banks over the long term and was not able to do another equity issue. Therefore, the board asked some investment banks to seek an interested party to acquire the firm or some parts. The board decided to support the offer from Alchemy Partners in order to ensure short-term solvency. They took the firm private in an IBO at an 85% discount on the last quoted share price before the announcement of the offer, at 1 pence.

11. Irrevocable commitments involve legally binding promises given by existing shareholders to agree to sell their shares to the bidder before the bid is announced. In the U.K., the City Code on Takeovers and Mergers includes both rules concerning the conduct of management buyouts of listed corporations and restrictions relating to irrevocable commitments in terms of the number of shareholders that can be approached to obtain irrevocable commitments, the prohibition of favorable treatment for those offering irrevocable commitments without Takeover Panel consent, and the disclosure of irrevocable commitments. Irrevocable commitments are thus part of the public bid process. While they may not formally be given until just before a bid is announced, obtaining them involves private actions by the bidder prior to the bid being announced.

12. See M. Wright, C. Weir, and A. Burrows, "Irrevocable Commitments and Going Private," *European Financial Management* 13, no. 4 (2006), 757–775.

13. As already suggested, the announcement of irrevocable commitments may make other potential bidders less likely to enter the contest with an alternative bid since the commitment ensures that, without any higher alternative bid, the agreement to sell the share becomes binding, although a higher bid can still undo the commitment if it is a so-called soft irrevocable. Research on irrevocable commitments suggests that investors proposing a PTP are more likely to gain the backing of other shareholders the greater the bid premium and the more reputable the private equity backer as indicated by the extent of their PTP activity. See ibid.

14. M. Wright, K. Robbie, S. Thompson, and K. Starkey, "Longevity and the Life Cycle of MBOs," *Strategic Management Journal* 15 (1994), 215–227.

15. R. Jelic, B. Saadouni, and M. Wright, "Performance of Private to Public MBOs: The Role of Venture Capital," *Journal of Business Finance and Accounting* 32 (2005), 643–682.

16. Ibid.

17. E. Nikoskelainen and M. Wright, "The Impact of Corporate Governance Mechanisms on Value Increase in Leveraged Buyouts," CMBOR Occasional Paper, 2006.

18. In the U.K. system, this process is known as receivership. The receivership rate varies according to vintage year, peaking at 21% for buyouts completed in the boom years of 1988–1990, which subsequently encountered problems in the recession of the early 1990s (see CMBOR, "Management," *Buyouts Quarterly Review,* table A39, [Autumn 2005], 73). The failure rate of buyouts completed during the first half of the 1990s was approximately 12% by Sept. 2005.

19. D. Citron, M. Wright, R. Ball, and F. Rippington, "Secured Creditor Recovery Rates from Management Buyouts in Distress," *European Financial Management* 9 (2003), 141–162. Approximately a fifth were sold as outright going concerns.

20. See, e.g., PricewaterhouseCoopers Global Private Equity 2004 for funds raised and invested between 1998 and 2003.

21. Over a fifth of respondents to a recent CMBOR survey of buyouts of family firms say they have done no succession planning.

22. For example, a generalist private equity firm may link with a second firm with specialist technology skills.

23. M. Wright and A. Lockett, "The Structure and Management of Alliances: Syndication in Venture Capital Investments," *Journal of Management Studies* 40 (2003), 2073–2104.
24. Issues remain to be resolved about the duration of the enforcement of standstill agreements and the extent of waiver of adequate protection rights by second-lien providers.

CHAPTER 15

Sovereign Wealth Funds

A Growing Global Force in Corporate Finance

SHAMS BUTT, ANIL SHIVDASANI, CARSTEN
STENDEVAD, AND ANN WYMAN

SOVEREIGN WEALTH FUNDS (SWFS) are government-created investment vehicles that are typically funded by commodity export revenues or the transfer of assets directly from official foreign-exchange reserves. In some cases, government budget surpluses and pension surpluses have also been transferred into SWFs.

With an estimated $3 trillion of assets that are projected to more than double over the next five years, SWFs are attracting considerable attention in financial markets and in capitals around the world. Understanding these funds can be challenging because of the vast diversity of objectives, investment philosophies, and political and economic ambitions. Compounding the difficulty, the funds themselves are in transition, with many undergoing restructurings, changes of asset allocation styles, and developing partnerships with both financial sponsors and corporations.

For public corporations, SWFs are becoming increasingly important as a potential source of capital, as a strategic partner in special situations, and as a major influence on trends that could affect a number of corporate sectors. Moreover, as illustrated in figure 15.1, the rise of SWFs is directly affecting not only global corporations and asset managers but also global policymakers. Because most SWFs are closely linked to their governments, political concerns have arisen in a number of countries, like the U.S., where companies have been on the receiving end of SWF capital. One concern is over the lack of information about them, which has created uncertainty about their ultimate objectives. More specifically, the pursuit of large positions in highly visible companies by SWFs has raised national security or broader strategic concerns. In some cases, moreover, the fact that investments by SWFs have been used to support their own national champions has raised questions about potential effects on international competitiveness.

FIGURE 15.1

Rise of SWFs Affects Several External Market Participants

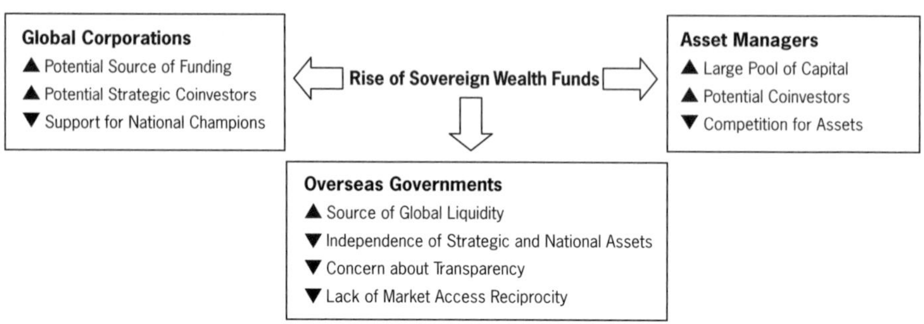

Source: Citi.

Also worrisome to some, acquisitions by entities supported by foreign governments appear to have the potential to reverse a trend toward privatizations that has occurred in many economies and could possibly undo some of the economic benefits that prompted these privatizations. And, finally, because SWF assets are concentrated in the hands of commodity-exporting countries and rapidly growing Asian countries, harsh regulatory responses against SWFs create the specter of a broader wave of protectionist trade policies and restricted access to sought-after growth markets.

The political debate has paid less attention to the potential benefits of SWF investments. SWFs have long-term investment horizons, and in most cases, they tend to rely on low leverage in their investments. These features make them a stabilizing long-term influence on global liquidity. In the current economic environment, there has been some recognition that SWF capital is playing an important role in stabilizing some sectors, particularly banking, where their funds have made several high profile investments recently. At the same time, it is important to note that despite the intense media focus on their M&A activity, the bulk of their assets are held in highly liquid instruments or invested with traditional money managers.

In this chapter we summarize the key characteristics of this growing pool of liquidity, introduce the major players, analyze the factors driving their investment choices, and discuss the implications for global corporations and governments.

Where Is the Sovereign Wealth Coming From?

Over the past five years, shifts in global savings and investment patterns have led to a widening of global current account imbalances. Observers differ on the root causes of such shifts, with some focusing on the increase in the net supply of financial capital from outside the industrialized countries, while others highlight the declines in public and private savings in the U.S. Regardless of the explanation, the result has been a sharp widening in the current account deficit of the U.S. and a rapid expansion of current account surpluses, particularly in Asia and in oil-exporting countries of the Middle East and elsewhere (see figure 15.2).

As these current account surpluses have built up, global foreign-exchange reserves have grown, increasing by 140% over the past five years (see figure 15.3). And today these reserves are approaching $6 trillion and are widely expected to continue to grow.

Creation of Sovereign Wealth Funds

Some of the largest SWFs, such as the Abu Dhabi Investment Authority, the Kuwait Investment Authority, and Temasek of Singapore, were established in the 1970s. Yet the number and size of SWFs have grown sharply in the last five years, in line with the rapid growth of the foreign-exchange reserves of largely non-Western countries.

As foreign exchange reserves have grown, many monetary authorities have concluded that these reserves are well in excess of their immediate needs and offer sufficient protection against sudden capital outflows. Thus, they have

FIGURE 15.2

Large Global Current Account Imbalances Underlie Growth in Sovereign Wealth (U.S. Dollars in Billions)

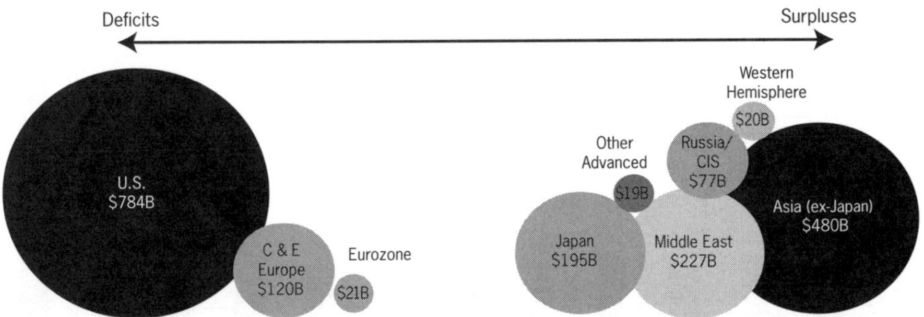

Note: There exists a global deficit of $94bn. There is a U.S.$93 billion discrepancy between the surpluses and the deficits which reflects errors, omissions, and asymmetries in balance of payments statistics on the current account, as well as the exclusion of data for international organizations and a limited number of countries.

Source: IMF: "World Economic Outlook" April 2007. (Estimates for 2007.) Accessed on 24 April 2007.

opted to "ring-fence" a portion of their foreign exchange reserves for other purposes, allocating a significant share to sovereign wealth funds. New funds have been created and existing funds have been reformed, or split into multiple vehicles for a variety of purposes. At the heart of these changes is the desire to diversify the holdings of this growing capital base and to seek a higher risk-return tradeoff.

As can be seen in figure 15.4, SWFs are one of many channels through which governments deploy their financial assets. At one end of the spectrum are the reserves of central banks, which are usually invested in highly liquid, fixed-income securities. Toward the middle of the spectrum are the SWFs, which are generally managed with a higher risk tolerance than official foreign exchange reserves, and can be classified into two broad groups: stabilization funds and savings funds. Stabilization funds are usually intended to provide budgetary support, particularly to insulate commodity-producing countries against the effects of declines in commodity prices. Savings funds have longer-term wealth creation and policy objectives that enable them to take larger risks than the stabilization funds.

Distinct from SWFs, but sharing many common elements with them, are a number of government-owned investment corporations that are active in purchasing ownership stakes in various entities. Finally, there are many large state-owned enterprises that, with support from their governments, are becoming increasingly active in strategic transactions across the globe.

FIGURE 15.3

Sharp Increase in Global Foreign Exchange Reserves (U.S. Dollars in Billions)

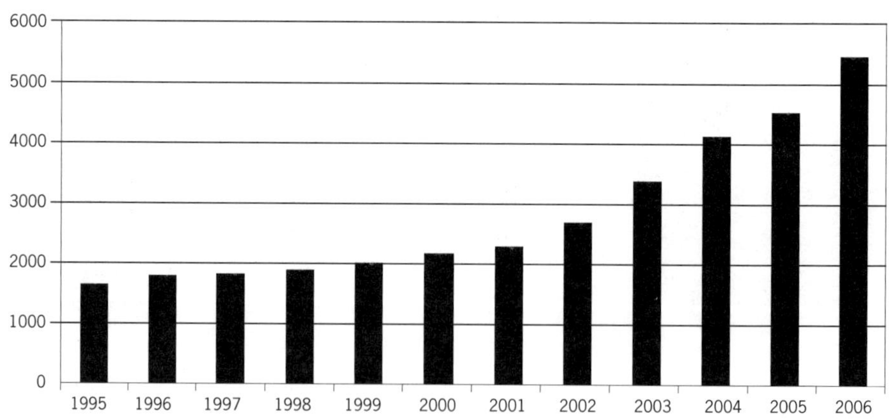

Source: Economist Intelligence Unit.

FIGURE 15.4

SWFs Belong to a Continuum of Sovereign Investment Vehicles

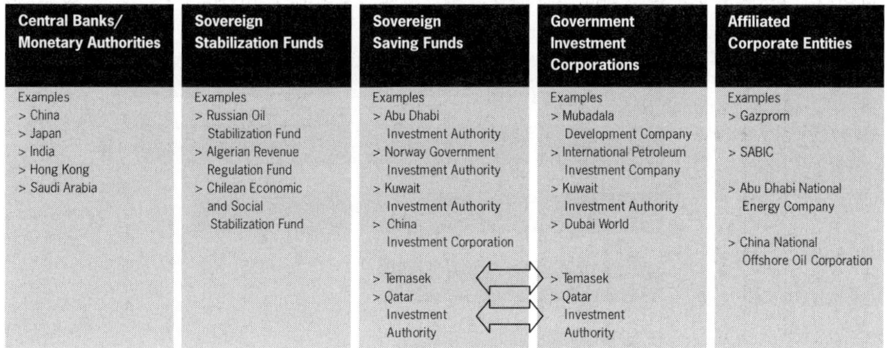

Source: Citi.

This report focuses primarily on SWFs and the large government investment companies.[1] Generalizing about such investors is difficult because of their distinct economic agendas, varying risk appetites, and investment time horizons. They are also less focused on the shorter-term financial and return metrics typical of public markets and private equity firms. In some cases, they have objectives that go beyond the purely economic, including the promotion of environmentally friendly strategies, industrial development, or the support of national champions.

What's more, as already noted, many SWFs and sovereign investment corporations are in a state of transition, rethinking their goals and strategies. The explosive growth of foreign exchange flows to Asian exporters and Middle Eastern and Russian commodity exporters has expanded the capital available to existing SWFs and motivated governments to restructure existing entities and create new investing entities. The result has been a blurring of the lines between the different types of sovereign investment vehicles.

Global Financial Clout of SWFs

Driven mainly by the increase in FX reserves, the number and size of SWFs have grown dramatically, reaching a level of assets under management at the end of 2007 that has been estimated at $3 trillion. The exact size can only be approximated, reflecting the limited disclosure of many SWFs and the differences in how SWFs are defined.[2]

Though SWFs control only a small percentage of global financial assets, they are large as an investor class. As shown in figure 15.5, their assets amount

FIGURE 15.5

SWFs Control a Fraction of Global Financial Assets but Are a Large Investor Class (U.S. Dollars in Trillions, 2006)

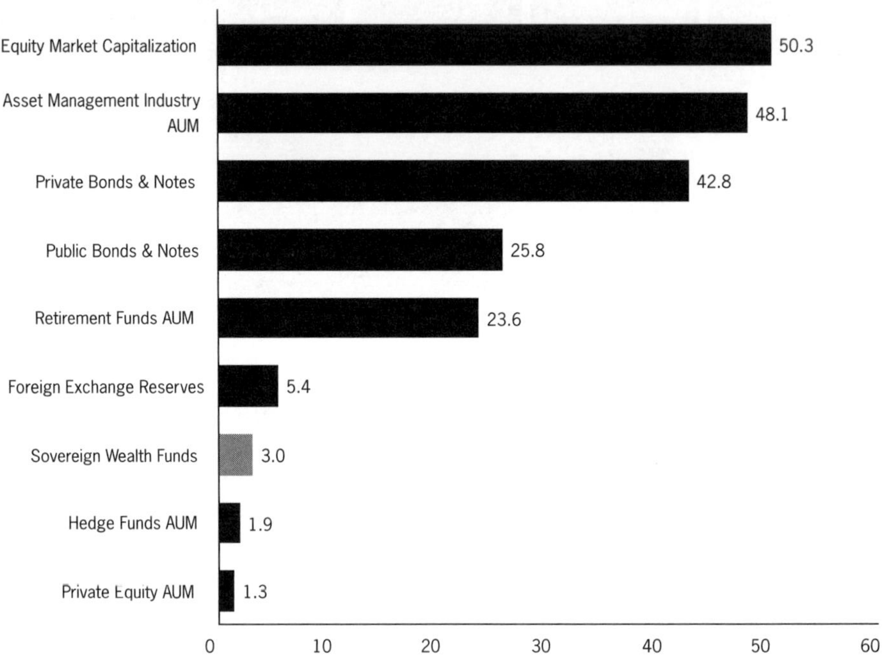

Sources: Cerulli Associates, EIU, Bank for International Settlements, EVCA Yearbook, Bloomberg, and Hedgefund.net.

to more than half of global foreign exchange reserves, 13% of global pension fund assets, 6% of the global asset management industry, and 6% of the world's stock market capitalization. As an investor class, SWFs rival the global hedge fund and private equity industry combined. Since the SWFs themselves have allocated funds to these various asset managers and asset classes, these numbers understate their true relative size.

SWFs are now poised to become even larger players over the coming years, as the capital inflows stemming from commodities and trade surpluses continue. Assuming that the SWFs' assets continue to grow at roughly the pace of reserve growth over the past five years, they should reach $7.5 trillion by 2012.[3] With the expected growth of SWFs thus outpacing the 9% annual growth rate forecast for global asset managers,[4] the SWF share of total assets under management could grow from 6% today to 10% in five years.

On an individual basis, as can be seen in figure 15.6, the largest of the SWFs—those from UAE, Kuwait, Norway, and China—have reached a scale that

Individual SWFs Are among the World's Largest Investors

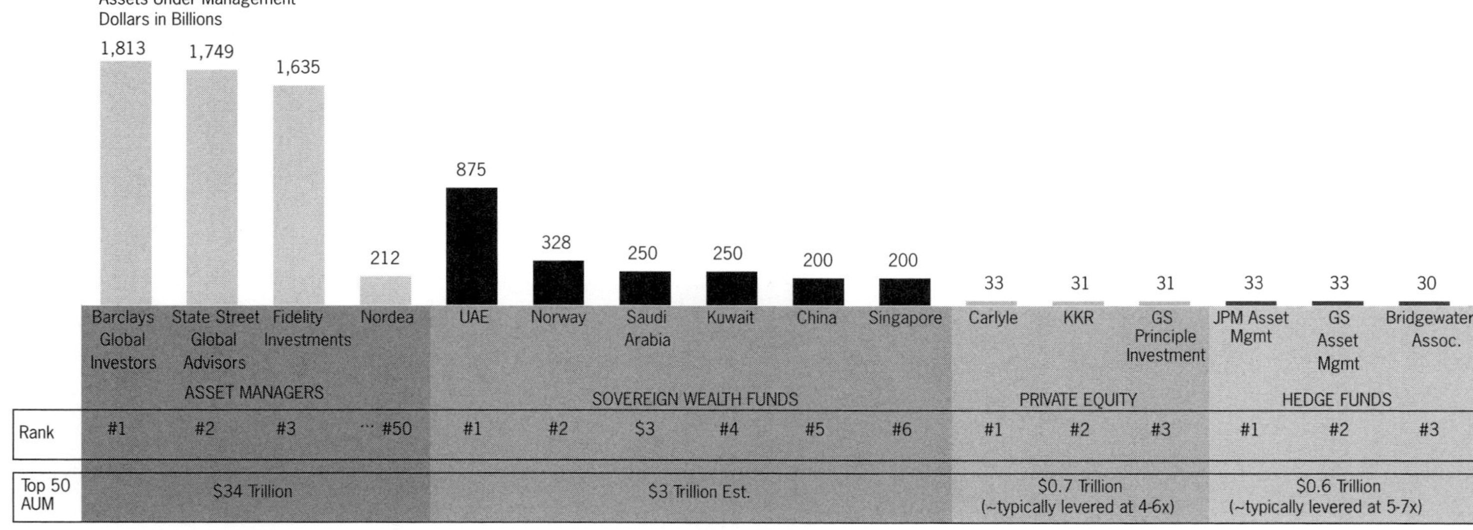

Sources: Alpha Magazine, Cerulli Associates, IMF, Private Equity International, public information, and Citi.

Size and Structure of Major Sovereign Wealth Funds (U.S. Dollars in Billions)

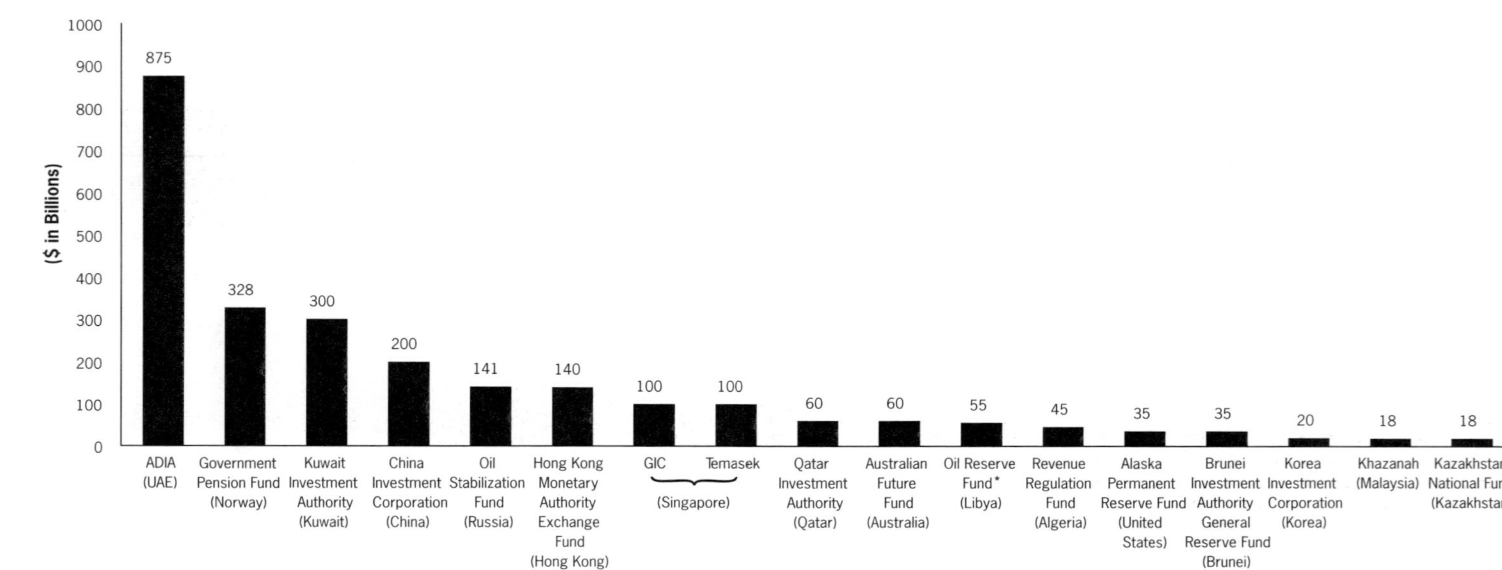

Source: IMF, public information from websites, Citi.

* Libya Oil Reserve fund includes assets worth $8bn of Long Term Investment fund.

is comparable to that of the largest global asset managers and the biggest private equity and hedge funds. Even when one accounts for the 4–7 times leverage typically employed by hedge funds and private equity funds, the *unlevered* portfolio sizes of the six largest SWFs are still about as large as the *leveraged* size of the top three private equity or the top three hedge funds. And while over three dozen countries have established SWFs, assets in this sector, as shown in figure 15.7, are concentrated in the hands of the few very large players listed above.

The managed investment companies set up by many governments have become a particularly important sovereign investor class as they have been among the most active with respect to M&A, strategic transactions, and the purchase of equity stakes in other companies. Some of these, such as Dubai World, Mubadala, and Istithmar (all of the UAE) are organized as holding companies or private equity firms. In other cases, such as Dubai Holding, they are owned by the rulers of their country. Istithmar, for example, has purchased U.S. retailers Loehmann's and Barneys New York, Mubadala has acquired stakes in Carlyle and Ferrari, and Temasek has long been active in purchasing companies and has holdings in several financial institutions (see figure 15.8.).

FIGURE 15.8

Investment Companies Have Adopted Active Investment Strategies

Qatar	Malaysia	Singapore	UAE (Abu Dhabi)	UAE (Dubai)	UAE (Abu Dhabi)	UAE (Dubai)	UAE (Dubai)	UAE (Dubai)
Qatar Investment Authority	Khazanah Nasionala	Temasek Holdings	International Petroleum Investment Company	Dubai World	Mubadala Development Company	Dubai International Capital	Dubai International Financial Centre Investments	Istithmar
5% stake in Lagardere (France)	Stake in Miyazu Seisakusho (Japan)	13% stake in Standard Chartered (U.K.)	64% stake in Borealis (Through a JV)	Via its subsidiary, DP World, bought P&O (U.K.) in March 2006 for GBP3.7bn	7.5% (U.S.$1.35bn) stake in Carlyle investments (U.S.)	100% stake in Doncasters (U.K.)	2.2% stake (U.S.$1.8bn) in Deutsche Bank (EU)	100% stake in Loehmann's (U.S.)
5% stake in Lagardere (France)	Stake in Apollo Hospitals Enterprise Ltd. (India)	8.3% stake in China Eastern Airlines (China)	70% stake in Hyundai Oilbank Co. Ltd. (South Korea)	9.5% stake in MGM Mirage for U.S.$2.4bn	35% stake in Piaggio Aero industries (Italy)	3.12% stake in EADS (EU)	3.48% stake in Euronext (EU)	100% stake in Barney's NY (U.S.)
	Stake in Parkson Retail Group (China)	7% stake in ICICI Bank (India)	17.6% stake in OMV (Australia)	50% in CityCenter Holdings, wholly-owned subsidiary of MGM Mirage for U.S.$2.7bn (U.S.)	5% stake in Ferrari (Italy)	2.87% stake in ICICI Bank (India)	Borse Dubai completing agreement on purchase of 20% of NASDAQ (U.S.)	

Sources: Individual companies' public websites and Citi.

a. Some government investment companies have been listed under sovereign wealth funds. They are listed as investment companies here, since some of their larger investments are strategic acquisitions, rather than more traditional asset allocation in capital markets.

b. Note that Sheikh Mohammed bin Rashid Al Maktoum as the Ruler of Dubai holds 99.67% of Dubai Holding.

Understanding Sovereign Wealth Funds and Their Investments

Despite their differences in economic and political agendas and their divergent investment styles, all SWFs share the objective of increasing returns on capital when compared with the very conservative, short-term investments made with central bank reserves. (For an overview of the investment objectives and risk profiles of a number of the largest funds, see figure 15.9.)

The primary purpose of stabilization funds, as noted earlier, is to provide budgetary support, particularly in the case of commodity-producing countries to offset the effects of declines if commodity prices fall. Their investments tend to be highly liquid and conservatively invested since they could be called on over a cycle of a few years. Since they are managed much like foreign exchange reserves, they will generally be of limited interest to companies seeking to raise capital. But as they increase in size, they may spin off more aggressive funds (as happened in the case of the Russian Stabilization Fund).

By contrast, savings funds typically have a variety of longer-term objectives:

- *Promotion of domestic or regional economic development.* For example, Singapore's Temasek focuses not only on domestic, but also on regional development. Korea's relatively new Korea Investment Company (KIC) has indicated that one of its main objectives is to develop the country as the financial hub of northeast Asia.

- *Instrument of industrial policy.* Several of the Gulf-based funds identify national development of certain industries as part of a strategy to diver-

FIGURE 15.9

Varying Investment Objectives and Risk Profiles of SWFs

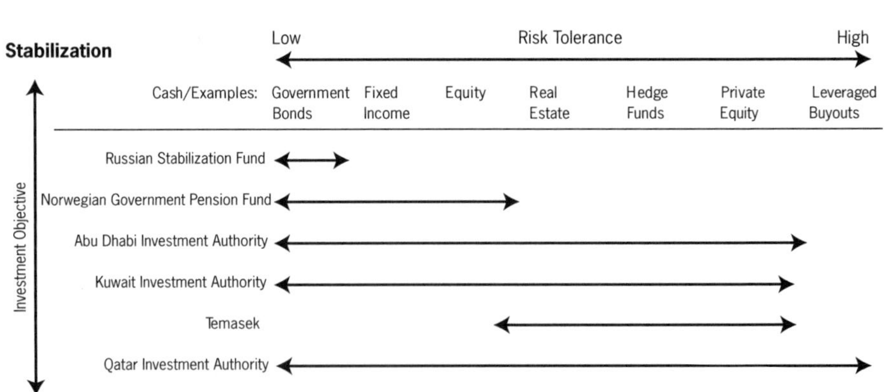

Source: Citi.

sify their economies from dependence on oil. This includes investment in such diverse sectors as health care, tourism, and financial services. In Russia, President Putin has called for investing excess oil reserves in domestic companies.

- *Endowment to replace declining natural resources.* A fund with an endowment structure aims to maximize returns to benefit future generations, with the primary objective of capital preservation. Underlying this objective is the premise that, with finite natural resources, an endowment can help ensure continued prosperity for citizens in future years.

- *Intergenerational savings.* This is an important goal of the Norwegian and Australian SWFs, where funds have been set aside and are being managed with a specific view of timing and size of future pension liabilities.

- *Foreign policy objectives.* While no SWFs have explicit foreign policy objectives, SWF investments can sometimes be used as an instrument of foreign policy—whether the aim is to accumulate natural resources or increase leverage with a third country. These objectives could clearly influence the sectors in which investment takes place.

- *Long-term macroeconomic objectives.* Some countries use their SWFs to promote long-term economic goals, such as the Australian Future Fund, which (among other objectives) has indicated that it seeks to increase the country's national savings rate.

- *Social objectives.* Norway's pension fund has sought to promote socially responsible investment through a set of ethical investment guidelines.

Where Sovereign Wealth Funds Invest

Most SWFs follow a traditional allocation approach that balances liquidity needs with a drive for greater returns. Various investment funds, as shown in figure 15.9, make allocations across the spectrum of asset classes, from the least to the most risky. China, for example, has made a significant investment in Blackstone through its new SWF, though press reports suggest that the fund will primarily follow a traditional asset allocation model and invest through other asset managers.[5] Both Asian and Gulf-based SWFs have invested in financial services, real estate, and the retail sector. In addition, these funds are increasingly considering the infrastructure sector since the long-term profile of these investments fits with their long-term investment objectives. As economic uncertainty and credit market conditions have challenged the financial services industry in the U.S., both Gulf-based and Asian funds have been actively investing in opportunities in the U.S. banking sector, with several high profile investments in major financial institutions.

These trends reflect the growing economic opportunities, the good historical performance of these investments and even better expected returns, as well as greater comfort with political risk. Increasingly, SWFs are evaluating investments in a manner similar to that of other major asset managers by choosing to invest primarily on the basis of economic opportunity, and regardless of the sector or geography. The rapid growth of the funds, the shortage of available investment targets, and the increased willingness to take risk inevitably mean that investment strategies are continually undergoing change.

SWFs Increasingly Involved in Strategic Transactions

It is useful to distinguish between the more proactive sovereign wealth funds and those that are continuing with less aggressive, though perhaps multi-asset, allocation strategies. Probably the most active among the former is Temasek, which has a long track record of strategic investments across a variety of sectors at home and abroad.

In the Gulf countries, the dominant funds—Abu Dhabi Investment Authority and Kuwait Investment Authority—do not generally hold large stakes in public companies. Rather, they invest primarily in private equity funds, and are occasionally co-investors in private equity transactions. The newer entities, such as Dubai Holding and its subsidiaries (Dubai International Capital and Dubai Group) and Dubai World and its subsidiaries (Istithmar and Dubai Ports), tend to be more aggressive with strategic investments. They are actively involved as investors in leveraged buyouts and co-investors in private equity investments. In many cases, their investments have served the dual objectives of wealth creation and support of the country's industrial policy.

SWFs and Financial Sponsors

Singapore and Middle East–based SWFs have had long relationships with financial sponsors as investors in private equity funds and as direct investors in deals. The 9.9% investment in Blackstone made by the China Investment Corp., Mubadala's 7.5% investment in Carlyle, and ADIA's reported interest in a minority stake in Apollo[6] deserve special note because they suggest the convergence of private equity and SWFs.

SWFs have been natural buyers for private equity firms looking to sell a minority stake due to their existing relationships as SWFs have been investors in funds raised by private equity firms for buyouts and other transactions (see figure 15.10). For financial sponsors, investment by an SWF can also help establish a pre-IPO valuation in the event of a future public offering.

FIGURE 15.10

Significant M&A Announcements Involving SWFs

Acquirer	Target	Announcement Date	Investment Amount (USD millions)	% of Company Sought
GIC[a] & Other Investors[b]	Citi Inc	15-Jan-08	14,500	NA
GIC	UBS AG	10-Dec-07	9,750	9%
Dubai World	P&O	29-Nov-05	8,833	100%
ADIA	Citi Inc	26-Nov-07	7,500	4.9%
KIC[c]/ KIA[d]/ Mizuho Corporate Bank	Merrill Lynch	15-Jan-08	6,600	NA
Dubai World	MGM/CityCentre Holdings	22-Aug-07	5,186	10%/ 50%
China Investment Corporation	Morgan Stanley	19-Dec-07	5,000	9.9%
Temasek Holdings	Merrill Lynch	24-Dec-07	4,400	<10%
China Investment Corporation	Blackstone	20-May-07	3,000	10%
Borse Dubai[e,f]	London Stock Exchange	20-Sep-07	2,710	28%
Temasek Holdings	Barclays	23-Jul-07	2,000	2%
Dubai International Capital	Madame Tussaud	23-Mar-05	1,495	100%
Mubadala [g]	Carlyle	20-Sep-07	1,350	7.5%
QIA	OMX Ab [h]	21-Sep-07	1,279	10%
Istithmar	280 Park Avenue, New York	6-Jun-06	1,200	100.0%
Dubai International Capital	Och-Ziff Capital Management Group	29-Oct-07	1,100	9.9%
Dubai International Capital	HSBC	2-May-07	1,000	0.5%
CITIC Securities Co., Limited	Bear Stearns Companies Inc.	22-Oct-07	1,000	6%
Istithmar	Standard Chartered	6-Oct-06	972	3%
Borse Dubai[h]	NASDAQ	20-Sep-07	928	20%
Istithmar	Barneys	22-Jun-07	942	100%
Dubai Group Ltd	Marfin Investment Group	24-Jul-07	653	9%
Mubadala Development Company	Advanced Micronic Devices	16-Nov-07	622	8%
ADIA	AP Alternative Fund (Apollo LBO Fund)	17-Jun-06	600	40%
Dubai Financial	Marfin Financial Group	15-May-06	489	32%
Istithmar	Knickerbocker Hotel	4-Jun-06	300	100%
Istithmar	MGM - Kerzner JV	12-Sep-07	300	25%
Dubai International Capital	Sony	26-Nov-07	NA	<5%

Sources: Bloomberg, Dealogic, Mergermarket, press reports, SDC, and Citi.

a. Borse Dubai is 60% owned by Investment Corporation of Dubai, the investment arm of the Government of Dubai.

b. Deal Value based on current market capitalization of NASDAQ & LSE.

c. Mubadala has also committed US$500 million to a buyout fund managed by Carlyle.

d. As a result of this transaction, Borse Dubai acquired an indirect stake in OMX AB.

SWFs have also been active as co-investors with private equity firms. For example, Kuwait Investment Authority invested $300 million alongside KKR and TPG in their buyout of TXU.[7] Thus, for the SWFs that are direct investors in private equity, the investment in the financial sponsor is mutually beneficial. It may provide preferential access to future private equity transactions both for themselves and also potentially for other government-owned private equity vehicles. The symbiotic relationship could go a step further in a tighter liquidity environment, with SWFs providing liquidity guarantees to support transactions that would in turn allow the sponsors to reduce their dependence on bridge loans from banks.

SWFs as an Alternative to Traditional Private Equity

The Qatar Investment Authority's attempted buyout of Sainsbury PLC through Delta Two illustrates the evolution of SWFs as they move from taking minority and non-controlling stakes to purchasing majority and controlling stakes in companies. As private equity activity slows, a sale to SWFs is likely to become an alternative strategy for some companies. While not all funds will act as direct investors in buyouts, some like the Qatar Investment Authority have been active participants seeking to be principals and engage in deals directly, as well as being major co-investors.

Nevertheless, there are some key differences between private equity and SWFs in buyout situations:

- Unlike most financial sponsor-led buyouts, investments by SWFs do not require significant financial leverage. Thus, an SWF buyout would be a financially feasible alternative for a broader range of companies, including those not suited for very high leverage. The financial and default risk in SWF buyouts is thus likely to be lower, making them more attractive alternatives in some cases. However, financial synergies in such transactions may also be lower.

- Many SWFs have a much longer time frame for managing investments than the typical private equity firm. Unlike financial sponsors, SWFs do not have a need to exit an investment through an IPO or sale and can take an ownership position longer than the five-to-seven horizon typical of financial sponsors.

- Since SWFs are at the early stages of entering into the buyout market, they do not yet possess the full suite of management capabilities that the leading private equity firms have. Thus, they are more likely to work with existing management teams provided their return expectations are being met. This is also reflected in SWFs' purchases of second-stage buyouts after a private equity firm has completed the initial restructuring required. But, as the SWFs continue to build out their direct investment capabilities, their investment preferences may also evolve to resemble traditional private equity funds more closely.

Strategic Implications for Global Companies

Due to their large and expanding asset base, sovereign support, growing risk appetite, and willingness to employ more leverage in transactions, SWFs are having an increasing impact on the M&A and financing markets. What are some of the key implications for companies of this trend? We describe four potential opportunities and three main challenges.

Potential Opportunities for Companies

First, SWFs can be key investors in IPO or pre-IPO financing as well as a source of follow-on funding for growth. To cite a number of examples, KIA invested approximately $700 million—and QIA and GIC (Singapore) invested smaller amounts—in the IPO of the Industrial & Commercial Bank of China. And press reports have indicated ADIA's interest in a pre-IPO stake in Apollo Management.[8] SWFs have also made sizeable investments in several public companies such as MGM Mirage, DaimlerChrysler, and Sony.

Second, SWFs can also be a source of capital for sizeable or transformative transactions. In some cases, the funds have broad mandates and sufficient flexibility to complement strategic buyers' investment plans. For example, part of Temasek's equity investment in Barclays PLC represented a conditional equity investment to support its proposed acquisition of ABN Amro. At the same time, many Middle East funds have sought to invest in industry-leading companies, with good management credentials and strong cash generation (as opposed to turnaround situations).

Third, a strategic partnership with a national fund may ease regulatory approvals and mitigate political risk. For example, Blackstone's agreement to buy a 20% stake in China National BlueStar (Group) Corp., a state-owned chemical maker, following CIC's investment in Blackstone, has come as private equity firms have encountered resistance from Chinese officials to the purchase of large stakes in government-owned firms.

Fourth, SWFs' longer-term horizon and ability to close deals with less leverage insulate them from both equity and credit market volatility. For example, QIA has continued in its plan to purchase Sainsbury, but has reduced the leverage in its most recent proposal.[9] And both QIA and Borse Dubai have continued to acquire shares in the London Stock Exchange and OMX despite equity market volatility.[10]

Challenges

In some cases, SWFs compete for assets and firms against strategic buyers. For example, Cathay Pacific lost out to Temasek and Singapore Airlines (a Temasek affiliate) in its bid to acquire China Eastern Airlines.[11]

The acquisition strategy of SWFs may support their national champion companies in their efforts to become stronger global players, which increases the competitive pressures on the leading companies from the developed markets. In some cases, this means helping to fund large transformational acquisitions. In others, it can mean providing smaller supporting stakes with the aim of transferring skills and know-how. For example, Chinese officials have cited the role of CIC in helping Chinese state enterprises to expand overseas.[12] And Temasek holds controlling stakes in a number of large Singaporean companies with a global presence, including Singtel, Singapore Airlines, and PSA International.

Finally, an increase in political and/or media risk for companies may accompany investment funding from certain SWFs, particularly in situations where the investment is deemed to be in a politically or economically sensitive area. Although there have been relatively few instances of attempted transactions actually being blocked, the potential for significant and potentially adverse publicity exists. Thus, companies considering strategic partnerships with SWFs—whether as an investor or a prospective partner in bidding for other assets—should prepare for this type of complication with a transaction. This consideration is more relevant for SWFs from countries that are not generally considered free-market democracies.

Key Considerations for Overseas Governments

The activities of SWFs have been the target of substantial political debate. Observers and regulators in Western economies have voiced concern that SWFs have an agenda that involves promotion of their countries' political interests more than the pursuit of profits. Apprehension about their opaqueness has led to substantial calls for greater transparency. Against a backdrop of financial market volatility, growing geopolitical uncertainty, and rising protectionist tendencies in the industrialized countries, this debate is gaining momentum.

SWFs touch upon several controversial themes dominating the political discourse in the industrialized world. The economic, political, and security implications of the rise of the petrodollar states and Asian economies have attracted substantial media attention. But there is also widespread concern about the impact of globalization on the industrialized world and its contribution to increased concentrations of wealth and rising income inequality. These themes have considerable resonance among the electorates of Western democracies, leading to increased demands for government action against a disparate range of targets. With the political debate surrounding SWFs, we are likely to see a shift in the investment strategies of SWFs away from opportunities in sensitive areas such as energy and defense, toward an increased focus on other sectors that carry less headline or political intervention risk, and in areas where their role is seen as promoting financial market stability.

Governments around the world are debating the implications of the surge in cross-border investments by SWFs. As they begin to formulate policy responses, five key issues are being debated.

First of all, transparency of the SWFs has become a key concern for governments whose companies and capital markets have become investment targets of SWFs. The dearth of publicly available information about many SWFs, and the lack of clarity about their ultimate objectives, creates uncertainty for host-country governments. Concerns have been raised about SWFs' institutional structure, investment policies, and risk management. Some policymakers have noted the potential for increased market volatility in certain asset classes as a result of SWF involvement. Over time, governments are likely to insist on greater regulatory scrutiny, and some policymakers are calling for an SWF "code of conduct." Some governments have begun to strengthen processes for examining foreign acquisitions or lowering the threshold for government scrutiny.

The second issue relates to the political ambitions of SWFs. Government concern about the political ambitions of SWFs is most observed in industrialized countries, but also arises in the emerging markets. In some cases, this resistance stems from concerns about national security, perceptions of growing income inequality, or fears of losing the "national jewels." These concerns are not new and have appeared in many cross-border transactions that did not involve SWFs, such as the prospect of a bid by China National Offshore Oil Company (CNOOC) for Unocal, the Bain/Huawei Technologies' proposed buyout of 3Com, and Hutchinson Whampoa's bid for Global Crossing. But as SWFs have become more involved in cross-border M&A, they have also come under this regulatory spotlight, as seen during Borse Dubai's planned purchase of a 20% stake in NASDAQ[13] or Thailand's response to Temasek's $3.8 billion takeover of Shin Corp.

Third, some commentators have noted that acquisitions by SWFs are reversing a 25-year trend toward the privatization of state-owned assets. As the economic and productivity benefits of private ownership have become broadly accepted, acquisitions by SWFs are raising the concern that assets will end up being controlled by governments or entities controlled by them, running counter to the intention of privatizations.

Fourth, industrialized governments are carefully weighing their responses to the advances of certain SWFs, given the potential for reciprocal treatment by governments supporting the SWFs. Protectionist reactions have the potential to elicit retaliatory responses by the SWF-governments and raise the broader possibility of reciprocal restrictions in international trade or market access. Since most SWF countries are either significant commodity exporters (e.g., Middle East, Russia) or from countries with attractive high growth markets for global corporations (e.g., China, India), any such reciprocal restrictions could have a significant economic downside for all parties.

Finally, overseas governments are weighing the benefits of welcoming this large source of liquidity into the global financial markets. SWFs are, by their nature, long-term investors who are likely to stick with asset allocation choices, perhaps even in the event of short-term losses. This can be an important stabilizing factor for companies and financial markets. Unlike private equity and hedge fund investors, SWFs do not usually rely on high leverage, do not face capital requirements, and are not likely to face pressures to rapidly liquidate positions based on withdrawals—all of which can make them more stable investors.

In light of the importance of these issues for global policymakers, one can expect continued public discussion about the need for international consensus on "best practices" for SWFs in the context of the future stability of the international financial system.

Notes

Reprinted with permission of Citi Global Markets Inc. (CGMI). Although the information in this chapter was obtained from sources that the authors believe to be reliable, CGMI does not guarantee its accuracy, and such information may be incomplete or condensed. All figures included in this report constitute the authors' judgment as of the original publication date.

1. There is an active segment of government pension funds in the United States, Europe, and Asia and these are generally considered a separate group of investors. While a number of SWFs are set up in part or whole to fund government pension liabilities (e.g., Norway's Government Pension Fund), we do not cover government pension funds extensively in this report.
2. The IMF has estimated that SWFs total US $1.9–2.9 trillion. Truman estimated that the largest sovereign wealth funds combined hold more than US $2 trillion ("Sovereign Wealth Funds: The Need for Greater Transparency and Accountability," August 2007). There is some disagreement over whether certain holdings of net foreign assets by central banks such as SAMA or HKMA, portions of which may be more actively and aggressively managed, should be included in the definition of SWFs if they have not been set up as a separate vehicle. We have opted to look at a slightly wider universe of funds.
3. The IMF assumes a somewhat slower growth path for total foreign assets under the management of predominantly emerging market governments, projecting a 50% increase to $12 trillion by 2012 from their current level of $8 billion. (April 2007 Global Financial Stability Report (GFSR), IMF, page 45.) The faster projected pace of accumulation of SWF assets can be attributed to several factors, including the increasing number of countries potentially setting up such funds (like Bolivia and Japan), as well as the likely increasing share of incremental reserves that countries will dedicate to SWFs, as their needs for traditional foreign exchange reserves are exceeded. While a drop in commodity prices could slow the pace of growth of natural resource–based funds, it would be counterbalanced by even greater current account surpluses for Asian commodity importers like China and India. A meaningful appreciation of Asian exchange rates could slow the pace of accumulation of foreign reserves, but this is not expected to happen quickly.
4. Cerulli Associates.
5. As reported by *The Wall Street Journal,* October 16, 2007.

6. As reported in *The Wall Street Journal,* July 6, 2007.
 7. As reported in *The Wall Street Journal,* August 24, 2007.
 8. See note 6.
 9. As reported in *The Financial Times,* September 25, 2007.
10. As reported by Reuters, September 20, 2007.
11. As reported by Bloomberg, September 25, 2007.
12. As reported by *The Wall Street Journal,* September 10, 2007.
13. As reported by Reuters, September 20, 2007.

About the Contributors

SHAMS BUTT is a Managing Director at Citi.

RAJESH CHAKRABARTI is Assistant Professor of Finance at the Indian School of Business in Hyderabad.

ART DURNEV is Assistant Professor of Finance in the School of Management at McGill University.

ALEXANDER DYCK is Associate Professor of Finance at Joseph L. Rotman School of Management at the University of Toronto.

FRANK H. EASTERBROOK is Chief Judge of the United States Court of Appeals for the Seventh Circuit.

JULIAN FRANKS is Professor of Finance at the London Business School.

PÉTER HARBULA is a Director of Deloitte Financial Advisory Services in France. He is also an accredited Senior Appraiser of the American Society of Appraisers and a member of the Société Française des Evaluateurs.

E. HAN KIM is Fred M. Taylor Professor of Business Administration and Director of Mitsui Life Financial Research Center at the University of Michigan's Ross School of Business.

WOOCHAN KIM is Associate Professor of Finance at the KDI School of Public Policy and Management in Seoul, Korea. Professor Kim is also a member of the Policy Advisory Committee of Solidarity for Economic Reform and a member of a group that serves as a consultant to the Korean Corporate Governance Fund.

COLIN MAYER is Peter Moores Dean of the Saïd Business School and Peter Moores Professor of Management Studies at the University of Oxford.

WILLIAM L. MEGGINSON holds the Rainbolt Chair of Finance at the University of Oklahoma Michael Price College of Business and held the Fulbright-Tocqueville Distinguished Chair in American Studies 2007–2008 at the University of Paris Dauphine.

RAGHURAM G. RAJAN is Eric J. Gleacher Distinguished Service Professor of Finance at the University of Chicago's Booth School of Business.

LUC RENNEBOOG is Professor of Corporate Finance at CentER, Tilburg University. He is also a member of TILEC (Tilburg Law and Economics Center) and the European Corporate Governance Institute (ECGI, Brussels).

MARK J. ROE is David Berg Professor of Law at the Harvard Law School.

DARIO SCANNAPIECO is Vice President of the European Investment Bank and former Director General, Privatization and Finance Department, Italian Ministry of Economy and Finance.

LOUISE SCHOLES is a researcher at the Center for Management Buyout Research, Nottingham University Business School.

ANIL SHIVDASANI is a Managing Director of Citi Financial Strategy Group.

TOMAS SIMONS is a Consultant at McKinsey and Company.

CARSTEN STENDEVAD is a Managing Director of Citi Financial Strategy Group.

RENÉ M. STULZ holds the Everett D. Reese Chair of Banking and Monetary Economics and is the Director of the Dice Center for Research in Financial Economics at the Ohio State University.

MIKE WRIGHT is Professor of Financial Studies and Director of the Centre for Management Buy-out Research, Nottingham University Business School. He is also currently a Visiting Professor at Erasmus University and INSEAD, and an editor of the *Journal of Management Studies*.

ANN WYMAN is a former Managing Director with Citi.

PRADEEP K. YADAV holds the W. Ross Johnston Chair of Finance at the University of Oklahoma's Michael Price College of Business. He is also Visiting Professor at Lancaster University in England, CFR Research Fellow at the University of Cologne in Germany, and a member of the CAF Board of Advisors at the Indian School of Business.

LUIGI ZINGALES is the Robert C. McCormack Professor of Entrepreneurship and Finance at the University of Chicago's Booth School of Business. He is also a faculty research associate at the National Bureau of Economic Research and a research fellow at the Center for Economic Policy Research.

Index